IN THE SERVICE OF PEACE IN THE
MIDDLE EAST, 1967–1979

Blessed are the peacemakers because they shall be called the children of God.

Matthew 5:9

ENSIO SIILASVUO

In the Service of Peace in the Middle East

1967–1979

HURST & COMPANY, LONDON

ST. MARTIN'S PRESS, NEW YORK

First published in the United Kingdom by
C. Hurst & Co. (Publishers) Ltd.,
38 King Street, London WC2E 8JT
and in the United States of America by
St. Martin's Press, Inc.,
175 Fifth Avenue, New York, NY 10010
Printed in Hong Kong

ISBNs
1-85065-139-6 (Hurst)
0-312-07151-5 (St. Martin's)

Library of Congress Cataloging-in-Publication Data

Siilasvuo, Ensio.
    In the service of peace in the Middle East, 1967–1979/Ensio
Siilasvuo.
        p.   cm.
    Includes index.
    ISBN 1–85065–139–6 (Hurst). — ISBN 0–312–07151–5 (St. Martin's)
    1. United Nations—Armed Forces—Middle East.   2. Israel-Arab
conflicts.   3. Siilasvuo, Ensio.   I. Title.
JX1981.P7S495   1992
327.1′ 72′ 0956—dc20   91–43329
                                                              CIP

This book is about the twelve years I spent in the Middle East serving the United Nations in different capacities. The first six years were a period of apprenticeship, when I got to know the area and its leaders. The October War in 1973 was a historical turning point that changed the general situation in many ways and paved the way for a peace process. To me the war brought challenging new tasks, as I set up a new UN force in Sinai and began my job as a mediator in the tent at Kilometre 101 and in Geneva. These were high points in my life.

I also had the opportunity to take part in the drafting and carrying out of the plans for the disengagement of Israeli, Egyptian and Syrian forces. I was happy to see the situation stabilize both in Sinai and the Golan. From 1975 onwards, as Chief Co-ordinator for UN Peace-keeping Missions in the Middle East, I took part in the planning of the second phase of disengagement in Sinai. In 1978 and 1979 I also tried to facilitate UNIFIL's difficult task in southern Lebanon.

These are my memoirs, not a history of the conflict in the Middle East. First and foremost I write about events in which I took part myself, and of which I have first-hand knowledge. I write about the people I met, my staff and my superiors, negotiations with ministers and generals, and meetings that I chaired. But I also write about things I read or heard, because without this background it would be impossible to understand the details of what happened on the military level and why certain solutions were reached. I also relate interesting occurrences and incidents that have taken place without my presence.

However, the book does not only deal with official matters; it touches on my personal life too. I write about my family, my home and the friends and acquaintances I made – all of whom have in one way or another influenced my public life and attitudes. It was difficult to keep one's private and public lives separate. Especially in Jerusalem and Ismailia, where we lived in the headquarters, they were intertwined in many ways.

I sincerely thank all those who, with words or actions, have assisted me in writing this book. The names of my UN comrades in arms, whose statements or stories I have quoted more extensively, appear in connection with the respective quotations.

I also want to thank my son Lauri, who checked the text of

v

these memoirs and to extend special thanks to my wife, Salli, for her intellectual and editorial assistance. Both during the long years in the Middle East and in the writing of this book, she has been my most trusted adviser.

Helsinki, May 1987   ENSIO SIILASVUO

Contents

Part II. THE OCTOBER WAR

PART III. TOWARDS PEACE

Illustrations

Maps

Abbreviations

HJKIMAC	Hashemite Kingdom of Jordan-Israeli Mixed Armistice Commission
ICRC	International Committee of the Red Cross
ILMAC	Israeli-Lebanese Mixed Armistice Commission
ISMAC	Israeli-Syrian Mixed Armistice Commission
MAC	Mixed Armistice Commission
NATO	North Atlantic Treaty Organization
NSC	National Security Council (United States)
OP	observation post
PFLP	Popular Front for the Liberation of Palestine
PLO	Palestine Liberation Organization
UN	United Nations
UNDOF	United Nations Disengagement Observer Force
UNDP	United Nations Development Programme
UNEF	United Nations Emergency Force
UNESCO	United Nations Educational, Scientific and Cultural Organization
UNFICYP	United Nations Peace-keeping Force in Cyprus
UNIFIL	United Nations Interim Force in Lebanon
UNOGIL	United Nations Observer Group in Lebanon
UNRWA	United Nations Relief and Works Agency
UNTSO	United Nations Truce Supervision Organization

Part I. The Middle East in the Aftermath of the Six Day War, 1967–73

1. Assignment to UN duty in Jerusalem

The deteriorating situation in the Middle East in the spring of 1967 was front-page news in the Finnish press. As one who was familiar with the region, I followed with interest and even some anxiety the development of events. I imagined, however, that all this was merely a question of sabre-rattling, which was so typical for the area and which would gradually quieten down. To my surprise, and probably many others', war did indeed break out, on 5 June 1967. Within six days Israel's mighty and skilfully led armed forces had defeated the armies of Egypt, Syria and Jordan. Even from faraway Finland one could conclude that Israel's crushing victory would cause profound changes in the area. The military hegemony achieved by Israel would mean the beginning of a new era in the history of the Middle East.

At the request of the UN Secretary-General, the government of Finland had, in August 1967, sent about ten military observers of the rank of major and captain to the crisis area. By granting this request, the Finnish government had followed its traditional policy towards the UN: one of strengthening the world organization and its ability to function. I imagined, however, that I myself would remain an onlooker this time. I was too old to become a military observer. My surprise was the greater, therefore, when at the end of September Secretary-General U Thant requested me by name to become the Deputy Chief of Staff of the United Nations Truce Supervision Organization (UNTSO). The message which was conveyed by our UN Ambassador, Max Jakobson, to the Foreign Ministry asked whether the Finnish authorities were willing to assign me to that post.

I knew beforehand that the headquarters of UNTSO was situated in Jerusalem. The Chief of Staff of the Organization was

1

Lieutenant-General Odd Bull, former Commander of the Norwegian Air Force. I had a presentiment that Odd Bull was behind this request, because I had served in his headquarters in UNOGIL (United Nations Observer Group in Lebanon) in the summer of 1958.

The idea of the appointment of a Finnish officer to a relatively high position in UNTSO was pleasing to the architects of our foreign policy. Finland had participated with enthusiasm in the UN peace-keeping missions since 1956, when Dag Hammarskjöld, in order to solve the Suez crisis, had set up the first armed UN force, UNEF I. A Finnish officer, General A.E. Martola, had helped him in this pioneering work. Peace-keeping had gradually become an important part of our foreign policy and the most visible and most significant form of Finland's involvement in international co-operation. In 1967 we had a battalion in Cyprus, military observers in Kashmir and, as mentioned above, in UNTSO too after August. General Martola was for the time being Commander of the UN force in Cyprus, but it was known that he would soon retire because of his age. For the position of the Deputy Chief of Staff of UNTSO to be held by a Finn was desirable from the Finnish point of view.

I, however, was not pleased with the idea. I had already served three times under the UN flag. Just ten years earlier, in 1957, I had commanded the Finnish company in the first UN force in Egypt. In the following year I had served with General Bull as a staff officer in Lebanon, which was then in the grip of its first civil war. My third period of service had been spent as the Commander of the Finnish battalion in Cyprus, 1964–5. So I imagined that I had done my duty to the United Nations. I also thought that I had more than enough of the international experience needed in an officer's profession, because during the years 1959–61 I had, between UN duties, served as a military attaché in Warsaw.

There was a more important reason for my negative reaction. The eldest of my three sons was due to finish secondary school the following spring, the middle one still had three years left and the youngest was finishing elementary school. From the point of view of the family, it was thus reasonable and desirable at this stage for father to stay at home.

It is easy to guess, therefore, that my family's response was not enthusiastic either. This unexpected development was all the more unwelcome because in all other respects things were going well. My career had progressed in a normal manner. After my time as Commander in Cyprus, I had had the opportunity to serve in a responsible and agreeable job as the Deputy Director of the National Defence Course at the Staff College. In the summer of 1967 I had been appointed Chief of the Foreign Department at General Headquarters. After a pleasant vacation at the family summer cottage in northern Finland, we moved to a new and larger official residence on the Helsinki waterfront. My own life and the life of my family were in order.

The law and other regulations did not oblige me to serve abroad. In this respect, as an army officer, I was in a different position than, for example, the officials of the Foreign Ministry. But the pressure was intense. It came from both the Foreign and the Defence Ministries. My bosses appealed to my military obedience and my patriotic feelings. When finally I was told that the Commander-in-Chief, President Urho Kekkonen, wished that I should accept the appointment, there was no alternative left to me. It was agreed, however, that the assignment should not last longer than a year. I would hardly have departed if I had known that it would in fact stretch to twelve years.

With this inauspicious beginning, I flew in mid-October towards Jerusalem, the centre of the Middle Eastern controversies. We landed in Tel Aviv at dusk, with the hot air of the Mediterranean night blowing the familiar exotic smells around me. I was pleased to be met by General Bull's Aide-de-Camp, Captain Alfonso Vitiello of the Italian Air Force, who cleared passport and customs formalities with experience and skill. Soon we were heading for Jerusalem.

The airport is situated in the town of Lod or Lydda, where, according to legend, Saint George was born. The next town along the road is Ramle, where Napoleon hid in the local church for fear of the plague. After Lydda and Ramle, we continued over the Judean hills towards Jerusalem. In the darkness little could be made of the scenery, but I knew the road from having visited Jerusalem as a tourist from Cyprus in 1964. It was curved and narrow. From time to time, the headlights of the car picked out destroyed armoured vehicles, mementoes of the War of Independence in 1948. During the hour and a half it took to make the trip, Captain Vitiello told me about UNTSO Headquarters and the life of the observers. Many points which had remained obscure in Helsinki were clarified now.

The magnificent headquarters of the United Nations in Jerusalem, still called Government House, had once been the palace of the British High Commissioner. It had been damaged in the Six Day War but repairs were now almost complete. The building also housed UNTSO Headquarters and, on its second floor, the residence of General and Mrs Bull. As, however, it was customary for military observers to spend their first few days in a hotel and then rent an apartment in the city, I began my stay at Shepherd's Hotel in East Jerusalem, which was favoured by the military observers.

2. Introductory phase

The history of UNTSO

The following morning, together with three other recently arrived officers, I embarked on the usual introductory phase, to get acquainted with UNTSO's history, organization and present modes of operation, the situation in the field, logistics and administration. We passed a driving test and received some items of equipment. They were rather scanty: a blue beret, two blue scarves and, surprisingly, a small feather pillow. At least there would be somewhere to lay my head.

On the first day I also met General Bull, who seemed to be pleased about my arrival. Longer discussions with him were left to a later time, because he had just returned from leave in Norway, so I did not yet know what my duties and position in UNTSO were to be. A temporary desk was, however, arranged in the office of Miss Moira Figgis, an English UN official. She was the Reports Officer of UNTSO who had been sent from New York some months earlier in order to write a report to the Secretary-General about the functioning of UNTSO and the status of the supervision of the armistice agreements. Then the war had intervened, UNTSO's task had completely changed and nobody was interested any more in a report which dealt with earlier times. Miss Figgis, however, did not return to New York, because she intended to retire soon. For me, discussions with this wise and experienced servant of the UN were priceless. She knew UNTSO better than many others. We had long conversations and she also brought documents for me to read so that I could become better acquainted with what was going on.

Little by little it became clearer what kind of an organization I was supposed to serve. UNTSO had originated after Israel's War of Independence in 1948, when the United Nations Security Council was seeking a solution to a difficult situation. At the beginning of May 1948, the Truce Commission established by the Council brought to its attention the idea of effectively supervising the cease-fire, asking the Council officially on 21 May to send military observers to assist it. At the end of that month the Security Council called for a four-week cessation of all acts of armed force and decided that the UN Mediator, Count Folke Bernadotte of Sweden, together with the members of the Truce Commission, should supervise the truce and for that purpose be provided with a sufficient number of military observers. This Resolution 50 (1948) would become the charter of the observer organization, although the name of UNTSO was not mentioned in it.

Bernadotte requested military observers and auxiliary personnel from the states members of the Truce Commission (Belgium, France and the United States) and from his own country, Sweden. During the first four-week truce about 90 observers arrived, but during the second truce which followed the numbers rose to about 700 officers and 600 auxiliary people. The work was difficult at the beginning. There were no contingency plans and the operation had to be improvised quickly. Nobody had any experience of how to direct a large observer operation. Communications were lacking and there was no proper logistics organization. But despite all the shortages the operation got off the ground in a satisfactory manner.

Then United Nations peace-keeping and UNTSO suffered a serious blow when members of the Israeli Stern Gang murdered Folke Bernadotte in Jerusalem on 17 September 1948. He had just been studying the suitability of establishing the headquarters of UNTSO in Government House, which had, since the departure of the British, been temporarily administered by the International Red Cross.

The next phase of UNTSO's history began in early 1949, when four General Armistice Agreements were concluded in the island of Rhodes between Israel and its Arab neighbours, Egypt, Syria, Jordan and Lebanon. The negotiations were brought to a conclusion after the murder of Bernadotte by his most senior adviser, Dr Ralph Bunche. This prominent and strong-willed statesman later received the Nobel Peace Prize for his work in the Middle East. Bunche went on to direct UN peace-keeping activities during the tenure of the first three Secretaries-General – Trygve Lie, Dag Hammarskjöld and Sithu U Thant – until 1971, the end of Thant's tenure.

The Armistice Agreements of Rhodes terminated the role of the Mediator. At the same time the autonomous task of UNTSO and its Chief of Staff began, centring on the provision of assistance to the parties in dispute by supervising the application and observance of the General Armistice Agreements. In addition, UNTSO was to maintain and supervise the cease-fire ordered by the Security Council in 1948. UNTSO carried out its task through the Mixed Armistice Commissions (MACs) set up in order to improve relations between Israel and its neighbours. The representative of the UNTSO Chief of Staff acted as Chairman of the Commission. It dealt with local incidents and the differing interpretations of the agreement on the basis of complaints by the parties. In addition, the UNTSO observers manned observation posts, patrolled cease-fire lines and investigated alleged breaches of the cease-fire. But their task was not only to observe and report on such breaches. They were also to act as go-betweens, promoting harmony between the parties and preventing the escalation of local incidents. In favourable conditions the UNTSO observers and their superiors were able to solve problems and keep the peace successfully. If, however, the controversies aroused were too deep, or if national honour was at stake, the work of the MACs reached an impasse, although in such situations their reports were the only reliable source of information available to the Secretary-General and the Security Council. The number of observers varied from 50 to 200. After 1953 Norway, Denmark, Ireland, Italy, Canada, Australia, New Zealand and the Netherlands also began to send observers.

The weakness of the system was that in the MACs the Chairman, who represented the UN, was allowed to vote. It would have been easier for UNTSO if the Commission members had tried to reach a consensus and the Chairman had not been obliged to take sides.

The structure of UNTSO

UNTSO Headquarters was divided into three parts: military, political and administrative. The military staff (usually ten officers) took care of operations, personnel affairs and medical care. Members of the political staff came from the UN Secretariat in New York. In 1967 there were four political officers, one legal officer and one press officer. As UNTSO's role altered, the need for political advisers was reduced because the Mixed Armistice Commissions were no longer in place. In 1970 we had only one political adviser, while the tasks of legal adviser and press officer were at times carried out by one person. The Chief Administrative Officer had as his subordinates a number of so-called field service officers, who took care of different administrative and logistics tasks in Jerusalem and at the field stations.

The actual operational echelon of UNTSO consisted of about 200 military observers from 17 countries. These observers did not carry arms. The experience of many years had shown that their unarmed status was the best guarantee of their security. Their status was well-known in the area of operations and no-one would attack an unarmed officer.

UNTSO headquarters, or Government House (till 1948 the residence of the British governor-general).

Leaders of UNTSO, spring 1970. *From second left*: Ramon Prieto, the author, Miguel Marin, Dennis Holland, U Myang.

The rank of the observers was either major or captain, but there were also a few lieutenant-colonels. The Deputy Chief of Staff of UNTSO was the only colonel. The officers were all on loan from their home armies and received the salaries from their jobs at home. The UN paid to each of them a *per diem* (in 1967 this was $10 a day) which was meant for board and lodging. The observers rented apartments for themselves in Jerusalem, Cairo, Damascus or Beirut. When they were in service at the observation posts they lived in caravans or mobile homes set up by UNTSO and bought and prepared their own food. From the point of view of the UN this system was practical, because the observers took care of themselves, and financially advantageous, because the participating countries paid (as salaries) the main part of the costs. The UN paid the *per diem*, the cost of transportation to and from the area of operation and some other minor expenses.

The position in the UN hierarchy of the Chief of Staff, Lieutenant-General Odd Bull, was Assistant Secretary-General. His deputy was Colonel Mick Johnson, of the US Marine Corps, from Texas. He was a tall, energetic officer, about 45 years old. Colonel Johnson told me that he was very fond of the Middle East, enjoyed the task of UNTSO and liked the peoples of the region, both the Israelis and the Arabs.

An opportunity for me to get acquainted with the other members of the staff arose at General Bull's staff meeting. There I met for the first time the grand old man of the political advisers, the Frenchman Henri Vigier, who had earlier been an aide to Bernadotte. He was one of those idealistic and exceptionally gifted people who wanted to further the idea of the UN and had therefore joined the world organization in 1945. People like him were already rare in 1967. Vigier had drafted the Armistice Agreements in 1949 and I was told that he knew everything worth knowing about the conditions, peoples and situation of the Middle East. However, his more than 80 years of age had begun to show and he seemed to live in his own world. During the meeting he did not say a word. Because of his great merits Vigier had been permitted to serve longer than the UN rules and regulations allowed, but he finally retired in March 1968 and died soon afterwards at his home in France.

Some months earlier a Spanish UN official, Miguel Marin, had arrived in order to replace Vigier. He was about 60 years of age. As a young man he had served in the Foreign Ministry of the Spanish Republic and had, among other posts, been assigned to the delegation of his country at the League of Nations in Geneva. As the Civil War in Spain ended with the victory of General Franco, Marin was exiled in 1939. After having started out as a professor of international law in Mexico, Marin had gone on to a long career in the UN Secretariat. He had been a member of delegations for political affairs in India, Pakistan and Papua-New Guinea. Marin's most visible quality was his great sense of humour, which appeared in the form of funny stories about his earlier UN tasks and in aphorisms and Catalan proverbs. Like his friend, the film-maker Luis Bunuel, he had a violent antipathy to the Catholic Church and the army. This, however, did not prevent him from spending entertaining evenings in Jerusalem in the company of priests and officers. "All my youth I fought against Generals," Marin would lament with a sigh, "and now in my old age I must serve under the Generals." But Marin's humorous aphorisms were often also aimed at instructing people. He was always a professor. Marin taught me what politics really were, stressing that in politics, like in love, there is never a "never" and never a "forever" and everything can change overnight.

Vigier and Marin were by no means the only important persons and original thinkers in the political department. One rather eccentric character was the Information Officer of UNTSO, Albert Grand. During the Second World War he had been a member of the French intelligence service, the Deuxième Bureau, and was intimately acquainted with the complex political situation in the Middle East. Albert Grand and I at once became good friends and conversations with him benefited me greatly. Speaking French with him was great fun for me and also very useful. It was obvious, however, that Grand had lost his faith in UNTSO and in the chances of the UN in general of solving the conflict in the Middle East. He would appear in his office unshaven and without socks and vanish again very quickly. Grand no longer had the strength to involve himself in his work and, like Vigier, he soon retired on pension.

The younger generation in the political department was represented by the Spaniard, Ramon Prieto, the legal adviser. Later, in the 1970s, he also took care of political questions and for a long time acted as my skilful and trusted aide.

The Chief Administrative Officer of UNTSO was an Englishman, Dennis Holland, who directed the civilian personnel with a strong hand and was responsible for logistics and administrative arrangements. During the Second World War he had been a signals officer in the British Army and he was thus professionally exceptionally competent for work in a military organization. His subordinates respected him greatly and probably also feared him a little. This was a good thing, in my opinion. Maintaining discipline, order and efficiency in a 200-strong international group of civil servants was not a simple task.

It took time before good and confidential relations were established between Holland and myself. At the beginning he treated me in a cool and suspicious manner. Maybe there was reason for this. The system of organizing and managing peace-keeping operations had been established in Hammarskjöld's time and remained relatively unchanged. I, however, had my own ideas on how the peace-keeping operations should be managed.

Administration was directed centrally from UN Headquarters in New York. The Director of Field Service Operation, the American George Lansky, was in charge of it. He co-ordinated the co-operation between the peace-keeping missions and the administrative departments of Headquarters. Thus UNTSO could not be in direct contact with the departments of personnel, finance and general services; all correspondence went through George Lansky. UNTSO could not influence the decisions very much, as matters were presented according to Lansky's ideas. I am sure that the system was practical from the point of view of Headquarters.

Lansky directed the work of the Chief Administrative Officer (CAO) using personal "Dear Dennis" letters which were not usually shown to the military leaders of UNTSO. The CAO answered the letters and submitted for Lansky's decision even the smallest details, such as the taking of home leave and the procurement of screws and nails.

I thought that the organization and management of the administration were bad. In Finland I was used to a system in which the Commander directs all activity and the Quartermaster assists him in matters pertaining to logistics and administration. Such a system only happened in UNTSO on paper, because there the CAO, following an established practice, dealt with most of the matters directly with Lansky, behind the back of the Commander. This practice was, in my opinion, intolerable because the Commander alone had total responsibility, including responsibility for mistakes made by the CAO. In addition, Headquarters in New York interfered too much in details. Once the General Assembly had approved UNTSO's budget, its implementation should have been left to us. In general there should have been more delegation of authority to the field, where decisions on details would have been easier to make. As we could see later, the delegation of authority would have been especially useful in times of crisis, because the people in the field knew better the needs of the mission and the requirements of a quickly changing situation.

In times of peace the system worked satisfactorily, despite all its shortcomings. UNTSO was an established mission where things ran smoothly and routinely. Holland himself was partly responsible for this success; during the tenure of weaker CAOs the shortcomings became more apparent.

George Lansky too was exceptionally able and energetic. This was another factor in the success of UNTSO's activities. He was, however, over-ambitious and dictatorial, and that caused friction at times. In a crisis the UN administrative system was too bureaucratic and slow, serving our needs in the field poorly. Yet from the point of view of the highest UN leadership it was obviously successful and freed the Under Secretary-General and his aides from many worries. They could trust that George would take care of them. It was difficult, therefore, to bring about the changes that those of us who worked in the field wished to see.

Thus the opinion of UNTSO's Chief of Staff in administrative matters was only asked if great questions of principle were involved. It followed that in Holland's view there was no need to ask me any questions; I was not even a member of the Secretariat. Fortunately my relations with Holland started gradually to improve. I learned to respect his long experience, great professionalism, determination and unwavering impartiality. Holland also came to the conclusion that it was worthwhile to discuss logistics matters with me. In this way we were able to progress matters to the benefit of UNTSO. Later I could see that Holland as a CAO was completely in his own class. He was more able and trustworthy than any of those who succeeded him in the twelve years I spent in the Middle East. We were all happy when, after a few years service in New York Headquarters, Dennis Holland returned once more to the field in the early 1970s.

In my opinion, administration was the weakest link in the whole UN system and the CAOs I met were mostly mediocre and even weak from the point of view of their ability and skill. It is true that Lansky was happy with his subordinates. He thought that they represented experience and continuity better than military officers who came and went. They also mastered better the complex UN administrative rules and regulations and the established working procedure. I believe, however, that such a grasp of the formalities should not have been the prime consideration in making an appointment, as it was a quality that any efficient officer could soon have acquired. It should have been more important for the CAOs to be competent and full of determination and initiative. Lansky did not want such people as his subordinates; humility and obedience were, according to him, the principal qualities of a real administrator.

The question of continuity came up later, too. When Lansky once again stressed the importance of continuity to the Commander of UNDOF, the Austrian Major-General Hannes Philipp, the latter wondered who in fact did represent continuity. Philipp had been Commander of UNDOF for a year and during that time he had had three CAOs, all of whom he had had to familiarize with their tasks.

A special organization, the Field Service, had been established in the 1940s as a working echelon of administration for UNTSO and other peace-keeping missions. At first, young, brisk and usually unmarried men were recruited to the Field Service in order to take care of logistics and administrative tasks in the difficult conditions of developing countries. Professionally these men were police and radio officers, radio technicians and vehicle mechanics and included many Scandinavians, Irishmen and other Europeans. The intention was to pay these men higher salaries than they would have received in their home countries, in order to compensate them for the difficulties caused by the hard conditions and long working hours. In the early days qualified and enthusiastic people had been recruited. The reputation of the organization was excellent and many fine stories were told about the achievements and bravery of the first pioneers.

Towards the end of the 1960s the Field Service unfortunately was no longer equal to the fame of its earlier times. A large group of experienced and able people were still in the service, but the youngsters of the 1940s had grown older and their enthusiasm had faded. They had acquired families and now felt it was time to start taking care of their children's future and their own pensions. They would no longer undertake overtime work without extra pay, while because of their children's schooling they were less geographically mobile. On the other hand, high-quality young recruits continued to arrive from different parts of the world. Among others, the first Finnish field service officers arrived in the late 1960s.

In the 1970s there was a significant change in the composition of the organization, as people from developing countries began to be recruited. Field Service changed from an European to a truly international organization. It was a step in the right direction, corresponding with the UN principle that all its member states should contribute to its operations. It is true that many people complained that the newcomers were inexperienced, but this was the only way that these young men could learn and develop. I gave the same answer later to those who complained that the UNEF battalions from the developing countries were not of the same standard as the soldiers from the developed industrial countries: one should be patient and give them time to learn.

In time, a major problem arose: how to offer field service officers the same kind of career development as other UN officials had. There were exceptional cases where the ability of some of the former made advancement possible, perhaps by placing them in higher administrative jobs. But the majority had such a poor basic education and limited professional training that they were not suited to more responsible tasks. Because of this poor career development, many field service officers became frustrated and so the working morale of the organization declined.

I thought that Field Service already belonged to the past, or at least that a thorough reorganization was needed. One alternative would have been to replace the civilians of the working echelon with noncommissioned officers, who would be recruited from the same countries and on the same conditions as the military observers. I am still convinced that this system would function well and would be much easier to handle from the point of view of the UN. Moreover, expenses would be much lower. Civilian personnel could be recruited to the higher administrative posts in the same way as other members of the Secretariat are. We had at least a glimmer of an idea of how this scheme might function when, at the end of the 1960s, we recruited four noncommissioned officers from the Finnish battalion in Cyprus as drivers of our Saracen armoured vehicles. In fact the Commander of UNDOF had had a military driver for his staff car from the beginning and this had worked well. Later I had to resort to a military driver in 1979, when a strike of the Field Service personnel made the use of civilian drivers impossible. During the years I had been very satisfied with my Field Service drivers, but my experience of using military drivers was wholly positive. Unfortunately, I could not persuade the administrative officers of UN Headquarters to accept my views.

George Lansky was himself very content with his organization. When he was visiting Jerusalem once, he told me that the organization was so good, and the field service officers so skilful, that UNTSO could run very well without its military observers. I answered that this was true if the task of UNTSO was just "to run". But if instead its task was to observe and to report on the breaches of the cease-fire, observers were also needed. Lansky replied that he must reluctantly admit that.

The local Palestinian workers were the third large group of personnel in UNTSO. They were employed in the workshops, the restaurant, the laundry, the garden, the tax-free shop and the offices. The majority of them worked at UNTSO HQ, because the workshops were centrally situated there. The Palestinians were known as skilful and hardworking employees. Their working morale was high and their attitudes positive. They considered their salaries, pensions and other benefits good despite the fact that these were, according to UN rules, linked to the local salary level and were therefore only a fraction of the salaries of the international staff.

I realized to my regret that there was in UNTSO quite a lot of open or hidden racism towards the local workers. It was probably inherited from the colonial past of Government House and, particularly when it emanated from those who came from the Nordic countries, was quite unnecessary. One example of this racism was the prohibition of local personnel from participating in joint social gatherings. Their presence would, supposedly, not be proper because tax-free drinks were served at those parties. When I remarked to Dennis Holland that in Geneva the local Swiss personnel were allowed to attend UN cocktail parties, he answered that this was a completely different matter. On another occasion, when the drawings for the enlargement of the workshop at Government House were presented to me for my comment, I noticed that the plan included separate washrooms and toilets for the international and the local staff. I said in my comment that the UN should be furthering the equality of nationalities in practice, not only by the resolutions of the General Assembly. I considered it intolerable that people who worked together could not wash themselves together. These ossified attitudes could not be altered overnight, but I did notice that by speaking continuously about the matter some changes could be achieved.

My new role

My own position and task in UNTSO became clearer. I met the General for a second time and we had an interesting conversation which lasted for two hours. The atmosphere was pleasant, as always in the company of General Bull. He always spoke Norwegian, his English pronunciation being slightly unclear. To begin with, the General read me a letter he had written to Dr Bunche, saying that while he greatly appreciated his deputy, the American Colonel Johnson, the Colonel's nationality had lately restricted his ability to function in the Arab countries, particularly in Egypt and in Syria. In the latter he was not received any more and even in the former his reception was cool. Therefore Bull wanted to appoint an officer with a more acceptable nationality to this job. He had in mind the Finnish Colonel Siilasvuo, whom he considered, based on his previous knowledge, to be suitable for the job. Bunche's reply to the letter was positive.

Finally General Bull mentioned the reasons why I had been asked to arrive at such an early stage, although Colonel Johnson's service contract was to end only at the end of March 1968. I could take care of a part of his tasks concerning Egypt and Syria, but above all I should spend the coming months in becoming thoroughly acquainted with the functioning of UNTSO and with the countries of the region and their leaders. Bull also told me that in November Colonel Johnson was going on home leave to the USA for a month and I would then act as his deputy. We spoke, too, about my programme in the near future and agreed that the following week I should go to acquaint myself with the conditions of the east bank of the Suez Canal.

My early arrival must surely have been annoying for my predecessor, but fortunately he adopted a calm and correct attitude. He was polite and friendly to me; the situation was not my fault. The overlapping of our tours ended on 1 April 1968 without controversy or mishap.

I pondered the reasons why this situation had arisen and wrote in my first letter to the Finnish Ministry of Defence on 12 November 1967:

It has become clearer what the UN leadership had in mind when they asked me to come here. The intention has been, on the one hand, to decrease the US contribution within UNTSO. Besides Colonel Johnson, one of the three officers in the Operations Branch is an American lieutenant-colonel, while in the field there are about ten Americans in different positions. On the other hand, I have noticed that Colonel Johnson (a US Marine Corps officer from Texas, over 6 foot 10 tall) is, because of his domineering character, often in disagreement with General Bull's principal political adviser. The general is naturally in a quandary when his military and political advisers disagree over almost every question and the general must, therefore, when he is making his decision, choose between two alternatives . . .

When I had returned from my first trip to the east bank of the Suez Canal, General Bull took me with him on his trips to Cairo, Damascus and Amman. The introduction to my new duties began in earnest. I awaited tensely my first encounter with Moshe Dayan, the Defence Minister of Israel and a famous war hero. I described this meeting in a letter to my wife:

> On 7 November I was at Tel Aviv Airport to meet General Bull returning from Cairo. We then waited in the VIP room for half an hour, Bull, Marin, Colonel Johnson and I, because Dayan was to receive us at 1800 hrs. So we departed in a column of three vehicles with an Israeli motor-cycle patrol driving in front of us. First came the general's car with the UN flag fluttering, then Colonel Johnson and, last, me, as fast as I could make it in my Volkswagen. I was able to follow quite well, although at our departure I had been a bit worried about whether the horse- and other powers would suffice.
>
> We were led directly to the minister's office. Besides him there was the Chief of Staff Itzhak Rabin (about 45 years old) and four or five young colonels. The Foreign Ministry was represented by Ambassador Joseph Tekoah, who would soon travel to New York as the Permanent Representative. The minister himself made a very powerful impression. No wonder that his popularity is so great. He was clad in simple cotton trousers, a summer shirt with an open collar and a leather jacket.

During the coming years I learned to know Moshe Dayan better and to hold him in great esteem. Even in Israel, where there is no shortage of able and dynamic people, Dayan was an exceptional talent. He was a creative man with great vision. Thanks to this, he also had the broadmindedness of a true statesman, which was not disturbed by the trivialities of everyday politics. Because of this, many people who regarded everyday politics as important had difficulties in tolerating Dayan. Soon after the Six Day War Dayan forced the passage of his idea of the free traffic of people and goods between the West Bank and Jordan. This so-called policy of open bridges turned out to be a brilliant arrangement which solved many problems. The Palestinians of the West Bank no longer felt that they were living in a closed prison camp, for their relatives in the Arab countries could now visit the West Bank and Jerusalem. Moreover, the agricultural and industrial produce of the West Bank could be exported to Jordan and, from there, to Kuwait and Saudi Arabia. This arrangement was beneficial to Israel too. Thanks to this commerce, the West Bank became self-sufficient and the state of Israel did not need to invest its own money in its economy. It was quite obvious that Moshe Dayan would have an important role in the peace process of the Middle East.

New friends in Jerusalem

In General Bull's hospitable home I got to know many people of note in Jerusalem. Since Biblical times there have always been representatives of foreign peoples in the City of David. Among the foreigners of today, the archaeologists were closest to the heart of General Bull. Thus it was no wonder that at the first dinner party I attended at his home I met a specialist on the ancient City of David, the Director of the British School of Archaeology, Mrs Crystal-M. Bennet. She had recently assisted the famous Chairman of the same school, Kathleen M. Kenyon, to excavate the ruins of that city near the Temple Mount. Also present were two scholars from the École Biblique, an institute of theology and archaeology for advanced students which was run by French Dominican monks. One of the scholars was Father Charles de Coüasnon, a specialist on the history and architecture of the Church of the Holy Sepulchre. He was energetically involved in the restoration of the church, a project that had lasted for decades and had, since 1959, been run jointly by the Roman Catholic and Greek Orthodox churches – a circumstance, as one could guess, not always without quarrels. Father Coüasnon's profound knowledge and extremely unpretentious character surely made him particularly well-suited for a task that required the diplomatic skills of persuasion.

The second professor from the École Biblique was the internationally still more famous Father Roland de Vaux, whose speciality was the research of the Old Testament, which meant that he was well-known in Israel. Father de Vaux's life work was in fact the writing of the ancient history of Israel. Its first part, describing the formation of the nation and the return to the promised land of Canaan, appeared in 1971, but the death of the author in the same year interrupted the completion of the work, which had been planned to consist of three volumes.

In Jerusalem it was impossible not to get enthusiastic about history and archaeology. I also soon realized that without knowing the past it was difficult to understand the present and its problems. It was a pleasure to accompany Father de Vaux on one of the historical walks he conducted monthly for the benefit of UNTSO staff, and to attend a series of lectures on the authenticity of the Christian holy places, given by Canon Every, a learned Anglican divine.

The city was also notable for the way it recalled the strong and indelible memories left by religious teaching in childhood. At each footstep one encountered something learned long ago, the name of each locality brought back a Biblical story. Events and places which one thought forgotten, returned fresh and vivid to the mind.

After General Bull's party I moved out of Shepherd's Hotel, where I had been living for almost a month. Hotel life had become strenuous and even expensive. I took furnished rooms in a house quite close to the hotel on the Nablous road, owned by Judge Jerallah, a member of a well-known Palestinian family, who administered justice at the Court of Appeals in Ramallah, a Palestinian town north of Jerusalem. His wife, the cheerful and energetic Hilda Jerallah, who was, unlike her husband, a Christian and belonged to the Assyrian Church, took in paying guests in order to have an income of her own.

I liked my new apartment, although it was modest. It consisted of a large bedroom and a living room from where a door opened on to the balcony.

The other occupants of the house were the American Medical Assistant, Chief Belcher, and two British ladies. I soon discovered that my British neighbours, Miss Helen Brien and Miss Carol Hunnybun, were in charge of a Roman Catholic welfare organization. I met them every morning at the breakfast table and always had most interesting conversations with them. I learned that theirs was the Pope's own organization, the Pontifical Mission, which maintained orphanages, old people's homes, schools for the handicapped and other social institutions in East Jerusalem, the West Bank and Gaza. These two ladies had both been in the region a long time and therefore knew the occupied territories thoroughly. They had real grass-roots information which could not be obtained from elsewhere and through them I learned to understand better the complex situation of the area. In time, a real friendship developed between them and my whole family.

In Jerusalem I often came into contact with Catholic scholars and priests. At the beginning I noticed that my attitude towards them was full of suspicion, probably as a result of the Lutheran education of my generation. In the books of the popular children's author, Zachris Topelius, well-known both in Finland and in Sweden, the picture given of the "Papists" was as negative as possible and according to him the Jesuits were the most abominable of all. In Jerusalem I was obliged to change my attitude completely, for I found that the representatives of the Roman Catholic Church, and many Jesuits in particular, were the most civilized and far-sighted of the people I encountered.

In the centre of our part of the city was the Mosque of Sheikh Jarrah, from whose minaret the greatness of Allah was announced early each morning. From the mosque, Saladdin Street, the best shopping street in Jerusalem, led towards the Damascus Gate of the Old City. Near the mosque was the most important sight in the whole area, the American Colony Hotel, which had originally been the palace of a Turkish pasha and his four wives, numerous children, retinue and servants. The atmosphere of this magnificent hotel was unique. It was favoured particularly by writers, artists and journalists.

The manager of the American Colony was Horatio Vester, an unchallengeable expert on Palestine. Born in Haifa at the beginning of the century, son of an American mother and a German missionary, he had worked when young as a teller at Barclay's Bank in Luxor, and had later lived in Jerusalem during the wars of 1948 and 1967. Marriage with the daughter of an English admiral had made him highly anglicized. Horatio's attitude to both the Arabs and the Jews was very positive. For my part, I found conversations with Horatio and his wife Val very instructive. From them I heard about matters relating to the region which I had not known before. I remember especially an assertion repeated many times by Horatio that the peace process could get under way only when Menachem Begin attained power, for as long as he was in opposition he would always prevent any efforts aimed at peace.

Jerusalem was the holy city of the Jews and Moslems and also of Christendom, which was therefore well represented in the city. There were three Patriarchs: the Roman Catholic, the Greek Orthodox and the Armenian, while the Pope had in addition an Apostolic Delegate as his personal representative. The Anglican Church and many other smaller churches were represented by an archbishop. Only the Lutherans had a rather unassuming representation, as they had arrived in Jerusalem later than the others. The German Emperor

Wilhelm II had visited Jerusalem in 1898, learning beforehand, to his great chagrin, that Germany had no worthy foothold there like the other great powers and that the only Lutheran church in the city, originally built by the Crusaders, had fallen into ruin. In honour of the emperor's visit this German Church of the Redeemer had been completely rebuilt, to a much higher standard than before, on its excellent site near the Church of the Holy Sepulchre. Space for the Lutheran community and a vicarage for the German Probst had also been built, while construction started on a hospital, bearing the name of Empress Augusta Victoria, on the Mount of Olives. That building now houses an UNRWA hospital and the office of the Lutheran World Federation.

It came as a surprise to discover that the Russian Orthodox Church of the Soviet Union also had a representative in Jerusalem. The Archimandrite of the Russian Spiritual Mission had his offices in the so-called Russian Compound in the very centre of Jerusalem, which had been acquired by the Russian Church in 1860. On the highest point in the middle of it there was a cathedral, whose green, onion-shaped cupolas and golden crosses could be seen from afar. Of the buildings which surrounded the cathedral and which originally had been built as hostels for pilgrims, most had been handed over to the state of Israel for the use of the Central Police Station and the High Court of Justice. The Russian Church also owned churches, convents and large areas of land in Jaffa, Ein Kerem and Tiberias. Israel had recognized the rights of the Patriarch of Moscow in 1948 in order to show its gratitude for the positive attitude of the Soviet Union to the founding of the new state. As a result, Jordan never again recognized the rights of the "Soviet" Church, the Russian Orthodox churches in Jordan henceforth belonging to the White Russian Patriarch of New York. When divided Jerusalem was reunited after the Six Day War a strange situation was created. In West Jerusalem and other parts of Israel all the Russian churches belonged to the Patriarch of Moscow, while in East Jerusalem places like the onion-domed Church of Mary Magdalene in the Garden of Gethsemane were the property of the Patriarch of New York. The White Russians later tried by court action to transfer the Moscow-owned churches to their possession, but the Israeli judiciary did not grant this request.

The Russian Emperor Alexander III (also Grand Duke of Finland) had built the church in 1888 in memory of his mother. The inside was decorated in pale colours and was, in my opinion, very beautiful. The iconostasis had been decorated by the Russian painter Vereshchagin and, among other icons, the church housed a copy of the famous Black Madonna of Kiev. I visited the church during a service and very much enjoyed the singing of the church choir, particularly its rumbling basses. I was told that one of the singers was a member of the Romanov family, as was the very old abbess of the nunnery behind the church.

The Soviet Union had broken diplomatic relations with Israel as a result of the Six Day War, so the Russian Spiritual Mission was now the only local link between these two states. With this in mind, a professional diplomat had been appointed senior aide to the Archmandrite. Diplomatic relations were also maintained by the Patriarch of Moscow, Pimen, who during my time visited Israel twice, meeting with the Israeli authorities on both occasions.

Extension of service

As Christmas 1967 was nearing, rumours from New York reached us, saying that both the Americans and the French were very much interested in filling the job of the Deputy Chief of Staff of UNTSO when it became vacant after Colonel Johnson's departure in March. The Secretariat had been able to fend off the French attempts, but the United States had referred to the fact that it paid 40 per cent of the costs of the UN and remained steadfast in its claims on the post. General Bull announced that the new colonel who was to be sent out from the USA should go to the field as an ordinary military observer; here at HQ he would not be needed. Then Colonel Johnson returned from home leave, relaxed and full of enthusiasm. We mentioned to him the possible arrival of the new colonel. His brilliant proposal was that he would not return home in March but would stay until my departure, i.e. till mid-October, when he could hand over the job to the new American. I began to feel that I would not be allowed to go back to Finland after the service of one year as I had planned. General Bull also began to explain how important it would be to the UN and UNTSO that I should remain here for one more year. Should I for the second time put the public interest before the interests of my family and myself?

At the end of the year it was time to draw up a temporary balance sheet. I had only been three months in my new job in the Middle East, but during this short period of time I had experienced many new things, met a great number of new people and perhaps learned to understand a little better the problems of the area. It already seemed obvious that I would not return home after twelve months' service, as I had planned. That would be sad news for my family. However, I was sure that, as a kind of a compensation, the future would bring new challenges and more interesting tasks than before.

3. Getting acquainted with the Middle East

Egypt

I awaited my first trip to Cairo with excitement, wondering what changes had taken place since I had visited it ten years ago while serving as the Commanding Officer of the Finnish Company in UNEF I. As I could have guessed, many things were much as before. Changes are slow to take place in a country like Egypt, where religion still has a strong influence on people and strengthens the hold on old traditions.

In Cairo one could see clearer than anywhere else the consequences of Egypt's immense population growth. Even an outsider could understand that the increase of about one million people every year was Egypt's real problem and the greatest worry for its government. Quite obviously, presenting Israel as the main problem had chiefly served the aims of Arab nationalism and the Pan-Arabic movement, and Nasser's position as the leader of the movement.

The capital of three million inhabitants that I had visited in 1957 now seemed a haven of peace to me, compared with the present hell of eight million people. Nobody in fact knew the exact population figures, but when I was driving in the traffic of Cairo I had the feeling that the city was about to burst apart at the seams. The problems caused by its enormous growth were no longer humanly manageable. The traffic jams were indescribable. Huge crowds poured out of the trams and buses. The international airport and the office of UNTSO were situated in Heliopolis, about 15 kilometres from the centre. Previously it would have taken half an hour to travel there; now it could take two hours. Telephone communications between the different parts of the city no longer functioned. The general poverty of the population was manifested in many ways. Children were begging in the streets and some parts of the city were dirty and miserable. The decay was so far advanced in some places that bulldozing the buildings seemed to be the only solution.

In the countryside, from where the additional population of Cairo had come, not much had changed in the last ten years. On my way to Ismailia I saw again the typical Egyptian farmer and his family toiling in the fields from early morning to late evening. Methods which had been established over the course of millennia had not changed. Camels and oxen were pulling the wooden ploughs. Behind the fields in the courtyards of the farmhouses rose the tower-like dove-cotes, while sailboats moved fast along the sweetwater canal. This carried the water of the Nile towards Ismailia and branched off from there to the north and south, towards the cities of Port Said and Suez. On both sides of the sweetwater canal there was a narrow cultivated strip, only about 1 km. wide. The road, following the course of the canal, was bordered by bushy and fast-growing eucalyptus trees. Closer to Ismailia, one could see mango orchards and date palms growing along the road.

Water was raised to the fields by hand or by pumps turned by oxen. They also threshed the corn, in the same way as in Biblical times. I also noticed the extraordinary industry of the people and their bright smiles and positive expressions which were evidence of happiness and satisfaction. One could believe that the inhabitants of the countryside, the Egyptian farmers, were the backbone of society and a guarantee of its continuity and stability. No revolution would be started in the rural areas.

I knew beforehand that Egypt was a country of great contradictions. There were considerable differences in income. Despite Nasser's revolution, the rich continued to be rich, while the majority of the people is very poor. Gross National Product in 1967 was only $200 per capita. For comparison, one could mention that at the end of the 1960s the GNP per capita in Egypt was only one tenth of the corresponding Finnish figure. Because the population of Egypt was ten times larger than that of Finland, the total GNP in each of the two countries was the same. Despite the poverty, however, nobody dies of hunger in Egypt; the police do not need to collect the corpses of those who died of hunger during the night, as they do in some really poor countries.

Thus Egypt is, above all, a developing country where the infrastructure is inadequate, the industrialization slight and the agriculture primitive. On the other hand, Egypt also has an ancient civilization, a growing educated middle class and a great number of skilled workers. Both latter groups have suffered during the years from inflation and retarded salaries and many of their members have moved abroad in the hope of a better income.

There are still master artisans in Cairo. When looking in Cairo's ancient palaces and mosques at their skilful woodwork and masonry, brass ornaments, tiles and mosaics, one might think that these crafts have become extinct. However, the reality is different. In the fire of the Al Aksa Mosque in Jerusalem, the pulpit donated by Saladin was destroyed. It was a masterpiece of carved ivory and ebony. When I doubted that there would be anyone to repair it, the artist in charge of the restoration told me that there were still masters in Cairo.

When Caliph Amr captured Egypt from the Byzantine Empire in 641 AD, most Egyptians were Coptic Christian ("Copt" is a corrupt form of the Greek word for an Egyptian). The Arabization of the country and its conversion to Islam were slow at the beginning, because the conquerors did not force anybody to it. Only in the eighth century did the rate of conversion increase, because now it was followed by economic and social benefits. Since the fourteenth century the proportion of Moslems and Copts in the population has remained the same: 10 per cent Copts and 90 per cent Moslems. Thus the number of the Copts in recent times has been about four million.

Although the Copts are, in an Islamic state, second-class citizens in a certain way, they play an important role in the economic life of the country and as civil servants. They are on average better educated and wealthier than the Moslems. Finnish businessmen and engineers gave me details of their experiences of the position of the Copts in Egyptian society. For example, in the Ministry of Electricity, where the Finns did a good deal of business, the highest directors were Moslems. Their task was to receive the guests and drink coffee with them. The number two men were Copts, who took care of the real business. Perhaps this impression was exaggerated and only showed the prejudices of the Christian Finns. In my opinion, one can draw from this story the conclusion that the Copts could not get the job of the number one man in the administration. I had also noticed, however, that there were no major quarrels between the religious groups.

Often one heard the Copts asserting that they were descended from the original population of Pharaonic times. But obviously those Egyptians who considered themselves as Arabs were also descended from them. Some people thought that 90 per cent of the population consisted of these descendants of the Pharaohs. This dichotomy of the past into the time of the Pharaohs and the time of the Arabs had led Egypt into a kind of an identity crisis, where appreciation of these two heritages varied in different ages. The geographical position of the country had a further influence on this confused sense of identity. Egypt is situated in Africa, but by its culture it is a part of Asia and the Mediterranean area. Many cultures have met in Egypt over the course of millennia. The identity crisis is complicated by the fact that both the Pharaonic culture and the Arab culture are great high cultures of humanity.

Appreciation of its national history really began in Egypt at the end of the nineteenth century, when Western scholars unearthed monuments of its ancient culture. Many Egyptians became very enthusiastic about the exploration of their national roots, although others jeered at this as Pharaonism. Perhaps behind the enthusiasm lay the desire to flee from the difficulties of the present. Since the sixth century Egypt had been under the yoke of a foreign conqueror and, as a reaction, people now sought comfort in the knowledge of their ancient splendour and position of power. The first history book in Arabic, which came out in 1868, gave information about this past.

After the Second World War there was a clear change of line in Egypt. Pharaonism and the admiration of Europe were condemned and Arabism became popular. The Arab League was founded with its headquarters in Cairo. It was stressed that Cairo was the brain of the Arab world and Mecca its heart.

The 1950s were the golden decade of Pan-Arabism, as Nasser tried to merge Egypt into the Arab world. He saw in this the means to increase the political influence of the Arabs. He also saw himself leading this new political movement, in which Egypt as the most developed Arab state would play a leading role. In the constitution of 1956 Egypt was declared a part of the Arab world. The majority of the people had no idea what this was about, but was satisfied that King Farouk had been overthrown. People regarded Nasser and his Revolutionary Council as the first Egyptians to rule the country for 2,500 years. In 1959 Egypt and Syria formed a union and the name of Egypt disappeared from maps, stamps and the coat of arms. The United Arab Republic was the first one of the many Arab unions in the Middle East which have proved impossible and so have been short-lived.

At Nasser's initiative the history books were rewritten. The Pharaohs were invalidated. All Semitic people except the Jews were retrospectively declared Arabs. In this way the Arab identity of the countries of the region and the importance of the Arabs in world history were stressed. The history of the Arabs was artificially lengthened by thousands of years. The peoples of Mesopotamia, the ancient Egyptians and the Phoenicians were also Arabs according to this school of thought.

The Arab conquest of the world which had started in the seventh century could now be explained as a liberation movement which had freed ancient Arab lands from the domination of Persia and the

Byzantine Empire. The use of the word "conquer" (*fataha*) in this context was abolished and replaced by "liberate" (*halla*). It was also said that the Arabs had lived in Palestine before other peoples, because its original inhabitants were Semites and thus Arabs.

In 1967 it became clear that the idea of Pan-Arabism which had started in Egypt and Syria had not materialized. It had been overtaken by military defeat. The Egyptians woke up to the realization that Pan-Arabism had become too expensive for them. In all the wars since 1948 Egypt had been Israel's main adversary and it had suffered from them most. Its casualties and economic losses had been greater than those of the other Arab peoples.

Because of the great disunity of and controversies between the Arabs, the whole idea of a united and politically influential Arab world has remained, for the most part, wishful thinking. The operational ability of the Arab League has often been paralysed because of a greater or lesser quarrel. The League has not been able to convene the summit meetings which are so popular with the Arabs. The union between Egypt and Syria, the United Arab Republic, held together only about a year. The defeat of 1967 signified a death blow to Nasser's dreams. Only the future will show whether the Arab states are able to arrive at a settlement of their disputes and overcome their disunity.

In the disunited Arab world Egypt was, however, the most significant state in 1967. Despite the losses it suffered in the war, it was militarily the strongest and politically the most important. Furthermore, Egypt was culturally superior. Well-educated Egyptians functioned as teachers, medical doctors, judges and engineers in countries such as Libya and the states of the Persian Gulf. In other words, Egypt was not simply a poor developing country suffering an excessive population growth. In some areas of life it was almost on the level of the developed European states. Despite losses and failures, it was a surprisingly steady and balanced country. It had existed as a state since the dawn of history and did not need to be worried about its future.

As a state it was more developed than any other Arab country in the Middle East. The location of Egypt in a remote part of the Ottoman Empire, and its semi-autonomous position within that empire, had made it possible for an authentic sense of nationalism to take root there more easily than elsewhere in the Middle East. In fact, in that area Egypt is the only national state, in the European sense, to have developed in the nineteenth century. The patriotism and nationalism of the

Egyptians are based more on their own history than on the heritage of Arab nationalism. The period of Pan-Arabism of Nasser's time remained a temporary phase. The free development of nationalism had been furthered in the latter half of the nineteenth century by the reformers and modernizers of Egypt, the Khedives Muhammad Ali and his son Ibrahim Pasha. Thanks to them, Egypt was greatly westernized and became an autonomous entity. The construction of the Suez Canal, the railway network and modern Cairo were high points in this development.

The glorious past gave the highest Egyptian leaders confidence in the future. Nasser and, later, especially Sadat clearly had a "pharaonic" view of their position and task. But lower leaders too, as for example the military officers and the officials of the Foreign Ministry whom I met in my work, had a strong faith in the future of Egypt. Nobody would be able to push the Egyptian people into the sea.

The Egyptians are a talented people. I had already noted that in my previous UN job. In my own sphere of experience, I greatly appreciated the functioning of the Foreign Ministry in particular. Israel's war machinery was superior, but Egyptian diplomacy was continually better planned, had more initiative and was more skilful. Perhaps Israel wanted to avoid taking the initiative at that stage and was therefore content with reacting to initiatives originating from elsewhere.

I had tried to become acquainted with the political situation in Egypt even before my first trip to Cairo and the west bank of the Suez Canal. I wrote home about it at the beginning of November:

Egyptian foreign policy seems to have two main objectives. Firstly, the demand, presented in the UN, that Israeli forces should withdraw unconditionally. Secondly, Egypt wants necessarily to open the Suez Canal. Egypt feels that it is in a stronger position politically and therefore considers that it is able to wait, even for a long time, for the development of a situation more favourable to it. The conference in Khartoum in August 1967, where Egypt received, among other things, economic support as compensation for the lost income from the Canal, has given it encouragement and strength. In addition, it hopes that the big powers will bring pressure to bear for the opening of the Canal to navigation.

The Egyptian officer and soldier have not yet fully recovered from the shock caused by the defeat. According to UN Military Observers they try now to invent different, supernatural explanations for Israel's success. They assume that the same supernatural forces could be on the side of Egypt next time. Finnish observers have also said that the Egyptians have not learned the lessons from their past errors when redeploying their forces. The deployment is again concentrated on the forward defended areas, and the first line is manned by soldiers in tight formation.

The appointment of Deputy Prime Minister Ali Sabry as the Minister in charge of the canal zone was in a way a symptomatic event. As the leader of the hawks in the parliament, Sabry has always followed an aggressive policy aimed at the destruction of Israel.

On my inspection tours I could see for myself the depressed mood of the Egyptians, although they did not easily expose their innermost feelings to a temporary visitor. Only from the memoirs of Anwar Sadat, which appeared in 1977, did the matter finally become clear to me. Sadat describes the period from June 1967 to September 1970 as one of intense suffering, unprecedented in the whole of Egyptian history. Sufferings and frustration forced the Egyptians into a struggle for survival. According to Sadat, this struggle was apparent, among other ways, in the surprisingly rapid rearmament of the army and in the way that the people continually looked to Nasser, who at that time still represented the only ray of hope in the otherwise hopeless situation. Sadat surely does not exaggerate too much, but describes truthfully the feelings of both the Egyptian ruling class and the ordinary people. The Six Day War had been a crushing defeat for all Egyptians. The armed forces had been beaten. Besides the large number of casualties, they had lost almost all of their equipment. The main sources of income of the state – the Suez Canal and the oil of Sinai – were gone. But the hardest thing to endure was the deep shame caused by the defeat. For the proud Egyptians this was an intolerable burden. Sadat describes his own feelings: "I myself was completely overwhelmed by our defeat. It sank into the very fabric of my consciousness so that I relived it day and night. As its real dimensions were daily revealed to me, my agony intensified – and my sense of helplessness."

For Nasser himself the three last years of his life were surely still more burdensome. That the country was driven into a war in June 1967 was mainly a consequence of his defiant and fanatic policy. The highest command of the armed forces could naturally be accused of incompetence, but the main responsibility for the military defeat was Nasser's alone. Moreover, none of his other initiatives now succeeded in the manner he wished. Egypt's relations with the rest of the world had been bad for some time, but now even relations with the Soviet Union did not correspond with Nasser's wishes. Weapons and ammunition meant to replace the losses of the June war arrived, in Nasser's opinion, very slowly and the Russians continuously warned the Egyptians against taking any new military action. Nasser's efforts to get the Soviet Union to hasten and increase its deliveries of armaments were not successful. The Soviets had decided, so Sadat thinks in his memoirs, to take care only of Egypt's immediate needs and to confirm the presence of the Soviet Union in the area. In any case, the Russians presumably would have had a different opinion on how speedily they were delivering these arms supplies, because before the beginning of November 1967 all the lost aeroplanes and 70 per cent of the army's heavy armament and tanks had been replaced.

The summit meeting in Khartoum in August 1967 was more successful from the Egyptian point of view. Relations with Saudi Arabia improved and the oil-producing countries, Saudi Arabia, Kuwait and Libya, promised to compensate Egypt's loss of income from the Canal. It was a further relief for Egypt that it was allowed to reduce the number of its troops in Yemen from 60,000 men. The summit meeting also made its famous decision of three nos: no peace with Israel, no recognition and no negotiations.

Because Nasser regarded the arms supplies from the Soviet Union as slow and insufficient, he finally had to turn to the United States. The initiative made in his speech on 1 May 1970 happened conveniently to coincide with the new American peace initiative, the so-called Rogers Plan of June 1970. According to this, the UN Mediator, the Swedish Dr Gunnar Jarring, would conduct negotiations during the cease-fire, which was to last 90 days. Although Nasser, based on his previous experience, regarded Jarring's success with some suspicion, he decided during his last trip to Moscow to announce his acceptance of the Rogers Plan. This was his last desperate attempt to exert pressure in order to increase and hasten the Soviet arms supplies.

In the last years of his life Nasser was a very sick man. As his last effort, he convened in September 1970 an Arab summit meeting with the aim of settling the deep disagreements between King Hussein of Jordan and PLO Chairman Yasser Arafat. It was a difficult task and the parties had unrealistic expectations and directed unfair accusations at him. Finally, Nasser's health gave out and he died during the meeting on 28 September 1970.

Syria

My earlier knowledge of Syria and the Syrians was quite superficial, consisting of a one-day trip to Damascus in the summer of 1957 while on vacation in Beirut. I had briefly visited the Mosque of the Omayyads, the National Museum and the bazaar. Now it was time to get to know the country from a different viewpoint from that of a tourist.

Even on my first trip to Syria many things became clearer. I travelled to Damascus in the company of General and Mrs Bull. The journey was more comfortable than usual as it was made in the air-conditioned limousine, UN 1. The time passed quickly in lively chat and in recalling our stay in Lebanon ten years ago. The car passed along the fertile West Bank of Jordan, through Bireh, Nablus and Jenin, which were very clean and prosperous. The difference between these northern Palestinian towns and those of Egypt or Gaza was noticeable. At noon we arrived at Tiberias, an ancient Roman bathing town on the shore of the Sea of Galilee. We stayed a few hours in the UNTSO control centre west of the town.

Guided by the Officer-in-Charge of Tiberias Control Centre, we visited an observation post on the Israeli side of the cease-fire lines and the badly destroyed town of Quneitra where UNTSO had an out-station. On the Syrian side we were met by the local Divisional Commander and the Syrian Liaison Officer, Commodore A. Abdallah. After another hour's drive we could see the lights of Damascus. The great city rising high on the slopes of the mountain was a glorious sight.

In a letter to my wife I wrote:

> In the evening we were invited for dinner in Commodore Abdallah's home. A grand home, gilded furniture and gaudy colours, somewhat in the same style of the Turkish Military Attachés we knew in Warsaw. The children, nice 10 and 8 year-old boys, came to shake hands. Madame was expecting her third. Both spoke English well, but French better still. I noticed for the first time that my knowledge of French is very useful. The table was beautifully laid and the food familiar from Lebanon: stuffed vine leaves or dolmas, chicken and rice. Extremely sweet puff pastries were served as dessert. They looked like our Christmas pies. The meal ended with grapes, apples and bananas of a particularly high quality. Such fine fruit is not available in Jerusalem.

The next day it was time to meet the Syrian military leadership. Accompanying General Bull, I first met General Soueidani. A guard of honour and bugle sounds met us in the courtyard of the Defence Ministry. The Minister gave the impression of being a strong and pleasant person. During the conversation it became quite clear that the Syrians deeply hated the Israelis. At one point, General Soueidani remarked that Israel could of course come and capture Damascus, but it would be recaptured, if not by him and his generation, then by their sons. In my opinion this was mighty and arrogant talk which seemed unwarranted after a lost war. As he was blamed for the defeat in the 1967 war, Soueidani was replaced by Hafez al Assad in March 1968.

During my later trips to Syria, and also in conversations with the Israelis, it became more and more clear that this hatred really was deep and mutual. The last 20 years had only increased the suspicion and distrust between these two peoples who both laid claim to the same piece of land. This was not only a question of the possession of the Golan Heights; the Syrians have always considered Palestine as a part of Syria and, consequently, the state of Israel as an obstacle to their expansionist aspirations and the unification of the Arabs. The Israelis, on their part, considered the Syrians as the most bellicose and implacable of their next-door neighbours. The hatred between these two peoples is instinctive and one could accurately describe them as arch enemies.

One conversation which took place in Damascus during a festive dinner describes the Syrian attitude well. The talk turned to national diseases. Somebody thought that the French suffer especially from their liver. Others thought that the English were plagued by gout and Americans by heart disease. I asked a Syrian general about the Syrian national disease. "It is Israel," came the gloomy answer.

Having visited Egypt just before my trip to Syria I was naturally comparing the qualities of these two peoples. The Syrians are very different from the Egyptians. Softnesss, a desire to please and a sense of humour are Egyptian qualities. The members of the Egyptian ruling class are often refined, cosmopolitan and blasé. They are used to a leading position in the Arab world and therefore their behaviour is self-confident. Nothing could shake them. The Syrians, on the other hand, are harsh inhabitants of a mountainous country, closer to nature and less sophisticated than the Egyptians. The Syrians are proud and easily offended. They want to be respected and have their merits recognized, reacting violently to any hint of condescension.

It was not easy to know Syria and the Syrians. An observer from the outside who did not speak Arabic felt especially isolated from the local environment. No newspapers or TV programmes in Western languages were available in the country. The Syrians treated foreigners with suspicion and did not volunteer information about the political or economic situation of their country. Fortunately, during my first trips to Damascus I became friendly with a Syrian businessman and his English wife. Over the years, many interesting discussions were held in their hospitable home. Despite this, I felt myself a poor and superficial expert on Syria.

As representatives of UNTSO, however, we were in a better position than many other foreigners, because the senior liaison officers whom the Syrian Army had appointed to assist us were all very helpful, enlightened and good at languages. During my tour of duty, Commodore Abdallah was followed by Colonel Hikmat al Shihabi, a very forceful and intelligent officer, trained at Fort Leavenworth. I was not surprised that he was Henry Kissinger's negotiating partner in 1974 in Washington, DC. He is now the Chief of Staff of the Syrian Army. Colonel al Shihabi was in turn succeeded by General J. Bitar, a Christian, who was a very civilized and polite liaison officer. Moreover, Mrs Bitar was, from our point of view, an important person because she was the headmistress of the international school in Damascus. Many children of UNTSO personnel attended it. Bitar was followed by Colonel (later General) Adnan Tayara, an experienced officer who had travelled widely. Before the 1967 war he was Military Attaché in Amman and in East Jerusalem had met his wife, who belonged to the well-known Palestinian Nuseiby family. Tayara was related to the very influential Foreign Minister Abd El Halim Khaddam, who later became Vice-President of Syria. Khaddam, an elegantly dressed, French-speaking gentleman, was known among diplomats for his acid tongue and rudeness. With his aggressive tone, he could easily insult an Ambassador or snub a visiting United Nations Under Secretary-General. To me he showed only his polite, gentle and friendly side and our relationship became warmer every year. This, of course, helped immensely in carrying out my duties.

That, however, was all in the future. On my first trip, when I was visiting the UNTSO observation posts, I also watched the Syrian Army. I formed a rather favourable impression of its discipline and fighting ability. It was difficult to believe that it had fought so poorly in the recent war. Fortifications were assiduously being completed along the entire cease-fire line. The UN observers said that this work was now better planned than it had been before the war. Until now there had been no firing between Syria and Israel since the Six Day War. The observers thought, however, that incidents could be expected as soon as the Syrians had completed the fortification of their positions. The terrain between the cease-fire line and Damascus was very difficult to defend. It was typical tank terrain and there were no narrow parts of passage. From the point of view of the attacker Damascus was just waiting to be taken. Israel, on its side, held all dominating points of terrain along the entire width of the cease-fire line.

Throughout the Ottoman period, Syrians identified themselves only by their religion: a Syrian is first and foremost either a Moslem, a Christian or a Jew. And in 1967 the transition into nationhood was not complete. As in other traditional societies, the most important structures were families and tribes. Religion was the most significant divider. Syria is preponderantly a Sunni Moslem society, with each of the principal minorities – the Alawites, the Christians and the Kurds – forming about ten per cent of the population. The Druse, the Ismailis and others total about six per cent. There are other groups too, for instance about 200,000 Palestinians (mainly Moslems) and about 5,000 Jews. The Christians are moreover divided into many different churches, like the Maronite, the Greek Catholic (who are part of the Roman Catholic Church) and the Greek and Russian Orthodox Churches, plus many Prostestant communities.

Another important divisive factor was the strength of local ties. Thus the Syrians could be natives of Tartus, Aleppo, Homs and so on. The long-standing Liaison Officer of UNTSO, General Adnan Tayara, originated from Tartus and was therefore jokingly called the King of Tartus. His task as a private person was to take care of the problems that the inhabitants of his home town encountered with the bureaucrats of the capital. Almost every day a delegation from Tartus was in his office to present all kinds of problems.

Perhaps a sense of belonging to one nation had not been able to develop because Syria had been under foreign occupation for almost its entire history. I had earlier noticed similar attitudes and the under-development of the idea of state in Poland. The last occupier of Syria was the Turkish Ottoman Empire, until Turkey lost its position in the Middle East as a consequence of the First World War. After that, the League of Nations gave Syria as a mandate to France. The last French troops left Syria in 1948.

I was surprised by the still quite strong influence of the French language and culture in Syria. Members of the older generation, and many of the younger, preferred to speak French rather than English, which quite a few did not speak at all. Young people would be sent to Paris to study if possible. The French themselves were admired and respected. One might have imagined that the Syrians would feel hatred, or at least antipathy, towards their former colonial masters. But there was no trace of such feelings. Naturally, the Syrians were satisfied with the French attitude to the Middle East conflict and de Gaulle's decision to stop selling arms to Israel. But this did not wholly explain the great popularity and authority of France in Syria. The short-lived mandate is not a sufficient explanation either.

In fact, French influence on the entire area of the Levant dated from almost a thousand years earlier. The Frenchman Godefroy de Bouillon, the Duke of Lorraine, led the first Crusade to the Middle East and founded the Kingdom of Jerusalem in 1098. During the reign of his successor, Baldouin II, Damascus, Homs and Aleppo had to pay tax to this kingdom. On the arrival of the French, the Arab occupation, which had lasted 400 years, turned Syria, Lebanon and Palestine into a mainly Arabic-speaking Moslem area where the Jews and the Christians were a minority. The Crusades signified the arrival of French civilization to the Levant. French gradually became the language of administration and business. Numerous mixed marriages strengthened the spread of French culture. French influence manifested itself in the Romanesque churches, castles and fortified farm-houses built by the Crusaders. The period of the Crusades, which lasted almost two centuries, saw Western culture strengthen. As a result of this, many Syrian families of French origin have preserved their names, their language and their manners.

There are many parallels between Syria and Egypt. Like Egypt, Syria also has its own culture, dating back thousands of years, which was broken by the arrival of the Arabs in the seventh century. And in Syria, too, people's interest in their own roots started to grow towards the end of the nineteenth century, when Western scholars excavated valuable evidence of the ancient cultures of the region from the sand. Syrian nationalism began gradually to appear in the struggle against the Turkish oppression. Moreover, the Syrians had their own identity crisis in the 1930s and 1940s. Nationalistic feelings were strengthened by the influence of the French. A "people's party", stressing Syrianness at the expense of Arabness, was founded in the 1930s, but suspended in 1940. The 1960s were a time of strong Pan-Arabism, which, thanks to Nasser, was a generally accepted line of thought in Syria.

For a long time Syria suffered from internal disunity. After it became independent, many competing factions struggled for power. The country experienced a series of revolutions, sometimes three a year. In 1957 parliamentary democracy was experimented with and for a short time a civilian government was in power. But by the following year the idea of a union with Egypt became attractive and the United Arab Republic was founded. It was hoped that Pan-Arabism would prevail in the Arab world under the leadership of Egypt and Nasser. This experiment too foundered in 1961 because of mutual disagreements.

In 1963 the Syrian Ba'ath Party came to power. Founded in the 1950s by Michel Aflaq, a Christian, it had grown into a major political movement. A large proportion of its followers belonged to the Christian and Alawi minorities. The three Ba'athist goals were the unity of all Arabs, from the Atlantic to the Persian Gulf, freedom and socialism. Arab unity was the most important goal, but Arab socialism was also a central Ba'athist doctrine. It did not include dialectical materialism or atheism, but was seen as the party's instrument for promoting the well-being of the under-privileged.

The Alawites occupied an important position in the Ba'ath Party. Since early times they had been a despised rural minority which mainly performed manual work. Many had joined the army because able men could make a career there. The influence of the Alawites increased greatly after the Ba'athist coup of 1966. Their position of power in internal politics is based on the discipline and unity of the group. In external politics it is founded on an uncompromising Syrian nationalism. Syrian military leaders must constantly be on the alert in case radical civilian leaders, using chauvinist fanaticism as their excuse, push them aside. Syria is unusual in that its civilians are more bellicose than its soldiers.

The Ba'athist coup and Syria's disastrous defeat in the June war of 1967 were followed by violent factional fighting at the top echelon of the Ba'ath Party. Hafez al Assad was named Minister of Defence and from that position he finally reached the top as President in 1970, appointing General Mustafa Tlas as Minister of Defence and General Chakour as Chief of Staff.

When I first visited the new Chief of Staff, who was a Christian,

I learned that he had previously been the Consul General of Syria in São Paulo, Brazil. On my remarking that I did not know Syria had interests in São Paulo to be cared for, General Chakour told me that, as elsewhere in South America, there were many Syrian immigrants in Brazil; for example, in São Paulo there were 60,000 people from the town of Homs alone. The inhabitants of Homs were predominantly Christian. Perhaps one could infer from General Chakour's story that many Christians had found their life as members of a religious minority so difficult that they had preferred life in exile. Later I discovered that these emigrants were not exclusively Christians; many Moslems had also left the country in the hope of freedom and a better income.

If the life of the Christians in Syria was difficult, what was the fate of the Syrian Jews? This question was often asked by the Israeli press. Often I too was asked, at diplomatic dinner parties and elsewhere, what I thought about the plight of the Syrian Jews. I was slightly bothered by this question, because I did not know the answer. After some fact-finding I realized that their position was not so exceptionally miserable after all. Many Israelis, however, did not want to believe my information.

On one occasion at the French Embassy in Damascus I saw a French-made film about the life of the Jews in Syria. My attention was drawn to nice pictures of Jewish children and of two Jewish schools in Damascus. One of the schools was run by the Alliance Française. As the film seemed to be something of an eulogy, and as I did not know on whose behalf it had been made, I decided to interview some UNTSO people who lived permanently in Damascus as well as some Jewish merchants in the bazaar whom I knew. There were many Jewish masters of the typical Damascene handicrafts, particularly copper-smiths who made brass plates and vases with silver and copper inlays. My interviewees told me that, for Jews, political activity was not possible; expressing Zionist opinions would land one in prison. Life was not always easy in other respects either, but my informants emphasised that the lives of Christians and Moslems were not without difficulties. Syria was at war with Israel. The government had dicta-torial powers and the police often resorted to hard measures.

At the end of the 1960s Syria was still a poor, agricultural country: a developing country. Its political system was unstable. Life in a tight police state and in the whirl of socialist economic experiments could be hard. The Six Day War had brought home, with a sense of shock,

how weak Syria still was militarily compared with Israel. But it clearly
had great political, economic and cultural objectives. It wanted to fulfil
the idea of Greater Syria, with Lebanon forming at least one part of it.
In order to achieve these political goals and to improve its security, the
armed forces must be strengthened. But Syria also wanted to improve
the educational level of its people and its national economy. For
instance, the great electric power plant that was under construction
on the River Euphrates would produce electricity for industry and
provide an opportunity to carry out plans for the modernization of
agriculture in the Euphrates Valley.

Lebanon

I knew Lebanon already, having spent a great seven-day vacation in
Beirut in the summer of 1957. At that time the UN paid the expenses
of such recreation trips for all UNEF soldiers. I had enjoyed the natural
beauty of the Lebanese mountains and the bustle of the big city. The
civil war had not yet spoilt the country and as a tourist spot it deserved
its fame as the Switzerland of the Middle East. However, although
the ordinary tourist might not be aware of it, below the surface matters
were coming to a head and the internal disputes were about to explode
into open war.

The first phase of the civil war had already broken out when,
in the summer of 1958, I came to Lebanon for the second time
in order to join the new United Nations Observer Group in Lebanon (UNOGIL). President Camille Chamoun had requested the United
Nations to investigate whether Syria had intervened militarily in the
civil war.

In the course of carrying out our job, we had the opportunity
to become familiar with the circumstances and internal problems of
the country. We visited northern Lebanon, where the population,
undeterred by the police, grew hemp and where the UN had to hire
a local gang of brigands to protect the security of its observers. At
the beginning of the operation we fetched new vehicles from Naqoura
on the Israeli border and on the way we familiarized ourselves with
southern Lebanon, which the supervision and care of the government
did not reach either. In that part of the country, too, the population
could live their poor and modest lives without the interference of anybody. However, the orange orchards along the Mediterranean coastal
road guaranteed a good income to their wealthy owners, who lived in

the cities. One could see from this and other matters that differences of income in Lebanon were great indeed.

During those first months I had made many Lebanese friends, Christians, Moslems and foreigners who lived permanently in Beirut, and I had spoken with them about the problems of the country. I had also heard in the cafés of the Hamra shopping street how the well-educated and elegantly dressed Beirutis spoke in three languages – Arabic, French and English – about their work and their most favoured hobby: making money. There was no time for or interest in anything else, except entertainment. In the opinion of the Beirutis, sitting in a night-club was the most amusing pastime. The cabaret programmes in the night-clubs, especially the famous Casino du Liban, were top class. But during these performances, many Lebanese were also surely thinking of how best to succeed in the hard competition of the business world.

The Lebanese were descendants of the ancient Phoenicians, but over the centuries many conquerors had taken possession of this area: Egyptians, Romans, Crusaders, Arabs, Turks and lastly the French. All these conquerors had left as a legacy, apart from cultural influences, traits of their character and appearance. I imagined that something also remained of the original Phoenicians. As we know, because of their business activities they had no time to defend their country, but recruited for that purpose foreign mercenaries and scientists, like Archimedes. Now we, the UN soldiers, were to take care of the security of the Lebanese.

This is illustrated by an incident from 1958. I was in a group of Swedish and Finnish officers on a patrol tour in the mountains near the cedar forest called the Cedars. In a restaurant a young Lebanese Member of Parliament came to our table and was wondering greatly that we had come so far from the north to his country. I remarked that, thanks to technology, distances had decreased, the globe had become smaller and therefore a faraway crisis could threaten our security as well. As Sweden and Finland had sent their soldiers, I thought the least that Lebanon could do was to reimburse the UN for the expense our deployment incurred. The thought simply terrified him and when he later passed by our table again, he exclaimed: "*Qui payera? Qui payera?*" ("Who is going to pay?")

The internal conflict in Lebanon was a struggle for social and economic power between two groups, something like the dispute between the Protestants and Roman Catholics in Northern Ireland.

The Christians of Lebanon traditionally had the economic power in their hands and, through it, a great influence in other matters too. When the French gave Lebanon its independence in 1941 they wanted to strengthen the Christians' position of power and therefore created the myth of the Christian majority. In reality this majority had ceased to exist by the 1940s and now in the 1960s the Moslems had a clear majority. The difference in the size of the two groups increased because the number of children in Christian families declined as their parents wanted to guarantee them as good an education as possible. In contrast, for religious reasons the Moslem families had many children. In order not to reveal the truth of this, a full census could not be carried out.

The presence of the Palestinian refugees in Lebanon upset the population balance because the majority were Moslem. Therefore many Christians were hostile towards them and wanted them to go. The Christians were also more nationalistic and were ready to do anything to preserve the independence of Lebanon, while some of the Moslems supported the idea of Arab unification. Thus their attitude towards Israel was radical: Israel opposed Arab aspirations and therefore had to be destroyed. The Lebanese Christians adopted a more positive approach to Israel. However, the difference in attitudes was not always as clear-cut as this. This was Lebanon and an outsider had difficulties in understanding its complexities.

The division of wealth in Lebanon did not run rigidly along religious lines. Among the Moslems were many wealthy families who in fact had the same objectives and interests as wealthy Christians. On the other hand, the majority of the Christians were poor and badly paid. In particular, the salaries of the civil servants, such as the police and customs officers, were bad. This was one reason for the widespread corruption which was one of the worst plagues of Lebanese society. Civil servants were obliged to resort to bribes because their salaries were not high enough to maintain the standard of living that a businessman could afford. Once, in front of the airport building in Beirut, I saw a police officer hurrying to his brand new Mercedes car carrying boxes of expensive Cuban cigars. I asked the UNTSO Air Transport Officer, who happened to be on the spot, how such luxury was possible. "When his monthly salary is about 1,500 Lebanese pounds [$400], one can guess from where the money comes," was his reply.

On the other hand, public opinion did not condemn bribery very strongly. It was considered part of the Levantine tradition. In fact a person was considered a little stupid if he did not, as a minister for example, accumulate his own wealth. Even the presidents of the republic were not always honest. President Franjieh once admitted in public that he was a crook. It was thought that the first honest person to occupy this high office was General Shehab, who was elected in 1958 after the first civil war and who belonged to a previously wealthy family. When he was looking for a trustworthy and honest adviser, Elias Sarkis, Professor of National Economy at the American University in Beirut, was suggested for the job. Sarkis in his turn was also completely honest.

In the constitution of the country drawn up by the French, the division of offices was precisely determined. Thus the President of the republic should always be a Maronite Christian, the Prime Minister a Sunni Moslem, the Army Commander a Christian and so on. This system was complicated and artificial. A real and just democracy could not be built on this basis. Furthermore, in Lebanon nothing was known of the Nordic welfare state: the state and the municipalities gave nothing free to their citizens; most schools and hospitals were owned by different churches, while education and public health had to be paid for and were therefore often very expensive.

Matters were further complicated by the division of the Christians and Moslems into numerous factions. The most important Christian denominations were the Maronites (about half a million) and the Greek Catholic (about 100,000), which were both under the authority of the Pope, and the Greek Orthodox (about 150,000). Most of the Moslems were Sunnis (about half a million). Smaller groups were the Shi'ites, who numbered about a quarter of a million, and the Druse (less than 100,000). The politico-religious groups had their own private armies. Moreover, corruption and other crimes were part of the way the groups operated, and mafia-style traits had become more and more apparent. In such circumstances the government's authority was limited and the weak and disunited army was of no help. The government simply had no means to maintain public order and security.

The Lebanese civil war originally had no connection with the broader conflict between the Arabs and Israel, but the presence of the Palestinians in Lebanon soon provided a link. Initially these refugees, some 100,000 people, had lived in Haifa, Acre and northern Galilee. At the end of the 1960s they numbered about 150,000. Since 1948 they had lived in camps around Beirut and in south Lebanon. The refugees were gradually becoming a factor in political and military power in Lebanon. The strengthening of the Palestine Liberation Organization (PLO), the birth of Palestinian nationalism and the excellent education given to the young refugees by the UN all had their effect. The miserable conditions in the camps and the desperate future faced by their inhabitants increased the feelings of hatred towards Israel and incited the youth to aggressive deeds. More and more often one could see that desperate people resorted to desperate acts.

During my first trips to Lebanon I observed that Beirut was outwardly as it had been before, but beneath the surface it was smouldering. When I went, together with my boss, to meet the Army Commander, General Boustany, he told that there had been a number of guerrilla attacks on Israel from Lebanese territory. He wanted more UN observers, in order to prevent Israeli retaliation. On my next trips I found that the situation was steadily worsening. In 1969 Lebanon was again about to dissolve. From this point of view the Cairo summit meeting proved fatal, because it decided that Lebanon should allow the Palestinian fighters to use its territory as a base from which to attack Israel. I thought it cynical that the weakest state in the region should be forced into such a difficult position. Larger and stronger Arab states, such as Egypt and Syria, refused to allow Palestinian guerrilla activities to be launched from their territories because they knew that Israeli retaliation would be very severe.

Jordan

The small, poor country of Jordan has a rich and varied history. During the period of Islamic dominance it was part of Syria and remained under the authority of Damascus and a part of the Ottoman Empire from the beginning of the eighteenth century to the First World War. After that war it became a semi-autonomous emirate, ruled under British tutelage by Abdullah, son of Hussein, King of the Hejaz. The members of this Hashemite dynasty were descendants of the Prophet in direct line. In 1946 Jordan became an independent kingdom. From the British, Abdullah inherited a well-organized administration and a small army called the Arab Legion. Under the leadership of its British Commander-in-Chief, this was developed into an effective and well-trained troop.

King Abdullah's objective was to form a union between Trans-Jordan, Syria and Palestine: a kind of Greater Syria, which would be the first step towards the birth of a larger entity, the Fertile Crescent.

Thus the Zionists, the Syrian nationalists and now also Trans-Jordan quarrelled about the possession of the territory of ancient Syria. The plan was supported by Iraq, which was ruled by the Hashemites, and by certain circles in Syria and Palestine. It was strongly opposed by the Zionists, who were already preparing for the foundation of Israel. Also opposed were Egypt, Saudi Arabia and Syrian nationalists. The plan foundered when the Arabs started a war against the newly founded state of Israel in 1948. As a result of this war the west bank of the River Jordan and East Jerusalem remained in the hands of the Arabs and, contrary to the resolution of the Arab League in Cairo, were annexed by the King of Trans-Jordan. The new state was named the Hashemite Kingdom of Jordan. But the dreams of becoming a great power had to be definitely abandoned when King Abdullah was murdered in Jerusalem in front of the Al Aksa Mosque in the summer of 1951. The assassin was obviously furthering the interests of those foreign groups which opposed the King's policies. The following year Hussein, the 17 year-old grandson of the old king, succeeded to the throne of Jordan.

The first years of Hussein's reign were not easy. He tried to maintain his relations with Britain, on whom Jordan was economically dependent. He also tried to follow a more conciliatory policy towards Egypt and Syria and to strengthen ties with Iraq, which was ruled by his cousin. Meanwhile, the radical Arab states, with Egypt led by Nasser to the forefront, enticed Jordan to join their camp by promising it economic support, while at the same time trying to destabilize Hussein's position. He was pressed to fire Glubb Pasha from his command of the Arab Legion and the union with Iraq collapsed because of the revolution and the murder of King Feisal in 1958.

On the eve of the Six Day War King Hussein apparently felt strongly that he belonged in the Arab camp and no warnings could change his decision. Daringly he joined the war on the side of Egypt and Syria. Although the Jordanian Army was well trained, it was still small in size and its resources were weak. However, solidarity with the Arab cause and confidence in Egypt's military might carried more weight with the government. Perhaps the youthful zeal and lack of experience of the 31 year-old King influenced the decision. The Jordanian Army fought bravely and skilfully but its weakness showed. The promised Egyptian help never arrived. East Jerusalem and the west bank of the River Jordan were lost. Defeat was bitter. Jordan's territorial and economic losses were relatively greater than those of Syria.

In November 1967 I travelled with General Bull to Amman for the first time. The trip itself was impressive. We descended from Jerusalem to the valley of the Dead Sea, almost 400 metres below sea level. As we approached the bottom of the valley the terrain changed to a barren moon landscape, with the Qumran area to the right and the northern point of the Dead Sea ahead of us. The road turned to the left towards Jericho, where the greenery of the orange orchards contrasted strongly with the surrounding desert. We continued over the Jordan River up to the mountains and towards Amman.

Discussions were held first with Prime Minister Ahmed Toukan, member of a well-known Palestinian family, and later with Crown Prince Hassan, who was deputizing for King Hussein during the latter's visit to New York. It appeared that the Jordanians were worried about possible retaliatory attacks from Israel. They feared revenge for Palestinian acts of terrorism on the West Bank. Both the Prime Minister and the Crown Prince stressed that Jordan could not be held responsible for incidents in areas conquered by Israel. On the other hand, they asserted that they had tried, by every means possible, to prevent the infiltration of the guerrillas from their territory to the Israeli side. They had detained hundreds of guerrillas and confiscated their arms.

As I mentioned before, Jordan differed from Israel's other neighbours in its refusal to allow military observers on its territory after the Six Day War. During our visit now General Bull decided to repeat his proposal to deploy observers along the Jordan River. The suggestion was received politely for study but Prime Minister Toukan doubted that a positive response could be given this time either. Jordan did not want observers because their presence would be interpreted as a *de facto* recognition of the Israeli conquest.

Despite his young age the Crown Prince made a very convincing impression. His briefing on the situation, presented without the benefit of notes, was brilliant in both content and style. I thought that very few 20-year-olds would have been capable of a similar performance. When I later had the opportunity to meet the King, which I did on several occasions, I realized that the Royal Family of Jordan was unusually gifted. Under the leadership of these two men an unprecedented programme of economic and social development had begun after the lost war. It seemed as if the people of Jordan sought, through hard work, to remove the shame which had been caused by the defeat.

Jordan, after the loss of the West Bank, was a country with a small population and an under-developed economy. Half of its one and a half million inhabitants were Bedouins, who, like the Hashemite Royal Family, came from the Arabian Peninsula. The word "Bedouin" in this context is slightly misleading, because only some of them were nomads. One such "Bedouin" was the Jordanian Liaison Officer to the UN, Colonel Tual. He belonged to a Christian Bedouin family which had given up nomadic life as early as 1890 and had settled down permanently in the cities of Amman and Madaba. The family had been very successful; for example, one of its members was the local importer of Ford cars. When I asked Colonel Tual when his family had converted to Christianity, he answered that he did not know the exact time. In any case, his ancestors had been Christian before the beginning of the seventh century or the arrival of Islam in the Middle East. During the Crusades in the eleventh century his family had taken the side of the Moslems against the Western intruders. Gratefully, the Moslems had given them all kinds of privileges.

The other half of the Jordanian population comprised Palestinian refugees. Since 1948 their numbers east of the Jordan River had risen to about half a million. As a consequence of the war in 1967 about 200,000 refugees were forced to leave their homes in the West Bank and Gaza, some of them exiled from here for the second time. Thus the total number of refugees in Jordan was about 700,000 people. Alone of the Arab countries, the Jordanian government had from the very beginning granted Jordanian citizenship to the Palestinian refugees. Despite this, the government in 1967 had its worries about the activities of the Palestinian organizations, as we had already heard. But matters only became worse. The new wave of refugees entering Jordan had strengthened the Palestine Liberation Organization's potential for action. It became apparent that the PLO's objective in Jordan was revolution: King Hussein was to be superseded and a republic of Palestine founded. Jordan's political future was under threat from within.

Moreover, the economic life of the country was in shambles as a result of the Six Day War. The most important occupation was still agriculture, the source of livelihood for 85 per cent of the people. Other sources of income were tourism and the production of phosphates and other minerals. Jordan's exports, however, were worth only 15 per cent of its imports. Thus the country was continuously dependent on foreign aid, which in the 1960s came mainly from the oil-producing countries and the United States. Yet one could see many signs that the Jordanian economy was improving. The reform programme initiated by the King had begun to produce results. New schools and hospitals were being built at a fast pace. Industry was encouraged. New and effective methods·were applied to agriculture in the same way as in Israel. As the result of various innovations and development work the economic self-sufficiency of Jordan improved. When I was travelling in Jordan during the coming months and years I was to see with my own eyes how the use of artificial irrigation increased and plastic sheeting was used more often to protect the plants. In my opinion there were three reasons for the progress made by this small poor country: skilful and inspiring leadership, with King Hussein and his brother Crown Prince Hassan at the helm; the utilization of the Palestinian labour force and its skill and industry, and sufficient foreign economic aid.

My visits to Jordan were always very pleasant. The officials and the people were friendly and regarded UNTSO in a positive light even though its observers were not welcome on the shores of the Jordan River. I learned over the years to appreciate the King's efforts. His task was not easy, for Jordan's internal politics required a balancing act between the Palestinians· and the Bedouin. Jordan also had no tradition as an independent state. Some people said in fact that it had none of the requirements necessary for independent survival: it was supposedly an artificial state which was doomed to live indefinitely on foreign goodwill and economic support. But one could say the same about Israel, too. Fortunately, however, the life and future of nations are not based only on such external factors: the spiritual qualities of their peoples are decisive.

It was easier for us, living in Jerusalem, to follow the events when Jordan Television was founded at the end of the 1960s and started regular broadcasts. English language news reported local and world events surprisingly truthfully. In addition we could enjoy the best entertainment and cultural programmes of the BBC. Israeli Television commenced transmission a little later, in black and white for economic reasons, but unfortunately they were incomprehensible to those who did not speak Hebrew or Arabic. In fact, I often wondered why not even the news was broadcast in English.

There was another reason why visits to Jordan were so refreshing. At almost every step one could see relics of earlier cultures. The capital, Amman, is mentioned in the Bible as the centre of the servants of Moloch. In Hellenistic times its name was Philadelphia. Legacies from the Roman era include an amphitheatre built to hold 6,000 spectators and the city of Jerash north of Amman, whose kilometre-long pillared street, temple ruins and large circus for gladiators are quite well-preserved. South-west of Amman, near the northern end of the Dead Sea, is the Biblical Madaba, the town of the Moabites, with its Byzantine mosaics. One of my favourite places, however, was Petra, the city of wonderful tombs, situated on the edge of the Great Rift halfway between the Dead Sea and the Gulf of Aqaba. Petra was the capital of the Nabataean kingdom from 100 BC to AD 150.

Jordan had recovered quickly and apparently painlessly from the traumatic experience of the Six Day War. Rather than simply grieving uselessly for its losses, the country had started to repair the damages of war and to rebuild, economically and culturally, a better place for both the Bedouin and the Palestinians. King Hussein was realistic about his role and surely did not imagine himself as a major influencer of events in the Middle East. Jordan's resources were too small for that. The King had burnt his fingers in the recent war and had reason to be careful now.

In Israel many people wished that the fate of the Palestinians on the West Bank could be solved within the framework of the so-called Jordanian option. To me too this seemed the most realistic solution. Its implementation was hampered, however, by the limitations placed on Jordan's ability to decide for itself according to its own interests. It had to take into account the views of the PLO, Syria and Egypt. Considering King Hussein's talents, however, one could imagine that in the future the Jordanian option might come to be viewed more favourably.

Israel

Before my arrival in the Middle East in the autumn of 1967 I had little first-hand information on or personal experience of Israel. When I had served with UNEF I, we were not even permitted to visit the country. I had, however, travelled to Israel from Cyprus in 1964 and during a few days' tourist trip I had become superficially acquainted with the western part of divided Jerusalem and with Tel Aviv and Eilat. However, I had from the very beginning followed the vicissitudes of the young state of Israel and wondered at its great military success. I had seen how the power of faith which had maintained the unity of the Jews for 2,000 years had finally led to the foundation of the state in its former historic area. A miracle had taken place: the dream of the Zionists was coming true through strong efforts and hard work as the desert was made to bloom. In addition to modern agriculture, a diverse industry had been created in the country and in many other areas there had been surprising progress too.

But there was also a negative side. For almost 20 years the people of Israel had in fact lived in an army camp, surrounded by hostile neighbours and an object of continuous guerrilla attacks and acts of terror. Israel had become a besieged ghetto where life was spiritually exhausting. Its neighbours had not even recognized the existence of the state of Israel. The very name of the country was not allowed to be mentioned; instead they referred to "the Zionist entity". The economic boycott declared by the Arabs continued and on the international stage Israel was severely criticized. Its existing borders, which were not easily defensible, added to the difficulties, for at its narrowest point Israel was only about ten kilometres wide and the main road from Tel Aviv to Jerusalem passed within about 100 metres of the Jordanian positions. Maintaining security was the most important objective of all political and military activity in Israel. It had become almost an obsession.

External pressure did not seem to discourage the people of Israel, however. Whatever they may have thought in their hearts, outwardly most people seemed to trust in Israel's better future. Yet I thought I observed in some Israelis a certain insecurity which I did not recognize in the Egyptians. The leaders of the people of Israel strengthened the faith in the future. Moshe Dayan used to say: "Our fathers founded the state of Israel. Our generation defended its borders in continuing wars. The task of our children is to take care of the future of Israel."

The external pressure was a factor which strongly united the people. It is possible that, without it, quarrels would have arisen between the different population groups – the Ashkenazim (Jews of Central and Eastern Europe) and the Sephardim (Jews of Spain and Portugal and their descendants in Asia and Africa) – the leftist and rightist parties and the different religious parties and factions, which ranged from ultra-orthodox to atheist. Some outsiders in fact thought that peace-making with Israel would be the best way to promote Arab interests as, when peace came, Israel would supposedly fall apart because of its internal quarrels. I don't believe such assumptions. I am sure that the clever and resourceful Israelis would somehow find the means to cope with the difficulties which peace could possibly bring.

For me the contrast between the Ashkenazim and Sephardim was completely new. I had in fact noticed the class differences already at

Tel Aviv Airport, where the "white" Ashkenazim were sitting behind the desks and receiving passengers while the "black" Sephardim were washing floors and carrying suitcases. I received my first lesson in this social problem from an Israeli liaison officer on a trip to the Suez Canal. This officer, whose rank was major, was in civilian life a social worker for youngsters in Beersheba. He told me how difficult it was to adapt to the modern competitive consumer society for people who had come from the almost Stone Age conditions of Yemen or the softer life of the bazaars of Morocco and Baghdad. Their social and cultural background was completely different from those who came from Europe. Although the Sephardim included many wealthy and educated families whose ancestors had lived in the area from time immemorial, the educational level, the professional and social position and the standard of living of the Sephardi majority was on average lower than those of the Western Jews. If the Israeli Arabs were second-class citizens, the Sephardim could be compared to a "class B" and the Ashkenazim to a "class A" sub-division of the first class. The educational level of the former rose slowly because their families were large and there was not enough money to educate the children. The weak cultural level of the family slowed down the children's development. The difference in starting points was visible as early as kindergarten, where the Ashkenazi children had a large vocabulary acquired at home and the Sephardi children had only a few hundred words. It was difficult to close this gap. Military service, however, could act as a melting pot where differences could be narrowed. Numerous mixed marriages also dispelled differences and so it is possible that after a certain amount of time they may have vanished completely.

There were many similarities in the cultural background, traditions and manners of the Sephardim and the Arabs; the only difference lay in their religion. One might have thought that the Sephardim of the older generation in particular, who often had positive experience of a peaceful co-existence with the Arabs in their former homelands, would have found ways to co-exist with them in Israel too. This was, however, not the case; on the contrary, the Sephardim adopted an even more negative attitude towards the Arabs than the Ashkenazim did. Perhaps the older generation wanted to emphasise their unity with the Western Jews by displaying similar negative attitudes. As far as the younger Sephardim are concerned, perhaps their inability to exist with the Arabs is a result of losing their roots and lacking information about their past.

The Sephardim had originally arrived from Arab countries whose political systems were authoritarian and where there was no knowledge of liberal or socialist ideas. Thus they now trusted more in a strong leader than in a seemingly weak democratic form of government. This was apparent later when many of the Sephardim joined ultra-rightist parties and chauvinistic organizations. Because of their high birth rate, the proportion of the Sephardim in the population was growing and overtaking the number of Ashkenazim. It was obvious that they were becoming an important political power in Israeli society. Their continuously rising level of education furthered their position.

At the end of the 1960s the Ashkenazim had an overwhelmingly dominant position in Israeli society. They held the most important jobs in the administration, in business and in the defence forces. Those officers who had been appointed to liaise with UNTSO were also Ashkenazi.

Early on I got to know our senior Liaison Officer, Shimon Levinson. He had begun his UNTSO tasks in the 1950s as a young captain and finished them as a colonel when Begin's government came to power. Both he and his wife were typical Ashkenazim whose families had originally come from Central Europe. Their attitudes and way of life were therefore very European. UNTSO had been lucky to have an able officer and diplomat as a liaison officer. There was no doubt that Shimon Levinson was a great patriot to whom Israel's interest was important in every possible way. But at the same time he was a flexible and ingenious person who arranged matters to facilitate the functioning of UNTSO. He tried to fulfil our requests, to interpret existing regulations and otherwise to support UNTSO's activities. However, he also took care that no harm was done to Israel's interests. The charming and intelligent Mrs Levinson, who by profession was a military psychologist, helped her husband in creating and maintaining good relations.

Although Israel was a part of Asia and was situated in the former area of the Byzantine Empire, it was, thanks to the Ashkenazi influence, greatly Europeanized, or perhaps, considering the number of Jews who had come from the United States, it was greatly Americanized. In many people one could observe the influence of different cultural backgrounds. For example, Golda Meir spoke with a distinct American accent and one could discern her background as a young teacher and Zionist in Milwaukee. But I was told that when she was addressing her Cabinet colleagues who had come from Russia, she also used her

Russian, a language which she had learned in the Pinsk of her child-hood. Incidentally, I noticed that the older generation in Israel still spoke many languages. The Jews have always been famous for their knowledge of languages and it was therefore somehow deplorable that many younger officers, for example those who had grown up in the kibbutzim, now spoke only Hebrew.

Walking along the coastal boulevard in Tel Aviv or relaxing on the sunny beaches of Israel, a visitor can easily forget that he is in Asia. Everything speaks a French, Spanish or Italian beach resort. In other places the atmosphere is like Eastern Europe. When for the first time I climbed up to the apartment of the favoured UNTSO car dealer in downtown Tel Aviv, I wondered where I had previously encountered the same dirty staircases and the same foul smell. I realized it had been in Warsaw, of course! Completely different pictures came to my mind when I travelled from the old and messy coastal town of Haifa to Mount Carmel. There one could imagine oneself in a small German town.

But the diversity of the people of Israel was more complex than this. Different religious attitudes, which ran from atheism to a fanatic ultra-orthodoxy, had divided the people into sects and factions whose relations were bad and sometimes even hostile. To the main trend belonged the Orthodox Jews, who through the religious parties often hold the balance of power in the Knesset and have thus legitimized many religious rules. The less religious consider, for example, the prohibition of civil marriages and limitations on activities on the Sabbath as disagreeable blackmail. To an outsider it also seemed strange that the religious majority group did not want to accept at all many movements popular in the United States, like Conservative or Reform Jews. In their view, these people did not fulfil the strict rules of *halacha* and therefore could not belong to the community of real Jews. The question of who was a Jew was important when interpreting the Law of Return promulgated by the Jewish state. According to that law, every Jew had the right to immigrate to Israel without restrictions. The definition of a Jew had, however, never been agreed to everyone's satisfaction and bitter quarrelling over this matter continued year after year.

The Hassidim formed their own ultra-religious sect. Many of them lived in the Mea Shearim quarter of Jerusalem, near the Old City. At dusk on Friday evenings at the beginning of the Sabbath, they marched in large crowds towards the Wailing Wall for prayers. The traditional temple locks, silk coat and magnificent fur-trimmed hat adopted from Polish noblemen distinguished them from the rest of the people.

The most fanatic in its convictions was the small but noisy sect of Naturei Karta. They were opponents of Zionism and did not recognize the state of Israel. According to them the foundation of the state before the arrival of the Messiah had been a grave sin. They sent petitions to the King of Jordan or appealed directly to the Secretary-General of the United Nations in order to turn the state of Israel onto the right path. They also viewed the use of Hebrew in everyday matters as a sin, because it was only meant for reading Holy Scriptures in the synagogue, and so the members of Naturei Karta spoke Yiddish among themselves.

As an outsider I often wondered why the peaceful co-existence which prevailed in Finland and many other Christian countries did not obtain between the secular and religious people in Israel. Why was there a terrible quarrel between people who had different views on religion? Why should the ultra-religious frenziedly stone cars which were running on a Sabbath? (I myself ran into a hail of stones when on my first Sabbath in Jerusalem I got lost in Mea Shearim.) And why should certain Jews ostentatiously drive their cars through Mea Shearim and other residential areas of the Orthodox Jews? Perhaps the cause of such co-existence in Finland was the religious indifference of the people. In Israel religion was important and a live issue. Sometimes one had the impression that the consecration of the Sabbath was the country's most important problem. Despite quarrels and stoning, Israel seemed to offer to different religious beliefs at least the possibility of existence. Perhaps the severe external pressure made it easier for different ideas to survive side by side.

In Israel, the aftermath of the Six Day War brought unrealistic expectations. The war did not bring recognition from its neighbours, but the land acquired was easier to defend. Many people in fact imagined that the occupied territories had finally brought the security for which the Israelis had so longed. Only very few understood that continuing possession of these areas would not further friendly neighbourly relations, nor would it lead to the recognition of the state of Israel. Real peace would be as far from realization as before.

When, however, the Arabs did not seem to recover at all from the loss of honour which the crushing military defeat had caused, the victorious euphoria continued in Israel at full pitch. Many thought that little Israel really had become a great power of the Middle East which had established its position conclusively. Accordingly, Israel also considered that it had the right to behave like a great power. Neighbours and countries further away could be punished and could even be given lessons by violent means.

The entire society was filled by a strange national defiance which prevented any realistic appraisal of the situation. The international standing of Israel began to deteriorate. Firstly, France declared an embargo on arms supplies. De Gaulle was annoyed because Israel had started the 1967 war contrary to promises. Many other traditional friends criticized Israel's politics. Some states went still further and broke diplomatic relations with Israel, including the Soviet Union and the other socialist countries (except Romania). Especially deplorable and economically harmful was the breaking of relations with most of the African countries.

Israel's victory in the war had been so overwhelming that it had blinded otherwise sensible and judicious people. They did not want to see that the political results of the war were bad and that it had not brought peace and security to Israel. People did not want to believe President Nixon, for example, in whose opinion the Soviet Union was the political victor of the war. He remarked that despite the defeat the friendship between the Arabs and the Soviet Union had become stronger and the United States was now the Arabs' real enemy. In my opinion the defeat had clearly strengthened the determination of the Arabs to prepare for a retaliatory offensive. The occupation of the west bank of the River Jordan and the Gaza Strip had increased Palestinian nationalism and made them a considerable political force.

We received information about Palestinian activities at the beginning of 1969. During the first 18 months after the war almost 1,300 terrorist actions against Israel took place. Of these, about 1,000 were near the Jordanian border, the rest along the cease-fire lines of Egypt and Syria, on the Lebanese border and in Gaza. Israel's casualties were heavy: more than 200 dead and almost 800 wounded.

A blind trust in the infallibility and ability of the political leaders and generals was one result of the great victory. Thus, although signs of the deterioration in the military and political situation became gradually apparent, the Israeli people and press received them without protests. The government and the army were above criticism, even when they defiantly fended off the peace initiatives which had been presented and declared that the makers of the initiatives were traitors.

At this stage my sympathy was with the ordinary people and particularly the young families with children both in Israel and in the neighbouring countries. They surely hoped for peace more than anybody else. I could imagine that worry for the future of their children weighed upon the minds of the parents. Would their children's generation also live in continual fear of war and time after time take part in new wars, each more destructive than before? I also identified worry and insecurity for the future in some of those who publicly acted unconcerned and arrogantly. Perhaps Israel's position was not as stable and secure as had been imagined.

Many Israelis found it hard to understand why they were so severely criticized around the world. Perhaps the main reason for the criticism was that Israel's policy was in contravention of two principles of international law, which had been generally accepted after the Second World War. Firstly, it contradicted the view expressed in the UN Charter that no state had the right to conquer territories by war. Secondly, it did not take into consideration the right of the self-determination of peoples. The importance of this human right had grown with the increasing number of former colonies that had become independent. Israel's behaviour was considered an anachronism. The world could not accept that, at the beginning of the 1960s, the clock would be turned back in former Palestine and there Israel would adopt the position and methods of past British colonial masters and the mandatory laws and regulations issued by them.

In this and other connections the Israelis complained that the world applied a different yardstick to them than to other nations. But perhaps one should in fact judge them more severely. During their long history the Jews have suffered oppression at the hands of other peoples. For me it was difficult to understand why they now, having freed themselves from such oppression, treated the Palestinians badly and unjustly.

The Israeli Defence Ministry and the General Staff operated out of the same building in Tel Aviv. On my return trips to Jerusalem after meetings there, I had plenty of time to consider the views I had heard. Despite my negotiating partners' strong faith in the future, the idea came to me that the security of the state is on fragile ground if it is based on military strength alone. It is true that Israel had many advantages. Its army was well-trained, equipped with technically advanced armaments and enjoyed excellent morale. It was supported by a home front which in questions of security was unanimous. The educational level of the people compared with that of their neighbours was high.

But there were also great shortcomings. The population base was weak: only about three million people. The country was poor and there were no natural resources worth mentioning – no oil, no coal, no metals, not even forests. The fact that the state of Israel had coped up till now with its heavy military and other burdens was mainly due to the generous military and economic aid of the United States. It could happen, however, that one day in the future the maintenance of its military strength might become economically untenable, foreign aid might decrease and the military capability of the Arabs might increase.

In my opinion, a better guarantee of security than mere military power would be good neighbourly relations based on friendship and confidence. This I tried to explain to my Israeli interlocutors. Nahum Goldmann, the President of the World Zionist Congress, had arrived at the same conclusion. In a series of articles in *Le Monde* in 1969 he wrote that Israel's two main problems were the normalization of relations with its neighbours and the continuation of the aid given by the United States and world Jewry. He thought that these two issues were connected in such a way that the aid would diminish if Israel were not able to resolve the first problem. Now, 20 years later, Goldmann's prediction has not yet come true but the future looks very alarming. The pro-Israeli attitude of the people of the United States, and particularly of its Jewish population, has been based on the view that Israel expresses the best moral values of the Americans. The continuing occupation of the West Bank and Gaza has shaken this view, however, and it is possible that with time Israel will lose its favoured position.

I thought that I had seen in Israel's fate similarities with the history of Finland: two small countries fighting for their existence. Many Israelis also remarked on this to me. The resemblance was, however, superficial and under closer observation the differences were great. Israel, unlike Finland, was the stronger party in the conflict. Despite its small size it was a regional great power. Finland, inferior in military strength and numbers, was forced to fight a world power, although during the Second World War we had been able to demonstrate our military prowess and will to remain independent. But the war had also taught us to recognize the facts and from that basis we had succeeded in striving for peace and in normalizing our relations with the Soviet Union.

The Israelis were proud of their democracy, which, apart from Lebanon, was the only one in the Middle East. There is, however, no real reason for this pride. In the first place, the population of the occupied territories is outside this democracy and without human rights. Secondly, the achievements of Israel's democracy in foreign affairs have been poor. In the Knesset it often happens, as in ancient Rome, that *maior pars meliorem vincit* ("The bigger party defeats the better one"). The people of Israel really need leaders who understand the demands of the future better than the majority of the Knesset do.

But in any peace-making process there are two parties and therefore new ideas and new leaders were also needed in the countries round Israel. At the end of the 1960s we did not foresee that in Egypt there would soon be an exceptional new leader who would be able to break the impasse and initiate peace.

The Palestinians

The Palestinian question was not born only when the state of Israel was founded. It already existed at the beginning of the twentieth century when the immigration of Jews into the area started to increase. The landless Arab agricultural labourers were obliged to give way to the farms of the new Jewish owners. The Arab population of Palestine began to worry for its future and often held violent demonstrations. The long-standing peaceful co-existence of Jews and Arabs came to an end. Meanwhile, British policies were wavering; at one time they favoured immigration, at another they put obstacles in its way.

The first Jewish immigrants arrived full of hope and in good faith. At last a solution had been found to the problem of the Jews of the Diaspora. The founder of Zionism, Theodor Herzl, had said: "I brought a people without a country, to a country without a people." The slogan sounded magnificent but its latter part was not true. Another people lived in the area, whose majority was Moslem. It was impossible for the Palestinians to understand that the Bible of the Jews gave the immigrants special rights to the land which they had tilled since time immemorial and considered as their own. When two peoples laid claim to the same piece of territory in this way, there was reason enough for a dispute. The quarrel was made deeper and more implacable by the fact that at different phases in the immigration programme large groups of Palestinians had to leave their homes and live for years in refugee camps.

In 1967 the Palestinian question had become a central problem caused by the Middle East conflict. If the peace process could not get started, the future of the Palestinians would not be solved either.

A smaller group of the Palestinians, the so-called Israeli Arabs, consisted of people who had not fled in 1948, but had remained in their homes in northern Israel. In the beginning there were about 150,000 of them, but this figure has increased every year by about 3 per cent and thus in 1987 they numbered 700,000, or 17 per cent of the population of Israel. They have rights of citizenship and representation in the Knesset, but do not perform military service. Despite their seeming equal rights, one could not fail to realize that the Israeli Arabs were second-class citizens. In leading positions, as ministers or as high officials for instance, there was not a single Arab, nor were there any Arab diplomats. Arab villages and towns were treated as poor relations and the funds they were granted were less than those given to the Jewish communities. The Arabs complained about the poor educational facilities in particular; at universities, for instance, some study programmes were reserved only for those who had done their military service. Despite all this, the Arab population had been surprisingly loyal to the state of Israel.

The war in 1967 had brought a large Palestinian population, altogether about one million people, under the Israeli military administration. Most of these people lived in their homes in the West Bank, Gaza and East Jerusalem, while some had been in the refugee camps of the West Bank and Gaza since 1948. Those in the most difficult position were the camp refugees, who were chiefly agricultural labourers and unqualified for any other job; many could neither read nor write. This was the poorest and most helpless stratum of society. Those refugees who had a profession or financial means never stayed at the camps, but continued on to Lebanon, to the oil-producing countries or elsewhere, where many succeeded in their new lives.

The United Nations Relief and Works Agency for Palestine Refugees (UNRWA) took care of the housing and ration distribution in the camps. The significance of the latter function diminished according to the ability of the refugees to find work outside the camps. These places are thus by no means a form of concentration camp surrounded by barbed wire; what they resemble most closely are heavily populated country villages where the houses are small and without amenities. The most important task of UNRWA was, however, to arrange schooling for the children and youths. In co-operation with UNESCO a good education has been given at all levels, from primary and vocational schools to university studies. Thanks to this schooling, a new educated class has been born in the camps. It is in fact no wonder that, frustrated by the miserable conditions in the camps, this class is now demanding rights for the Palestinians.

I realized that the Palestinian question was a thorn in the flesh of the Israelis. Many feared that its just solution would shake the foundations of the Jewish state. For the Israelis themselves the right of possession was an important right. It was feared that the Palestinians, appealing to their right of possession, would begin to demand to have back areas of land and property which had passed into Jewish hands. The feeling was that if the Palestinians were given an inch they would take a mile. While I knew that the Israelis were basically a people of conscience, I guessed that finding the right solution would be difficult and so they would prefer to fend off the entire Palestine question.

It seemed that the occupation of the conquered territories and the maintenance of the continuous military administration were also great problems. The Israelis often stated that their military administration was exceptionally humane and liberal. Such an administration had supposedly not been experienced in connection with any previous occupation. This was, however, only partly true. The police and the army were soft and flexible when everything ran smoothly and the population meekly followed their instructions. But in the event of the smallest incident the attitude of the authorities changed and counter-measures were merciless and harsh. Violence was repaid with a still greater violence, including collective punishments, the blowing up of houses and the terrorization of the population. Many Israeli parents were worried, for good reason, that these severe measures should be carried out by conscripts less than 20 years old and feared that the ethical development of the youth would suffer from it. I was not the only one who thought that something should be done quickly in order to solve the problems caused on both sides by the occupation.

The hard treatment of the Palestinians was manifested in many ways. At its least severe it could be seen in the checking of identity cards at army checkpoints and by the police at road junctions and crossroads. For example, the Arabs living in the villages on the outskirts of Jerusalem, like our Palestinian cook Ata, had to prove their identity on each trip to and from work. If something special had happened, people would be ordered out of the buses and made to stand with their hands up against the walls of the houses. Then the police apparently carried out body searches. In addition to these checks there were nightly searches in the villages and people were detained for police investigations which often included heavy-handed treatment. These were all acts which were considered completely normal and necessary from the point of view of state security. They always take place in states where a part of the population has no human rights and is obliged to live in conditions similar to those of a police state. The Palestinians found it extremely humiliating and frustrating to experience such treatment in their own country.

Sometimes politically active people were banished to Jordan. This was carried out under the emergency regulations inherited from the time of the British Mandate which had originally been intended for disciplining the Jews. They were now used on Arabs for a similar purpose. One might have thought that a forced transfer of an Arab from his home would have weighed quite specifically upon the conscience of the Israelis. One might have imagined that memories of the events which had happened to them and their relatives quite recently would have touched their Jewish consciousness. When, in accordance with the same emergency regulations, houses were blown up, quite often innocent bystanders suffered too. The seizure of land by different means caused a particular bitterness among the Arab population. The legal basis of the procedure was often very questionable. The Israelis defended the confiscation of areas known as the Sultan's lands by claiming that this land had now been transferred into the possession of the Israeli government. The Palestinians' response to this was that they had an ancient right to till the common lands or the Sultan's lands and that occupation cannot change ownership.

Palestinian feelings in the delicate question of the possession of land is well described by the following anecdote from a West Bank village. The *mukhtar* of the village was so old that he had lived under the domination of three occupying forces. When he was asked what the difference was between them, he answered, "The Turks were hard and cruel. If somebody opposed them, he was hanged at once. The British were also hard but they hanged more seldom. The Israelis do not hang anybody, but they have touched our land. It is the worst of all."

If such a confiscation concerned an energetic and influential person, the seizure of the property did not always succeed. I saw an example of this with my own eyes in the autumn of 1967. In front of the house where I lived in the Sheikh Jarrah quarter of East Jerusalem stood the house of the Atallah family. Mr Atallah had been a minister in the Jordanian government. He had obtained permission from the Israeli authorities to travel to Amman to arrange money matters for the Palestinians. Because of the war, the connections of the banks in the West Bank with Amman had been broken and the people were in difficulties. Presumably the monetary matters were resolved somehow, but as well as his official task Mr Atallah made a speech in the Jordanian parliament in which he severely criticized Israel. Again using the emergency regulations inherited from the British, the Israeli authorities decided to banish Atallah. The following morning the police appeared at his house and nailed on the front door a declaration according to which the house now was "absentee property" and had been transferred in trust to the Israeli authorities. The energetic Mrs Atallah pointed out that she was not an absentee but still lived in the house. She managed to contact an influential enough official and the confiscation order was cancelled. An ordinary man in the street in a similar situation would perhaps not have been so lucky.

Visitors to the Holy Land are usually well shielded from the bitter realities of life that are the daily bread of the Palestinians in Israel and the occupied territories. If the subject of the Palestinians does arise, it is usually put into that context which much of the Western world has already come to accept, namely that the Palestinians are poor, illiterate people who have resorted to terrorist activities in a futile and pathetic drive to reverse the tide of destiny and history and drive the Jews into the sea. These propagandist claims are not true. The Palestinians are on a higher social, educational and economic level than many other Arabs. But the propaganda war also describes them as bloodthirsty killers. Therefore many people consider them to be an unusually violent people. This is a complete misunderstanding; in reality they are a well-meaning, deferential people who have a strong desire to please. Many have the character traits of successful tradespeople. They resort to violence reluctantly, for it is an activity which is contrary to their character. But the character of the Palestinians is also the reason why their land has been so easy to occupy from Israel's point of view. There have been incidents, but a sustained resistance or campaign of civil disobedience has not taken place. Israel has therefore not had any real reason to revise its occupation policy. I am sure that the occupier's situation would have become untenable if instead of the Palestinians the West Bank was peopled by, for example, Yugoslavs or Finns.

Soon after the war Moshe Dayan initiated the policy of "open bridges", with the aim of giving the residents of the West Bank and Gaza, besides the free right to travel, at least some kind of chance of a normal life, without unnecessary harassment and humiliation. In this the military administrators did not succeed, if they even tried it. A still greater shame was that Dayan's idea of a unilateral declaration of autonomy did not receive wider support. According to this plan, Israel would grant autonomy to the Palestinians in much the same manner as the Russian Tsar Alexander I in his time granted it to us Finns. Under Dayan's plan the Israeli authorities would annul the military administration and withdraw the occupation forces from residential centres to remote, uninhabited areas. The Palestinians would then be obliged to determine the central and local administration of the area themselves. In my opinion this arrangement would have solved many problems and for my part I recommended it to all my Israeli contacts. I thought that Israel as a democratic state had a special obligation to arrange autonomy for the Palestinians. I noticed that in this matter I have been of the same opinion as President Jimmy Carter, who writes in his memoirs:

> The continued deprivation of Palestinian rights was contrary to the basic moral and ethical principles of both our countries. In my opinion it was imperative that the United States work to obtain for these people the right to vote, the right to assemble, and to debate issues that affect their lives, the right to own property without fear of its being confiscated, and the right to be free of military rule. To deny these rights was an indefensible position for a free and democratic society.

4. The role of the United Nations in the Middle East

UNEF I

By the end of the 1960s the United Nations had participated in the political life of the Middle East for 20 years. Carrying out the resolutions of the Security Council, it had tried to maintain a balance in all situations and to promote peace. However, peace-keeping activities had not achieved permanent results; three times the illusory peace had been shaken and a war had broken out between Israel and its Arab neighbours. After each war the UN had devised new methods for supervising the truce.

UNTSO, founded in 1948 as the first peace-keeping mission of the UN, had carried out its tasks well. Despite temporary difficulties it had been able to assist the parties in maintaining the cease-fire. Soon experience showed, however, that a fairly small and unarmed observer operation like UNTSO was far too weak in the face of a more severe and wider conflict. There was a need for an armed military force which would be properly organized and equipped and would include logistics and other supporting elements. Thus, like a real military unit, it would be able to operate independently, would be logistically self-sufficient and could defend itself when necessary.

It took some time before the idea of such a force was ripe for introduction. In November 1955, General E.L.M. Burns, the Canadian Chief of Staff of UNTSO in Jerusalem, had discussed with a high-ranking British diplomat, Anthony Nutting, the possibility of interposing UN troops between the armed forces of Israel and Egypt. Burns said at the time that he did not think this would be possible without prior intervention by the great powers. "This turns out," Burns wrote later, "to have been a good prediction."

At the time of the discussion between Burns and Nutting it had become clear to everybody that the UN had not quite succeeded in its main task, the maintenance of world peace. The organization's founders' dreams of a strong and well-functioning world government had collapsed with the Cold War. The unity between the allied nations had already begun to crack during the last years of the Second World War and was now nowhere to be found in a world divided into two hostile camps. Any one of the great powers could have prevented the deployment of a UN armed force anywhere by using their right of veto.

Behind all this was the fact that the Second World War, despite the tragic events it had caused, had not changed people's attitudes, particularly those of the great powers. Only the small and militarily weak states favoured the idea of a peaceful solution to conflicts. Great powers, and often also smaller states, resorted first to force.

As was obvious, the policy of the two superpowers had not changed either. It was directed by the struggle for spheres of influence and by narrow national interests. The competition between the superpowers was a fact that dominated the situation in the Middle East. Each wanted to arrange alone the affairs of this region and the whole world, employing as assistants only those states which were members of its own alliance. The opposing power and its allies were to be kept away from the arrangements of the region. The superpowers did not need the help of the UN either. They did not want to delegate their authority to the UN and its Secretary-General.

After having taken over the post of the Secretary-General in 1952, Dag Hammarskjöld had followed with great concern the development of the overall world situation. As a counter-balance to the policy of the great powers he wanted to strengthen the authority of the UN and to increase its sphere of action. In the autumn of 1956 the worsening conditions in the Middle East, which were about to develop into a grave international crisis, seemed in Hammarskjöld's opinion to offer an occasion to experiment with completely new methods in order to solve the crisis. The UN could perhaps be developed into an instrument of multilateral preventive diplomacy. If this could succeed, the authority of the UN would increase and his own position as Secretary-General would be strengthened.

In brief, the Suez crisis of 1956 was caused by the joint attack of Israel, France and Great Britain on Egypt in order to punish President Nasser for the nationalization of the Suez Canal. The British and French operation was not successful, however, and when the United States added the voice of its opposition to the entire operation, the matter was, exceptionally, brought for discussion to the General Assembly. The Security Council was at that time paralysed because the Soviet Union was boycotting its meetings. After a long discussion the General Assembly decided that an armed UN force should be established in order to facilitate the withdrawal of the attacking armies.

In pursuance of the task entrusted to him by the General Assembly, Hammarskjöld developed and implemented the idea of an armed peace-keeping force. He planned the composition of the UN force, defined the principles of the operation and directed the functioning of the first Sinai force with great success. It consisted of national infantry battalions and logistics and other support units. The battalions were organized for independent action and were logistically self-sufficient. They were armed with light weapons for self-defence only. The system developed by Hammarskjöld is still the basis of the composition and functioning of the UN troops today.

Egypt had voluntarily agreed to the arrival of UNEF (the UN Emergency Force) and to its deployment on its own territory. This decision was based on the fact that the General Assembly had accepted the unlimited sovereignty of Egypt regarding UNEF. In addition to this, Hammarskjöld had demanded that UNEF should be allowed to remain in Egypt for as long as it took to complete its task. Nasser, however, did not want to agree to such a limitation of Egyptian sovereignty. In the second memorandum between Hammarskjöld and Nasser it was stated: "UNEF could not stay or operate unless Egypt continued to consent, although it was understood that Hammarskjöld's approach to the question of the UNEF had been based on his understanding of Egypt's acceptance of the General Assembly resolution of 5 November 1956 which created the Force." This vagueness was to lead to all kinds of interpretations and misunderstandings ten years later, when Nasser demanded the withdrawal of UNEF.

At first UNEF regulated, according to its mandate, the withdrawal of foreign troops from the Suez Canal area and later it supervised the Armistice Demarcation Line between Egypt and Israel. For more than ten years UNEF carried out this task with great success. Attacks on Israel from Egyptian territory stopped. I am not sure whether the termination of Palestinian *fedayeen* activity was due only to the presence and functioning of UNEF, or whether this was influenced by the measures taken by the Egyptian government, who, in order to avoid politically delicate incidents, apparently prevented the Palestinians from launching attacks on Israel from Egyptian territory. In any case the area remained peaceful and its economy flourished. UNEF was praised for its actions.

But attitudes changed and world public opinion strongly criticized Secretary-General U Thant when UNEF, at Nasser's demand, was withdrawn from its area of operation in May 1967, on the eve of the Six Day War. Nasser referred to the agreement between him and Hammarskjöld. The Secretariat could perhaps be criticized for agreeing too quickly to Nasser's demands but the greatest culprits were the Security Council and its permanent members, who were sluggish and did not come to an agreement on the necessary measures before the beginning of the war. The United States' foreign policy during the entire month of May was cautious and unconcerned about the danger of war. President Lyndon B. Johnson did not believe that Nasser was serious and therefore did not act energetically to restrain the parties and to keep UNEF in place.

When the critics spoke about the bankruptcy of peace-keeping, this was based on a misunderstanding of its basic nature. Thanks to UNEF, Sinai had been outwardly quiet for more than ten years and this illusion of peace had given a false impression of the possibilities of peace-keeping. It was assumed unrealistically that a small, lightly armed UN force could make Egypt adhere to the agreement, as was envisaged in Chapter VII of the UN Charter. The fact that peace-keeping was outside the framework of the enforcement provisions of Chapter VII was forgotten. Above all, peace-keeping was based on the voluntary acceptance of the parties. Thus UNEF could be useful only as long as Egypt wanted to keep the agreement and gave UNEF its support and co-operation.

The criticism occasioned by the withdrawal of UNEF was, in my opinion, exaggerated and over-emphasises inessential matters. I suspect in fact that no measures could have changed the course of events. Protests would have been significant only as matters of principle. In practice any appeal by the Secretary-General or resolution of the Security Council would have remained ineffectual, considering Nasser's defiant attitude and the already far-reaching Israeli preparations for war. Perhaps the war could have been prevented had Israel accepted the proposal of U Thant and the United States that UNEF should be deployed on the Israeli side of the demarcation line.

In spite of its abrupt and controversial withdrawal in May 1967, UNEF was a brilliant innovation and an extraordinarily imaginative departure in the affairs of the United Nations. The peace-keeping operations were on the way to becoming one of the few activities in which the UN had been successful.

The initial success of UNEF I was probably one of the main reasons that the UN in the early 1960s embarked on two major operations, in the Congo and Cyprus. The effects of its success were still apparent in the 1970s, when three new UN forces were set up in the Middle East: UNEF II in Sinai, UNDOF (UN Disengagement Observer Force) on the Golan and UNIFIL (UN Interim Force) in southern Lebanon.

New duties for UNTSO

The June war of 1967 was not fatal only to UNEF. It also led to a complete change in the role of UNTSO, which had to adapt itself quickly to the new situation caused by the withdrawal of UNEF. As a result of the war, the Israeli forces had pushed on into Egypt, Syria and Jordan far beyond the former cease-fire lines. Only the border with Lebanon remained the same. In Israel's opinion the armistice agreements were not valid any more. Although the UN could not accept such an unilateral interpretation, in practice it had to resign itself to the fact that, for example, the Mixed Armistice Commissions could no longer operate. New methods of operation had to be found. In order to fulfil the task given it by the Security Council and in co-operation with the Israeli and Syrian armies, the first job of the UNTSO observers was to define on the Golan the forward defended localities of both parties and the cease-fire lines running through them. At the same time it was agreed with Egypt and Israel that the east and west banks of the Suez Canal would also be cease-fire lines. Along the cease-fire lines in both areas, UNTSO set up a number of observation posts. Two observers of different nationalities were on duty at each post in order to observe and report on breaches of the cease-fire. The observers were assisted by a liaison officer sent by the parties. The operation was directed by control centres established in Damascus and Tiberias and along the Suez Canal in Ismailia and Kantara. The Officer-in-Charge of the control centre and his small staff collected the reports and sent them to UNTSO Headquarters in Jerusalem. From there they were sent on to New York for the information of the Secretary-General and the Security Council. The control centre in Damascus continued to be called the Israeli-Syrian Mixed Armistice Commission (ISMAC) and its Officer-in-Charge the Chairman, because according to Syria the armistice agreement was still valid.

The Israeli-Lebanese Mixed Armistice Commission (ILMAC), situated in Beirut, and its out-station in Naqoura on the Israeli border, both remained in place and maintained contact with the Lebanese authorities. The Commission was not convened for years because of opposition from the Israeli authorities, but its machinery was available

UNTSO AREA OF OPERATIONS

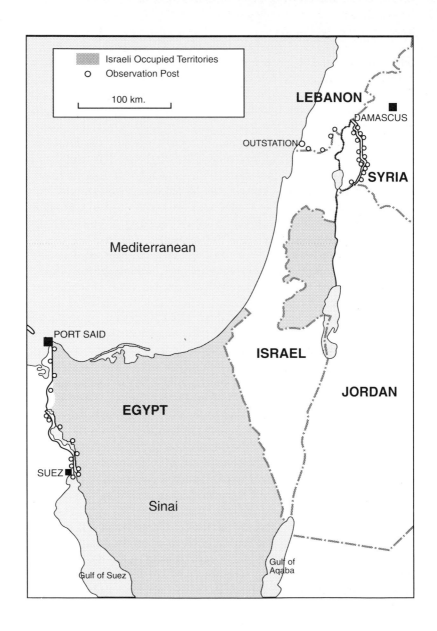

in the 1970s when the Israeli authorities wanted to use it as a forum for discussing mutual problems.

Similarly, the Headquarters of the Hashemite Jordanian Kingdom-Israeli Mixed Armistice Commission (HJKIMAC) remained in East Jerusalem, thus symbolizing the UN view on the permanency of the armistice agreements. UNTSO's representative in Amman was a liaison officer of lieutenant-colonel's rank. For its own reasons Jordan did not want observers along the River Jordan.

UNTSO had once again proved to be a flexible and innovative organization in a changing situation. Recovery from the profound changes caused by the June war had surely not been easy. UNEF's rapid and unexpected departure from the scene had not made things easier. It had reduced the authority and credibility of the United Nations.

There were other reasons for UNTSO's lack of popularity, apart from the miserable fate of UNEF. In the opinion of many Israelis, the UN was a hostile organization whose General Assembly, year after year, had become more anti-Israeli. In the General Assembly all Arab countries and most of the developing countries, supported by the socialist states, formed an "automatic majority" which condemned Israel's policy in the voting. Particularly in the defiant atmosphere after the 1967 war, it was difficult for the Israelis to admit that there was often reason for the criticism.

I could also very well understand that for the Israelis, proud and conscious of their strength, it was difficult to tolerate the presence of foreign soldiers in their own country. UNTSO's presence in Jerusalem could not pass unnoticed. Our white jeeps and blue UN flags were clearly distinguishable in any street scene. But perhaps their antipathy was not only a question of disliking the presence of foreigners. It may also have been that Israel, militarily strong and successful in many areas of human activity, found it hard to admit that it had not been able to normalize relations with its neighbours, and that the assistance of international UN soldiers was necessary for this task and for the maintainence of peace on the borders.

Many judicious Israelis, however, made a distinction between the hostile UN organization in New York and UNTSO, which was useful from Israel's point of view. UNTSO could not be held responsible for the voting results of the General Assembly or the Security Council. On 6 December 1968, at the Independence Day reception of the Finnish Embassy, a junior official of the Israeli Foreign Ministry remarked to me that there was no need for UNTSO's presence. The new Chief of Staff of the Defence Forces, General Chaim Bar-Lev, who had followed our conversation from the side, interrupted his countryman and remarked sharply that the UN officers were doing an useful job which was also in the interest of Israel.

UNTSO was clearly more popular in the Arab countries. After the severe defeat which they had suffered, the Arabs felt themselves to be the underdog and hoped that somehow the UN could support and help them in case they were again placed in a difficult position. Obviously the Arabs, for exactly the same reasons as the Israelis, did not really love UNTSO, but their more positive attitude was based on realistic calculations. This was clearly evident in the October War in 1973, when in the victorious opening phase of the war the Egyptians began to treat UN soldiers in an arrogant and unfriendly fashion. A few weeks later, when their defeat was already looming, the popularity of the UN grew greater than ever.

But the 1973 war had a sobering effect too on the people of Israel. The great danger caused by the initially successful Arab offensive made the value of our role very clear. The important role we played in the peace process also enhanced our popularity not only among the leaders of Israel but among ordinary people too.

Whether or not UNTSO was popular, we had to be very cautious and considerate. We were not allowed, not even inadvertently, to insult or irritate the representatives of the parties. In my briefings to newcomers I stressed that we should treat the leaders, soldiers and ordinary citizens of all the parties politely and impartially. I thought that this was necessary because we could not succeed without the co-operation, confidence and respect of the parties. We should never give the impression that we were representing some kind of colonial power which was above the law, treated the population arrogantly and gave orders to sovereign states. A peace-keeping mission is not an occupation army; it performs certain limited tasks which have been jointly agreed with the parties. Thus, in delicate circumstances we should emphasise diplomatic consideration. We should be careful on every level.

When I entered UN service in October 1967, UNTSO was seeking new forms of action and procedures. Its organization was also changing continually, because the centre of the operation had moved to the Suez Canal zone. The gap left by the departure of UNEF obviously had to be filled. However, UNTSO had already overcome the worst difficulties and was again quite an effective and able organization. Some friction was apparent too. In particular, UNTSO's longest serving civilian members found it hard to get used to the idea that the situation really had changed. For the soldiers this was easier. Generally, very few of them stayed in UNTSO longer than a year. I noticed too that newcomers could adapt themselves more easily to changing circumstances.

UNTSO was still the Security Council's only reliable source of information and now it was again the only peace-keeping mission in the Middle East. But people in the region had become accustomed to the changing role of the United Nations. At times it had a decisive significance, as during the foundation of the state of Israel in 1948, after the Suez crisis in 1956 and again in the years after the 1973 war. At others its role was less significant. UNTSO has not always been able to promote the peace process but it has only maintained the status quo by its continuous presence. Thus it has unwillingly furthered the aims of those groups in whose opinion there need be no rush to make peace. I think that after the 1967 war we were in such a phase.

Since its establishment, however, UNTSO has been an important mission. Three factors have enhanced its political significance. Firstly, there is no time limit on its presence in the area. In other words its mandate does not need to be extended every six months, as in the case of armed UN forces. Secondly, UNTSO is not geographically limited, but covers Israel and its four neighbours. Thirdly, its observers are not drawn only from small or medium sized countries but from three great powers as well. The United States and France have been represented from the beginning, while the Soviet Union became involved in 1973, adding to the universality of UNTSO and strengthening its political significance. In 1986 there were rumours that China also wanted to join UNTSO; its participation would probably have a balancing effect and make UNTSO politically stronger. I should hope also that the United Kingdom, the fifth permanent member of the Security Council will eventually take part, as the reasons why it kept out of UNTSO 40 years ago have become far less important now.

I think that in the beginning I myself did not quite understand the great political importance of UNTSO, or how much the presence and functioning of UNTSO was in the interest of the parties and the world organization and did not depend on the role which the UN might have played in the Middle East at different times. The overall political situation in the years after 1967 seemed hopeless. The weak peace efforts had dwindled. No ray of hope could be seen, nor had UNTSO any means to promote the cause of peace: it was impossible because the parties lacked the political will needed for it. Disappointed and frustrated, I did not take into account that in the Middle East situations change fast. The task of UNTSO itself could change and its share in the political life of the region could increase.

I remember a conversation at the dinner table in my home in the spring of 1970. Among our guests was the political adviser to UNTSO, Mr Miguel Marin. My wife, who was as frustrated as I because of the overall situation, happened to remark to him, "I think that UNTSO no longer has any meaningful task and therefore has very little time left." "No, no, Mrs Siilasvuo, UNTSO and Israel are eternal," was Mr Marin's reply.

5. Endeavours for peace

Resolution 242 and Jarring's peace mission

The Middle East conflict was not only a regional problem; its effects extended around the world. Two formidable antagonists, the United States and the Soviet Union, contended there for influence. The region's oil resources provided one of the reasons for the fierceness of this competition. In the opinion of the Soviet Union, its geographical closeness gave emphasis to its legitimate interests in the Middle East. The long-term objective of American foreign policy was to stop the advancement of the Soviet Union and to lessen its influence.

After the Six Day War the United States continued to side with its traditional allies, Israel, Jordan, Saudi Arabia and other oil states. The Soviet Union had suffered a setback in the war when its allies Egypt and Syria had been defeated and had lost almost all their Soviet-made military hardware. It tried, however, to compensate for its lost influence by sending new arms and advisers to Egypt and Syria. It obviously succeeded in its endeavours and the dependence of these two states upon the Soviet Union became greater than before. The possibility of the United States participating in the peace process appeared more remote when Egypt and Syria broke diplomatic relations with it. Now dialogue between the United States, Egypt and Syria could be held only with the Soviet Union as an intermediary.

Of all the results of the Six Day War the increase in Soviet influence in the Middle East was surely the most unpleasant and least expected in the United States and Israel. However, Egypt and Syria had no alternative but to continue to seek the assistance of the Soviet Union. This development had begun during the Suez crisis in 1956, when the United States had discontinued its economic support for the construction of the Aswan Dam in order to punish Nasser for the nationalization of the Suez Canal. With this act, intended to put an end to the Suez crisis, the United States pushed Egypt into the Soviet camp. At the same time it caused unforeseen future problems for itself.

There were many obstacles on the road to peace. Radical Syria and the Palestinians, locked in their extremist attitudes, did not want to hear of negotiations. The Israelis wanted a binding peace, as if any pact has ever guaranteed the permanency of peace. In the numerous peace treaties between Sweden and Russia "eternal peace had been sworn and

73

the cross kissed", but a new war had soon broken out again. Nasser as usual demanded impossible things: Israel should act as if it had lost the war and withdraw unconditionally from all occupied territories; only then would he begin to discuss the termination of the state of belligerency. About peace and recognition he did not want to talk.

Gradually political wisdom began to gain ground in Egypt and Jordan. It was understood that pigheadedness would only prolong the occupation of the occupied territories. While they continued to demand Israel's withdrawal from Arab lands, as a *quid pro quo* they hinted at a declaration of non-belligerency, the right of each state to a secure existence and the recognition of Israel. These, according to the Arabs, extremely significant changes to previous attitudes did not satisfy Israel. It demanded in addition face-to-face negotiations, secure and recognized boundaries (by this term Israel meant border changes), frontiers open to trade and travel, and free navigation through the international waterways. In Israel it was hoped that direct negotiations would be the first step towards recognition and that they would prevent the danger of big-power attempts at an imposed solution.

The first peace initiative of the autumn came from the United Nations. The adoption of Security Council Resolution 242 on 22 November 1967 was a great political achievement (see Appendix 1). It had been accepted by the Soviet Union, which represented Arab views, and by the United States for its ally Israel. The document was a seemingly clear and easy-sounding attempt to solve a complex and difficult problem. In reality its wording was so obscure and ambiguous that it could have meant anything. The United Kingdom Ambassador to the UN, Lord Caradon, who had drafted the Resolution, was justifiably proud of his achievement. When he was asked what the clause in the document concerning the "withdrawal from occupied territory" really meant, he replied oracularly, "It means, what it means."

The Resolution spoke of a "just and lasting peace" within "secure and recognized boundaries". It called for an "end to all states of belligerency", for Israeli withdrawal "from territories occupied in the recent conflict" and for acknowledgement of all states' "sovereignty, territorial integrity and political independence". It soon became apparent that the parties could accept these ambiguous expressions only because each could interpret them as it pleased. Egypt and Jordan interpreted the clause "withdrawal from territories" as requiring Israeli withdrawal from all Arab land. In Israel's opinion the missing definite article "the" in the English text meant that the withdrawal would not apply to all territories – not wanting to accept the French text in which the withdrawal from all the territories was expressed unambiguously. The Israelis also maintained that "secure and recognized boundaries" meant the right to border changes, for they thought that giving up certain territories would mean weakened security. Therefore they demanded compensation from the opposing party. The Arabs on the other hand thought that Israel should withdraw unconditionally because the land belonged to them.

The Resolution also affirmed the necessity "for achieving a just settlement of the refugee problem". When the text was being drafted, it obviously seemed the easiest way of reaching an understanding to speak only of the refugee problem. The fate of the Palestinians could be passed over as an insignificant secondary question, although it was gradually becoming the core of the Middle East conflict. In the autumn of 1967 the Palestinians were not able to demand anything else. The majority of them did not fully understand themselves that they formed a nation; nor did anybody else. In Israel Golda Meir, among others, claimed that the Palestinians did not exist. In her opinion the real refugees were the Jews who had fled from the Arab countries to Israel. Palestinian nationalism was still only embryonic. The political weight of the PLO was minimal and in the other Arab states there was insufficient interest in promoting the Palestinian cause.

The totally contradictory views on the real significance of Resolution 242 led gradually to an impasse. Its wording became a nonsensical peace liturgy which was repeated daily in propaganda speeches and writings. Real negotiations were not possible and no results could be achieved as long as the views of Israel and the Arabs were so far from each other.

For somebody like me, who had recently arrived in the area, the discussion sounded surprisingly irrational and emotional. Each word of the Resolution seemed to acquire a magical meaning, as if a correctly selected word could solve the problem. Perhaps people imagined that by repeating the words often enough the objectives which they described would be fulfilled. The words obscured the aims of the parties instead of clarifying them. I did not understand at first that this was the Middle East, where the Byzantine tradition was still strong. It had left its stamp on both Judaism and Islam. I did not understand either that, particularly for the Arabs, emotions and emotional reasons were an essential part of reality and as valuable as the rational reasons which we Westerners, in our own opinion more rational and pragmatic, valued more.

I tried to ponder what were the ultimate reasons for the conflict between Israel and the Arabs. Its foundation must be more than a dispute about the possession of certain territories, or the fate of the Palestinians. The Six Day War had only brought these matters more markedly to the forefront. Besides, the territorial questions only touched Israel's neighbours; in Saudi Arabia, for instance, they were just matters of principle. The roots of the conflict lay deeper. I believe that its causes in fact were psychological and above all arose from different cultural backgrounds. Israel was regarded as a foreign Western intruder who had no place in the Arab environment of the Mediterranean. It represented democracy, pluralistic liberalism, equality between men and women and other Western ideas which the Arabs could not accept. Particularly horrifying, in the view of the conservative Arab states, was the socialist trait which was characteristic of Israeli society especially in the early years. All in all, Israel represented values which would only spell misfortune if they were to spread in the Arab world. Therefore the Arabs should fight against Israel and, if at all possible, the Israelis should be expelled from the area. Thus the conflict would not vanish simply by solving the Palestinian problem and returning the occupied territories. It would be too optimistic to believe this.

I thought, however, that it would be better to start the attempt to solve the Middle East conflict from somewhere, by attacking these problems. It would be the first step on the road to adaptation and co-existence. The Israelis could then demonstrate that they were able to live in peace with the other peoples of the area. This adaptation would be easier if the Israelis were gradually to become Mediterranean people. I thought I saw signs of such a development. In time, changing attitudes in the Arab countries would help as well. There were signs of this development too, as a consequence of an improved educational level and democracy.

An alternative scenario would be Israel's complete isolation from the eastern Mediterranean area and a political, economic and cultural union with Europe. Signs of such endeavours appeared, for instance, in an agreement with the European Community and in participation in Eurovision song contests. I believe that such a policy of isolation would end very sadly. It could lead to a fate similar to that of the Algerian French, who imagined that Algeria was a part of France and Europe.

Resolution 242 requested the Secretary-General to designate a Special Representative who would talk with the parties and try to get negotiations started. U Thant chose for this task the Swedish Ambassador to Moscow, Gunnar Jarring. He set up his headquarters in Cyprus and began his work with energy and assiduity. He became in fact a pioneer of Middle East shuttle diplomacy; by the end of 1968 he had toured the capitals of the region 22 times. Jarring finished his job in April 1969 by sending to the parties a written questionnaire in which they were asked to define their positions. After many months of waiting they finally gave Jarring the same negative views that had been repeated many times in public statements.

After Jarring's appointment I described the Middle East situation in my report home in early December 1967:

The contents of Nasser's great speech in Parliament was, in brief: No peace, no negotiations and no opening of the Suez Canal!

Israel for its part maintains strongly its previous stand demanding face-to-face negotiations separately with each neighbour. Moshe Dayan defined Israel's peace objectives in his speech on 12 December 1967. Firstly, the Jewish character of the State of Israel must be maintained, regarding both its composition and the proportion of the number of Jews. Secondly, its neighbours must clearly recognize Israel as a sovereign Jewish state. Thirdly, Israel must achieve in the region an equal juridical status which includes the right of free navigation through international waterways. Fourthly, the boundaries must be defined in such a way that they express the affinity of the Jewish people to their historic homeland. Fifthly, one should strive to have peace agreements with the Arab states which would provide a framework within which to solve the problem of Arab refugees.

My report continues:

It is difficult for me to predict what would be Israel's final territorial demands, but in my opinion it would not in any event want to give up the strategically important Golan Heights on the Syrian border, united Jerusalem and, in connection with it, the so-called Latroun area along the road from Jerusalem to Tel Aviv, and not the Gaza Strip either. But instead it might be willing to give up most of the Sinai Peninsula. The so-called West Bank conquered from Jordan is a different story. The non-Jewish inhabitants of this area do not consider themselves as true Arabs but as Palestinians. A large part of this population was in years past rather dissatisfied with the internal policy of the Jordanian government. To the Palestinians the government of Jordan represented a foreign conqueror and they do not accept the Jordanian people as their relatives but call them the Bedouin. There is apparently much reason for Palestinian dissatisfaction. The taxes collected from the regions and the foreign currency from the tourists mainly benefited the capital of Amman, the Royal Family and East Jordan. It is thus possible that the West Bank could become an autonomous area under Israeli domination.

As already mentioned, Jarring's mission has got to start its work amid signs which inspire very little hope. Syria has announced that it will not receive Jarring at all. In Egypt's opinion Jarring is welcome as a person but there are no concessions to be expected from the Egyptian side. Jarring is at present here in Israel and continues on 16 December via Amman to Cairo. Although the situation concerning Jarring's chances looks rather hopeless in the light of the public statements of the parties, there are a few bright spots in sight. The great powers are willing at this moment, each for its own reasons, to reach a settlement in order to put pressure on the parties, at the same time as Jarring's first contacts are on their way. On the other hand, people here in UNTSO think that if Nasser, the most realistic of the Arab politicians after all, could have the freedom of choice, without outside pressure, some form of negotiations could be arranged. Jordan and Syria would not benefit very much from possible negotiations, because the Israeli demands would be hard. But for Egypt the opening of the Suez Canal would be a great advantage compared with the present situation.

Jarring had arrived in the Middle East in a characteristically optimistic mood and full of hope. I think that he learned little by little that there was no reason for optimism. When he came to the area for the second time, I wrote home in mid-January 1968 as follows:

The overall political situation has remained unchanged. Both parties stick strictly to their previous demands, in other words, the Arab states demand absolutely that Israel should withdraw from the occupied territories. Israel for its part wishes to have direct negotiations separately with each of the neighbours, before it will give up an inch of the territories it is occupying.

The second round of negotiations of the Jarring mission is going on at present. Following a principle he adopted at the beginning, Jarring does not talk about the results of the negotiations, but I think that nothing worth mentioning has been achieved. The only information which has become public concerns the fifteen commercial vessels remaining in the Suez Canal, whose fate Jarring has negotiated with the parties, with positive results. It might be expected in the near future that the boats in question will be able to sail away from the canal in the direction of the Gulf of Suez.

It happened in a different way, as I wrote in my report home in mid-February:

The long-lasting endeavour to free the fifteen stranded ships in the Suez Canal ended badly, as many experts here had predicted. An irreconcilable conflict arose mainly from the Egyptian position that it alone has the right to decide what is happening in the canal; while Israel, considering that its troops are on the canal, is of the opinion that any changes must be agreed with it. The chain of events connected with the freeing of the ships culminated in a serious incident at the canal on 30 January 1968.

On 2 February Cairo announced that the freeing of the stranded ships in the Suez Canal was no longer a subject of negotiations. The ships will be freed only when the Middle East crisis has ended and normal navigation has started in the canal.

I was sorry that Jarring's effort to free the ships did not succeed. It would have meant a small step towards restoring normality. Perhaps his credulity was a partial reason for the failure. His actual peace mission was such a thankless job that hardly anybody else could have succeeded in it. In the United States Jarring was blamed for too much caution. I do not believe, however, that daring and imaginative initiatives would have led to better results. The distrust between the parties was too deep and there was insufficient political will to start meaningful negotiations.

I thought Ambassador Jarring deserved a better fate. I had learned to know him as a wise person and a skilful diplomat. When U Thant decided not to run for re-election in 1970 I thought that Gunnar Jarring should have been elected Secretary-General of the United Nations. As Max Jakobson, for other reasons, could not be elected to this office, Gunnar Jarring would, on the merits of his incorruptible character, ·great talent and brilliant intelligence, have been the best choice. His election would have been an excellent solution from the point of view of the world organization. The great powers, however, wanted Kurt Waldheim as the Secretary-General.

The Soviet, French and American peace plans

Jarring's mission was not the only peace effort in operation. At the end of 1968 the Soviet Union presented its own peace plan with the aim of implementing Resolution 242. It reflected Arab demands for total withdrawal and defined the peace in such narrow terms that one could not imagine Israel accepting it. According to the plan, negotiations would be conducted between the Soviet Union and the United States outside the framework of the United Nations. Europe also wanted to join the peace process. The French proposal in early 1969 spoke of four-power negotiations, with the Soviet Union, the United States, the United Kingdom and France as participants.

The newly elected President of the United States, Richard Nixon, who according to his election promises was willing to initiate the participation of his country in the peace process, decided to pursue both options. The matter was also discussed with representatives of the parties. The Israeli Foreign Minister, Abba Eban, Nasser's foreign political adviser, Mahmoud Fawsy, and King Hussein of Jordan all presented their views during their visits to Washington. Their positions were still far apart. The cause of peace did not progress, but everybody thought that there was no hurry.

In Israel's opinion time was on its side. Its possession of the occupied territories was a fact to which the world would become accustomed little by little. One should also take into consideration that the sudden death of Prime Minister Levi Eshkol and the subsequent wait before elections could be held so that the new Prime Minister Golda Meir could stabilize her position, was bound to add to the delay. In the opinion of Egypt, too, there was no hurry for negotiations. According to Nasser, Egypt's political position was so strong that it could afford to wait. Moreover, Nasser came to realize that each successive American peace proposal came nearer to Arab demands and so it was worthwhile to wait.

Not even the United States, however, was whole-hearted in its participation. The Presidential Security Adviser, Henry Kissinger, and the President himself thought there was no hurry because the continuation of the impasse would weaken the position of the Soviet Union and would show the Arabs that the alliance with it would not bring a "just and lasting peace". It would also demonstrate that the continuation of the peace process depended solely on the United States. The start of the negotiations must therefore be delayed.

In Kissinger's view there were additional internal political reasons for the delay. Conditions of peace which Israel could not accept, or pressuring Israel to make peace, would create strong opposition among the politically active and influential Jewish population of the United States.

Perhaps it was not completely unexpected that the slowdown on the negotiation front in the early spring of 1969 should be accompanied by increased action on the military front. A real war was being waged in the Suez Canal sector, where the 1967 cease-fire was no longer in place. In the border area with Jordan, Israel carried out counter-attacks in order to prevent Palestinian guerrilla activities and even Lebanon declared a state of war in its fruitless efforts to prevent Palestinian attacks against Israel from emanating from its territory.

The credibility and authority of American foreign policy was weakened by the hard struggle for power between the Security Adviser Henry Kissinger and the Secretary of State William P. Rogers. The question was, who would direct foreign policy – the State Department or the National Security Council? Rogers wanted rapid action. In his opinion the United States should define the peace objectives in some detail and use its influence to persuade the parties to agree. At the same time as Kissinger tried to slow down the negotiations, Rogers and his energetic aide Joseph Sisco actively carried the matter forward in both the two-power and the four-power negotiations. Before Christmas 1969 they had already progressed so far that the Secretary of State published a peace plan, which was called the Rogers Plan after him. Rogers emphasised that the plan was balanced and that both sides should make concessions. He also insisted that the obligations required by the peace had to be clearly defined on such matters as sovereignty and freedom of navigation. The parties, assisted by Jarring, should agree on security arrangements.

Rogers' formulation of territorial questions received more attention than anything else. According to him, the United States thought that the parties should define the recognized political boundaries and agree on them. Changes to pre-existing lines should not reflect the weight of conquest and should be confined to minimal alterations required for mutual security. The United States did not support expansionism, believing that troops must be withdrawn as Resolution 242 provided. It supported Israel's security and the security of Arab states as well. Applying these principles to an agreement between Egypt and Israel, Rogers proposed the withdrawal of the Israeli forces to the international border.

In Israel the Rogers Plan caused a storm. Prime Minister Meir considered it scandalous and that it would lead to great misfortune. The government of Israel decisively rejected the American proposals.

But the Egyptian press too condemned the proposal as an American attempt to drive a wedge between them and the Soviets and to mislead the Arabs into believing that the United States was an impartial peacemaker.

Jarring's peace mission had ended without results. The two-power and four-power negotiations had met their end and America's own attempts had been buried.

I wrote home on 24 March 1969 about the Israeli situation:

Many signs point to the fact that Israel does not consider it possible to achieve an agreed settlement. After Nixon's rise to power the Israelis are deeply worried about the obvious change in the attitude of the United States. Therefore they have hurried to explain that Israel will not accept any imposed settlement but that matters can be solved only by direct, locally held negotiations between Israel and its neighbours. On the same grounds, the idea of the planned Four-Power negotiations has been condemned here. They cannot lead to anything good, especially considering the hostile anti-Israeli attitude of the Soviet Union and France. Also the idea of UN peace-keeping troops has been condemned by the authorities as still-born. The only activity to which the Israeli government gives its unconditional support is Doctor Jarring's mission. Perhaps it is thought here that it is the surest way to prolong and delay matters.

At the same time measures for long-term possession of the occupied territories and their possible final annexation continue and become more effective. New Jewish settlements are being set up in the Golan Heights and the West Bank of Jordan. Efforts continue to connect the economy of the occupied territories with the economy of Israel, extensive Jewish construction activity in East Jerusalem is in progress and the Suez Canal sector is being fortified very effectively for long-term defensive battle.

One could ask with hindsight whether the slow progress and deliberate delaying of the peace process was after all in the interest of Israel and the United States. Did it only give the Arabs time for rearmament, training and other war preparations? Did it irresistibly lead to a new war? Was a new war in fact necessary in order for a real peace process to begin?

To this last question my answer is affirmative. Later experience showed that the 1973 war was the only one of the Middle East wars whose consequences served the cause of peace.

6. Hostilities at the Suez Canal

Despite Soviet warnings, the Egyptians commenced military activities at the Suez Canal towards the end of October 1967. They began in dramatic fashion when the Egyptian Navy used a rocket to sink the Israeli destroyer *Eilat* near Port Said on October 21. This was the opening shot in a new military phase. According to the *Jerusalem Post*, Moshe Dayan said that the sinking of the *Eilat* meant the renewal of hostilities. The Egyptians rejoiced and the Israelis were furious. Heavy casualties added to the anger and sorrow of the Israelis: 16 dead, 45 wounded and 36 missing. The joy of the Egyptians was short-lived, however, because three days later, on United Nations Day, the Israelis retaliated by bombing and setting fire to the oil refinery in Suez. This was a blow to the economy of Egypt, which was already shaky, and forced the government to introduce temporary rationing.

The Security Council acted fast and condemned all breaches of the cease-fire. Simultaneously, it decided to increase the number of observers at the Canal to 90. With this number we could man nine observation posts on both sides of the Canal. The Secretary-General also recommended that UNTSO should have at its disposal four patrol boats and four helicopters, as we had proposed, and the right to send coded messages in by military radio. Unfortunately the parties did not accept these, in our opinion, reasonable proposals which would have greatly enhanced UNTSO's ability to function. The views of the parties were reflected in the remark of Defence Minister Moshe Dayan when we went together with General Bull to meet him: "From the boat you see too little and from the helicopter too much."

During the incidents in October I was myself for the first time on an inspection tour of the UNTSO military observers on the east bank of the Canal and I saw with my own eyes the magnificent but depressing fireworks in the city of Suez. I thought it was not a proper way to celebrate UN Day. I wrote home on 27 October:

> So the trip to Suez was long and wearying, though exciting in parts. The day of our arrival was still peaceful, although the sinking of the Israeli destroyer "Eilat" on Saturday gave a presentiment that something was going to happen soon. On the following day the cease-fire was broken in the southern part of the canal area and soon the big oil refineries in Suez were in flames. I went to the area on

the following day. The flames were still blazing and a big pillar of smoke rose to the sky. On Wednesday and Thursday the atmosphere was obviously excited on both sides and there were repeated small exchanges of fire.

Occasional shooting on the Canal escalated, on the initiative of the Egyptians, into increasingly intense fighting. Single shots from light weapons gave way to automatic fire and then to powerful artillery duels. From the very beginning the Egyptian casualties were many times higher than Israel's. The west bank of the Canal, occupied by Israel, was an uninhabited desert except for the small town of Kantara, but the densely populated east bank and the large Egyptian cities of Port Said, Ismailia and Suez had to be evacuated in order to prevent still heavier casualties.

The artillery duels also took their toll on the Israeli side. In the first encounters of 1968 a total of 25 soldiers died and 50 were wounded. The severe casualties forced Israel to begin extensive fortification work on their side of the Canal. Gradually the so-called Bar Lev Line was born, for the purpose of protecting all the first-line soldiers from Egyptian artillery fire. All firing positions and living quarters were fortified and fortified trenches were built between them. For further protection, a sand wall was built along the entire length of the Canal. It was 25 metres high, 200 metres deep and ran very steeply to the edge of the Canal. By this monumental sand wall, firing positions for tanks were built at distances of 100 metres. The tanks could drive to these positions and provide flanking fire along the Canal and its eastern bank.

The exchanges of fire at the Canal continued during the spring and summer of 1968. In August we witnessed a new type of military activity. Egyptian commando patrols had crossed the Canal one night and laid mines on the opposite bank. An Israeli jeep had then driven over a mine and in the subsequent ambush two soldiers were killed and a third taken prisoner and brought to the other side of the Canal. Israel demanded the immediate release of the imprisoned soldier. When we went with General Bull to meet Defence Minister Moshe Dayan, he wanted an assurance from the Egyptians that this would not happen again, or otherwise Israel would be obliged to take the necessary steps in order to protect its soldiers. Israel brought the matter to the Security Council for consideration too.

The tension burst into an exchange of fire along the entire Canal on 8 September 1968. Such firing had not been seen since the sinking of the *Eilat*. Casualties were heavy on both sides.

Despite Israeli warnings, the Egyptians did not desist from commando activity and attacks against Israeli transports and patrols continued on the Canal's east bank. As a result tension along the Canal grew and another powerful artillery duel began, again on Egypt's initiative. Israel's retaliatory action was reported in the newspapers of 4 November: helicopter forces had attacked deep in Upper Egypt; a power plant and two bridges south of Luxor had been destroyed. The meaning of this warning was clear: the next attack could be directed at vital Egyptian targets, such as the power plant and dam in Aswan.

In 1969 further exchanges of fire took place. In March Nasser declared that he would reject the cease-fire and the so-called war of attrition began on the Canal. Shots were exchanged almost every day. In a letter to the Secretary-General we tried to analyse Egypt's objectives: perhaps it intended to demonstrate to the Security Council how serious the situation was; perhaps it wanted to improve the morale of its soldiers and to show how efficient the new weapons were. Whatever the truth of those hypotheses, Egypt also wanted to prevent the Israeli fortification work from continuing.

At the same time, Israel's counter-measures became more severe. In early May its commando troops again attacked bridges and power lines in Upper Egypt and the Israeli Air Force started to attack Egyptian positions, which posed a risk to the safety of the UN observers. In July, U Thant warned the Security Council that no alternative remained but to propose the withdrawal of the observers if the shooting did not stop. The warning fell on deaf ears as the daily exchanges of fire went on. In addition, the Egyptians continued their patrolling on the Canal's east bank and the Israeli artillery and Air Force hit back as well as they could. UNTSO became a target of fire too. Between June 1969 and the spring of 1970 the UN observation posts were shot at 284 times from the Egyptian side and 61 times from the Israeli side.

In January 1970 Israel launched a series of air attacks that penetrated deep into Egypt, near Cairo and in the Nile delta, in order to demonstrate Nasser's impotence and to force him to stop the war of attrition. The bombing of a steel factory near Cairo, where 70 workers were killed, was a serious warning of the dangers of this war. It also showed that air defence was still the Egyptians' weakest spot. Now the Soviet

Union was finally ready to help and promised to send the first SA-3 batteries earlier than promised, i.e. before the beginning of March.

The continuing war on the Canal and the heavy casualties it caused began to play on the nerves of the parties and their supporters. But as always, they all – Egypt and the Soviet Union, Israel and the United States – had their own objectives and problems. Should they try for a final peace settlement or should they be content with merely a cease-fire as the first step?

In the spring of 1970 the United States government began to think seriously about what could be done. However, the situation was difficult because the President's National Security Council and the State Department had quite different views on the character of the problem. The latter favoured swift action. The problem would be solved if only the Arabs and Israelis could reach an agreement on the issue of the possession of territories. In the opinion of Henry Kissinger and the National Security Council, which he headed, the problem was much more complex than that: the settlement of territorial questions alone would not lead to real peace. It would be wiser to proceed slowly and to ensure that the cease-fire would not just promote Soviet interests. Kissinger considered these matters very important and according to him the core of the problem lay here. At the same time, he believed, the USA should ensure that the Israeli Air Force got the deliveries of arms that it needed. Its latest shopping list included combat planes: 25 F-4 Phantom jet fighter-bombers and 100 A-4 Skyhawk attack-bombers. The State and Defense Departments, however, considered that its present level of equipment was sufficient and that additional deliveries were unnecessary.

At the beginning of March 1970 the Soviet representative, in Egypt's name, proposed a cease-fire on the Canal and on 17 March Israel accepted this. On the same day, however, it was revealed that a large consignment of weapons had arrived in Egypt, consisting of the most modern SA-3 anti-aircraft missiles, together with about 1,000 Soviet soldiers to operate them. A strong American protest had no effect.

The matter was discussed without results all through the summer. It became known that in addition to the Soviet instructors previously in the area, there were now fighter pilots and missile personnel numbering perhaps 10,000 people. The UNTSO observers also noted the arrival of new Soviet experts, who could be distinguished by their dress: an Egyptian uniform without insignia of rank and elegant civilian shoes instead of heavy military boots. At the end of July the Egyptians and Russians began to construct an anti-aircraft system parallel to the Canal, comprising two SA-3 and eleven SA-2 missiles, which would be able to protect the firing positions of the artillery shooting across the Canal. Egypt's strategic position had improved decisively. It could even launch an attack across the Canal to Sinai. Soviet policy had been superior; while the others only talked, it had supported Egypt efficiently. Israel was worried, for good reason, fearing that its possible counter-measures would lead to direct encounters with Soviet pilots.

At the end of July, when the situation was at its most tense, Nasser announced that he would accept the American cease-fire proposal made in June, together with the offer to start peace negotiations under the auspices of Jarring. After tough negotiations, persuasion and promises of arms supplies, the Israeli government was also ready for negotiations and accepted the cease-fire on 6 August 1970.

The cease-fire and the military standstill connected with it were to take effect the following day. The United States and Israel had agreed what this standstill would mean in practice: a 50 km.-wide zone west of the Canal where the deployment of missiles and the construction of concrete sites would not be permitted. The matter had not been negotiated with the Egyptians and they had their own views on it, saying that the missiles close to the Canal had been transferred there three weeks before the cease-fire. Israeli intelligence claimed that the forward deployment had continued after the cease-fire had taken effect. Egypt repeatedly denied claims of breaches of the agreement. It thought that the measures it had taken had been in conformity with the Egyptian interpretation of the agreement: that it would not introduce additional missiles into the zone but would reserve the right to rotate missiles in and out to maintain their existing level; that it would not construct any new missile sites, but would reserve the right to maintain and repair the existing ones; that Israel was violating the cease-fire agreement and that American arms supplies ran counter to Rogers' assurances and the agreement itself.

Israel protested strongly against the Egyptian breaches it had detected, but the American statements were cautious and understanding. This the Egyptians exploited unscrupulously. One had the impression that, for the Egyptians, the strengthening of the anti-aircraft defence of the Canal zone was more important than participation in peace negotiations, the results of which seemed uncertain.

In an outsider's opinion the situation was annoying and I was not surprised that the Israelis, offended by the Egyptian behaviour, refused to come to the negotiating table. The hopes for a wider peace process had once more turned out to be futile. Israel got the planes and other military equipment it had wanted. It was quiet on the Canal for a long time.

7. UNTSO squeezed between the parties

The many phases of the war of attrition, from the autumn of 1967 to the cease-fire agreement negotiated by the Americans in August 1970, were a difficult time for the parties. But the conditions on the Canal were also awkward for UNTSO military observers. They had no weapons with which to defend themselves, had played no part in starting the war, but had simply been placed there to supervise the cease-fire agreed after the 1967 war. The war of attrition was a continuing and deliberate violation of that cease-fire. It was somewhat absurd that UNTSO, in its daily detailed reports, tried to maintain the fiction that the cease-fire still existed. These reports were sent to the Security Council, but I don't know whether anybody read them.

Thus the military observers had to operate under the continuing fire of the parties, like a kind of voluntary target. In trying to protect themselves from the accurate fire of the Israelis on the West Bank, the Egyptians had pushed their battle positions so close to the UNTSO observation posts that most of the fire was directed straight at the observers. Mistakes were difficult to avoid, although the Israelis tried not to shoot directly at UN targets. We presented the Egyptians with the demand that their combat positions should not be built closer than 50 metres to our sites. The matter was discussed for years but our efforts had no effect. The Egyptians did not want to change their practice.

On the Israeli side this problem did not exist. There were generally fewer of their soldiers in this area and their combat positions were far away from each other and from the UN sites. Life at the observation posts on the east bank of the Canal was still very dangerous, because the Egyptians did not select their targets but as a principle fired at everything that moved. Trips to and from the observation posts were therefore especially dangerous. In comparison, staying at an observation post was safer, because during the firing the observers could go into the shelter.

We tried to do our best to improve the safety of the observers. The shelter construction programme was completed in 1968. The Kantara Control Centre, where for weeks the staff had to work underground, was transferred 50 km. east from the Canal bank to the village of Rabah. We received four Saracen armoured personnel carriers from

British stores in Cyprus. I recruited four UN soldiers from the Finnish Battalion in Cyprus to drive these cars. It turned out to be a good arrangement, because in this way we could transport the observers safely to the observation posts on the Canal's east bank.

We also considered the possibility of closing all the observation posts along the Canal and leaving only the control centres operating. Even alone, without the observation posts, they would have been able to observe and report the fact that there was shooting on the Canal every day. However, the Secretary-General could not accept this idea because he considered the continuity of UNTSO's presence important. It would have been politically difficult to reopen the closed posts. Our only remaining resort remained the possibility of closing, without asking anybody, those posts which were under the heaviest fire. By the end, only five out of the original nine observation posts on both sides of the Canal were still operating.

Despite the dangers, the UNTSO observers came through remarkably unscathed. During the war of attrition the parties' casualties were high, with thousands killed or wounded. In the same period, UNTSO lost only two officers killed, while a few were wounded. With some very rare exceptions, the mental endurance of the observers remained at a high level and every day we had new proof of their courage. They really deserved the expressions of gratitude which the Secretary-General and the Security Council sent them.

On my inspection tours of the Canal zone I had personal experience of the dangers involved. On the west bank of the Canal the trip went rather pleasantly, because the careful and logical Israelis found out in advance the exact details of my route and time-table and adjusted their daily firing plan accordingly. Often the firing would stop abruptly when I arrived in the area of a certain observation post and would start again when I had left.

Sometimes I happened to come to Ismailia Control Centre at times when artillery duels continued throughout the night and the staff of the centre worked in the basement shelters, which were reinforced with sandbags. I could then follow the work of the Officer-in-Charge of the control centre and his personnel in almost warlike conditions. Young officers gained an idea of how each of them would behave under fire, an experience which they would not have had during normal peacetime manoeuvres.

My inspection tours of the east bank of the Canal were often full of surprises because the Egyptians were not so polite that they would change their firing plans for the sake of my travels. I remember many cases when my party and I had to seek shelter from direct and indirect fire. Once, near Kantara, we were fired at by light weapons and one of our cars was hit. On another occasion, north of Kantara, I drove into the middle of light mortar fire; grenades exploded in front of and behind our car. The only thing to do was to order the driver to press the accelerator flat against the floor of the car.

Many times I was really scared, more than I remember having been scared as a young man in the Second World War. Perhaps life seemed more valuable when there was less of it left. Perhaps it was also that in the war one did not have time to worry so much about oneself when one had responsibility for the success of one's unit and for the well-being and life of its soldiers. The military observers on the Canal were in fact responsible only for themselves. In that respect their work, and the courage and bravery they showed, deserved a quite special admiration and respect. For my own part I can honestly confess that my condition improved and the gnawing feeling at the bottom of my stomach disappeared when the car headed for Jerusalem and we were out of the reach of artillery fire.

The war of attrition on the Canal, which lasted for years, was one of the most difficult phases of UNTSO's history. Because of its severity and long duration it put the military observers to perhaps a harder test than ever. It demanded the life of two able and courageous Swedish officers, Major Roland Bo Plane and Lieutenant-Colonel Jens Bögvad. Many observers were wounded, some seriously. The war of attrition was mentally and physically strenuous for all of them, but it was also frustrating. It was hard for the observers to understand whether the presence of the UN along the Canal in these circumstances was at all necessary. Were their willingness and self-sacrifice of any concrete use to the cause of peace? Were their lives and health endangered for insufficient reasons? The observers had come to the Middle East to supervise the cease-fire, but instead they were stranded, against their wishes, in the middle of a war. They had the right to wish that the Security Council would carefully weigh their position and at least give them a new task.

I thought at the time, and later too, that these questions were justified. From the point of view of the world organization's credibility it was essential that UNTSO remained steadfastly in place to carry out its extremely difficult task: a task that required great courage. Despite the political and diplomatic character of its mission, UNTSO

Meeting with Moshe Dayan, spring 1970.

Gunnar Jarring on a visit to Government House. Behind are his aides Ian Berendsen and Rémy Gorgé.

was a military organization whose operations were directed by general international military traditions. UNTSO observers knew when they entered service that there was not a pleasant holiday trip ahead, but that service could include great risks. During the war of attrition on the Suez Canal they were, however, near the absolute limits of military demands. If the casualties suffered by UNTSO had been heavier, I am sure that the Security Council would have had to urgently revise its mandate.

I have been obliged in my later work for the UN to give consideration to the problem of casualties. When assigning duties, I have always stressed the importance of caution. Commanders of UN battalions should, in my opinion, do their utmost to avoid unnecessary casualties, that is to say those which are incurred in the course of an operation or job that does not further the UN's objectives or duties. On the other hand, casualties must be accepted in a situation where they cannot be avoided without endangering the task of the mission.

I have in fact been obliged to take a position on the question of casualties. I was on leave in Finland in the summer of 1974, when Turkish forces landed in Cyprus. In the course of this, the Finnish UN battalion had suffered casualties, and the Helsinki newspapers wrote that it should be immediately withdrawn and sent home. Our men had not been sent there to be killed.

I discussed the matter with Finnish officials who wanted to know my opinion. I told them that, according to information I had received, the Finnish battalion had acted very ably and courageously in a difficult situation. By doing so, it had helped in carrying out the task of UNFICYP (UN Peace-keeping Force in Cyprus). The casualties were very regrettable but they could not have been avoided. They were sustained while the Finnish battalion was performing its duties and so were a part of those duties. I had also observed that our UN soldiers were fully aware of the risks involved in their job and were, despite the casualties, enthusiastic and ready to continue. I ended by saying that we should be ready to accept possible casualties in the future if we considered participation in peace-keeping to be an important part of our UN policy.

On the first day of May 1970, at a stage when there was no sign of an end to the war of attrition, I was appointed Chief of Staff of UNTSO. In UN circles it was not usual for the second in command to be appointed to the number one job. However, the year 1970 seemed to be exceptional in this respect, because at UNRWA Headquarters in Beirut, to replace the American Lawrence Mitchelmoore, his deputy, the British Sir John Rennie, was appointed as the Commissioner-General. The spirit of the age was manifest even in the Roman Catholic Church, because when the Latin Patriarch died, his nearest aide, Monsignore Beltritti, was nominated as his successor.

My appointment was completely General Bull's idea, and he had talked about it with me and probably with others for a long time. He succeeded in persuading me to stay for another year in the colonel's job in UNTSO. Otherwise the post would have passed to an American. I was naturally glad of the confidence he showed in me. The appointment to the office of an UN Assistant Secretary-General would radically change the situation; it would mean an independent and responsible job and the beginning of a completely new career. My financial difficulties would end. On the salary of a Finnish colonel, I had had to maintain two households, one in Helsinki and the other in Jerusalem. Similarly I had had to pay, among other things, for the travels of my family to Jerusalem and back. I was also glad that the appointment would mean moving to Government House, where the Chief of Staff had a beautiful residence on the uppermost floor.

Now it would be meaningful to remain in Jerusalem for a longer period of time. When the news of General Bull's coming retirement at the end of 1969 was published, the Finnish authorities also became enthusiastic and quickly started to take steps. It took me completely by surprise to be promoted to major-general on Finnish Independence Day 1969. The government wanted to remove the formal obstacle to my appointment to a new position.

However, the matter became more complex and a decision was postponed. According to Bull, the parties had nothing against my appointment, but attitudes in New York were sour. Perhaps some members of the Secretariat looked askance at the zeal of the Finnish authorities. The matter was further complicated by General Bull's postponement for six months of his departure on pension. The waiting was long but in the course of the spring the situation was clarified and the Secretariat abandoned its opposition. On May Day I could start my new tasks, although at first only as Acting Chief of Staff. At the last moment General Bull had for personal reasons changed his plans. He first went on a three months' leave and then returned in July for farewell visits and finally to hand over his job.

What kind of a man was my boss, General Odd Bull? I had learned to appreciate him as the Chief of Staff of UNOGIL in Lebanon in 1958. My admiration and respect only increased when I had the opportunity to work with him more closely. In negotiations with the parties he was impartial and honest; one could not doubt his intentions and goodwill and he had therefore gained the confidence of the parties.

The most visible traits of Odd Bull's character and behaviour were friendliness and consideration, which he generously showed to his subordinates as well. At official receptions and private parties he was a charming host who always helped his guests enjoy themselves. The genuine modesty of his character could be seen in his desire to shun the spotlight of publicity. One could also observe that he found it hard to blame or even criticize his subordinates, as much as it was necessary at times. Gradually a practice developed between us according to which I took care of disciplinary matters within UNTSO.

On General Bull's departure, the *Jerusalem Post* published a very positive editorial praising his "integrity, honesty and objectivity". According to the paper Israelis never lost their respect for General Bull, not even when the authority of the United Nations was at its lowest after the Six Day War. The *Post* ended its editorial thus:

> Israel regrets having to bid goodbye to this untypical representative of the United Nations. He worked hard for peace. Now that a glimmer of hope looms on the horizon, the job has fallen to the Finnish General Siilasvuo who will be shouldering a major post if and when the cease-fire takes effect. One would wish that the successor of General Bull should follow in his footsteps, which is a sufficient tribute to the retiring, quiet Norwegian.

8. The Jordanian crisis, September 1970

At the same time as the guns fell silent along the Suez Canal, relations between King Hussein of Jordan and the Palestinians began to deteriorate decisively. One had thought that a more favourable phase had begun in the Middle East; Nasser had expressed his willingness to reach a political agreement and optimists thought that Gunnar Jarring could begin his shuttle diplomacy again. But the cease-fire on the Canal set free forces which prevented the peace efforts and led to a severe crisis. The events in Jordan were an internal Arab affair and were not really part of the Arab-Israeli conflict, but when the Jordanian crisis was at its worst the political leadership of the United States realized, to its surprise, that the Arab country's relations with the Soviet Union had become strained.

The Palestinians embarked on a period of vigorous terrorist activity at the beginning of September, with an attempt to assassinate King Hussein. This was followed by clashes with the army and on 6 September the Palestinian action reached its peak to date when four passenger planes were hijacked in Europe, although the hijacking of an El Al plane so far remained only an attempt.

Of the hijacked planes, one, a Pan Am flight, was forced to land at Cairo Airport, the passengers were set free and the plane was blown up. The TWA and Swissair planes had to land near the town of Zerka in Jordan and their passengers remained on the planes as hostages.

Responsibility for the hijackings was claimed by a radical group, the Popular Front for the Liberation of Palestine (PFLP), which presented a number of demands to the owner states and to Israel. If their demands were not accepted, they said, the planes would be blown up with their passengers.

All authorities, including the Security Council, tried their best to liberate the passengers. In the intolerable heat of Zerka Airport, the conditions in which the passengers were kept were inhumane. For six days these 280 people had to suffer, until finally the majority of them were freed thanks to the negotiations carried out by the Commander of the Jordanian Army. The planes were blown up at the airport. The last 40 hostages were set free only after the Jordanian troops had overpowered the prison camp where they were kept.

During 1970 the Palestinians had strengthened their position in

Jordan and undermined the authority of the King. They had become almost a state within a state. The cease-fire that had been reached on the Canal now threatened their plans. There was a danger that their previously loyal supporter would make an agreement with King Hussein and try to come to a political solution at their expense. In August the National Council of Palestine met in Amman. In the course of this meeting, radical groups demanded the immediate dethroning of the King. Moderate groups, particularly Al Fatah, tried to put on the brakes. Then the leader of the PFLP, Georges Habash, as unpredictable as always, carried out the hijackings of early September and demanded that Israel should hand over a large number of imprisoned Palestinians.

King Hussein was faced with a difficult decision. Violent measures against the Palestinians would be strongly condemned in other parts of the Arab world. He also had to consider the possible reaction of the Syrians and of the 17,000 strong Iraqi division which had remained in Jordan after the June war. On the other hand, inactivity would undoubtedly lead to a personal defeat for the King.

On 15 September the King formed a new government by replacing the civilians with soldiers. At the same time he informed the United States, via the British, that he intended to take forceful measures against the Palestinians. President Nixon, who as a reaction to the PFLP demands had taken preparatory military steps, now gave the order to move the aircraft-carrier *Saratoga* to the eastern Mediterranean near the Lebanese coast. The aircraft-carrier *Independence* was there already. In addition, some air transport troops in Germany were placed on alert and more cargo planes were sent to Turkey.

The situation developed into bloody clashes in mid-September. In the outskirts of Amman the King's troops had the upper hand, but a few days later the Palestinians received support from Syria, whose armoured troops crossed the border in the north near the town of Irbid. The worried President Nixon warned that the United States and Israel might be forced to take military measures if the Syrians would not withdraw. Nixon wanted to demonstrate clearly that Syria (and its supporter, the Soviet Union) could not attack an ally of the United States without being punished. It so happened that Prime Minister Golda Meir and Ambassador Itzhak Rabin were at that time on a fund-raising tour in New York and in the course of talks with them it became obvious that Israel was ready for air and ground operations against the Syrians.

The certainty that help was to be expected gave King Hussein new enthusiasm and the courage to take action. He gave the order to his small air force to attack Irbid. The results were surprisingly successful and the Syrians suffered heavy casualties and losses of equipment. The Syrian Air Force and the Iraqi division did not react. When in addition the political and diplomatic counter-measures organized by the United States began to bear fruit, the Syrians had to withdraw with a bloody nose. The Palestinian revolt was harshly subdued.

UNTSO had an excellent window onto the events of the Jordanian civil war. Our Liaison Office was situated in a central area of Amman. It was manned by the Liaison Officer, his assistant and two field service officers. A curfew had been ordered in the city and therefore diplomats could not leave their embassies. But UNTSO liaison officers in their uniforms and white jeeps, blue flags fluttering, could move freely in the streets of Amman. They could report their observations to UNTSO Headquarters because the radio link between Jerusalem and Amman continued to operate. Thus UNTSO could keep the Secretary-General and Security Council well-informed of the situation.

Besides UNTSO, Jordan also housed the offices of the United Nations Development Programme (UNDP) and the United Nations Relief and Works Agency for Palestinian Refugees in the Near East (UNRWA). The Resident Representative of UNDP, the Haitian Jean-Claude Aimé, was in charge of the security of the UN officials and their families in Jordan. In order to be able to carry out his duties better, he moved to the UNTSO house for the duration of the crisis. From there he had better communications in all directions and the liaison officers could help him in many ways. It was a pleasure to follow his energetic and courageous performance via the radio set at UNTSO HQ. In this way I first became acquainted with the man who later became my political adviser.

The King emerged victorious from the crisis and he could be content with the results. The Palestinians had once again been the losers. Their fate was in my opinion pitiable, particularly as their defeat had been suffered in a struggle against another Arab people. For good reason this phase remained in the memory of the Palestinians as "Black September". The PLO's wrong appraisal of the situation and failing policy were the main factors in its defeat.

Now I realized for the first time how incompetently the PLO, as the *de facto* government of Palestine, carried out its duties. It lacked a clear programme with realistic objectives – its aim was everything or nothing – and its great internal disunity made it hard to reach unanimous decisions. Discipline and order were bad and were not much improved by the dismissing of Georges Habash and his group after the hijackings.

The PLO's methods of operation were inefficient and psychologically badly considered. Obviously, it was important to arouse the attention of the world and in that respect the hijackings surely made their point. At least now people were aware of the existence of a Palestinian people who desperately sought a just solution to their problems. But the other objectives of the hijackers were not achieved because their demands were not accepted, while irredeemable harm was caused to the organization's image and fame. Particularly in the Western countries, the PLO's methods could not be understood at all and were still less condoned. The opponents of the PLO could be happy: the Palestinians would not achieve their goals by such means.

President Nixon and Secretary of State Kissinger were very satisfied with the end results of the Jordanian crisis and considered it a great victory for American diplomacy. The faithful ally Hussein was firmly in power, the Palestinian guerrillas had been beaten and all the hostages set free. Yet perhaps Jordan itself had a greater share in the success that had been achieved. Fortunately, it had been able to repel the Syrian attack without the help of the United States and Israel, whose intervention in the Jordanian civil war could have had unforeseen consequences for Hussein. The rest of the Arab world would not have forgiven it.

The United States was also convinced that, as a result of its show of force, the Soviet Union had given up its policy of direct intervention. I doubt that the Soviet Union ever seriously considered taking any direct action in this crisis. In general, the American and Israeli assessment of the Jordanian crisis over-emphasised the threat from the Soviet Union and the worldwide character of the crisis. It was really more of a regionally limited clash between Syria, Jordan and the PLO.

The Jordanian crisis had a favourable effect on relations between Israel and the United States, a process that had already begun with the obvious Egyptian breaches of the cease-fire on the Suez Canal. Israel had strengthened its position as an important strategic ally which was needed to keep the policies of Egypt and the Soviet Union in check. The latter was, in Kissinger's view, double-faced. Israel had given valuable assistance in different phases of the Jordanian crisis. By its mere presence it had been able to prevent the Syrians from using their air force. Moreover, by deploying armoured troops in the Golan area, Israel had expedited the Syrian withdrawal. Now Rogers' balancing policy would be forgotten and Israel would get a good deal of military and economic assistance from the USA. Relations really flourished in the next three years.

The events in Jordan also had an indirect effect in the fatal deterioration of Nasser's health and his sudden death. Shaken by the bloodbath suffered by the Palestinians, at the end of September he had convened an Arab summit meeting to mediate between Jordan and the Palestinians. Nasser had drafted a proposal for a solution which he felt both parties could accept. Both should make concessions because in his opinion both had made errors. President Anwar Sadat writes in his memoirs, however, that during a private meeting at Nasser's hotel suite Arafat flew into a rage. This saddened Nasser and he wanted to leave the meeting then and there. In Sadat's opinion Arafat's behaviour was very unjust, because in fact Nasser had done his best to promote the Palestinian cause. With great effort, Nasser was persuaded to remain at the meeting and a kind of a compromise was reached. Although completely exhausted, Nasser still forced himself to go to the airport to say goodbye to his prominent guests. This farewell was his last because he died on the same evening, 28 September 1970.

A large group of world notables gathered in Cairo on 1 October 1970 for the solemn funeral of President Gamal Abdel Nasser. Among the guests were kings, presidents and prime ministers, from the Emperor of Ethiopia, Haile Selassie, to the Prime Minister of the Soviet Union, Alexei Kosygin. I too was there, in my capacity as the Chief of Staff of UNTSO and the Representative of the Secretary-General of the United Nations. Nasser's funeral was the magnificent and dramatic final act of an era. Hardly any of the participants could have guessed, however, that we were approaching an important turning point in the history of the Middle East and that the ending of Nasser's presidency would also be the beginning of a new era which would lead towards peace.

I had arrived in the grieving Cairo the evening before the funeral. The city, where usually a multitude of people was thronging the streets, was now a ghostlike desert. The Cairenes stayed in their homes and only near the mosques did I see groups of religious people, who, carrying banderoles and Islamic green flags, displayed their sorrow by singing and dancing. I had never before experienced such a deep and impressive Moslem celebration of sorrow.

Fortunately I had a room in the venerable Omar Khayyam Hotel on Gezira Island. It was historically the most remarkable hotel in Cairo because it had been built for the opening festivities of the Suez Canal. The rooms were grand in size but the gilding was already worn. From here I could, in case of emergency, walk to the starting point of the funeral procession, which was on the same island in the courtyard of the palace of the Revolutionary Council near the Kasr El Nil Bridge. Not far either was the Sheraton Hotel, where I intended to go that evening. That is to say that I had heard in Jerusalem that my former boss, Lieutenant-General Jorma Järventaus, was also in Cairo and hoped to see me. As the Military Adviser of the biggest Helsinki newspaper, *Helsingin Sanomat*, he had intended to interview Nasser, but death had intervened. It was refreshing to listen to Järventaus' conversation, which was always witty and to the point. I had not had the opportunity to enjoy it for a long time. He is really a master conversationalist. We talked about the issues of our home country, the Middle East and the entire world. Time was passing, and it was already late when my host saw me to the outer door.

The following morning the crowds in the streets of Cairo were almost impenetrable. I was told that at least two million people had come from the nearby countryside to catch a glimpse of the funeral procession. I was among 800 invited guests sitting on gilded chairs in huge funeral tents which in the traditional Egyptian manner were decorated with colourful embroideries. We were waiting for the helicopter carrying Nasser's coffin to land in the palace courtyard, listening to the funeral prayers of the *imam*, and drinking cold water which the waiters brought us. A young Egyptian soldier, wild with sorrow, had climbed onto the roof of the funeral tent and from there greeted his dead leader with the words "*Maas salami, Rais!*" (Go in peace, leader!). The soldiers of the guard of honour also had tears in their eyes as the funeral procession went by.

But the cortège could not even reach the bridge. The exceptional multitude of people blocked the road and the situation got out of the control of the soldiers and the police. The important guests had to return to where they had set out. I saw King Hussein first, followed by the others. The drama of the situation was increased when the tall President of Sudan, Jaafar Nimeiri, carried the Egyptian Vice-

President, Anwar Sadat, on his shoulders. I was told that Sadat had been taken ill.

There was nothing else to do but patiently wait for the crowds to disperse. The situation was unexpected because the cars and even the security men attending all the notables had moved in advance to the other side of the Nile. Most probably many guests, like myself, were contemplating the future of Egypt and of the entire Middle East. Sadat seemed like a makeshift choice as Nasser's successor; political observers believed that Nasser had viewed Sadat as a mediocrity, only giving him religious ceremonies to take care of.

Little by little the throng began to ease and, together with the Resident Representative of the UNDP and the Director of the UN Information Office, I proceeded towards the latter's office on the other side of the Nile. On the road we saw others who had also decided to walk; the British Foreign Secretary, Lord Home, with his party, was in front of us. Cairo was returning to normal.

The conclusion of Nasser's funeral ceremonies meant a return to daily routine for me too. I had decided to fly back to Jerusalem the same evening. There were in fact no urgent tasks in sight because the situation had been politically and militarily quiet for some time. I knew, however, from experience that this could change overnight without any warning.

It appeared, however, that the prospect of stability was better now than it had been for a long time. Even the Suez Canal zone had been peaceful for many weeks and the cease-fire, negotiated by the Americans in August, seemed to be holding. All the signs were pointing to a long period of peace for UNTSO.

9. Quiet days, 1970–73

Even during the quiet days the Chief of Staff of UNTSO had enough work to do. UNTSO was a large and complex organization and it operated over a wide area. The wheels had to run whether there was much or very little to report along the front lines. The headquarters had to function smoothly and efficiently and to send its daily reports to the Secretary-General promptly and ensure their contents were reliable. In these respects UNTSO Headquarters had a good reputation, dating back to old times, which had to be maintained. The high standard of UNTSO's staff work depended mostly perhaps on the fact that we were allowed to choose our staff officers ourselves, picking the most suitable military observers from the contingent of over 200.

However, UNTSO could not be directed only from its headquarters; the Chief of Staff had constantly to be on the road. He had to make inspection tours of the Suez Canal, the Golan and Lebanon. He had to meet with military observers and field service officers and take care of their families. In my opinion, the special duty of the Chief of Staff was to maintain the working morale of UNTSO personnel and the United Nations spirit. In the quiet times he had to pay more attention to these questions than usual, to make everybody understand that the work was meaningful and promoted the cause of peace in the volatile region of the Middle East.

In the quiet period disciplinary problems increased. I had had the same experience in the Second World War; when people do not have enough to do, they have time to plan all kinds of forbidden things. In UNTSO smuggling was a very tempting crime. During my time one of the most peculiar cases was an attempt to smuggle a rather large amount of gold from Beirut to Cairo. One of our field service officers was caught at Cairo Airport with 12 kilos of gold hidden in a belt around his waist. From the point of view of UNTSO's reputation the case was annoying. But the culprit's prospects were grim: he would lose his job in the United Nations and in the police force of his own country; the gold had been confiscated and in addition legal action in an Egyptian court was awaiting him. An extenuating circumstance, I was told, was that the man was in a desperate situation. His wife was fatally ill, the family's means had gone on medical expenses and money had to be found from somewhere. I thought that the case was lost but then, at the request of the culprit, Michel, the Cairene owner of a travel agency and a general factotum employed by UNTSO personnel, took an energetic interest in it. Now it so happened that the judge trying the case had been a fellow student of Michel and the verdict was that the gold should be divided into three equal parts: one to go to the judge, one to Michel and the third to the UNTSO man.

Another favourite activity of the quiet times was complicated love affairs, which on occasion had to be resolved by the Chief of Staff. Once it happened that the 15 year-old daughter of a Nordic observer of the rank of major had fallen in love with a Syrian captain. The affair was made delicate by the information I had received that the Captain was a member of the Syrian intelligence service. I summoned the Major to my office and asked how it was possible that the parents could have allowed the association of such a young girl with a much older man. The father assured me that the daughter was well-developed for her age and the parents did not want to be an obstacle to her happiness. I told the Major that I would immediately transfer him from Damascus to Tiberias on the Israeli side of the border and that I would also forbid him or the members of his family to visit Damascus in the future. I also told him that I would cancel the family's UNTSO identity cards, which were needed to cross the border. The Major pointed out that his wife and daughter were free citizens and that supposedly I had no right to limit their movements. To this I answered that they were free indeed, but the Major himself was not, as he was in the service of UNTSO. If it appeared that he could not prevent his family from returning to Damascus, he should prepare himself for an immediate return to his home country. I had the feeling that the Major was relieved by my decision. When a few moments later I went downstairs to the restaurant to have my lunch, I saw the ladies of the family there. If looks could kill, I thought, I would have been a dead man.

But of course I had other duties than dealing with smuggling and love affairs. Of these the most important was to maintain contact with the authorities in the area of operation. Depending to some extent on the nature of my problem, I would generally hold meetings with the Defence or Foreign Minister and often also with the Chief of Staff or a senior official in the Foreign Ministry. I discussed with them the general situation, specific events in each area and the role of UNTSO. I would then tell both the Israelis and the Arabs what was happening on the other side of the line and present my own evaluation of the situation. By doing this I tried to dispel misunderstandings and distrust and to promote the maintenance of peace.

In Egypt the arrangements at first were not satisfactory, for UNTSO had no direct contact with the political and military leadership of that country; the principal contact person was the Under-Secretary of the Foreign Ministry, Salah Gohar. Since 1948 he had served in the Armistice Department of the Ministry, which took care of UNTSO and in 1956–67 of UNEF too. Gohar tried his best in his dealings with us, but his authority was not enough to influence the decisions of the military leadership in particular. In 1970, however, when I took over the command of UNTSO, Gohar was transferred to be Ambassador to Vienna. The new and energetic Commander of the Egyptian Army, Sa'ad Shazli, started direct contacts with me. A little later the Defence and Foreign Ministers of Egypt also began to receive me and communications became as flexible as they were in the other countries of the area.

Gradually I began to know the most important leaders of the area and to understand their temperament, character, manners and attitudes. For the sake of my own work it was perhaps still more important that they found out what kind of a man I was and what they could expect from me. It was the starting point for future co-operation.

From the very beginning I tried to keep close links with the embassies of the region, particularly with the representatives of the United States and the Soviet Union and of those countries which sent observers to UNTSO. To help with the smooth running of affairs, it was right for these member states to get information directly from the field.

The Chief of Staff had to take care of the guests of UNTSO and show them hospitality. There were guests enough on ordinary days; when the situation became tense their numbers multiplied. The most significant of the local guests were diplomats: ambassadors from Tel Aviv and a few from Jerusalem, consuls general from Jerusalem (representing France, the United States, the United Kingdom and Belgium). For diplomats, UNTSO was the most useful source of information, especially concerning the Arab countries. Other important guests were the representatives of the International Red Cross, UNRWA and the media. The Defence and Foreign Ministers of the countries that sent observers to UNTSO particularly wanted to call: during my time representatives of the Nordic countries, for instance, visited us many times. There were guests from other parts of the world as well; from Canada, Austria, the Netherlands, Belgium and even from Australia. In conversations with the ambassadors I stressed the importance of such visits and invited new visitors. I had noticed that the visits of such dignitaries refreshed and encouraged the observers and heightened their motivation. In addition, these visits enhanced knowledge of the work and conditions of the observers and so could be used to promote the standing of the observers in their home countries and to improve their social conditions.

If guests were served a lunch or a dinner, this was most often in our private home. If the party was so large that we could not accommodate them there, however, the meal was given in the dining-room and ballroom downstairs.

As I had guessed, one of the bright features of my new job was the move to the residence of the Chief of Staff on the uppermost floor of Government House. This solemnly beautiful palace had been built in the 1920s as the residence of the British High Commissioner. The construction had been expensive, the budget had been exceeded and the whole matter had been criticized in Parliament. Downstairs were the formal rooms – a ballroom with adjoining smaller halls, a large dining-room – and a kitchen. On the first and second floors there were about 20 bedrooms. Jerusalem had very few hotels at that time, but in Government House the visiting notables, like the British Foreign Secretary or the King of Trans-Jordan, could be accommodated in a dignified manner. Even the everyday life of the house was solemn and formal. In fact it was much like a vice-regal court.

In UNTSO's time only a beautiful, slightly faded relic was left of the previous splendour and life had become more unassuming. The bedrooms had become offices, the dining-room and kitchen served as a cafeteria for the personnel, while in the ceremonial rooms guests could be received and joint parties arranged on great holidays. At the top of the house was our private apartment, surrounded by a balcony from which there was an unrivalled view of the Old City, the Valley of Kidron, the Mount of Olives and the village of Bethany.

The new and more spacious home made it possible for the children, relatives and friends from Finland to come more often to visit us in Jerusalem. Our youngest son, Pekka, spent two years (the eighth and ninth grades) in the Anglican Church School of Jerusalem. The fact that English was the medium of instruction in the school caused him some difficulty at first. Therefore we did the homework together and studied, among other things, the book of Joshua, which was the subject of Pekka's Scripture lessons. I had not had any earlier acquaintance in such great detail with the ancient history of Israel.

The kitchen was managed at first by Sophie, a Christian Palestinian from Ramallah, a somewhat difficult character and not very competent. She was followed by Ata, a pensioned sergeant who had got his training as a cook to British officers in the Jordanian Army. Ata was professionally able and could cope alone with cooking and serving a dinner for eight. When there were more people at the table, Ata got waiters from the kitchen downstairs to help him.

Ata lived in an Arab village close to the main road to Tel Aviv. He had a respected position in his village because he had acquired a generator and in the evenings distributed electricity to his neighbours for lights and watching the television. I often took my guests to see the conditions in Ata's village. We would meet Ata's wife and mother, both dressed in traditional national costumes, the mother with blue tattoo marks on her face. It was foolish to imagine that women in this family or in the village community played a submissive role. No decisions were made until the wife and, particularly, the old mother had said the last word. With his small salary Ata had given a good education to all his six children. He and his family were a new type of modern Palestinians who wanted to make a better future for their children and spurred them to success at school.

For many years we were also served by Hertta, a religious Finnish girl from a kibbutz who temporarily needed to earn money. Hertta took care of our home, endlessly washed and ironed table-cloths and napkins, arranged flowers and when necessary also laid the table for special occasions beautifully and artistically. Ata's and Hertta's relations were good because, being humble by nature, Hertta did the more tedious kitchen work, washed the dishes and peeled the potatoes. One day Hertta looked wondering at the devotedly religious Ata who according to the rules of the Koran was praying on the balcony. "This one there prays to somebody who does not exist," Hertta said to my wife and was surprised when she assured her that Ata prayed to the same God of Abraham as we did.

The life of the people in the Middle East was not easy even during the years of quiet. The cause of peace did not seem to progress. The governments were lacking the political will to start negotiations and nobody, not the Arabs or the Israelis or the great powers, were in a hurry to speed up the peace process. They imagined that the maintenance of the status quo would be in the interest of all the parties.

Therefore it was vain for us in UNTSO to hope that we would be able to promote peace. Living continuously amidst the conflict was hard, although we were not ourselves a party to it. We were especially conscious of the difficult situation in Jerusalem, where the Arabs and the Jews were continually and directly in contact with each other. Here one could almost literally touch the conflict. We foreigners were acutely aware of their mutual distrust, antipathy and often even hatred.

Fortunately Jerusalem had its great positive features too. It is one of the most beautiful cities in the world. With the power of its great past it influences its inhabitants and even temporary visitors deeply. The city is full of museums and historical monuments, but it is a living, modern city as well, with its own culture and ways of life. It also has more to offer in the way of culture, in the European sense, than almost anywhere.

For the fun and recreation of the UNTSO people we organized our own cultural activities on a modest scale. The standard of the annual exhibition of UNTSO's amateur artists was surprisingly high, particularly the work submitted by our Japanese friends. Very refreshing too were UNTSO's historical walks, which were organized in the winter season to sites in Jerusalem and further afield. Our expert guide was the Irish Father Jerome Murphy-O'Connor, a Professor at the École Biblique. In our wanderings we were able to see the monuments and other remains left by many different cultures. All of them have left their mark, but none has lasted for ever.

Part II. The October War

10. On the eve of war in Egypt

My new aide, the Senior Staff Officer of UNTSO, Colonel P.D. Hogan, and I were in Cairo at the beginning of October 1973. He had arrived from Dublin in September to take over from his country-man, Colonel R.W. Bunworth. On his briefing tour, Hogan had already visited Damascus and the Golan Heights. Now it was the turn of Egypt. We had decided to go together to Cairo and the Suez Canal in order to assess arrangements there. It was pleasant to travel with Colonel Hogan, a man with a deep knowledge of history and an exceptional command of the English language.

Early in the morning of 4 October we departed from the UNTSO Villa in Heliopolis. As our expert guide we had the Egyptian Chief Liaison Officer, Brigadier Adlai Sherif, always a very amiable but at times an absent-minded gentleman. We drove along the so-called agricultural road towards Ismailia, a route that runs alongside the irrigation canal which carries water from the Nile to the Suez Canal zone. It was getting hot, as October in Egypt is still a month of great heat. The scenery was beautiful and there were many people both on the road and in the fields. The sweetwater canal was bordered by narrow cultivated strips of land, whose greenery was accentuated by the barren desert surrounding them. The grass looked emerald-green against the darker background of the mango trees. On both sides of the road huge eucalyptus trees gave some shadow. The people working in the fields looked as smiling and content as always.

We saw no more soldiers along the road than usual; the military traffic from Cairo to Ismailia passed along what was known as the desert road, where we as officers of UNTSO were not allowed to travel, although once Adlai Sherif, as a sign of special courtesy, had taken me along this road to Cairo. On a normal day the road was empty and there was nothing to be seen but a vast sandy desert on both sides of the road.

On our way I showed Hogan the excercise areas where the Egyptians had spent the last months and years training their soldiers for the conquest of a fortified position and the crossing of the sweetwater canal by different means.

Soon we arrived at the Ismailia Control Centre, whose Officer-in-Charge, the French Major L. Woloch, was already awaiting us at the gate. Woloch was of Ukrainian origin and spoke fluent Polish as well. He had real war experience, gained in Algeria, which most UNTSO officers lacked. In Algeria he had also learned Arabic quite well, another rare skill in UNTSO. I held Woloch in high esteem both as an officer and as a person. We agreed on most matters too. The only matter on which we held different views was the question of when war might break out. Woloch was absolutely sure that there would be a war in the next few days; I for my part did not believe this. Little did I guess on that beautiful sunny morning in Ismailia how soon it would become clear which of us was right.

We continued to drive northwards along the canal road from Ismailia. Our intention was to spend the day travelling to Port Said and to inspect the northern observation posts between Ismailia and Port Said. Military activity in the Canal zone had become much busier since my last visit. There seemed to be a great many soldiers about; in fact they were swarming all over. The fortifications in the area had begun to look as if they were complete. I had concluded that they were a response to the construction of the Bar Lev Line which the Israelis had been working on for years. They also demonstrated the energy and ability of the new Chief of Staff of the Egyptian Army, Lieutenant-General Sa'ad Shazli.

I had met Shazli several times. He gave the impression of being an able and modern leader of international standing. Many Egyptian officers had also expressed respectful and admiring opinions about him. None the less, our Liaison Officer Adlai Sherif described his task as almost impossible. According to him the Egyptian Army had almost no traditions of its own; some were adopted from the British, but most from the Turkish Army. Therefore, Shazli had been obliged to start from quite elementary matters; for example, how an officer should behave in the office of the Chief of Staff: he should not begin by asking about the health of the General and then that of his family, instead he should go straight to his subject, present it briefly and then get out. The stories which Sherif told us in the car may or may not be true, but the fact was that Shazli had been able to create in the Egyptian Army unprecedented enthusiasm, energy and initiative during a very short period of time.

As we continued our trip we saw something else in the Canal zone. Numerous new roads had been built close to the bank. Artillery pieces had been transferred forwards. Tanks and anti-tank guns had been dug in in sheltered positions. Everywhere we could see the preparatory signs of a large-scale offensive, signs which are probably mentioned in the field manuals of all armies. Would Major Woloch be right? Did the Egyptians really intend to attack?

We spent the night in the Ismailia Control Centre. At the dinner table the conversation centred on these latest developments. We spoke with Major Woloch and his staff until late in the night. The atmosphere was clearly tense.

Our intention was to continue our trip on the following morning and to study the southern observation posts. In the morning, however, we learned from the Egyptians that the inspection tour had to be cancelled, for there had been an accident during the night which had cut the road. This information sounded strange to us. There was, however, no other choice but to cut short our trip, return to Cairo and wait for a better day.

Many people have wondered afterwards how I could have been so badly mistaken about the intentions of the Egyptians and to have worn such rose-tinted spectacles that I failed to see the clear signs of the preparations for war. It was not a question, however, of whether or not I had seen these signs; they were so clear that one could not avoid seeing and hearing them. It was a question of interpreting the signs.

Since 1971 President Sadat, in many of his speeches, had publicly announced that Egypt would attack in the very near future and had declared in a threatening voice that it was now "the year of decisions". Nobody took him seriously, however. So I said after the war that it was more or less the same if a statesman speaks the truth ten times: if people do not want to believe him, repeating the truth will not help.

Towards the end of March 1973, President Sadat gave an interview to Arnaud de Borchgrave, the editor of *Newsweek*, in which he repeated that negotiations had now finally failed and that war was necessary. After discussions with the world's great powers, he believed there was only one conclusion:

"If we don't take our case in our own hands, there will be no movement . . . There is no sense turning the clock back. Everything I've done leads to pressures for more concessions. I was even told by Rogers that my initiative for a final peace agreement with Israel was very courageous and had transformed the situation. Every door I have opened, has been slammed in my face – with American blessings."

"I can conclude, from what you say," said de Borchgrave, "that you believe a resumption of the hostilities is the only way out?"

"You are quite right. Everything in this country is now being mobilized in earnest for the resumption of the battle – which is now inevitable."

I was not the only one who doubted the military capabilities of the Arabs. Many prominent military experts were unanimous before 1973 that Egypt and Syria lacked the ability to reconquer the occupied territories by armed force. Therefore there would be no war. The same thing was said in a different way by concluding that the Arab armies were bound to lose and therefore they would not attack. Afterwards many people said that the premises were right but the conclusions were wrong. But apparently even the premises were not quite right. Perhaps we had all exaggerated the military weakness of the Arab armies and forgotten that success in war depends on other factors too: motivation, determination and offensive spirit. We had not understood the Arabs' war objectives. Only later did it become clear to us that the restoration of the honour lost in the 1967 war was the most important matter to the Arabs – more important even than the reconquest of territory.

11. War begins; departure from Cairo

On 6 October 1973, at about 1400 hours, Colonel Hogan and I were just finishing our lunch in the dining-room of the Sheraton Hotel in Cairo. After lunch we went together to the hotel's tax-free shop, for I wanted to buy a new suitcase which I had seen on sale there. From the rear of the shop came the shouting voices of an Arab news broadcast. Suddenly all business stopped and I heard in Arabic the words: "*Harb, harb!*" ("War, war!"). The manager of the shop began to explain excitedly that according to the news the war had broken out. Israeli naval units, supported by the air force, had attacked Egyptian positions in the Bay of Suez. The Egyptians for their part had retaliated for this "provocation".

The news sounded unbelievable. It was in any case Sabbath and Yom Kippur, the holiest religious holiday of the Israelis, when the streets of Israel were empty, nobody took their cars out and people stayed either in the synagogues or at home, praying and meditating. Even in the Israeli Defence Forces, all action stopped except for the most essential services.

As the matter did not seem to become any clearer, Hogan and I decided to go to the office of UNTSO in Heliopolis, where there was at least a communications link with Jerusalem and the Canal. Perhaps we would be able to obtain more information there.

On the first day of the war additional information was just not available. No-one answered the telephone in the Egyptian Liaison Office. Nothing was heard from the Canal zone and we no longer had radio contact with our observers there. Later it became clear that at the start of the offensive the Egyptian liaison officers had used forceful means to interrupt the functioning of the observation posts and of Ismailia Control Centre. UNTSO Headquarters in Jerusalem at this stage had no more information than anyone else.

From the BBC English language news, which earlier had been our only reliable source of information, we learned in the first hours only that a major joint attack had been launched by the Egyptian and Syrian armies on 6 October 1973 at 1400 hours. On the following day, which was a Sunday, the BBC told us that the Egyptians had reached a continuous line on the east bank of the Suez Canal at a distance of about 10 km. from the Canal.

The Syrians had also achieved excellent initial success. The strategically important positions on Mount Hermon had been conquered and the main attack proceeded north and south of Quneitra.

The next day the first military observers who had been serving on the east bank of the Canal started to arrive at the UNTSO Villa. Many of them had undergone hardship; they had been taken for Israeli officers and treated accordingly.

I wrote to my wife on 14 October:

The Egyptian attacking forces apparently did not even know what the UN was. In most cases it was a great miracle that our men, in general, survived. [At Observation Post Copper the French and Italian officers were missing.] The boys were glad when in the early days of the week they reached Cairo. They had been kicked and beaten, but were very much alive in any case.

It was fortunate that I was by chance in Cairo when the war started, because the military authorities of victorious Egypt became arrogant and difficult towards the UN. "You are not needed here any more. Your officers are at present observing the backs of our valiant soldiers as they liberate their fatherland from the yoke of the enemy," Adlai Sherif remarked to me. In Cairo I could solve many difficult problems on the spot. I could personally keep in contact with the Egyptian military authorities and defend the interests of UNTSO and the observers. From Jerusalem this would have been almost impossible, because radio contact with Cairo was very poor, due to atmospheric disturbances. Often we had to wait hours before a message was received in New York and an answer had arrived.

The letter to my wife on 14 October 1973 continues:

The Egyptians in their euphoria were rather swinish to us. Everything was naturally accompanied by Sherif's hypocritical smile and assurances of friendship. [Colonel] Hogan and [Major] Windsor, who are less experienced at this, were at first surprised and then furious. The only way of demonstrating our feelings a little was that not one of us went to a dinner arranged by Sherif and Colonel Helmy. I said only that we were not in festive mood, because a Norwegian colleague and his family had died in the bombardment [in Damascus] and the two officers from Observation Post Copper had probably met the same fate.

Our first difficulty arose from the evacuation of the observation posts. The Egyptians demanded, in much the same way as they had of UNEF in 1967, that they must be emptied immediately. In order to gain time I requested that they should contact the Secretary-General directly in this matter, because it was he who in July 1967 had received from the Security Council the task of deploying observers on the Canal. I also wanted the evacuation to take place in an orderly fashion and the valuable property of the UN to be secured. Nothing helped, however, but Colonel Helmy sent the military police to remove the observers by threatening them with arms. The same applied to the building of the Ismailia Control Centre too. I did, however, get agreement from Sherif that a small group could stay in Ismailia in order to prepare for the evacuation and that Major Woloch [who at the beginning of the war was in Cairo] could drive a truck over there to collect the equipment. Woloch told me that, when they then left Ismailia, bringing with them the most valuable property, the most difficult to replace, the trucks of the raiders were already ready to start the plundering.

The last difficulty with the Egyptians was their demand on Tuesday 9 October that the military observers in Cairo should leave with their families immediately. I protested strongly, saying that the war was still going on, the Security Council was in session at present and therefore it was not yet time to make such decisions. I also pointed to the fact that UNTSO may still be needed in Egyptian territory in one way or another. Therefore it would be better that the observers remain in Cairo. I was pleased to hear on Thursday [11 October] that my point had prevailed, at least until further notice.

The second day of the war was coming to an end. It had been hard. I had been particularly worried about the fate of UNTSO, the observers and their families. I had moved away from the Sheraton, as the trip to the hotel was too long and difficult, and Captain Kaarlo Iivanainen had invited me to come and live in his house. It was a great relief to be a guest of him and his family. It was also pleasant to relax in the evening in the sauna on the roof of the UNTSO Villa. I was later told that once in the hot room of the sauna I had said, "It seems that these Egyptians are chasing us away from here now. But you can bet that in two weeks' time they will be on their knees praying us to come back."

When UNTSO's affairs in Cairo were in some kind of order, I had to find out what was happening in Jerusalem, Damascus and Beirut. Getting out from Cairo in the midst of a raging war was not easy, however. At first it looked quite impossible, because Cairo Airport was closed even to UN planes. Although UNTSO's Falcon jet was as fast as a Mirage fighter and needed only ten minutes to leave Cairo air space, the missile umbrella covering the airfield apparently could not be removed. According to the Egyptians, ten minutes without missile cover was too long a period for the city's safety. The port of Alexandria was also closed. At one stage I planned to drive the 1,400 km. to Benghazi in Libya and from there to take a commercial flight to Beirut or Nicosia. Then the UNTSO Falcon would take me on to Jerusalem. It would have been a real adventure, perhaps involving being stranded at the Libyan border because of passport and visa problems.

Fortunately the Egyptian authorities suddenly changed their minds. Fourteen military observers who had served on the Israeli side of the Canal had to be moved out of Cairo at all costs. I believe that behind this was the fear of spies, which because of the war had become hysterical. In fact our liaison officers were themselves in the service of counter-intelligence. When it was a question of such an important matter, it appeared that Cairo Airport was available after all. Thus two Falcon flights could be arranged, the first on Wednesday and the second on Thursday. I decided to go by the later flight, because New York wanted me to resolve the problem of the observers remaining in Cairo.

On the afternoon of 11 October we were sitting in the transit hall of Cairo Airport waiting for departure. The large building was entirely deserted, apart from a few soldiers here and there. The restaurants and tax-free shops had been evacuated. We were told that the Italian-made landing system had also been placed under shelter. A pair of Russian transport planes was unloading. About 4 o'clock we were sitting on board the Falcon, piloted by Captain Jetzer, and we landed without mishap at Tel Aviv Airport. Dennis Holland and Tatsuro Kunugi came to meet us.

Rémy Gorgé, who had interrupted his home leave and had fortunately arrived on Sunday, four days earlier, was awaiting us in good humour at Government House. Together with the Chief Operations Officer, the American Lieutenant-Colonel Nicholas Krawciv, he briefed me about the situation. I was particularly interested in the events on the Golan, of which it had been difficult to get a clear picture

on the basis of radio news. It appeared that the control centres in
Tiberias and Damascus were still operating despite the raging battles.
The only places that had been forced to close were the out-station in
Quneitra and the observation posts on the main road from Quneitra
to Damascus.

On 14 October I made a return journey to Tiberias, where I gave
a briefing to all personnel, who were both brave and enthusiastic. There
I learned that in Damascus the mood was low and the leadership had
not been able to maintain morale. I should get there as soon as possible,
before anything irrevocable occurred. Together with Paddy Hogan
and Dennis Holland, I then travelled by car to Damascus via Beirut.
Damascus was strangely peaceful; there was very little traffic and the
Syrians we met, like our Liaison Officer, Colonel Adnan Tayara, were
proud of their success in the war.

In the MAC House, as the Control Centre was still called, the
mood was sombre and both soldiers and civilians were pessimistic. I
could understand this, because Damascus had been bombed, the families
evacuated and a Norwegian officer and his family killed. In addition
the Officer-in-Charge, the Swedish Lieutenant-Colonel Sven Svensson,
had been on leave when the war started and had only just returned.
His people had been adrift in his absence. I spoke to the staff, a mixture
of encouragement and admonishment. I also spoke over the radio with
all the officers at the observation posts. Their morale was high and
their enthusiasm great, despite the danger of being killed and the lack
of food and drink. Once again it became clear that it is easier for a
human being to endure deadly peril than inactivity and monotony. My
trip had been useful. Perhaps it had gone some way towards improving
morale and refreshing the mood. I left Colonel Hogan in Damascus
for a few days to support the leadership there.

After a heavy day we spent the night in the Semiramis Hotel in
the centre of the city; quite a bad hotel, but a tired man slept well
there.

In the afternoon of 18 October we travelled from Damascus to
Beirut. The city was peaceful, as if no war were going on around it.
Twice I negotiated with the Commissioner General of UNRWA,
Sir John Rennie, who was responsible for the security of UN personnel
in Beirut. I also gave a briefing to the UNTSO people in ILMAC.
There I received an urgent message: the Egyptians were demanding
that the UN radio station in the UNTSO Villa be closed immediately.
I gave the order to reply to them that the radio station in Cairo was

a part of the worldwide communications network of the United Nations and could only be closed by the order of the Secretary-General. I was very angry at the behaviour of the Egyptians. I did not think we had deserved it.

In the evening I wrote to my wife:

The families from Damascus are here. Anne Lindgren flies with her sons to Finland on Friday. The brave Heljä Pantzar said on the phone that she is not going anywhere as long as Hasse is here. Hasse continues at the observation post for the third week now. We have not been able to rotate this OP yet; food and water have been sent there, however.

ILMAC will soon be the only part of UNTSO left to be handed over to a successor. Naturally it is too early to speculate about the possible future tasks of UNTSO, but it has always managed to get back on its feet before. Strange that Syria and Israel have let the observation posts continue to operate?

The experiences of the early days of the war in Cairo and the heavy round trip to Beirut and Damascus were taxing. The flu had already started on the way to Damascus; my eyes and nose were running. It did not get better during the trip, of course, and on 19 October, having returned to Jerusalem, I went to bed at noon in my own home. Our Austrian Medical Assistant, "Doctor" Leubnegger, prescribed his usual medicines – Penbritin, a multi-vitamin and a hot drink – and asked me to remain in bed. In the evening the fever had already gone and I started to feel better.

I wrote home on 21 October:

Leubnegger's effective medication and two days in bed have done wonders. Today I feel healthy and have been up a little. Despite the fact that it is Sunday there have been visitors: before noon M. Henry [the French Consul General] and in the afternoon Jongejans [the Dutch Ambassador].

Yesterday's happy news was the evacuation of OP Winter, whose people finally got back to Tiberias. Harri Pantzar and the Dane Hansen had been at the observation post since 4 October. During the last days there was no food or water, only a few biscuits and two cups of water per man per day. Nick Krawciv went to meet the boys and said that they were as thin as the victims of Buchenwald;

their wrists had got too thin to wear watches, which slipped over their hands. Otherwise they were in a brave mood and to start with we've put them into the good care of the Finns and Danes in Tiberias. Today Harri is already in Beirut with Heljä and the children.

Something about the military situation: in the Syrian area it has remained the same for a week now. Having fended off the ferocious and, for Israel, dangerous Syrian attack (which reached up the Quneitra-Rosh Pinna road to the Yarmouk River close to the famous Benot Jakov Bridge), the Israelis pushed along the Quneitra-Damascus road about 20 km. west of the village of Sasa and they now have in their possession an area, 20 km. wide and 20 km. deep, east of the former cease-fire line in the direction of the road leading to Damascus. For the rest of the way the front follows the former cease-fire line. We have four observation posts in operation on both sides, also the Quneitra out-station. One could say that the situation there has stabilized and apparently Israel has transferred the main part of its forces from the Syrian front to Sinai.

About the situation in Sinai I don't know more than what the papers and the radio are saying. Israel has a bridgehead on the west bank of the Canal south of Ismailia and obviously has the initiative. However, the operation has been very slow and the destruction of the Egyptian Army is not going to be an easy task, as it has dug in to static defensive positions on the east bank of the Canal.

It is difficult to say anything about the future. I would hope that after this war, more reason will prevail. Whichever way the war ends, this has been a bitter lesson for Israel and evidence that the policy of the last six years has been wrong; it also shows the underestimation of Arab military power, of which many others (including me) have been guilty. Something other than a solution based solely on military might should now be found, because in the next war things would really go badly for Israel.

The fate of UNTSO is also shrouded in darkness. One can believe that in Syria our operation can continue more or less as before, similarly of course in Lebanon, where nothing has changed. Sinai is a question mark. Perhaps the Egyptians don't want us any more. If the Russian idea of joint United States and Russian troops is not accepted, perhaps Israel will have observers on that line of theirs, when the fighting finishes in due course.

A propos, we are very popular in Israel at present. People are waving from their cars etc. But popularity shifts easily, as always. By the way, New York has been very happy with us.

I cooked a casserole of salted Baltic herring and have been eating it yesterday and today. I stopped in Herzliya on my way back from Damascus and got salted Baltic herrings from Helga.

12. Summary of the October War

As I lay in the grip of the flu in Government House on about 20 October, I tried to keep myself informed about what was happening. On the basis of press and radio information, a view, still somewhat dim at this stage, was being formed that the war had already reached its peak and that the representatives of the great powers were feverishly looking for ways to prevent a conflagration and find an "honourable" end to the war. I did not guess, however, that the fighting would end in a few days.

After the first hours of the war UNTSO had practically no sources of information of its own to enable it to follow events. The observation posts on the Canal had been overrun by the attacker and subsequently withdrawn. The same had happened in the area of the main attack on the Golan, while the posts still operating on the flanks could not get any idea of the different phases of the war.

But an overall picture, based on different sources, was forming all the time and much that was uncertain was clarified after the war at least. It was obviously necessary for us in UNTSO to have a clear idea of the course of the war, the shifting balance of victories and defeats, the alternation between euphoria and depression. Otherwise it would have been difficult or even impossible to understand the entire postwar situation, the attitudes of the parties and the demands which they presented in the later negotiations.

I drew up the following outline of the events of war on the Golan and in Sinai:

After careful political and military preparations Egypt and Syria had decided to start their attack simultaneously and thus force Israel into a battle on two fronts. Clear signs of the preparations for a large-scale offensive had been observed in both countries, but they had been interpreted wrongly. It was true that, as far as Syria had been concerned, there had, as always, been reason to worry a bit. In keeping with tradition, the Israeli Defence Minister, Moshe Dayan, had visited the Golan Heights and inspected the troops there on the eve of the Jewish New Year on 26 September. As a consequence of his visit Dayan had transferred back to Golan the famous 7th Armoured Brigade, which had been in the reserve. This was the most significant preparatory measure on the Israeli side before the outbreak of war.

THE SYRIAN OFFENSIVE
6 OCT. 1973

Area occupied by Syria

UNTSO Cease Fire Line   20 km.

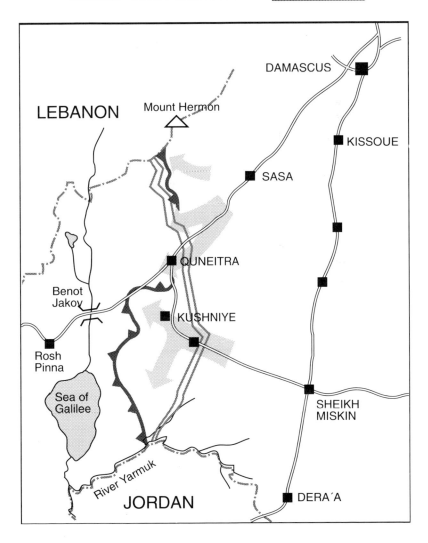

The parties had succeeded in keeping the timing of the attack secret. When the Syrian Mig 17 fighters swept past the front lines and started the attacks a few minutes before 1400 hours on 6 October 1973, the surprise was as great in the Israeli bunkers along the cease-fire line as it was among the civilian population in the new fortified settlements of the Golan and in the Druse villages of the area. The military observers of UNTSO could hardly believe their eyes when the armoured columns, their hatches open as if this was a peacetime parade, rolled towards Quneitra and Rafid. There may have been 700 tanks in the first wave. Many observers had never in their life seen such a number of tanks. The Finnish Captain Harri Pantzar, whose observation post was south-west of Quneitra on the Syrian side of the cease-fire line, reported:

The sixth of October began like any other day, there was nothing to report. The flocks of sheep and shepherds were missing; somewhere an obstacle had been put in the way of their grazing. I am quite convinced that our Liaison Officer had no knowledge of a war breaking out . . .

Normal routine work stopped at 1357 hours, when the Syrians started firing at a strong Israeli position near Quneitra directly in front of us. They began with an air attack. We counted eight Migs at the height. At this stage the most amazing thing for us was that we did not observe any counter-actions from the Israeli side.

We were not able to follow the events above ground for long. A Syrian major, apparently the Commander of a tank battalion, rushed into the observation post and headed straight for our telescope. We made him understand that he was in completely the wrong place, but when he was going out he made it clear that he did not want to see us on observation duty. We believed that he was serious when our main antenna was shot down by a hit from a tank cannon.

We spent our time in the shelter and found out, based on monitoring the sounds, that on both sides of the observation post tanks were pushing west. In the darkening evening we went out and observed that quite near our quarters, between us and the Syrian stronghold, red lights had been installed to guide those who were coming up from the rear. Just this easiest route through the rocky terrain had been reconnoitred by two officers the day before. We marked that the forward movement continued and that a

122 mm. battery had been deployed near us, less than 100 m. to our north.

During the night we did not get a clear picture of how the attack had proceeded, but when some supplies were carried forward past us we assumed that some kind of success had been achieved. In the morning of 7 October we saw a lot of destroyed Syrian equipment in the terrain ahead of us . . .

On the third day of the war the Syrians pushed still more troops and equipment forwards as soon as darkness fell.

Another military observer, Captain Heikki Tilander, gives his story:

The sixth of October 1973 on the Golan Heights was sunny and hot. I was doing the last turn of service of my one-year stint with the UN, which took place on Observation Post Zodiac on the foothills of Mount Hermon. My observer colleague was the experienced UN veteran, Major P-G. Björlin, and as Liaison Officer we had a young Syrian, Second Lieutenant Yashin. Zodiac was at an elevation of 1,300 m. and from there one could see for kilometres.

It was the penultimate day of my turn of service.

After lunch we usually sat outside in the sunshine, wearing only shorts, reading, discussing and at the same time observing. The sixth of October was no exception. Yashin had, against regulations, carried the stretcher out of the shelter and fallen asleep on it. It was quiet on the cease-fire line.

At 1358 hours the quiet suddenly came to an end. From the radio speakers we heard the warning of alarm, "Air attack!" from Observation Post Winter to our south. We rushed to the observation platform. We saw explosions on both sides of the cease-fire line. At the same time four fighter-bombers swept low over us. At first I thought them to be Israeli – I had never seen the Syrians fly in that manner. When, however, the fighters fired rockets at the Israeli positions in front of us, we realized to our surprise that the planes were Syrian. At the same moment the Syrian anti-tank cannons near us started firing past us. The Israelis retaliated immediately with tank fire. In less than 60 seconds the entire 70-km.-long cease-fire line was a sea of fire. Our observation post also came under fire and we had to take cover. The fire of the Syrian artillery and rocket-launchers seemed superior.

The first Israeli planes appeared in the area within 2–3 minutes. Four Skyhawk fighters came in low in the direction of the lower part of the mountain. Before the planes had time even to operate, Syrian rockets brought two of them to the ground right before our eyes.

After about ten minutes Syrian tanks crossed the cease-fire line. On the road running south of the observation post a unit attacked, comprising ten T 55 tanks, thirteen BTR 152 armoured vehicles and a great number of logistics vehicles. The unit proceeded by short stages towards an Israeli stronghold, from where Centurion tanks, surprisingly, opened fire. In a few moments four of the first Syrian tanks were set ablaze by a direct hit, and the advancement of the unit stopped for a long time.

Further to the south, in the area of Quneitra, we saw amidst smoke, dust and explosions a huge Syrian tank formation, whose number of tanks it was impossible to count. It moved westwards and seemed to push without opposition towards the heartland of Israel.

When we were listening to the BBC radio news at 1500 hours, we heard that "large-scale hostilities had broken out in the Middle East". It was reported that all details were uncertain and that "impartial information was available only from the UN Military Observers in the area". At that moment I felt that we were carrying out a historic task.

During the first night the battles in our area continued to 3 o'clock and started again at five. We hardly slept.

The northern Syrian spearhead, consisting of about 300 tanks, proceeded from Damascus along the main road to Israel towards Quneitra, while the southern, a tank division of about 400 tanks, came from Sheikh Miskin towards Rafid. Altogether, about 7,000 infantry men, with their armoured personnel carriers, took part in the operation. The first aim of the offensive was apparently to divide the Golan area into two parts and to cross the Yarmuk River using the Benot Jakov Bridge.

The Israeli defence system – two tank brigades, with about 175 tanks – was rather inferior in numbers. The armed and fortified agricultural settlements which had been set up on the Golan rapidly collapsed. Similarly, the southern tank brigade was in distress and splintered badly. The northern, or the 7th Tank Brigade, which was in a better position opposite Quneitra, held up better. Particularly worrying from the point of view of the Israelis was that Syrian commandos and helicopters captured their observation post on the Mount Hermon ridge. This deprived Israeli troops of their gunnery spotting ability and at the same time enabled the Syrians to range their artillery on the Israeli positions.

For me it has remained a mystery why the Syrians, despite their initial success, halted their offensive. If they had continued at this rapid pace of advancement, the southern group would have surely reached the Lake of Tiberias and the Valley of the Jordan. Perhaps the reasons were logistical: shortage of fuel or ammunition, for instance. Perhaps the Syrian commanders imagined that they could continue the attack on the following morning after redeployment and distribution of supplies. Perhaps they had no contingency plans in the event of an unexpected success. Whatever the reason, the standstill was fatal. It gave the Israeli reserves enough time to arrive at the spot and start their counter-attack.

The basalt plateau of the Golan was littered with volcanic rocks of different sizes and it was therefore difficult to move in such terrain, but the difficulties applied to both the attackers and the defenders. Both parties sustained heavy casualties; the Israelis had never experienced something like that before. As an example, on the first day of the war Israel lost 30 Skyhawks and 10 Phantoms to the Syrians' new SA-6 and SA-7 anti-aircraft rockets and ZSU 23 batteries of anti-aircraft artillery.

But five days later the same UNTSO military observers who had seen from their observation posts the gallant departure of the Syrian armoured forces, now witnessed the miserable return of their remnants. In ferocious, almost desperate but always unrelenting battles which lasted five days, the Israelis had decisively defeated the attackers and thrust recklessly at the gates of Damascus.

Captain Harri Pantzar's story from OP Winter continues:

> Israel's counter-measures began actually to be visible. The withdrawal of the Syrians, at least for the part we saw, was miserable to watch. Troops without leaders; if there were leaders in their midst, one could not see any sign of leadership. We also saw with our own eyes how indifferently a Syrian soldier treats his wounded comrade.
>
> Although we were in a central area, we were not overrun by the actual battles. The Israeli counter-attack swept past us at a safe distance. No Israeli artillery or any other heavier weapon was

THE ISRAELI COUNTER OFFENSIVE 11 OCT. 1973

Israeli Forward Line
Syria Forward Line
UNTSO Cease Fire Line

20 km.

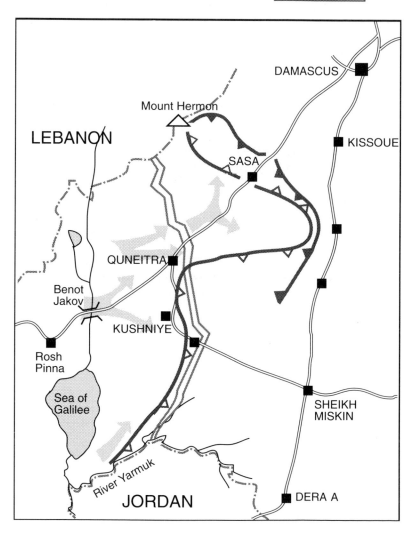

directed against our post at any stage. For a few days, a Syrian anti-aircraft battery was deployed round us, next to the wall of the observation post. These anti-aircraft men caused harm only to us, because they left their weapons and rushed into our shelter as soon as the sound of aircraft could be heard. It was very impressive to watch the performance of the Israeli Air Force. If they had difficulties with the Syrian rockets in the initial phase, they were later fully superior, particularly in the case of an air battle.

In some ways the Syrian Army created the impression that it was lacking front-line commanders. One had the feeling that the battle round Quneitra was led from somewhere in the rear. The Syrian soldier knew little about his task and even any slight interest died in the phase when casualties started to occur.

If one of the reasons for the defeat was inadequate planning and lack of professionalism, surely another was the ignorance of the troops and junior commanders about the general situation, their objectives, supporting weapons, etc. It was difficult to understand the senseless squandering of artillery ammunition and rocket-launchers in an area empty of enemies, an air attack against our own positions and the movement of vehicles to the area of operations in daylight. And so forth. When the Sasa salient had been formed we had nothing to do but await evacuation. We had almost nothing to report and life became tedious.

Captain Heikki Tilander from Observation Post Zodiac in the foot-hills of Mount Hermon continues his tale:

Israel's counter-attack and breakthrough in the Golan took place on Thursday 11 October. It had been decided to carry out the attack in the northernmost part of the Golan because the left flank of the attacking forces would lean on Mount Hermon.

We woke up to intense Israeli air activity which started at seven and continued all morning. The Skyhawk planes attacked in pairs, one pair after another. They strafed the Syrian positions and moving troops with rockets, napalm bombs and guns. The planes flew very low in the valleys between the mountains. Sometimes they flew around Mount Hermon and hit their targets from behind. Relentless air attacks crushed the Syrian resistance piece by piece.

At 11 o'clock we saw the first Israeli tanks. Two long columns of Centurion tanks advanced from the west towards the former

cease-fire line. After the war I read that this was the 7th Tank
Bridgade, one of Israel's élite units.

The tanks wound along curved roads up the mountain slope to
the plateau beneath us, spread out into a line and continued their
advance at distances of 20 metres, firing time after time as they
moved. The Israeli fighters formed a ceiling of thunder above the
tanks. Syrian resistance was paralysed. They tried to fire their
artillery in the area of the attacking tanks, but the scattered fire did
not even force the Israeli tank commanders to take cover.

The first tanks crossed the Israeli cease-fire line at 1220 hours
and after three hours the attack had already advanced 4–5 km. We
counted 10 Israeli tanks taking part in the attack. When darkness
descended over the Golan, 20 armoured vehicles were still burning
in the foremost areas.

In the evening the BBC news told us that Israel had broken
through the Syrian lines and was advancing towards Damascus.

During the October War we spent twelve long days and nights
in a small bunker, with not even a door, when two modern armies
were fighting around us. We were often frightened and in the
final stages, when food ran out, we were hungry all the time.
However, throughout all this we were able to work and to report
our observations.

The outbreak of hostilities took even us by surprise. On the
morning of the Day of Atonement I did wonder about two things.
Why were the Moroccan soldiers near us wearing helmets? Why
did an Israeli fighter carry out a patrol flight over the area at about
10 o'clock on Yom Kippur, when they did not fly even on a regular
Sabbath? We had the answers a few hours later.

The rapid defensive victory on the Golan Heights was decisively
important from the point of view of the final outcome of the war.
It made it possible to divert troops to take counter-measures in Sinai.
It also removed the threat directed at the heartland of Israel. Unlike
the Egyptian front, there is no wide buffer area like Sinai between
Syria and Israel. The entire Golan area is only 30 km. deep and the
distance from Tel Aviv to Damascus is only about 200 km.

In Sinai the surprise was, if possible, still greater. Nobody could
imagine that Egypt would start an attack at all. Nobody believed either
that it would be able to cross the Suez Canal on a broad front and
to break through the Bar Lev Line. The high sand walls and the strong

bunkers looked insuperable. At least, that was the impression the press had given.

The attack began with a strong artillery barrage. In the initial stage two tank divisions and two infantry divisions were involved. The assault was concentrated along three main stretches: below Kantara in the north, round Ismailia in the middle, and south of the Bitter Lakes from Shalufa to El Kubrit.

The sheer physical weight and great superiority of the Egyptian attack broke the resistance and the defenders had to give in. Luckily the Israelis had enough space in Sinai to gain them time. In this regard the situation was different from that in the Golan.

The Finnish military observer, Captain Pekka Viskari, who served at Observation Post Red opposite the city of Suez, gives his initial experiences on the Suez Canal:

> After lunch our Israeli Liaison Officer, Lieutenant Ben-Ami Roth, climbed onto the roof of the shelter to sunbathe and the Swedish Major Ingvar Torefalk and I started to change the oil of the generator down in the pit. After the change of oil there was an explosion which caught us in the act. Twelve Egyptian Mig 21 fighters crossed the Canal in a formation that almost touched our antenna masts and, having passed us, they fired all their weapons somewhere in the direction of the Bar Lev Line. At the same time the artillery began to fire from the other side of the Canal and grenades were also dropping near the observation post.

Manning the Bar Lev Line were reservists of the 116th or the Jerusalem Brigade, which had won its great fame in the storming of Jerusalem in 1967. The brigade had recently taken over from the regular garrison on the Canal. Normally its strength was 800 men, but a few hundred had been given leave for Yom Kippur.

Thus the Egyptians crossed the Canal in strength.

According to their information, as part of the defence apparatus of the Bar Lev Line there was a system of oil-pipes, which, if ignited, could turn the entire Canal into a sea of fire. The Egyptians claimed that their commandos had blocked the oil-pipes with cement and thus sabotaged the whole system. The Israelis for their part asserted that the system could not function because of technical difficulties and that therefore it had been abandoned. The Egyptian soldiers in the first wave were equipped with two new Russian portable anti-tank weapons: the RPG bazooka and the Sagger anti-tank missile. Their

THE EGYPTIAN OFFENSIVE
6–7 OCT. 1973

 Egyptian Forward Line

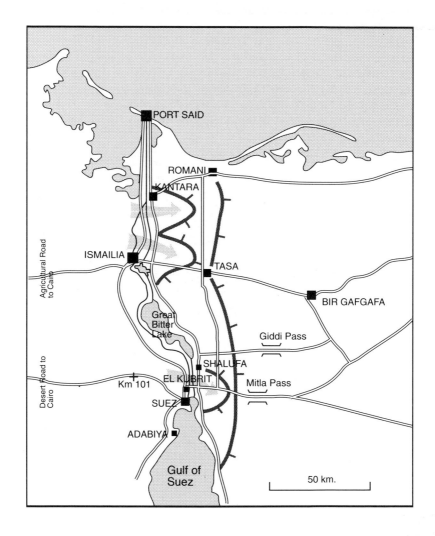

task was to destroy the tanks dug in at the sand wall for protection. The next wave was to concentrate on the destruction of the fortifications of the Bar Lev Line. At the same time, the third wave was to push past them to a line about 10 km. from the Canal. There they were to dig in and remain in place. With their anti-tank weapons and SA-7 anti-aircraft missiles they were to fend off tank and air attacks on their positions and so gain time, at least 12–24 hours, to facilitate the crossing of the tanks and heavy weapons of the main forces.

In order to make holes in the high sand walls, first on their own bank and then on the other side, the Egyptians had developed an ingenious method, a real secret weapon. The holes were opened with high-pressure water-pumps. The jets of water cut through the walls in three to five hours. To have done this with a bulldozer or with explosives would have taken twice as long. Sixty holes were needed, which meant that 90,000 cubic metres of sand had to be removed. To cross the Canal, the Egyptians used for the first time a new Russian pontoon system which enabled their engineers to bridge the Canal in just under half an hour. Altogether, the engineers' achievement on the first day of the assault was immense: in six to eight hours they bored 60 holes in the ramparts, built ten pontoon bridges and put 50 motorized pontoon ferries in operation.

At dawn on Saturday, the Egyptian infantry used their new weapons to fend off counter-attacks from tanks and low-flying fighter-bombers, holding the area they had captured without the support of heavy weapons. The road was clear for the crossing of the Egyptian armoured troops.

Later, however, the Egyptians were surprisingly passive and their efforts did not lead to the capture of the Giddi and Mitla Passes, so important for the defence of Sinai. The battles had been hard and the Israeli resistance persistent. The losses of equipment give some kind of picture of the severity of the battles: for example, the Israeli 14th Brigade lost 150 of its 250 tanks.

At the same time, the Israeli reserves started to arrive in Sinai. On Sunday, before noon, Major-General Arik Sharon had deployed his 20,000-strong force in front of the area of the passes. When this had been done, the immediate danger in Sinai was over.

The successful Israeli counter-attack on the Golan had put the Syrians in distress. They requested an attack from the Egyptians to relieve the pressure. Hesitating and unwilling, General Ismail agreed to the idea and gave an order for an attack to begin on 14 October. The two tank divisions held in reserve crossed the bridges and advanced as the spearhead of the offensive toward the Mitla Pass and Abu Rudeis. The attack failed completely. Outside the range of Egyptian missile cover, the Israeli Air Force made free with the Egyptian attacker, while armoured troops put an end to the attack by using their new American anti-tank missiles. The Egyptians lost 230 tanks.

Now it was time for the Israelis' great counter-attack. Deversoir was chosen as the crossing-point; this is the place where the Canal opens onto the Great Bitter Lake. Intelligence had shown that in this area were deployed the core of the Egyptian 2nd and 3rd Armies, neither of which had taken sufficient care of defence arrangements for the area. According to the Israeli plan, one tank division was to capture a bridgehead on the west bank of the Canal and then to build the necessary bridges. Two other tank divisions were to advance from the bridgehead towards the south and try to cut the rear links of the 3rd Army on the east bank of the Canal.

The massive Israeli offensive did not at first go as planned. The difficulties were caused by local Egyptian counter-attacks, both on the bridgehead and in the area of departure. The Battle of the Chinese Farm (an irrigated area on the East Bank) broke out. The Israelis' objective in this battle was to re-establish a connection with the crossing-point and to get bridge matériel forwards. Early in the morning of 17 October the troops of the following wave succeeded in opening the road to the crossing-point and to build one bridge. Advancement continued to be slow and only late in the evening did the Israeli tank division cross the bridge.

It was only now that the highest Egyptian leadership woke up and realized the great danger caused by the Israelis' penetration on the West Bank. Retaliatory measures started slowly and were insufficient. In spite of this, the first Israeli efforts to enlarge the bridgehead and advance along the sweetwater canal failed. Only in the afternoon of 18 October could the new assault division continue southwards, advancing about 20 km. from the bridgehead and destroying several missile sites. The attack against Ismailia failed on the following day, but the main attack towards Suez and the rear of the 3rd Army continued. When the first UN-declared cease-fire was due to take effect on 22 October, the Israelis were able to cut the other road from Suez to Cairo, while their second attack group reached the Suez Canal at Shalufa.

In the confused situation north of Suez, a real cease-fire could not

THE ISRAELI BRIDGEHEAD
22 OCT. 1973

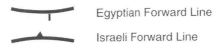

Egyptian Forward Line

Israeli Forward Line

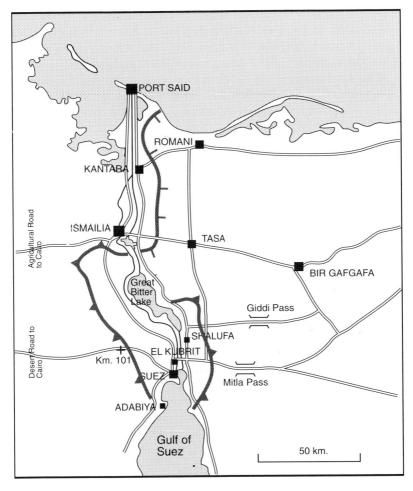

be established, although it was adhered to in other areas quite generally. Taking advantage of the general confusion, and despite the cease-fire accepted by the Israeli government, the high command of the Israeli Army ordered the continuation of the attack to isolate the city of Suez. The attack group reached the coastal area of the Gulf of Suez at the oil refinery south of the city before the evening of 23 October, and in this way severed Suez's connections with Cairo. During the night the second attack group pushed towards the south and before the morning of 24 October reached the Gulf of Suez at Adabiya. This operation isolated the part of the 3rd Army that was in the city of Suez from the main part of the Army east of the Canal.

That same morning the Israelis decided to press on with the capture of the city of Suez. Although their tanks were able to advance to the centre of the city, the resistance was so furious that they were forced to discontinue the attack and withdraw. Almost all of their tanks were destroyed. They were still smoking when the Finnish UN battalion arrived in the area three days later. The isolated Israeli soldiers had only succeeded in getting out of the city of Suez on the evening of the attack, and firing continued until the arrival of the Finns.

At the same time, on the northern front, just before the first cease-fire agreement took effect, the Israelis recaptured their observation post on Mount Hermon.

There has been much discussion about the special factors which affected the course of the war. The most important have been mentioned – the improvement of the professional standard and the fighting morale of the Arab soldiers, the significance of the Israeli fortifications and the defensive tactics of the Egyptians. The observers on both the Suez Canal and the Golan bore witness that there had been a decisive change in the performance of the Arab soldiers. Gone was the primitive, helpless, illiterate soldier weakened by bilharzia and tuberculosis who had been seen in 1956 and 1967. Gone also was the easily panicking coward who was ready to flee at the first approach of the Israelis. The rapid transformation, which was probably chiefly the result of efficient training and the elevation of morale, surprised the Israelis as well as many other observers. Even I had asserted a few years earlier in a conversation with the Soviet Ambassador in Cairo, Sergei Vinogradov, that at least one generation would need to pass before the Egyptian soldiers would be better trained.

The rapid breaching of the Bar Lev Line caused consternation and disappointment among the Israeli public. I think that one of the reasons for the disappointment was the press, who during the years had presented the actually not very dense and thin chain of bunkers as an invincible fortified system. I believe that the Israeli defence leadership had never intended the Line to be such a system, even though much work and money had been expended there over the years. The defence of Israel was still based on the mobile warfare of fast and superior armour, for which the vast Sinai offered excellent possibilities, not on a fortification system similar to the Maginot Line which had caused only trouble in the Second World War. As far as I know the Bar Lev Line was at least initially intended to offer protection to the limited group of soldiers who constituted a kind of early warning system along the Canal. The war of attrition, commenced by the Egyptians at the end of the 1960s, had caused too many casualties and something had to be done to improve security. The Egyptians afterwards exaggerated the significance of the Bar Lev Line into a mighty and complete fortified system, naturally wanting to stress the great difficulty of the Canal crossing and the importance of their own achievement. The Israelis for their part afterwards belittled the Line. In my opinion the dispute about the Bar Lev Line has no essential significance. The achievements of the Egyptians in the initial phase of the war were so superior that they overshadowed everything else.

The fortifications on the Suez Canal and the Golan fulfilled their purpose. They delayed the advancement of the attacking troops, made possible the counter-attacks of local reserves and gave time for the arrival of the mobilized reserves from Israel. Thus the Israeli forces were able to delay the attack at the start and, finally, to stop it.

I have already mentioned the Chief of Staff of the Egyptian Army, Lieutenant-General Sa'ad Shazli, whose dynamic influence was widely felt. Shazli's superior, the Minister of War, General and later Marshal Ali Ahmed Ismail, had perhaps a still greater influence as the creator of the new self-confidence and fighting spirit. I only met him after the war had already started. Ismail was in many respects a contrast to Shazli, being calm, well-meaning and even something of a protecting father-figure. During Nasser's time he had been kept in the shadows, but Sadat elevated him to the War Ministry in 1971. Relations between Sadat and Ismail were close; Ismail understood Sadat's ideas and had gained his complete confidence.

The difference in Ismail and Shazli's characters led inevitably to disagreements. Shazli wanted to continue the advancement definitively, in order to take advantage of the success of the first three days of the offensive. Ismail for his part was of the opinion that the attack should be discontinued at the objective which had been achieved, i.e. on the line about 10 km. from the Canal. The initiative should then be handed over to the Israelis, the Egyptians should wait to see how the enemy would act and adapt their own actions accordingly. Ismail's decision was exceptional and did not follow the usual theories of warfare.

Ismail's behaviour has caused much criticism and some have considered it to be the main reason for the ultimate failure of the Egyptian Army. The Israelis in particular seemed to have difficulties in understanding Ismail's lack of action at the moment of a great success, which was completely different to their own conduct in a similar situation. Others thought that Ismail's decision was correct and almost a stroke of genius; I was myself of exactly this opinion. Ismail knew his instrument, the Egyptian Army, and its limitations. Sending it out of the safe haven of the missile zone deep into the Sinai Desert could have meant a total disaster. It would have been destroyed by the professionally superior Israeli armoured troops. It was thus wiser to give the Egyptian soldiers a defensive task instead of offensive objectives. In 1973 the standard of the Egyptian infantry was, after all, rather weak; it was more suited to defensive operations than to attack.

Ismail and President Sadat knew that Egypt had achieved its political goals on the first day of the war merely by crossing the Suez Canal with strong forces. The legend of Israel's invincibility had been crushed and the shame of the Arabs had been wiped out. Now it was possible to sit down at the negotiating table on an equal basis. This was Sadat's intention.

Nobody but Ismail understood Sadat's objectives so clearly. They were not so much military as political and psychological and so could not be much affected by military adventures in Sinai.

13. The 22 October cease-fire; UNTSO's new role; crisis and compromise

Israel's successful counter-attack had put the Egyptians in a militarily insecure position. At the same time the situation was getting out of hand in other respects too. The war, which until now had remained regional, threatened to pit the great powers directly against each other. The danger of a world war was imminent. The troubled Kissinger tried, on his visit to Moscow on 21 October, to persuade the Soviet leadership of his view that a settlement imposed by the great powers would not improve matters. He said that the United States strongly opposed the idea of military intervention in Sinai, which the Soviets were considering carrying out either alone or in concert with the Americans. He also tried to assure the Soviet Union that a durable peace could be achieved only through direct negotiations between the parties. Peace should be striven for step by step, because there were many obstacles on the road to a comprehensive settlement and the whole matter was too complicated to be solved in one meeting.

Kissinger's Moscow negotiations led to positive results, because on the following day, 22 October, the United Nations Security Council adopted the trend-setting Resolution 338 (see Appendix 2). This called on the parties to cease all firing immediately and to begin negotiations under appropriate auspices with the aim of establishing a just and durable peace in the Middle East.

I too was in favour of direct negotiations and later tried to promote the idea when I had the opportunity. For the time being there was nothing to be done. The recent Resolution of the Security Council did not produce instant results; the battles continued on both fronts.

Appreciating the continuing deterioration of the military situation, President Sadat embarked on a phase of determined diplomatic activity. Firstly, delegates were sent to the most important Arab capitals to explain why an immediate cease-fire was necessary and why he was now obliged to abandon the strong demands which he had till recently presented to Israel.

At the request of Sadat the Security Council convened a new emergency session on Tuesday 23 October and adopted Resolution 339 (Appendix 3), confirming the decision on the cease-fire and urging that the forces of the parties return to the positions they had occupied at the moment the cease-fire became effective. It also requested the Secretary-General to dispatch military observers to the region, to be deployed between the parties.

Now I had to speed up matters. Israel played a key role in this respect. Through the Liaison Officer, I made contact with the military leadership of Israel and asked whether there was any obstacle to sending observers to the front to supervise the cease-fire. Moshe Dayan agreed to my request provided that a real cease-fire came into effect before 0700 hours the following morning. The Israelis would stop firing at that time if the Egyptians would give a similar promise.

Moshe Dayan received me at 7 o'clock on 24 October, when the cease-fire was due to come into effect. He gave me a map which showed the Israeli positions in Gebel Ataqa and Adabiya, among other places. Dayan said he was still awaiting the Egyptian acceptance of the cease-fire. After the meeting I returned immediately to Cairo. An hour later Colonel Hogan telephoned Dayan and told him that he had received the Egyptian answer by telegram. It said: "We agree. We agree. We agree." When Dayan asked whether the Egyptians really had answered three times with the same words, Hogan answered drily, "If you really wish to know, they answered four times."

The new Resolution gave UNTSO a task again and I was naturally very glad of that. We had been impatiently waiting for the time when our assistance would be called for. Also impatient, and worried too, were the expressions of our Egyptian Liaison Officers, Brigadier Sherif and Colonel Helmy, when they appeared in the UNTSO Villa to find out what I intended to do. Gone was the euphoria and pride of the first days of the war. Dirty and unshaven, they were a miserable sight. The prediction I had made in the sauna at the beginning of the war was coming true.

In considering the tasks that were to be given to the observers, I could guess that they would have difficulties in finding out what the real state of play was on 22 October and where the lines of the parties actually were on that particular day. Disputes about that lasted for days.

The fire ceased during the morning of Wednesday, 24 October. Just before that, Syria announced that it too would accept the cease-fire. Although it added in its announcement that it presupposed the Israeli withdrawal from the territories it had occupied in 1967, something new was that Syria was now ready to accept a UN decision which referred to Resolution 242 and direct negotiations with Israel. These had never before been accepted in Damascus. It was a sign to inspire hope.

In accordance with Resolution 339, on the morning of 24 October seven UNTSO patrols departed from Cairo towards the Egyptian front line. Each patrol consisted of two officers of different nationalities and an Egyptian liaison officer. The presence of a liaison officer was traditional, but was now surely very useful, as otherwise the patrols would hardly have come close to their objectives. We decided as well to reactivate Ismailia Control Centre and it reported being operational at 4 o'clock.

I thought that UNTSO had acted fast and efficiently. The Egyptians, however, were not satisfied. With good reason, they were worried about military developments and they had even had time to complain to the Security Council about our supposed slowness. I could understand their nervousness.

Before the evening was over, two patrols had crossed the Canal and settled down on the East Bank in the area of the Egyptian 2nd Army: one east of Port Fuad and another south of Kantara. Two other patrols were lodged on the West Bank near Ismailia, along the road leading to Abu Suweir and Abu Sultan. Three patrols which should have gone to Suez never reached it, for Israel did not want the presence of outsiders at this stage. On their way to Suez the patrols were stopped about 35 km. from their destination and they were able to see and hear that an open war was going on and that the fire had not ceased. According to the UNTSO daily report, "they had to withdraw to the west because of the heavy exchange of fire of tanks and artillery between the Egyptian and Israeli forces".

In Israeli-occupied Sinai, too, UNTSO observers prepared themselves for action. Kantara Control Centre was operational in Rabah and planned to send six patrols. Israel would not allow this, however. We did not yet know that the operation to encircle the Egyptian 3rd Army was still going on. In the middle of our own small worries we did not know either that a major political battle was taking place in New York which would end on 25 October at 21.15 GMT (23.15 Sinai time). As a result there would be a new Resolution which would radically change the role of the United Nations in Sinai.

My preoccupation at the time was with the question of how to make UNTSO more effective. I had at that moment 90 military observers in Sinai: in Ismailia there were six groups divided into seven patrols and in Kantara three groups and six patrols. I reckoned that I needed 40 additional officers and sent a request to New York accordingly.

In the afternoon of 25 October two Kantara patrols, accompanied by Israeli liaison officers, crossed the Canal near Deversoir but could not come close to Suez at all. Artillery fire stopped them in the same area where the patrols from Cairo had been stuck the day before. The other Kantara patrols did not receive permission to proceed from the Israeli Army.

On the Egyptian side the northernmost patrol was stationed 8 km. south-east of Port Said and had nothing to report. The Ismailia patrols were also in place. I had ordered one of the southern patrols to advance via Gebel Ataqa to the coast at Adabiya but this had not yet been successful.

From the point of view of the observers, 26 October was a more fruitful day. North of Kantara the Israelis allowed one patrol to proceed to the front line to observe from the east the bridgehead of the Egyptian 2nd Army. Meanwhile, in the south two patrols had come close to the bridgehead of the 3rd Army.

On the West Bank one of the Ismailia patrols had pushed through to the Canal bank 14 km. north of the Deversoir bridge. This gives an idea of the narrowness of the Israeli bridgehead. In the south, the two patrols had excellent observation posts from the eastern slope of Gebel Ibeiwid.

Despite our efforts, the UNTSO observer operation was improvised and disconnected. It did not cover all of Sinai and the observation reports were inadequate and trivial. UNTSO had not achieved the objectives set in Resolution 339. Better results were needed, but UNTSO was too weak. A more forceful presence was required.

Having received the latest reports on the deteriorating position in the city of Suez and the humiliation caused to the Egyptian 3rd Army by its encirclement, President Sadat once more requested a meeting of the Security Council. He gave instructions to Foreign Minister Zayat in New York to demand the Soviet Union and the United States send troops to Sinai to supervise the cease-fire, which would otherwise be useless. In order to make the cease-fire effective, something more than a few UN observers was needed.

The Security Council meeting began on the evening of Wednesday, 24 October in an atmosphere of irritation. The Soviet Ambassador,

Jacob Malik, let it be understood that the duty of the great powers now, as the sponsors of the two previous Resolutions, was to send troops to supervise their implementation. The United States Representative, John Scali, for his part asserted that any joint military action by the great powers would not further the peace process.

The Finnish Ambassador in Cairo, Pekka Malinen, told me that he had heard from his Soviet colleague that they intended to send to the area troops "which would tear the Israeli and Egyptian forces apart".

As the Security Council continued discussions in this manner till past midnight without reaching an agreement, a crisis was being created in Washington. There were possibly other reasons for this crisis apart from the worry about the fate of the Middle East. The Watergate scandal which had upset American internal policy for some time had now almost reached its peak. A dispute over the manipulation and destruction of the tapes was raging. People began to call ever more loudly for the impeachment of the President. In such circumstances it was naturally difficult to carry out a strong and consistent foreign policy. However, President Nixon, assisted by his Secretary of State Henry Kissinger, aspired to this very thing, hoping that success in the sphere of foreign policy would bring relief to internal problems.

The outline of the crisis was as follows:

Early on the Wednesday morning the Soviet Ambassador to Washington, Anatoly Dobrynin, brought the State Department a message from Brezhnev in which he took a supportive position on Sadat's proposal of joint action by the great powers in Sinai. Kissinger fended off the idea on the same grounds which John Scali had already given in the Security Council.

At about 11 o'clock Dobrynin returned, bringing with him a message whose tone was even angrier. The Soviet Union threatened unilateral action if there was no agreement on co-operation. This message initiated the crisis.

A short telephone conversation between Kissinger and Nixon followed. The President accepted the idea that the Soviet message should be responded to with both political and military means. The National Security Council (NSC) was convened to consider the matter. Satellite intelligence thought it had detected preparations for troop movements. The picture was not clear, however, and later the information proved to be wrong. In any case the Council decided to upgrade the state of preparedness of the United States armed forces. This would be one step higher than the normal readiness and so one step lower than the readiness during the Cuban missile crisis. By about midnight all the services had been alerted worldwide. Among others, Strategic Air Command was alerted and its B-52 bombers were on the airfields ready to take off. The NATO allies were told about the matter in the early hours and Kissinger finalized the answer to Brezhnev's message, warning that the United States would not tolerate unilateral action by the Soviet Union and that an attempt to bring troops to the Middle East would harm the cause of world peace. Finally he proposed co-operation within the framework of the UN. No mention was made of the alert, but it was assumed that the Russians would be aware of it through their own intelligence. It is also possible that Nixon mentioned it to Brezhnev when they spoke that night.

In the television news on Thursday morning (25 October) the alert was the lead story. A soldier from a nuclear base told an interviewer that this was the first time since 1962 that the missile silos had been in such a state of preparedness. To Kissinger's annoyance the news had been leaked. In his press conference at noon, Kissinger explained to the flabbergasted audience how the policy of détente had during one night changed to a nuclear threat. He tried all means, however, to belittle the seriousness of the confrontation.

There was good reason for that, because the real crisis was already over. The meeting of the United Nations Security Council had ended with a compromise. The decisive Resolution 340 (Appendix 4) had been adopted and the decision to set up a new United Nations Emergency Force (UNEF II) had been made. The members of the Security Council, and in fact the entire world, could sigh with relief. The threat to set the world on fire had been successfully avoided.

There was later much discussion about whether the nuclear threat was real, or only a political gamble characteristic of Kissinger. Neither is it possible to determine to what extent the intention was to support President Nixon's shaky position. It is part of the nature of the matter that the great powers accused each other of leading the world to the brink of war. Similarly, they each accused the other of deceit and dishonesty. What was important, however, was that a decision was made to establish UNEF and so to promote peace.

Once again the UN was the last straw which the great powers grasped when no other means would serve. Brian Urquhart comments:

The fact of the matter is that the UN still is the best available last resort when things go wrong. It is the best available safety net when daring high-wire acts of bilateral diplomacy fail to deliver. There is always the Security Council to fall back on or even the General Assembly, if necessary, and this is an immensely valuable resource. The question is whether people will be inclined to ask, as they used to do, for practical UN involvement in peace-keeping operations on the ground.

Part III. Towards Peace

14. Establishment of UNEF II

The meeting of the Security Council

It would have been interesting, even exciting, to be present at the meeting of the Security Council on 25 October at 1515 hours, when the decision on the establishment of UNEF II was made and Resolution 340 (1973) was adopted (see Appendix 4). Two superpowers had reached agreement on the means by which the explosive situation in the Middle East could be defused. But, as often before, the non-aligned members of the Council also played an important role in this agreement. The eight non-aligned members at that time (Guinea, India, Indonesia, Kenya, Panama, Peru, Sudan and Yugoslavia) proposed that an Emergency Force be sent to the area. Member states would provide its troops, but the permanent members of the Security Council would not participate.

The result of the voting was unique. For the first time in the history of UN peace-keeping the establishment of the new Force was supported by an almost unanimous Council. Fourteen members voted for, no-one voted against. China for its own political reasons did not want to participate in the voting.

The Chinese had already, on 23 October, in the discussion leading to Resolution 339, expressed their views on the policy and methods of the two superpowers:

> The Chinese delegation firmly opposes such a malicious practice of using the United Nations Security Council as a tool to be juggled with by the two superpowers at will. In our opinion, this also shows utter disrespect for the other State Members of the Security Council.

The significance of this unanimity was clear from the very beginning. It guaranteed the new Force the political and economic support of the entire world. The Force could not be withdrawn from the area by the unilateral decision of one party, as had happened in the case of UNEF I in the summer of 1967. The miserable fate of our predecessor often came unwillingly to my mind when I planned the setting up and deployment of UNEF II and thought of its future.

During the next months I had personal experience of how the full support of the Security Council gave UNEF II moral strength and authority, which many previous peace-keeping operations had been lacking. I felt that I had the support of the Chinese too, because one day the local representative of the Chinese Government Press Agency came to see me. He began by saying that the non-participation of China in the recent vote was due to its own reasons, on which he did not want to touch. Despite everything, he said, my work was well-known in China and was highly appreciated. He added that the Chinese people followed the achievements of UNEF with interest and that his reports had millions of readers.

I am sure that I was not alone in experiencing this growth of moral power and authority. We all, military and civilians, private soldiers and commanders, had a strong feeling that we were there for the sake of the entire world. We felt that we were privileged because we could serve world peace in a concrete manner.

The Secretary-General was to draft his report within 24 hours and he announced to the meeting of the Security Council that he hoped that it would form the basis for the establishment, task and functioning of the UN Force, so that the Council could accept it.

The mandate

The document dealing with the outline of the functioning of UNEF II, or the report of the Secretary-General, was ready in the afternoon of 26 October, when it was also accepted (see Appendix 5). According to this document, UNEF II was to supervise the observation of the cease-fire and use its best efforts to prevent a recurrence of the fighting. UNEF and UNTSO were to act in close co-operation. Consequently, in the early phase UNTSO was the most important provider of personnel, radio equipment and motor vehicles for the new Force.

The report went on to say that three essential conditions must be met in order for the Force to be effective. Firstly, it must at all times have the full confidence and backing of the Security Council. Secondly, it must operate with the full co-operation of the parties concerned. Thirdly, it must be able to function as an integrated and efficient military unit. These three principles dated back to the outline that

Dag Hammarskjöld had drawn up for UNEF I. The experience of years had shown their value.

Having in mind these past experiences, the Secretary-General suggested as a guideline for command arrangements:

> The Force will be under the command of the United Nations, vested in the Secretary General, under the authority of the Security Council. The command in the field will be exercised by a Force Commander appointed by the Secretary General with the consent of the Security Council. The Commander will be responsible to the Secretary General. It is my intention to keep the Security Council fully informed relating to the functioning of the Force. All matters which may affect the nature or the continued effective functioning of the Force will be referred to the Council for its decision.

The text of that paragraph sounds complicated and obscure. One can read into it the background of the disputes between the great powers which had continued since Hammarskjöld's times, coming to the fore time and again in the committee of 33 states which dealt with peace-keeping. The question chiefly concerned the independent authority of the Secretary-General, which the Soviet Union and France particularly had not wanted to concede to him. The command arrangement of UNEF thus entailed a considerable concession on the part of these two member states; they did not demand, for example, the institution of some kind of a committee to exercise command authority; instead the Force was directly under the command of the Council. This arrangement meant, however, that the Secretary-General must provide full information to the Council and particularly to the representatives of the great powers.

In the field I was never aware of any difficulties in questions relating to command. In my relationship with the Secretary-General, we occupied the clearly defined roles of a superior and a subordinate. In addition, I tried to maintain close contact with the ambassadors of the permanent members of the Security Council and the troop-contributing countries in Cairo, Damascus and Tel Aviv. Continuing confidential relations, particularly with the representatives of the United States and the Soviet Union, were very useful. When I had difficulties with the parties, they were the only ones who could at least partly influence their attitudes.

In his report the Secretary-General appointed me as the interim Commander of the Force. From that decision, one might have assumed that his intention was later to propose some other person for the job. I was told, however, that this was not so; the appointment of an interim commander was only a tactical means to speed up matters. My appointment as permanent Commander took place on 12 November 1973.

In this appointment the UN resorted to an earlier precedent. In 1956 the then Chief of Staff of UNTSO, the Canadian Major-General E.L.M. Burns, became Commander of UNEF I. UNTSO and UNEF worked in close co-operation then, too. In his previous role Burns had been negotiating closely with the parties about breaches of the cease-fire and other problems. He knew the area and its leaders and they knew him. All this was very useful for him in his new job.

Paragraph 4 of the Secretary-General's report included the demand that the Force must enjoy freedom of movement and should operate separately from the parties. This paragraph also dealt with the composition of the Force. In selecting the contingents, adequate geographic representation had to be borne in mind. There were no agreed principles on this question, however, so the final selection of troops came after tough negotiations and included, for instance, the participation of Warsaw Pact Poland side by side with Canada, a member of NATO. In the Secretariat this innovation was greeted with pleasure because it was interpreted as a more positive attitude towards peace-keeping on the part of the Soviet Union. Now we could be sure that the Soviet Union would also participate in paying the expenses of the Force. For myself, the involvement of the Poles was particularly pleasing. During my years as a military attaché in Warsaw, I had learned to appreciate them highly.

Paragraph 4 (d) defined the principles of the use of force and weapons: "The Force shall not use force except in self-defence. Self-defence would include resistance to attempts by forceful means to prevent it from discharging its duties under the mandate of the Security Council." The new definition of the use of force, which was wider and stronger than that given in previous peace-keeping operations, was a good and useful innovation. It would surely increase respect for UNEF, because the parties knew now that it could not be prevented by forceful means from discharging its duties.

Paragraph 4 (e) stressed the impartiality of the Force and the fact that it was not a party to the conflict.

These were the most important political paragraphs of the report. It included in addition a number of practical instructions. In my opinion the directions given to UNEF were clear and formed a solid ground for future operations.

The news reaches UNTSO

It sounds strange in retrospect that no information was leaked to the field about the discussions of the Security Council before the adoption of the Resolution. The highest UN leadership in New York did not dare even to hint about the matter, because premature publicity could have endangered the acceptance of the decision.

Anyway the decision on the setting up of UNEF took us in UNTSO completely by surprise. It reached us late in the evening of 25 October. The appointment as Commander of UNEF meant once again a complete change in my plans for the future. It had in fact been intended that I should return to Finland in the spring of 1974. The surprise was great, too, for the members of the Secretariat serving in UNTSO – Rémy Gorgé, Dennis Holland and others. The general view had been that the Congo and Cyprus operations would have been absolutely the last in the history of peace-keeping. In the Congo the dispute between the Secretary-General and the Soviet Union had led the organization to its most difficult crisis, while problems of financing Cyprus were still a heavy burden. It was even more apparent that the Secretariat had not had a great influence in the political decisions.

There was no time for wondering, however, for I had immediately to start planning the composition and tasks of UNEF for these details to be included in the Secretary-General's report.

My plan was based on the following assumptions:

1. Both sides would agree to stationing part of the UN Force within areas under their control.
2. There would be freedom of movement to cross the military lines and the Suez Canal.
3. UNEF's task would be to enforce the cease-fire by interposing its units between the belligerents, with the aim of achieving initial disengagement.
4. Subject to political developments, in a second phase UNEF's task would be to facilitate the withdrawal in stages of the Israeli forces.

All these assumptions proved later to be correct, except that the freedom of movement did not fully materialize in areas controlled by Israel.

In making my assumptions I wanted particularly to stress the importance of the crossing of the Canal. For years we had suffered because we had been unable to do that. I also wanted thoroughly to change Israel's attitudes toward UN peace-keeping. In order to succeed in its job UNEF needed Israel's full support. Therefore I wanted, for political but also for purely military reasons, to station about half of the Force on the Israeli side and also to support it logistically from there.

On the basis of the assumptions I proposed a Force of about 7,000 men, comprising a headquarters, two brigades and logistics elements. The idea of two brigades was influenced by the problems caused by the Suez Canal and the fact that UNEF would operate in areas controlled by two governments. One brigade with its three battalions would be on the east bank of the Canal and the other brigade with four battalions on the west bank.

I also brought up the idea of two headquarters: the main UNEF HQ in Cairo and a smaller UNEF office, a kind of liaison office, in Jerusalem or Tel Aviv. Naturally I also said that a headquarters company was necessary to take care of the logistics service and communications needs of the headquarters. Finally I proposed that in his report the Secretary-General should demand freedom of movement, including the right to cross military lines, for the troops of UNEF. I hoped, too, that he would stress the importance of communications and the right to send coded messages. In UNTSO the sending of such messages in the internal radio traffic of the mission was prohibited.

In a cable to New York a few days later I developed my plan further, especially the idea of two brigades. I thought that the brigades should be operationally and logistically independent. UNEF Headquarters in Cairo should include the operations, information, logistics and administrative staff. It should also take care of the central workshops and of communications, both internally and to New York. The brigade staff would exercise detailed operational and logistics control of its battalions. Consequently the initiatives I proposed to New York were as follows:

1. Provision of Force HQ including HQ Company;
2. Establishment of West Brigade HQ and the reinforcement of the Austrian, Finnish and Swedish battalions;
3. Provision of a fourth battalion for the West Brigade;
4. Establishment of an East Brigade HQ;
5. Provision of three battalions for East Brigade.

The programme I presented was far too complex and difficult to be implemented. In New York there were simply not enough staff to draw up such a plan and present its detailed requirements to the troop-contributing countries. Political considerations had priority in New York. Practical and military viewpoints were secondary. In New York's opinion, the most important thing now was for even a small group of UN soldiers to be visible in the area of operation and for UN flags to be fluttering. Now was not the time for detailed planning; rather, one should improvise, play by ear and see what time and the changing situation would bring. I definitely did understand the great importance of symbols in the early phase, but not that plans were not necessary.

As an example, nobody there seemed to have time to think about where and how a headquarters company for UNEF would be provided. None of the contributing countries wanted to be saddled with such a problem. For us in UNEF it was, however, one of the most important matters, and it was never properly resolved. Except for the Finns, the battalions had no additional personnel for detachment to Headquarters Company UNEF. When we later heard that the Canadians would provide the main logistics component, I asked them also to arrange a headquarters company for UNEF. But the Canadian authorities asserted that they did not have enough people for that; the provision of the logistics unit was already straining their resources to the utmost. I looked back nostalgically to my times in Cyprus, where at Force Headquarters British soldiers had filled the lower-level staff requirement at HQ Company, while the higher posts had been divided equally between representatives of the contributing countries.

The Brigade Headquarters and their headquarters units had no better luck. A Peruvian and an Indonesian general had been appointed as brigade commanders and in that way the problem of "the equal geographic distribution" had been partly solved, but nothing was known about the rest of the staff. It took months before we could get even one of the brigades operational. We had to abandon our efforts on the second one, because of the lack of people.

This criticism of UN Headquarters in New York is in a certain sense unjustified. I was well aware that the numbers of personnel and the other resources of the Office of the Under Secretaries-General dealing with peace-keeping affairs were very small. In these matters the Secretary-General was advised by two Under Secretaries-General, Roberto Guyer from Argentina and Brian Urquhart from the United

Kingdom. The Director of the Office was F.T. Liu from China. In addition there were three or four senior officials and the Military Liaison Officer, Colonel and later Major-General Lauri Koho from Finland, assisted by one officer. All of them had long experience and thorough knowledge of the political aspects of peace-keeping in particular.

The military expertise was much enhanced by the military background of Brian Urquhart, who, during the Second World War, had served with great success as an officer in the British Army in Europe and North Africa, ending the war with the rank of major. Moreover, thanks to his great gifts, exceptional experience and unwavering judgement, he was the backbone of the entire UN office. His influence reached into other spheres of the UN too, because the Secretary-General took advantage of his advice in other questions. As his style of writing was excellent, he himself wrote all reports or instructions worth mentioning which left the office. Despite his high rank, Roberto Guyer's share in the functioning of the office was minimal. Together with the rest of the staff, he prepared matters and took care of the routine affairs. In any case the small size of the office made thorough preparations and advance planning difficult even in peaceful times. In an emergency situation like the setting up of UNEF it had an impossible task. They had to be content with *ad hoc* improvisation.

When I later wondered why New York had not had any contingency plan for the establishment of a force like UNEF, Urquhart remarked that it was difficult to institutionalize peace-keeping operations for political and budgetary reasons. One would have to be content with temporary arrangements in the future too. It was also very difficult to make contingency plans in the way that national defence forces do, because advance planning within the UN would be regarded as a political act. It would have been considered an attempt by the Secretariat to involve itself in independent political activity, which the great powers particularly would not tolerate. Only when the Security Council had made its decision in each specific case, and funds for that case had been allotted, could the planning be started.

For my part, I suspect that one of the reasons for the lack of advance planning in the autumn of 1973 could have been that nobody in the Secretariat believed that another UN force would be established. The major operations of the 1960s, the Congo and Cyprus, had caused difficulties whose implications were still being dealt with. Nobody believed either that the great powers could reach an unanimous decision on the setting up of an operation. This had never been achieved before.

I admit that advance planning may be politically delicate. But these difficulties should not be exaggerated and used as a pretext for doing nothing. The success of the operation should not be based only on the ingenuity and the improvisatory ability of the commander. And "success" should not mean that the troops at the early stage of the operation must suffer from cold, hunger and thirst. There must be some way that they can be adequately provided with food, accommodation, transportation and communications equipment.

Planning directed at a specific area of operation can readily cause suspicions and criticism. That I am ready to admit. But all operations have so many features in common that preparing a general outline should be possible. If there is insufficient personnel to draw up this general outline, the task could be given to the military authorities of a member state, for example one of the Nordic countries. Likewise, the forces now in operation could be given planning tasks.

The errors and negligence of 1973 served as a lesson to everybody and fortunately planning has improved greatly in recent years. This was clearly visible at the beginning of the 1980s, when preparations got underway for a force to be possibly sent to Namibia. According to information I received from the Finnish authorities, planning was now very careful and the instructions to possible troop-contributors, like Finland, were detailed. When Brian Urquhart visited Finland in 1980, it was a pleasure to accompany him to the Finnish UN Training Centre in Niinisalo and see how far Finland had progressed in the reservation of personnel, in the provision of vehicles and other equipment and in their preparation for transportation. One could also see that the instructions the Finnish authorities had received from New York had now much improved.

The first day of UNEF II, 25 October 1973, was full of surprises, enthusiasm and much work. I described events and feelings in a letter home:

> I tried to sleep a little but then a phone call from Commodore Wikberg [Commodore Stig Wikberg was at that time the Chief of Military Affairs Department at the Defence Ministry who spoke to me about the setting up of the Finnish battalion] woke me up completely.
>
> So many things have happened since my last letter. The supervision of the cease-fire in Sinai, which I have tried to arrange these last days and nights. A quick trip to Cairo and back yesterday,

meeting with Acting Foreign Minister Fahmy, a completely chaotic situation along the front. Brigadier Sherif completely out of his mind. On top of all of this the meeting of the Security Council yesterday evening, the decision to set up the new UNEF and Waldheim's order to me to begin to command it. There is surprise after surprise.

Today on 26 October I fly again to Cairo, perhaps for a lengthy stay. The Headquarters of the new UNEF will probably be stationed there. The nucleus of the staff will come from here: Gorgé, Holland, Hogan, Windsor, Jankowyj, etc.

Sophie [our Palestinian maid] must be given notice today. Our home remains here in Jerusalem for the time being. When it gets a little easier, I shall come and start packing.

Despite the sleeplessness, I am in good and brave condition. The flu is over. Don't worry, darling. Everything will be all right, I am sure.

15. Beginnings of the Force

Setting up headquarters

When I left for Cairo on 26 October 1973, I took with me a team of experienced people from UNTSO Headquarters. They became ·the nucleus of my new staff. Of course I had with me Rémy Gorgé from Switzerland, my able political adviser for many years. A few days later James Jonah (of Sierra Leone), a senior official from Brian Urquhart's office in New York, joined the advisory group. Jonah had previously been an aide to Gunnar Jarring and knew the Middle East well. From Cyprus came Ramon Prieto as a legal adviser, whom I knew well from his earlier years in UNTSO.

Another important group of civilian officials came from Jerusalem, led by the Chief Administrative Officer of UNTSO, Dennis Holland of the United Kingdom. He would temporarily take over the equivalent job in UNEF. Holland brought with him Leif Skolem (Norway), Chief Communications Officer; Joseph Woods (Ireland), Chief Transport Officer, and some more junior field service and general service officers. Holland also took under his personal command the security, transport and radio officers serving in Cairo and Ismailia.

In the group of soldiers the senior officer was Colonel P.D. Hogan (Ireland) who became the first Chief of Staff of UNEF. Major Allan Windsor (Australia) and Captain Helmut Jankowyj (Austria) set up the Operations Branch. There was also my Aide de Camp, Commander Seppo Laessaari (Finland). Colonel Keith Howard (Australia) was appointed Acting Quartermaster and he was assisted by Captain B. Studdart (Ireland) and Janis Mieritis (Sweden), who were originally UNTSO military observers in Ismailia. The officers of the Ismailia Control Centre who had manned the radio room at UNTSO Villa in Cairo continued as the first duty officers of UNEF's Operations Branch.

It was naturally a great advantage that we had UNTSO personnel available. Without it, UNEF Headquarters would not have been operational almost immediately. In this way we had a group of experienced UN officers who knew the area of operation and the procedures used in UN staff work. In addition they were used to working together. Had the staff officers arrived directly from their home countries, it would have taken a week before the staff was operational and still longer before the staff members were familiar with the new conditions of work and with each other.

The first group of soldiers and civilians convened in Cairo was more a kind of a working team than a properly organized headquarters. In the first days the division of work was not fixed; everybody did what was important at the moment. The small size and improvised character of the headquarters were not a drawback at all. Considering all the many other problems against which UNEF was struggling in its first hours and days, there would have been no meaningful use for a larger number of personnel, and it would not have increased the headquarters' ability to function.

UNEF Headquarters was at first accommodated in the UNTSO Liaison Office (UNTSO Villa) in Heliopolis, a suburb of Cairo. The location was excellent, near the airport and the meeting of the roads to Port Said, Ismailia and Suez. The house itself, a beautiful private villa surrounded by a garden, was, however, far too small for its new purpose. There were only eight rooms altogether and even the "Mini HQ" of the first days was almost suffocated by shortage of space. On the first evening, in my office where previously the UNTSO Liaison Officer had sat all by himself, six people were now trying to work: Gorgé and Prieto with their secretaries and I with my secretary Maria Zingaretti. Cramped and primitive working conditions hampered the smooth functioning of the new force.

As a working environment Heliopolis was excellent. It was a modern city with wide avenues and many gardens. The streets were bordered with flame, tulip and jacaranda trees imported from South America and India. Near the centre was the Royal Palace of Kubbeh, surrounded by a large park. There President Sadat received state visitors. The modern Heliopolis was born at the beginning of this century on the initiative of a Belgian businessman, Baron J. Empain, whose ugly, mixed-style palace still stands, although this "Monster House" has been abandoned and empty for years.

At first we all lived at the Sheraton Hotel in downtown Cairo, because at that time there were no suitable hotels in Heliopolis. The trip to the hotel through the crowded traffic of Cairo often took more than an hour. There was no restaurant in our building when we started. Was it hunger which made me one day shout so furiously that the CAO quickly organized a cafeteria on the roof of the villa? (As we know, the roof already boasted the splendid sauna built by the Finnish military observers.)

One of the most difficult problems of the early days was the poor communications between Cairo and Jerusalem and New York. Our radio equipment was old-fashioned. Sometimes I said jokingly that it dated back to the Boer War and had already been superseded in the First World War. The fact was that the newly recruited UNTSO radio technicians did not know how to use these radios, which in their home countries could be found only in museums. In addition, the atmospheric conditions that autumn, particularly at night-time, were unusually difficult. We therefore needed cable or satellite links with Jerusalem or New York, but in 1973 these did not exist in Cairo for public use. Even making ordinary long-distance phone calls from Cairo was almost impossible until the 1980s. One had to book the call well in advance; at the earliest it would come through on the following day, but often one had to wait for several days. For UNEF this system was much too slow and uncertain.

On the evening of 26 October, when no messages from New York had arrived – for example, I had received neither the mandate for UNEF nor the report of the Secretary-General – I finally became so desperate that in the middle of the night I drove to the Foreign Ministry to ask the assistance of the Acting Foreign Minister, Ismail Fahmy. This visit and his unusual friendliness and helpfulness have remained imprinted on my mind. Ismail Fahmy was sitting behind his desk. On a side-table there seemed to be a modern telephone exchange with its signal lights. The phone rang at short intervals and Fahmy spoke with many people. From the change in his tone and the term of address "*Rais*", I could guess when he was speaking with President Sadat. Apparently Sadat was using the energetic Fahmy as a kind of factotum and a chief executor of his ideas.

When there was a suitable pause, I was able to present my case. After a few pushes of the buttons, contact was made with New York and I got the information I had been missing. It was also agreed that in the future Colonel Lauri Koho would phone me daily and keep me informed. In New York it was thought that the Finnish language would be a secure enough code even for dealing with delicate matters.

After this Fahmy began to organize a telex connection with Geneva for us. A free telephone line was found from the Telegraph Office but telex machines were not available anywhere. After brief persuasion the War Ministry promised to give us one of theirs on loan. Fahmy's efficiency seemed unbelievable and when I left I still suspected that something would happen to complicate the matter. My suspicions were, however, unfounded because an Egyptian technician was installing the telex machine when I came to the office in the morning. After a few minutes we had direct contact with Geneva and, through there, with New York and Jerusalem too.

The technical backwardness of the United Nations worldwide communications network had been public knowledge for a long time. The communications problems of UNEF in the autumn of 1973 gave a significant impetus to innovations, a drive that was led in New York Headquarters by the Assistant Secretary-General for General Services, Robert J. Ryan, an able and experienced former administrator in the State Department of the United States. Energetically, he made the rebuilding of the communications system a real aim of his life. The results soon began to show. In 1975 in the courtyard of UNEF in Ismailia and at Government House in Jerusalem a paraboloid antenna was installed, directed at a satellite hovering above Africa and through this we were able to telephone Geneva and New York.

Communications between UNEF Headquarters and the battalions was another serious problem. We did not yet have a signals company to take care of these connections. We therefore had to resort to temporary arrangements and improvisation. The UNTSO military observers had Motorola radio sets in their jeeps, but we had not been able to repair their powerful link station near Ismailia, which had been damaged in the turmoil of the war. Therefore we stationed observers on high ground between Cairo and Suez, on Gebel Ataqa among other points, in order to be able to transmit the messages from jeep to jeep and finally to UNEF Headquarters. In this manner we organized a temporary radio network. Later, when the Austrian battalion was deployed in the Ismailia area, we were able to use their modern telex equipment to arrange a connection between Cairo and Ismailia. This was also used by the Swedish battalion stationed in Ismailia. The Austrian telex machines had an on-line coding system so that outsiders could not listen in.

First troops arrive in Cairo

In order to get UNEF operational as quickly as possible, the Secretary-General decided to transfer the nucleus of the new force from Cyprus. Having obtained the permission of the governments concerned, he instructed the Commander of UNFICYP, the Indian Major-General Prem Chand, to form without delay special units (each about

200-strong) from the Austrian, Finnish and Swedish contingents under his command, and to send them immediately by air to Egypt. Feverish activity commenced in Cyprus in order to carry out the instructions. The units arrived from New York on 26 October at 0300 hours, the advance parties landed in Cairo on the same evening, the Finnish main body at 2330 hours; after them came the Swedes and the Austrians in the early morning of 27 October. The Irish, whose participation had also been planned, were as yet unable to leave because the Irish Parliament had not given its acceptance. The entire transportation operation ended in the morning of 28 October, 48 hours after UNFICYP had received its order. General Prem Chand and his staff had acted commendably quickly and ably.

But we had not spent our time in idleness either. I had gone ·to see the War Minister, Ismail, now promoted to the rank of marshal, and obtained from him permission to use some parts of the Military Academy near the airport to accommodate the troops. Using UNTSO military observers, we formed a temporary traffic control group and an accommodation group. We borrowed trucks from the Egyptians for the first transports of personnel. All this we tried to create out of nothing and to improvise as best we could. We were forced to do this, because our own resources were quite non-existent. The operational plan for the use of the incoming troops was not a very complicated task. The situation in the Suez area was apparently the most threatening, so the Finns, arriving first, must be directed there. The next most alarming situation was in Ismailia: the Swedes must go there. As long as we had no headquarters company we also needed a reserve unit which would take care of signals, supply and transport tasks. We must use the Austrians for these tasks.

I was at the airport when the first Finns, under the leadership of their Commander, Lieutenant-Colonel Aulis Kemppainen, disembarked from the VC 10 of the Royal Air Force. In the dismal atmosphere of Cairo it was encouraging to see my young countrymen and their Commander, my old colleague. I had got to know him five years earlier when he was an UNTSO military observer in the very same Cairo and I knew I could trust him.

While I was greeting the Finns, an Egyptian lieutenant-general appeared at the airport as a special messenger from President Sadat. His short message was: "To Suez as fast as possible!"

From Kemppainen I heard that the Finns had brought with them food for a month, the necessary field kitchens and 14 Landrover four-wheel-drive vehicles. We would get tankers for transporting fuel and water from somewhere. From the airport we moved to UNEF Headquarters, where I gave an order to Aulis Kemppainen and to the chief of the advance party, Major Martti Jokihaara. Giving the order was not an easy task, because my own information about the situation in Suez was insufficient. According to legend, the order was: "Go to Suez if you can! Deploy between the parties if you dare! Make peace if you are able!" Somebody had later formulated this more incisive version on the basis of my original order.

In reality the order ran more or less as follows: go to Suez to restore the peace, nothing else. My additional instructions are: go to the city of Suez, contact the Governor and make the presence of the UN known. Arrange a base for the battalion. Start patrolling in three directions: along the main road from Suez to Cairo up to Kilometre 100, on the east bank of the Canal up to Shalufa, i.e. to the area of the former UNTSO Observation Post Lima. If you don't get through to Suez, try to get as far as you can. Be careful and do not take unnecessary risks.

I decided, however, that the Finns would depart only in the morning, for the troops needed a rest now. By hurrying we would only cause confusion. The night was dark, the terrain unfamiliar, we had no maps and the situation at their destination was unknown. It was wiser to wait for daybreak and let them depart refreshed and with new strength.

I went to my headquarters at the UNTSO Villa to continue working. I had to arrange for the Finns what small help UNTSO could give. In the vehicles of the Battalion Commander and his staff, Motorola radios were installed for communication with Ismailia and via it to Cairo. A few additional vehicles – tankers for fuel and water, among others – were provided by UNTSO. Equipped in this manner, the Finnish advance party would depart at 5 o'clock in the morning, as I had agreed with their Commander.

After midnight the telephone rang and the Acting Foreign Minister, Ismail Fahmy, was on the line. At first he expressed his displeasure that UNEF soldiers were only sleeping when they should have been on the road to Suez. After that he announced that 50 truck-drivers were needed for supply transportations to the 3rd Army. I answered that the matter was not that simple and had to be investigated. First we would have to find out whether we had enough soldiers with a truck-driver's licence. This I could not do until the following morning because it was not my intention to wake up the soldiers to find out. In Fahmy's opinion this was childish talk, because in Egypt at least everybody was able to drive a truck. I answered that that was quite apparent in the muddled traffic of Cairo. Next I asked, already quite angry, how long he had known that drivers were needed. Fahmy replied that the matter had been discussed and agreed with Kissinger a few days ago. "And you have the nerve to phone about it at the last moment and in the middle of the night. Believe me now, there will be no drivers," I answered and ended the phone call.

Soon I began to regret my bad behaviour. One does not answer a Foreign Minister like this. I was restless and wondered whether I should call back and apologize. "Never apologize!" was the calm advice of Rémy Gorgé, who was sitting opposite me.

Perhaps ten minutes passed, then Fahmy was again on the line. "I realized a while ago that you were angry and for good reason, General. Could you not reconsider the matter again, however?" "Never mind. The drivers will come tomorrow," I replied.

I believe that it was after this discussion that Fahmy and I became good friends. I had heard many foreign ambassadors complaining that Fahmy was rude and unfriendly to them. To me he was always especially polite, helpful and friendly.

The Finnish battalion moves on to Suez

I had received a message, through the Israeli Liaison Officer, that Defence Minister Moshe Dayan wished to see me north-west of Suez on Saturday morning, 27 October, at 11.30. I took with me Rémy Gorgé and, as a driver, Captain Pekka Kujasalo from UNTSO, who knew the area well and was familiar with the use of the Motorola radio in the car. We departed, the UN flag fluttering, in the Chevy of our Liaison Officer. It was not the best possible vehicle if we needed to drive off the asphalt road, but there was just no other choice; my own cars were still on the other side of the Canal in Jerusalem.

We came without mishap to the Israeli checkpoint at Kilometre 101. I paid no attention to this marker, which later became the symbol of historic negotiations. There we met the Finnish advance party, who had waited in vain for three hours to be let through to Suez. They told us that their journey had gone well. They had met two UNTSO patrols and the Egyptian Liaison Officer had been left behind their first line. But the Israeli guard would not let them pass.

The area of no-man's-land in front of the position was a sad sight. Several Egyptian tanks and other vehicles had apparently been destroyed quite recently in an air attack and they were still smoking. A dead Egyptian soldier lay in the middle of the road in front of the Finnish unit. Many other corpses could be seen nearby; the stench of death was nauseating. I saw that Gorgé and Kujasalo were shaken. For both of them this was the first experience of a battlefield: unpleasant but instructive.

The guards and the chief of the position had apparently been informed of our arrival because we were let through without any more formalities. A liaison officer accompanied us to the meeting-place, a crossroads about 10 km. north-east of Suez. As we drove, we could see further relics of the battlefield. There were destroyed tanks and other vehicles everywhere. The road had been cut in many places and we had to by-pass these points by driving off the road. We were particularly surprised by the accuracy with which these culverts had been made; each was the work of one single bomb. Only afterwards did I learn that the Israelis had received up-to-date precision weapons from the Americans.

We saw a helicopter landing, but it was not Moshe Dayan who stepped out of it; it was his military assistant, General Shlomo Gazit. At the last moment Dayan had been obliged to cancel the trip because of a Cabinet meeting.

I had been a little worried about the meeting all morning. Would the Finns be allowed through to Suez or would other pretexts be produced to slow down their advance? My suspicions, however, proved to be needless. Gazit's very first words made it clear that Israel was ready to co-operate with UNEF. Our carefully prepared speech, outlining the operational plans for UNEF and the Finnish battalion, could be set aside. When the Defence Minister has already made his decision, such details become superfluous. The meeting was short, the atmosphere pleasant and all matters were speedily resolved.

Off the record I asked General Gazit why things had happened like this. How had the Egyptians been driven to such distress in the final phase of the war? According to Gazit the Egyptians had fought like lions, ably and systematically, in the first phase of the war. The Israelis could not believe their eyes. When the tide of military success turned, the Egyptians reverted to their old ways. The action became muddled and ill-planned and this was the end.

Finally Gazit grabbed the radio and said he was giving the necessary orders to the Commander of the Southern Group. Having given his instructions, he boarded his helicopter and took off for Tel Aviv. I decided to remain on the spot to ensure that everything happened as agreed. It was important for the sake of UNEF and Egypt that the Finns should start to act as soon as possible. I remembered the urgent message I had received from Sadat the previous night. I also remembered my own war experiences. In really decisively important situations the Commander must personally supervise the course of events and use his authority to overcome any obstacles.

My decision was right because it soon appeared that nothing was happening. The local Israeli Commander, a very friendly and helpful colonel, explained that the checkpoint where the Finns were waiting had not received any order from its own division.

A battle of wills ensued and lasted four hours. I had no contact with the Israeli authorities, but the helpful local Commander transmitted my messages to the headquarters of the Southern Group. Sometimes I appealed; sometimes I threatened. I promised to inform the whole world about the matter through the Security Council. I even heaped abuse on the friendly local Commander, who was obviously completely innocent and felt his position to be confused and embarrassing. Sometimes I wondered why my own headquarters, which had contact with the Israeli authorities via Jerusalem, did not do anything. Finally I said that I was deeply disappointed. I had not previously realized that I could not trust the word of an Israeli general. This finally had an effect. The problems disappeared and at 1530 hours the Finnish advance party started its march towards Suez.

During the day I had sent radio messages to Cairo in order to keep the Secretary-General informed. The messages were sent on by an UNTSO patrol on Gebel Ataqa. I noticed with amusement how the soldier transmitting the messages, an Irish-sounding military observer, quite automatically rephrased messages from Gorgé or from me into more idiomatic English. I asked the observer to report to me the following morning and so began the long co-operation between the Irish Captain Joseph Fallon and myself.

When we returned to Cairo I met Colonel Hogan, who wondered why nothing had been heard from us all day. We both went to the radio room, where it appeared that the new and inexperienced duty officers had received the messages and logged them word for word. But nobody had thought to transmit them on to their superiors.

As can be imagined, I was not completely satisfied with my staff's performance.

The following morning I described the events of Saturday in a letter home, beginning with a kind of summary:

> The first opportunity during these three days in Cairo to put at least a few words down on paper. They have been full of work and worries day and night. Last night for the first time I slept uninterruptedly for six hours without anybody waking me up. Usually the night's sleep has lasted only one or two hours. I have been doing surprisingly well physically and even mentally. The reason for this, probably, is that despite all the terrible difficulties and all kinds of friction I have so far succeeded better in my task than one might have expected.

UNEF calms the situation

According to the order it had received, the Finnish advance party began to move towards the city of Suez on Sunday morning, 28 October. The tiny unit, 50 men strong, was led by the determined and resourceful Major Martti Jokihaara. The situation was volatile. Battles and firing continued in the outskirts of the city. A crowd of hysterical people thronged the streets. Sometimes the Finns were greeted as liberators of the city, with people kissing their arms and even the sides of their cars. Sometimes they were taken for Israelis and the attitude of the population became murderous. But the Finns coolly continued their advance. They moved from bunker to bunker and managed to get the Egyptian soldiers to stop firing and to return to their barracks. Gradually the tension abated and the firing stopped. A miracle had happened.

In the afternoon the main body of the Finnish battalion from Cyprus arrived in Suez under the command of Lieutenant-Colonel Aulis Kemppainen. Even this unit was not very large, comprising only about 150 men. Nevertheless, the presence of the UN in the city became more obvious and the situation calmed down. The first contacts with the Governor of Suez and the local commanders were established, the course of the Egyptian and Israeli front lines was agreed, and the formation of a buffer-zone between the parties was initiated. The width of the buffer-zone was only a few dozen metres, running from the Gulf of Suez, across the coastal avenue, to the railway station area.

Its length was about 700 metres and a street ran along the middle of it. Three observation posts were established for the supervision of the buffer-zone.

The sending of patrols across the Canal to the area of the 3rd Army was initially unsuccessful, because the Egyptians were afraid that information about their position would reach Israeli ears. It was two days before the Egyptians allowed the patrols to cross. However, they did not receive permission to advance through the positions of the 3rd Army up to the Israeli forward line, as I had hoped.

For the next few days the Kemppainen group concentrated its action within the city of Suez. By 3 November, eight observation posts had been established north, west and south of the city, and continuous patrolling of the east bank of the Canal had been organized.

It was a powerful and pleasant experience to visit the Finns in Suez and to follow their activities. One could see how enthusiastic both the officers and the men were. Real men's work had finally begun. They had witnessed a great battle in all its spine-chilling harshness, they had been in great danger of their lives, having landed in the middle of a raging battle, but they had also succeeded in calming the situation in a city which at first had been completely chaotic.

There were so few men that the supply company had to be used as infantry. In fact it was not needed for logistics tasks because that part of UNEF was not yet functioning. Even the battalion chaplain carried out messenger tasks with great enthusiasm and vigour. Spiritual work could wait for a while. The achievements of Kemppainen's battalion speak for themselves. For the sake of the UN and the parties, it was very fortunate that we had at our disposal such experienced, able and courageous UN soldiers just at a moment when they were most needed.

The new Finnish battalion which had been raised in Finland began to arrive in Cairo in late October and early November and immediately started to take over the tasks of the Kemppainen group. I knew the Commander of the battalion, Colonel Reino Raitasaari, very well. He had had an outstanding career in UN jobs at home and abroad, beginning as a military observer in Kashmir 1962–3; then as a staff officer in Cyprus in 1964; appointed the head of the UN office at the Defence Ministry 1967–9 and next the Commander of the Finnish battalion in Cyprus 1969–70. We did not have a more experienced UN officer in Finland.

Raitasaari's battalion, which in UNEF was called Finbatt, was

600-strong, composed of three ranger companies and the supply and headquarters companies. It began to carry out its duties on the lines laid down by the Kemppainen group. As it was three times larger, it was able to increase the number of its guard positions and to intensify its patrolling. There were even enough people for a reserve unit, to be used when incidents occurred. Now the UN presence in the city of Suez and its surroundings was no longer merely symbolic.

In early November I visited Colonel Raitasaari and his battalion. It was a pleasure to see how energetically the Finns worked to improve their accommodation, to construct communications lines and to take care of the logistics arrangements. The last task was the most difficult because until now UNEF had not been able to provide anything. The battalion was living on the tinned food it had brought from Finland. Naturally, this grew monotonous in time. The strange thing was, however, that nobody complained. Everybody was so enthusiastic about the new task, not a single thought was left for such trivialities. Each Finn, from the Commander down to the youngest private soldier, felt that he was taking part in a historic event which could perhaps be a turning point in the Middle East conflict.

It was also a pleasure to follow how the battalion carried out its proper peace-keeping task. The situation seemed to become calmer still and the confidence of the parties in the battalion increased. They began to believe that this unit would be able to fulfil its duty. I could see in everything the influence of an experienced commander. In the battalion a firm and undisputed order prevailed, but at the same time there was a happy and positive spirit.

By the time Colonel Raitasaari came to Sinai as a commander, Finland had had more than 15 years' experience of peace-keeping. The earlier battalions had had many problems, mainly connected with alcohol and the disorders it had caused, not all of which had been solved satisfactorily. Fortunately Raitasaari stayed in his job for three years. During that time he was able to find solutions and to establish practices which are still followed today. Raitasaari gave up the previous restrictions on the sale of alcohol, because it was easily and cheaply available in Suez. On the other hand, he restricted its use tightly. It could now be consumed only in the messes. The same rules which the airlines had set for their pilots now applied in the battalion too. Nobody was allowed to drink in the six hours before their shift of duty started. These restrictions were accepted. All were content that there were clear rules on alcohol.

Raitasaari's justness and impartiality were characteristics which I valued highly. I was very much satisfied with his work. The Finns now had an exceptionally distinguished commander, a fact which would have a bearing on the success of UNEF.

The advance party of the Swedish battalion arrived from Cyprus late on the evening of 26 October, and was accommodated in the Military Academy. The Chief of Staff of the battalion, Lieutenant-Colonel Stig Edgren, acted as its commander. The following morning at the UNTSO Villa he received an order from me which, according to Edgren's notes, ran as follows: "We don't know where the front line runs [in Ismailia]. Move there! Deploy yourself between the parties. Solve the problem using your own ability and ideas. Any questions?" "No, General."

Furnished with this order, the Commander of the advance party and his unit moved to Ismailia, a Swedish military observer acting as their guide. At their destination they began the process of reconnaissance and planning for the deployment of the battalion.

The main body of the Swedish battalion, of the same strength as the Finnish, arrived a few days later under the command of Lieutenant-Colonel Lennart Önfelt. This battalion was lodged in the buildings of the Suez Canal Company, where the accommodation facilities were splendid. Led by their fatherly and able Commander, the Swedes took up their tasks with enthusiasm. Fortunately the situation in Ismailia was not as critical as it was in Suez, but here too the parties were positioned close to each other and despite the cease-fire the firing had continued. Unlike Suez, the Israelis had not been able to cut the agricultural road to Cairo. They had tried their best but when the cease-fire came into effect the first Israeli troops had still been 200 metres from the road. Therefore the Swedes operated in an area entirely in the possession of the Egyptians, which made their job easier.

On reaching their destination, the Swedes began to deploy strongholds of ten men between the front lines of the parties. I visited the Swedish battalion at the beginning of November and witnessed their vigorous activity, which enhanced the confidence of the parties. Thanks to this, the situation in Ismailia gradually became calmer.

During my visit to Ismailia I also met Colonel P.O. Hallqvist, who just had arrived from Sweden to take over from Lieutenant-Colonel Önfelt. I had met Hallqvist already in Cairo, greeted the advance party of his battalion and given a short speech. In Ismailia Colonel Hallqvist complained to me that he had not received proper orders for his new role. I explained to him that matters had been clear enough when he had received the order to take over the area of operation from his predecessor. I had nothing more to add. I noted that Hallqvist was a strong-willed and determined officer. He was a commander to my liking: taking good care of his men and tough in relations with his superiors.

Both in Suez and in Ismailia we experienced once again the fact that in peace-keeping operations the size of the force is not decisive; speedy action and the symbolic presence of the UN flag are more important. Success is decided, however, by the ability and determination of the commanders and the courage and enthusiasm of the men.

The Austrian battalion, which was the same size as that of the Finns and the Swedes, was stationed as the reserve unit of UNEF in Cairo. It was supposed to arrange transports, communications and the first contacts between the parties and in general it was to perform the work of a headquarters company. Secretary-General Waldheim, who was always more interested in how things looked, was not satisfied with this. In his opinion, reserve duty was not glamorous enough for the Austrians and several times he pushed for the Austrians to be moved to the front. At the beginning of November the Austrians started to reconnoitre in their sector south-east of Abu Suweir. The headquarters of the battalion was in the city of Ismailia and its Commander, Lieutenant-Colonel Erich Weingerl, created a most favourable impression.

It was indeed time for the Austrians to go to the front, although we had been unable to avoid keeping the battalion in Cairo initially. Now we could gradually detach small groups from each battalion to take care of the reserve duties. There was no other solution in this phase, because UNEF still had no headquarters unit.

At the same time as the battalions were starting their activities, I was myself busily on the move and negotiating with the parties. During the last days of October I travelled back and forth between Cairo and Jerusalem. I met the Israeli Defence Minister and the Egyptian War Minister and Foreign Minister. I explained to them the planned composition and the operational plan of UNEF. I told them that the basic idea was to deploy the troops now available to us between the fighting armies, mainly in the areas of Suez and Ismailia.

I also requested their acceptance and support for my plans. In principle their formal acceptance was not needed, but in my opinion it was more polite and wise to present the implementation of UNEF's mandate in this manner. Without the backing and co-operation of the parties, the objectives of Resolution 340 could not be achieved and UNEF would not succeed in its task.

The Acting Foreign Minister of Egypt, Ismail Fahmy, accepted my plan on 28 October, noting and greeting with pleasure my idea to station troops in Israeli-controlled areas as well. Defence Minister Dayan accepted my idea on 29 October and offered Israeli airfields for the use of UNEF troops. He also agreed that we could cross Israeli-occupied military lines when we were carrying out our operational and logistics tasks.

Having noted this encouraging attitude, I decided to make use of it before it might possibly be changed. Therefore I decided to move the newly arrived parts of our fourth contingent, the Irish battalion, by road from Cairo to the east bank of the Canal. From there the battalion would march to its future base in Rabah. The rest of the battalion would fly directly from Dublin to Tel Aviv and then move on to Rabah from there. In early November difficulties arose, as I had suspected, with Israel announcing on 4 November that the Irish could not be received in Tel Aviv within 48 hours. The Irish did not want to wait, but flew instead to Cairo, as had been originally planned. The problems continued; Israel did not allow the Irish battalion to cross the Canal on 3 November. The efforts of the Secretary-General and myself, which lasted more than a week, were needed before the Irish could cross the Canal. Once more we could see how the local command of the army in Sinai sabotaged the decisions of the Defence Ministry, in much the same way as these authorities had prevented the arrival of the Finnish battalion in Suez.

In this manner the Irish paved the way for the battalions of Peru and Panama which arrived in mid-November. They flew directly to Tel Aviv and continued by car to the village of Rabah on the east bank of the Canal.

Amidst the flurry of activity relating to the deployment and establishment of UNEF, I received a purely political task from the Secretary-General. I was to approach Defence Minister Dayan and, referring to Resolutions 338, 339 and 340, demand that Israel withdraw to the line where its troops had been on 22 October at 1650 hours. I could guess as I left that this would be a fruitless journey.

Moshe Dayan received me in Jerusalem at the King David Hotel, where he had a temporary office. He came there from Tel Aviv on those days when he had a Cabinet meeting in Jerusalem. We did not go inside, however, but instead Dayan asked me into the garden of the hotel, where there were no other people. There in the remotest corner we sat down and I presented my case. Dayan replied that the matter in question was such that he would have to refer it to the government but his own opinion was negative. This was probably my shortest encounter with him.

In his memoirs Dayan writes that not even the United States and the Soviet Union had been able to force Israel to withdraw. How then would the UN be capable of accomplishing this? Surely more order was needed now in the filing system of the Security Council, such as it had not achieved in the battlefield. Dayan thought that Israel would manage to get along with the peace-keeping force. It would not be very useful but would not do any harm either.

I had noticed already that Dayan could not tolerate idle talk. When we met he would never ask, for example, how the family was or something similar. He was such a busy man and took his job so seriously that he had no time for such niceties. When I came to his office many others were often present too: the Chief of Staff, the Chief of Military Intelligence, a representative of the Foreign Ministry, several generals and colonels. I, however, was only accompanied by one assistant. I complained once to the Liaison Officer that in Dayan's office I felt like an orphan. I had to behave as if I were addressing an audience and I could not think of having a confidential or off-the-record conversation. The Liaison Officer explained to me that this was simply a question of practicality, so that all those concerned got information about the substance of the discussion at the same time and the Defence Minister did not need to give a separate briefing after my visit.

When I went to see Dayan the next time, there were again at least ten people in his office. Dayan himself arrived last, looked around and cheerfully remarked to me: "We seem to be in the majority here again!" My message had at least reached him.

I met Dayan for the last time when he was Foreign Minister in the government of Menachem Begin. I went to see him a few weeks after his return from a state visit to Finland in the spring of 1979 and was received by Ambassador Eytan Ron, who told me that in the fortnight after his trip to Scandinavia, Dayan had talked only about Finland. No other object of the trip could compete with Finland. Particularly in Lapland, where he had been the guest of the frontier troops, he and his wife had experienced real warmth and hospitality. I was pleased to hear that, because I had read in the Finnish papers about the cool official reception he had received. When I entered Dayan's office his first words were: "Listen now, General Siilasvuo. What are you still doing here in Israel? If I had a country as beautiful as yours, I would not stay here a day longer."

Early difficulties

I have already said how cramped the conditions of my staff were in the early days in the small UNTSO villa. Unfortunately the Egyptian authorities were not able or willing to help us with our accommodation problems. I thought this was strange, because Heliopolis was full of large barracks areas. I was told that the British had space there for an army of 100,000. It was a question of attitudes, however. The War Ministry did not want to cause inconvenience to its own troops. Soon they were chasing us out from the Military Academy, claiming that the cadets needed their accommodation back. The War Minister, Marshal Ismail, looked offendedly at me when I proposed that the cadets could live in tents, for that is what we would do in Finland in a similar situation. The Egyptian attitude became clear from the talk of the liaison officers: the "rich" UN could get its housing in the private sector and pay the going rate for it.

At one stage the authorities offered us a tourist hotel, closed because of the war, on top of Mount Mokattan opposite the Cairo Citadel. This would have been an ideal solution, for there would have been space for the logistics base and good communications in every direction. We only had one night to enjoy this offer, however, because on the following day it was withdrawn. The site was too close to a top-secret army communications centre.

It took some time before the Chief Administrative Officer found a fairly large private villa in Heliopolis to use for our headquarters. It was situated in a quiet place near the beautiful Merryland Park and was named Merryland Villa. In Finland it would have been considered a palace, but the 15-room house was clearly too small for the needs of a large headquarters. In addition to the Commander there would only be room for the Chief of Staff, the Chief Administrative Officer, the political and legal advisers, the operational branch and some other important elements of the staff. We had to continue to look for additional space for the large logistics and procurement branches. For them we found a five-storey building still under construction a few kilometres from Merryland.

The Merryland Villa was owned by an Egyptian police general who was in prison for political reasons. I explained to my guests that in Finland generals do not usually live in such magnificent houses, but very seldom do they go to prison either.

I could already guess the difficulties which would be caused by dividing the headquarters between two buildings. Moreover, it was not easy to find a suitable site for the Canadian-Polish logistics base. The only choice proved to be the race course near the building of the logistics and administrative branch. We called it Shams Camp. The private residents of the area made protests, however. The situation became critical, because on the following day, 15 November, the first parts of the logistics contingents were supposed to land in Cairo, and we had no place where they could lay their heads. Now Marshal Ismail finally realized that we were in a quandary. The matter was arranged then and there and when I wondered who would pay the high rent of the race course, the War Minister said jokingly that he would pay it out of his own pocket.

Accommodation for our personnel also caused worries. There were no hotels in Heliopolis in those days, so that the growing numbers of UN personnel, from the Commander of UNEF down to the most junior civilian official, continued to live at UN expense in the elegant Sheraton Hotel in Cairo's city centre. This arrangement, which was meant to be temporary, was not only expensive but it also made for bad feeling among the military officers of UNEF Headquarters, because the Chief Administrative Officer forced them to rent their apartments privately in Heliopolis. Unfortunately, a misplaced sense of solidarity and a lack of courage prevented the CAO from obliging the civilians to do the same. When I took up the matter with him, he explained that UN administrative regulations presupposed the accommodation of the officials in a good hotel. It was my fault that I did not after all force him to make other housing arrangements. But at this stage I had other worries and I had neither time nor strength to make a major issue of this.

I did decide, however, to move from the hotel to a rented apartment in Heliopolis, by way of setting an example. Rémy Gorgé and some others followed my example at once. I also decided that this miserable charade would never be repeated. When UNDOF was set up in Damascus in the following year, the civilian personnel were obliged to find apartments in the city and the UN arranged that military officers at UNDOF Headquarters should have both housing and a restaurant in buildings the UN had rented.

Because of these problems, but also for operational reasons, it was decided during the first visit of Messrs Brian Urquhart and George Lansky to UNEF that the headquarters would be moved to Ismailia, where we had temporary possession of a group of multi-storey buildings owned by the Suez Canal Company. They had plenty of room for offices and housing and were at present used by the Swedish and Austrian battalions. The repair work, however, took longer than expected and it was only in August 1974 that the headquarters in Ismailia became operational.

Impatient with the housing difficulties, I proposed that the UN should reach an agreement on this issue with the host country at the time when the setting up of a new UN force was discussed in the Security Council.

The arrival of the Canadian and Polish logistics contingents was delayed for various reasons, so they were ready to handle UNEF's logistics requirements only in mid-December 1973.

Afterwards it seems quite unbelievable that despite its growing number of personnel, UNEF had to wait one and a half months without logistics troops and that it coped without them. Improvisation was of course the only way of ensuring that the troops had at least some kind of logistics and administrative backing. Everything had to be started from scratch and temporary arrangements for supplying the troops had to be made.

Little by little the Chief Administrative Officer, the Chief Procurement Officer and the Acting Quartermaster struck deals with Egyptian suppliers for the provision of fresh meat and vegetables. In this connection, it must be remembered that Egypt in 1973 was an underdeveloped agricultural country, where there were no large marketing chains and dairies with air-conditioned stores and trucks. Supplies for Cairo's millions of inhabitants were based on market-places and bazaars. UNEF's suppliers were small merchants on the level of Western shopkeepers at market-places. The poor quality of fresh food and the lack of refrigeration meant that the meat and vegetables were rotten before they reached Suez and Ismailia. On the east bank of the Canal our battalions were in a better position. There Shekem, the wholesale firm of the Israeli Defence Forces, provided supplies in refrigerated trucks directly to the battalions.

Fortunately, the first Austrian, Finnish and Swedish battalions had brought food for a month with them. When in addition the governments of these countries took good care of their troops and were swift to send them food, spare parts and equipment by air or by ship, they came off well, despite the lack of UNEF supplies. Without the attentiveness and generosity of these governments, the entire UNEF operation could have ended badly.

The logistics difficulties of UNEF's early days contain lessons for the future. The idea of battalions bringing food rations for 30 days was a step in the right direction. It would be better still if the contributing countries were obliged to take care of their battalions for the first four or five months, i.e. until the moment when the UN can take over the logistics responsibility. At the same time one could consider whether the battalions could take care of the maintenance and repairs of their vehicles as well. In UNEF we had favourable experiences of this policy in practice.

UNEF and the media

Very early on, UNEF Headquarters obtained important reinforcements when we were joined by the Chief Information Officer, the Yugoslav Rudolf Stajduhar, and his assistant Birger Halldén of Sweden. Stajduhar was an experienced journalist, a vigorous UN information officer and a public relations man. His first task was to change his Commander's attitude to information. In my own army I was used to taking a very cautious approach. Preferably one should not say anything to the press, but if a statement had to be given, General Headquarters should agree with its contents. In UNTSO we had followed exactly the same policy: UNTSO did not give its own statements to the press, it reported to the Secretary-General, who alone took care of information.

Now the old policy was no longer adequate, for it was much too slow in the new situation. We needed fast communication of news on the spot. New York was too far and the information officers there had no immediate contact with events. Information needs were, moreover, immense. On both sides of the Canal there were about 400 journalists, radio and TV editors, top-class people from the largest press agencies in the world. They buzzed around us continuously like wasps, always seeking more information.

Stajduhar gave other reasons for changing our information policy as well. For the success of our operation it was necessary that the press should treat UNEF positively. Therefore our relations with the press had to be carefully looked after and information given to it as much as possible. Stajduhar held a daily press conference at the Hilton Hotel, where he presented UNEF's press statements and answered the questions of the journalists.

Every morning Stajduhar came to my office to have the press release accepted. It was often very short but was followed by a longer section saying that in answer to the questions of the press the UNEF Information Officer gave the following replies. When I asked how he knew these questions in advance, Stajduhar answered, "If the journalists do not understand the right questions to ask, one should put them into their mouths." Then he explained to me that in the press statement one could not always tell the whole truth for political and other reasons, but that the questions asked by the journalists must always be truthfully answered.

The new information policy proved to be a direct hit. The press were almost literally eating out of our hands. During my whole time with UNEF I almost never saw a negative report on the operation of the Force.

On 3 November Stajduhar thought that now, after UNEF had been in action for a week, it would be proper to give the press a longer report on its operations. I drafted an outline for the report at 5 o'clock in the morning at the hotel and then in my office I dictated it to my secretary. To begin with, I explained that the shortness and meagre contents of the press releases had been caused by the highly complex situation in the area. But now the time had come to give the press a summary of UNEF's past and present activities.

I reminded them that UNEF was still a force of less than 600 men and that therefore one should not expect miracles. Then I described how the actions of the small Finnish advance party had lessened tension in Suez. I also outlined the first meetings of the military delegations and our assistance to the supply transports of the 3rd Army. Having then explained the deployment of our three battalions, I gave a few examples of their operation:

A dispute had arisen between Israeli and Egyptian forces in the area north of the city of Suez, regarding their forward defended lines, with a threat of a breakdown of the cease-fire. The Commander of the Finnish contingent arranged for a meeting on 31 October between the Israeli and Egyptian local commanders. As a result of the meeting a practical solution was agreed, in order to ensure a "neat, straight line". Under the arrangement Egyptian military personnel within the area to be occupied by Israeli armed forces withdrew, along with their equipment, to the agreed line. The same was done by the Israelis. A commitment was made by the local Israeli Commander to permit freedom of movement of civilians north of the city, back and forth between the villages and the city, through the forward defended lines.

Confidence-building was uppermost in the minds of both the Force Commander and his contingent commanders. It was most important that the parties should have confidence in UNEF's ability to fulfil its duties.

The process of building this confidence began on the level of company and platoon commanders. As in the example above from the Finnish battalion, the first measure was to create good relations between the local commanders on both sides. The Commander of the Swedish battalion, Lieutenant-Colonel Önfelt, describes how this was done:

> After the relative quiet of the first days of our arrival in Ismailia, the exchange of fire became a daily routine. The reasons for these incidents could be an Israeli bulldozer which had started to work on fortifications, or, on the Egyptian side, that some soldiers had during the night encroached into no-man's-land and built a new position. The uselessness of these exchanges of fire soon became apparent to my soldiers. They were the ones who were caught in the middle and had to spend hours in the shelters. Finally they decided to start a campaign in order to stop the unnecessary firing; they visited the parties daily, had tea with them, tried to gain the confidence of the Israeli and Egyptian platoon and company commanders and slowly achieved results. After some time, it became a habit of the parties to telephone our positions at the beginning of an incident which previously had usually led to an exchange of fire. The position commanders, usually young corporals and sergeants, tried to convince the parties not to start firing. Then they began to negotiate. Shuttling between the Egyptians and Israelis, they tried to find solutions which could be accepted by both parties. Surprisingly, they were very often successful.

The following story is from the Austrian battalion:

In the desert south-west of Ismailia, a detachment of Austrian members of UNEF are stationed at OP Foxtrot. Less than 1 kilometre away, Israeli and Egyptian units are dug in.

The Austrian soldiers watch and wait. A sudden burst of fire from one side is answered from the other; the duel grows fierce, and machine-gun fire is soon augmented by bursts from tank-mounted guns.

A moment of silence is seized upon by an Austrian lieutenant, who contacts the two sides by telephone, jumps in his jeep and leads the officers from the Israeli and Egyptian camps to his tent to talk it over.

The confrontation is tense at first. One of the opposing officers tells the other to stop putting up barbed wire; the response is a threat that any more firing would be met by tougher measures. The Austrian lieutenant serves whisky and coffee. Gradually the conversation becomes more relaxed; the lieutenant points out that barbed wire is useful only for defensive purposes. Within an hour the hostile mood of the Israeli and Egyptian officers has worn off; they even exchange a few jokes. They agree to hold their fire and return to their positions.

16. UNEF grows

Life in hotel rooms

In the early days of UNEF I lived in the Sheraton Hotel, located in the Dokki quarter favoured by wealthy people and diplomats. I could see from my windows the colonial-style buildings and beautiful park of the Soviet Embassy. The residence of my old friend, the Finnish Ambassador Pekka Malinen, was within walking distance. The hospitable home of the Malinens was good to visit for an exchange of information and for an airing of views. Often also Pasi Rutanen, Malinen's knowledgeable number two man, took part in the discussions. For a change it was nice just to relax in the sauna and the pool in the company of the Malinens.

The large hotel was almost empty. Cairo Airport continued to be closed to general air traffic. Businessmen and tourists were not seen. There were hardly any guests but UNEF people. In the lobby downstairs a large group of security men swarmed in the Egyptian manner. I had a small suite on the top floor, but very little time to enjoy it, because I came to the hotel late in the evening and left it early in the morning. During the day I had met so many people that there was no need for even more society. Therefore I did not go to the restaurant, but ordered a snack from room-service and after a quick bath went to bed. But the sleep lasted only a few hours. My head was full of UNEF matters. I had to think of them day and night. Sometimes, because of some trouble during the day, I became so angry that I could not sleep any more. I tried, however, to force myself back to sleep, because I needed rest to cope with the ordeals of the coming day.

Despite 16-hour working days I remained brisk and in a happy mood. I wrote home on 16 November 1973:

> I continue to be in excellent condition physically and mentally. My weight remains at 75 kilos, my clothes are loose around my waist. My good condition is naturally a result of the continuous feeling that I do something concrete and useful and that my work has had great success.

But hotel life had its drawbacks in the long run. The trip to the hotel and back through the crowded Cairo streets took at least an hour in the morning and in the evening. I wrote home on 20 November:

179

I live my life as if I were in a monastery. In the evening, tired to the hotel, a little food in the hotel room and then to bed. Besides the Malinens I have met hardly anybody else but Egyptian and Israeli authorities, people in our own house and press people. I have not once visited the city and the bazaars, or visited the Finnish observer families . . . But everything will change when the pressure is only relieved a little.

The misery of the war was reflected by the hotel personnel. One evening I went to the hotel cashier to exchange a large banknote for smaller ones to use for tips. These small banknotes in Egypt are unusually dirty, old and crumpled. Counting the money, the cashier philosophized, "We Egyptians are very tired of this war." After a short pause he added, "Even our banknotes are tired of it."

A more suitable home was sought for weeks. To find a house of a suitable size and good condition was not easy. I was presented with palaces and villas of all kinds, but they were dirty and shabby, the furniture impossible, gilded and terrible colours, and I said no. I was afraid that I would have nightmares in them. Finally I proposed: "Shouldn't we abandon the idea of a house and take an apartment as a temporary solution? I shall move to a better one if we find it."

My Aide-de-Camp, Seppo Laessaari, then found an apartment in an elegant new house along the main street leading to the airport. It was about 3 kilometres from the UNTSO Villa in the direction of the airport. It had a combined sitting- and dining-room, three bedrooms, a kitchen and two bathrooms. There were large balconies on two sides.

I moved to my new home at the beginning of December and after the hotel it felt good. Everything was new and tidy. The furniture and colours were not completely impossible. Not "Louis Farouk" style, which in Cairo was more popular than Louis Quinze or Louis Seize, as I was joking to my guests. The apartment was also well-furnished and included china and bedclothes. I realized the drawbacks only later. After the air traffic returned to normal, the noise of the aeroplanes was immensely disturbing and when the summer arrived the apartment was as hot as an oven. Fortunately we would move to Ismailia in August.

Only now was our home in Jerusalem closed and our things packed. The last weekend of November I spent in Jerusalem. Together with my Aide-de-Camp, we arranged the things for packing. Those which I would later send to Finland would remain in boxes in the UNTSO store. My wife's and my own clothes, some kitchen utensils, some paintings and other ornaments would be taken with us to Cairo. Among the paintings there was a Japanese *kakemono*, an elongated Buddhist text, painted on paper, which I had bought from the exhibition of UNTSO's own artists. It had been painted by Mr Ida of our Registry. According to the artist the text of the painting, translated into English, was: "Originality out of nothing". I thought this was very suitable as a motto for UNEF.

Personnel problems

As in all large organizations, personnel problems caused troubles in UNEF from the very early days. The international character of the Force, the need for equal geographic distribution, the representation of the contributing countries (particularly in higher posts) and the tension between NATO and the Warsaw Pact brought their own particular problems to UNEF. Very seldom was the question simply the ability of a certain person to carry out a job.

The first controversy between the UN administrative leadership and myself was caused by the appointment of the Chief Administrative Officer of UNEF. I had taken Dennis Holland with me from UNTSO and believed him to be particularly well-suited to set up a new UN force in difficult circumstances. He was respected by his subordinates and as a reserve officer he also had a solid military background.

George Lansky, who co-ordinated the administration of the peace-keeping missions in New York, had a different view, however. Holland was to remain in UNTSO in his former but now much diminished role. A new administrator was to be appointed to UNEF, a man whom I also knew very well from his time in UNTSO. I had already said to Lansky then that I did not want him as my subordinate in the future. I thought he was completely unsuitable for his new job and could not understand why Lansky wanted to force him on me. When my acceptance of the appointment was requested, my answer was negative. This put New York in an awkward position, because the autocratic Lansky had sent him on his way without waiting for my reply and he was, as I heard, already in Cyprus.

Holland for his part explained that he might now be in big trouble. If I would not change my attitude towards his successor, his UN career would suffer, because he would be suspected of having initiated my protest and of having promoted his own interests. Finally I gave in. I sent a cable to New York in which I promised to agree to the change of administrators. It was one of the greatest errors I made in UNEF. I did not follow my father's advice that one should never be tender-hearted in personnel affairs and should place the interest of the organization before personal interests.

The new Chief Administrative Officer remained in his job less than six months, until an illness forced him to resign. His successor was an elderly gentleman, already retired, who as an Assistant Secretary-General had previously been in charge of an UN agency. This appointment proved to be a still greater mistake. The difficult task of the administration of UNEF became too much for him. I could not have imagined such inefficiency. Fortunately, he also left us after six months. We were extremely pleased when he was replaced by the able and experienced Dennis Holland.

I sometimes wondered how we managed the great administrative and logistical difficulties of the first year with such weak administrators. Fortunately, the situation was much improved after the arrival of the Canadian and Polish logistics contingents in December 1973. Then we had as a counter-weight to the weak Chief Administrative Officer the highly professional and determined Canadian Quartermaster of UNEF and his Canadian-Polish Logistics Branch. The Commanding General of the Canadian logistics contingent also played an important role. During my time, there were three of them: Major-Generals D.E. Holmes, Bob LaRose and Blake Baile. They were all very competent officers. With their authority and professionalism they were able to correct and balance the logistics situation.

Not only did the first two administrators of UNEF fail in their jobs, but among their subordinate administrative officials were many incompetent people as well. This entire affair was difficult to understand, because all the other civil servants coming from New York, such as the political and legal advisers, information officers and all the secretaries, were with very few exceptions high-class people.

On the military side of UNEF Headquarters, the early shortage of personnel gradually ceased to be a problem. We received new people from the contributing countries and day by day our working team began to resemble a real military headquarters.

As a first step to improve the staffing level, I had requested Austria, Finland and Sweden each to send one senior Staff College-trained officer, and based on my personal knowledge I had mentioned some names as desirable candidates. The response did not meet my expectations completely. None of the candidates I had mentioned was available.

Finland proposed Colonel Tauno Kuosa, my comrade in arms from the Cadet School and the war years. Besides other merits, he had long UN experience, so I gladly accepted him. Sweden announced that their candidate, Colonel Liedgren, would arrive only in December. Austria had misunderstood my request and sent a captain who had no Staff College training and who was originally meant to replace an UNTSO observer, now returning home.

Finland was the only country to have included in its contingent a group of staff personnel. From that group, one lieutenant-colonel, four majors, two captains and a few non-commissioned officers reported for duty in UNEF Headquarters in the first days of November. This was a very welcome supplement, but when I heard at the same time that Finland was about to send a second group of officers, I had to ask the Finnish authorities to cancel their arrival. I could not very well make UNEF Headquarters completely Finnish.

The arrival of the Canadian and Polish logistics contingents solved the personnel problems of the Logistics Branch, because these countries had been requested to send the necessary staff officers too. Colonel Howard and his assistants could be returned to UNTSO after a job extremely well done.

It was now becoming clearer what the final composition of the new UN force would be and from which countries its troops would originate. Only now was it possible to begin the reorganization of Headquarters and to bring the numbers of personnel up to full strength in a systematic manner. However, this was a very difficult and complicated process which could only be completed after the first six months tour of duty came to an end. Some countries (for instance, Senegal and the Latin American countries) were never able to send the requested staff officers because of a shortage of English-speakers. Some others demanded for reasons of prestige that they should have an officer of colonel's rank in UNEF Headquarters. We already had colonels lined up and we had been obliged to create new jobs for them, such as the Assistant Chief of Staff and the Deputy Chief of Staff.

The struggle for prestige could have its amusing side. One day I received a cable from New York, announcing that Nepal wanted to send a colonel to my staff. I replied that this was not possible; UNEF had too many colonels already. On the following day a new cable arrived: "The King of Nepal wishes personally that UNEF would place his Colonel. The name of the Colonel in question is Rana and he has previous UN experience." At once I remembered Major Rana from my time in UNOGIL in Lebanon in 1958 and wished him warmly welcome. The family of Rana was a really great family in Nepal and had earlier provided the hereditary prime ministers of the country for centuries.

The choice of Colonel Rana proved to be most successful. His general joviality made him particularly suited for delicate, diplomatic tasks of mediation, which were in his line of affairs as the Deputy Chief of Staff.

The commanders of our two brigades, the Peruvian General Gaston Ibanez O'Brien and the Indonesian General Himawan Soetanto, had arrived in Cairo without a staff or a staff company. With good reason, they were unsure of what their role would be. We tried to scrape together personnel for the brigades from the battalions, but with the best will in the world the latter found it difficult to give up their people to put at the disposal of the brigades, because they only had sufficient personnel for their own needs. It was not easy to get additional personnel directly from the contributing countries; even when they agreed, the people were slow to arrive. We were never able to make the western or southern brigade operational and it was dissolved in due course. However, the eastern brigade, whose name was changed to the northern brigade, was finally operational in the spring of 1974. It served a good purpose when we needed a headquarters for UNDOF, the new UN force to be sent to the Golan.

The operational idea of brigades, which had been part of the original plan, was never fully completed and tested. Experience showed that commanding the battalions without an intermediary echelon worked well. On the other hand, the brigades could have been more useful if they had been full-sized and operational from the very beginning. Taking into consideration that most of the UNEF battalions were completely inexperienced in peace-keeping, the brigades could have given the battalions guidance in the performance of their tasks, helped them in logistical problems and co-ordinated their activities in other ways as well.

It was no wonder that even at an early stage General Ibanez realized the frustrations of his position. Obviously highly regarded in his home country, this officer had arrived with great haste in Cairo at the request of the UN, only to see that he was not given an instrument through which to fulfil his role. It was no wonder that he asked his government to recall him as quickly as possible. This was a pity, for at the turn of the year he acted for me when I was obliged to stay away from Cairo for long periods of time because of negotiations in Geneva.

More troops arrive

The Finnish and Swedish battalions arrived in Cairo during the first week of November, as we have seen. The strength of each battalion was about 600 men and they were well-equipped. They had vehicles and radio gear, at least for their immediate needs, and food for 30 days. In addition, more equipment arrived from home as required. Lieutenant-Colonels Kemppainen and Önfelt and their men could return home around 10 November after a job very well done. They had stayed two weeks in the area but for the sake of later action these weeks were decisive. The foundations of the operation's success were laid down then, as calm was restored to the area and the atmosphere became more conducive to negotiations.

The Austrian authorities sent additional people to their unit of 205 men which had arrived from Cyprus. Russian cargo planes brought 184 men and 60 tons of materiel to Cairo. More flights in December increased the strength of the battalion to 611 men. The Austrian battalion was very well-equipped and its signals equipment particularly was of high quality. Commander of the battalion from the very beginning was Lieutenant-Colonel Erich Weingerl, who in a quiet and unassuming manner commanded his battalion most effectively.

Part of the Irish battalion, 129 men, had arrived in Cairo from Cyprus on 31 October, led by Lieutenant-Colonel Peter Allen. The rest, a further 129 men, arrived straight from Dublin on 4 November. Even with the additional troops the battalion remained very small and in addition it was poorly equipped. The group arriving from Cyprus had only ten Landrover four-wheel-drive cars, while the group arriving from Dublin was completely without vehicles. Perhaps the authorities thought that the UN would arrange proper vehicles for the soldiers of a small and poor country and did not at all foresee UNEF's great difficulties. UNEF tried its best, however, and from its scarce resources gave the Irish battalion eight Russian ZIL trucks, loaned from the Egyptians and in very bad condition. In January, five more ZILs were given, but they proved to be completely unserviceable. The Irish battalion at this stage had only two trucks in addition to the Landrovers, but borrowed four trucks from the Austrians. In March, after the first disengagement, UNEF was finally able to adopt a more permanent solution, with the Irish getting on loan from the Finns five two-and-a-half ton trucks of Finnish origin. To compensate them, the Poles gave the Finns five of their own heavy trucks on loan. When I followed from the side-lines these arrangements of UNEF's logistics people, I often thought that the shortage of equipment, and the improvisation that it necessitated, in many ways resembled circumstances in the Finnish Winter War, when the emergency forced us to invent ways of compensating for the shortage of materiel.

The air transport of the additional troops was arranged so that the Swedes and Norwegians took care of the transportation of the Swedish battalion, the Soviet Union was responsible for that of the Finns and Austrians and the United States for that of the Irish. In this way the great powers and other member states provided assistance to UNEF, whose establishment they had unanimously supported. This free transport service by member states continued when the other UNEF contingents were being transported to the areas of operation. They saved at least $15 million of UN funds.

In conclusion one could say that by about 10 November, or in the phase when we began the negotiations on the Six-Point Agreement at Kilometre 101, the strength of UNEF's infantry was 1,600 men. Only small reconnaissance groups from the logistics contingents were in the area.

My opinion was not asked in the selection of new participating countries; this was decided by the Secretary-General together with the Security Council. The grounds for selection had obviously become clear during the discussion concerning UNEF's operational instructions which the Secretary-General had drafted. The great unanimity of the Council, which had not been the case in the setting up of previous peace-keeping forces, made the selection easier. The Council did not want to leave it to the two host countries, Egypt and Israel. The Soviet Union emphasised the principle of equal geographic distribution and the right of the Council to decide on the composition of the force. On 2 November the Council published a document on the consensus it had reached, requesting the Secretary-General to approach Ghana, Indonesia, Nepal, Panama and Peru and, in addition, Canada and Poland, representing different regional groups. The latter two were to take care of the logistics of UNEF. Senegal was later added to the list.

The idea of not asking the opinion of the host countries at this time seemed a fine principle on paper, but in practice it caused difficulties which UNEF had to bear. Israel accepted the composition of UNEF because it had no alternative, but at the same time it announced that it would not allow the soldiers of Poland, Ghana, Senegal or Indonesia to move in areas controlled by it, as Israel had no diplomatic relations with these countries.

This at once limited my freedom of action because the battalions of Ghana, Senegal and Indonesia could not be deployed east of the Canal. Still greater harm was caused by the fact that the Poles, who were to take care of UNEF's long-distance transport, were not allowed to move on the Israeli side. I had planned that UNEF would be supplied equally from Egypt and Israel. Now this plan could not be fully implemented.

The Secretary-General continuously complained to the Security Council about the attitude of Israel and the Soviet Union in particular thundered its condemnation. But the complaints and condemnations did not help, as Israel stuck steadfastly to its position. The theoretically sound principles of the Security Council were undermined by the harsh reality of practical life. Israel had of course the free right to demonstrate its disapproval of those countries with whom it had unfriendly relations, but I thought it was unjust that UNEF should suffer from the protest.

The freedom of movement which the UN had always considered as one of the main principles of peace-keeping did not always materialize in the case of other participating countries either. We have already seen how difficult it was for the Finns to get to Suez and for the Irish to get east of the Canal. We also saw how the Egyptians prevented the Finns from advancing through the positions of the 3rd Army to meet the forward line of the Irish. Similarly, Israel did not allow the Irish to set up observation posts between the parties in the northern sector. These problems were resolved only when UNEF was deployed in its own buffer-zone and was placed squarely between the parties. UNEF was finally its own master.

During UNTSO's time both parties had always been able to prevent patrolling, for example, by announcing that a liaison officer was not available. Now I tried to end this system of using liaison officers which greatly hampered our freedom of action. We succeeded quite well in this on the Egyptian side. UNEF's personnel and vehicles could now move in the front-line areas and towards Cairo without written permission and other restrictions. But in Israel the authorities did not want to give up all restrictions. So here, for instance, we always had to be accompanied by a liaison officer on the coastal road from Tel Aviv to the Canal, when we drove through the zone of Israeli battle positions.

This was Defence Minister Moshe Dayan's unconditional demand and he would not move from this position, despite my many attempts to change these regulations. Did fear of espionage lie behind this precaution which so much hampered the UNEF operation? Perhaps the reason was Dayan's obsessive wish to emphasise Israel's authority in the areas it controlled. Nobody would move in them without his permission and strict supervision.

I was worried about the standard of equipment of the incoming battalions because they came from the poorer, developing countries of the Third World. I was also worried about logistical support for the new contingents before UNEF's own logistics troops had arrived and were operational. Therefore I cabled New York on 4 November:

> . . . at present, except for some locally provided transport and tentage, all units of the Force are living on the resources carried in with them and will therefore face critical problems when these are exhausted. Especially in view of difficulties relating to local procurement, a large proportion of UNEF's needs will have to be provided from outside for some time to come. This particularly applies to transport and communications equipment, repair facilities of all kinds, tentage and furniture. The Force Commander has therefore recommended that when the four contingents now composing the Force [the Austrian, Finnish, Irish and Swedish] have been brought up to full strength, the arrival of new contingents should be closely co-ordinated with the provision of logistical support.

My cable had no effect. The Secretariat now considered it more important that the participating countries should not be irritated with requests to postpone their arrival. They could become downright annoyed. How UNEF would take care of these problems seemed not to worry anybody. Anyway, UNEF had always solved its problems before.

So it happened that the battalions of Panama and Peru arrived in late November and early December. They were not needed then, and neither was the Indonesian battalion which arrived at the end of December. These three battalions would only have a meaningful role when disengagement had been completed and UNEF had moved to its own buffer-zone in Sinai.

In many cables that I had sent to New York I had stressed that the battalions arriving straight from the participating countries should be properly organized and equipped. They should bring with them food for at least 30 days, enough vehicles and radio equipment. They should be logistically as self-sufficient as possible and therefore able, for instance, to carry out basic maintenance and repair work on their own vehicles, to nurse the sick in their own small hospitals and to survive winter conditions in the desert with adequate tentage and clothing. We could soon see that nobody had had time, or perhaps they had been unable, to pass these instructions to the representatives of the participating countries in New York. The miserable vehicle situation of the Irish has already been described. In addition, the transport and communications equipment of Ghana and Senegal were very defective; the Peruvians arrived without field cots, tentage, warm clothing or blankets; the Nepalese had no vehicles, radios or other equipment. Only the Panamanians were well-equipped, arriving with field cots, food rations, refrigerators and so on.

In summary I can conclude that the establishment of UNEF was poorly planned and its implementation was left to chance. The Secretary-General's report of 26 October had solemnly stressed Hammarskjöld's third principle, according to which UNEF should be "an integrated and efficient military unit". New York did not exert every effort to fulfil this objective. We in UNEF tried our best to correct the situation.

Arrival and deployment of the logistics units

We had heard rumours that the diplomats had had disputes in New York about the arrangement of UNEF's logistical and other support. Originally the intention had been that Canada alone would take care of everything; but on 30 October it was decided, following a demand from the Soviet Union, that the logistics tasks would be divided on an equal basis between Canada and Poland. The Canadians were not at all pleased with this decision and became difficult in the negotiations under the chairmanship of Brian Urquhart. The Poles were easier because they had a strong wish to participate for the first time in UN peace-keeping. So much was achieved, however, that the reconnaissance parties of both countries arrived in Cairo on 7 November. In mid-November, as a temporary decision, it was agreed that Canada would send a signals company and Poland an engineer company, but it was only on 23 November that the final decision on the division of responsibilities was made. Canada would send a service unit, consisting of a supply company, a maintenance company for Western-type vehicles, a movement control unit and a postal detachment. In addition they would send an aviation unit. Poland would send a road transport unit including a maintenance element for Eastern-type vehicles, a water purification unit and a field hospital.

The negotiations in New York over the division of responsibilities had lasted 17 days. Such a delay is difficult to understand when one considers that while these were going on the soldiers of UNEF were operating in harsh conditions and living merely on the resources carried in with them.

After all this I was naturally worried about how the co-operation between the Canadians and Poles would work out in the field. Fortunately, my suspicions proved to be groundless. From the very beginning the soldiers seemed to find a way of establishing a good working relationship. The chief of the Canadian reconnaissance team, General Nicholson, who commanded the Canadian contingent for a short time in the beginning, was a civilized and fine gentleman who probably never quarrelled with anybody. His successor was General D.E. Holmes, a cheerfully free and easy and extrovert officer who just had returned from Warsaw where he had spent three years as a military attaché. He was able to create good relations with the Commander of the Polish contingent, Colonel Piotr Jarosz, and the co-operation between the contingents of these two countries was better than I had been led to expect.

The first part of the Canadian contingent began to arrive in Cairo on 12 November. Half had arrived before the end of the month and the rest, about 600 men, on 10 January 1974. The Canadian supply company was operational in mid-December. The first part of the Polish contingent arrived on 23 November and the rest on 10 January 1974.

The new troops were guided from the airport to Shams Camp, where a Canadian-Polish tented city was soon erected. There was very little storage space in the spectator stand of the race course, but still less equipment to be stored in the early days.

I myself knew both the Canadians and the Poles very well in advance. I greatly respected my first UN Commander, Major-General E.L.M. Burns, the Commander of UNEF I. In Cyprus in 1964–5 I had served under another prominent Canadian officer, Brigadier-General Norman Wilson-Smith, and during the years had become friendly with a large group of Canadians.

Again, the arrival of the Poles brought back pleasant memories from my own time as military attaché in Warsaw in the years 1959–62. When I now told the Polish officers that half of my heart had been left in their home country, I hardly exaggerated. During my time in Warsaw I had diligently studied Polish and then thought that I would scarcely need it later. Now it proved to be a useful knowledge, because the English of most of the Polish officers was non-existent. Just as we Finns appreciate the efforts of foreigners who study our language, the Poles too were very happy to hear their Commander make a speech in Polish at a parade.

The arrival of the logistics troops was naturally a great relief for us all, although it did not automatically remove all the reasons for worry. Now the weaknesses of the UN administrative system appeared more clearly than before. In normal circumstances the main task of the UN administration was to take care of the established needs of the New York Headquarters and the specialized agencies. This stiff and bureaucratic system could not easily be adapted to meet the urgent and unexpected needs of a military emergency force. The administrative rules and regulations were very inflexible. The methods were fully centralized and they gave little authority to the Force operating in the field. The procurement of materiel was made on the basis of worldwide bidding and only in an exceptional case could authority be given to the Force for the local procurement of anything other than fresh food. The complicated and time-consuming rules and a lead time of six to eight months led to the urgently needed materiel arriving very slowly at the area of operation. As a result of this we had very little in the way of goods to be distributed, although the stores and the distributing units were ready. Similarly, vehicles could not be repaired because of the lack of spare parts, even though the workshops were otherwise operational.

The continuing shortage of equipment in the first months forced the administrative chiefs and quartermasters of UNEF to improvise, using all kinds of means. Necessity obliged us to carry out local procurement even though regulations did not allow it. Not much was available in Egypt, but fortunately the more developed economies of Israel and Lebanon offered assistance. It took time, however, before our logistics system was operating in a satisfactory manner and it was only at the end of the first six months that we had recovered from the worst logistical difficulties.

A happy Independence Day in Cairo

Finnish Independence Day in Cairo in 1973 remains in my memory as a feast day. I was promoted to the rank of lieutenant-general, which was both a happy event and a surprise. It showed that the Finnish authorities had recognized my work in the Middle East.

In Cairo the festivities had already begun on 5 December, i.e. the eve of Independence Day. The delegation of the Polish contingent came carrying a huge flower-basket, and in the morning I was present at a reception given by our Finnish Military Police Chief for his Canadian, Polish and Swedish military police colleagues. Then began a party organized by the Finnish military observers for the Finnish colony in Cairo, attended by the Ambassador and Mrs Malinen and the embassy staff.

On the morning of the 6th I was on my way to the Finnish battalion and Suez. But first there was a parade, which included a religious service, my own speech celebrating the occasion and a march-past, with the Israeli and Egyptian armies looking on in astonishment. The whole ceremony was extremely touching and I doubt if anyone who was there will forget it. Then followed a festive lunch, beautifully arranged outdoors, for about 50 people including representatives of the officers, NCOs and other ranks.

In the evening it was the turn of a reception hosted by the Finnish Ambassador. Besides the Nordic Ambassadors, the only foreigners present this time were those from the higher echelon of UNEF military and civilian staff. There were many Finns, however: the military observers and their wives, 40 people from the battalion and other members of the Finnish colony.

During the party Colonel Raitasaari came to me and asked me to take a look at the draft of a cable he intended to send to the Defence Ministry in Helsinki. It was a list of the most important materiel which the battalion urgently needed. I read the paper and noticed that it was written in the straightforward style so characteristic of Raitasaari. I said that the list was good in my opinion, but he could leave out a few curses.

Life returned to normal the following day, and according to my diary the programme was as follows:

08.00 Yugoslav correspondent.
08.25 Hearst Press.
08.50 Polish correspondent.
09.30 The UN television team.
12.00 Meeting with General Gamassy.
The afternoon in Ismailia. Visit to the Swedes and to the new base of the Poles.
20.30 Dinner given by the Swiss Ambassador.

17. The Six-Point Agreement

Kissinger's first shuttle

Thanks to UNEF's quick, determined and successful action, feelings became calmer, the sombre atmosphere lightened and new hopes gained ground. Thus the negotiations could gradually begin.

While UNEF continued to do its best to further peace and maintain the fragile cease-fire, new activity began on a higher level in November. Henry Kissinger arrived in the Middle East for his first shuttle between Israel and several Arab countries. The aim of the trip was to promote the ideas presented in Resolution 340 and more permanent peace arrangements.

Kissinger had dealt with the most urgent problems of the day in Washington in late October and early November during the visits of Egypt's Acting Foreign Minister, Ismail Fahmy, and Israeli Prime Minister Golda Meir. The Egyptians' main worry was the transport supplies to their encircled 3rd Army and the transfer of the control of the Cairo-Suez road to the UN. In their view, retaining control of the latter was important as a symbol of Egyptian sovereignty. It was easier to swallow a temporary transfer of the road to the control of the UN than to accept a lengthy occupation by Israel.

Mrs Meir was not enthusiastic at all and agreed only grudgingly to Kissinger's proposals. Israel was the victor, she said, and in her view one could not trust the Egyptians in any case. Only after strong persuasion did Israel agree as a temporary measure to allow one supply convoy through to the 3rd Army under the auspices of the Red Cross and the UN. Mrs Meir never ceased to be worried about the fate of the prisoners of war. She also demanded that Egypt should open the Strait of Bab el Mandeb for navigation.

Kissinger's first talks with Sadat in Cairo and his aides' negotiations in Jerusalem led to the conclusion of the first agreement, the so-called Six-Point Agreement between Egypt and Israel. In the field we had no idea that an agreement was so close. But at the end of October 1973 we took part in arranging the first meetings between Israeli and Egyptian soldiers.

First encounters between Israeli and Egyptian soldiers

Kissinger had agreed with the parties that details of the supply convoys
to the 3rd Army would be agreed by Israeli and Egyptian soldiers
on the spot. The talks would be held near the city of Suez at Kilometre 119. Nobody had remembered, however, to tell UNEF about
the matter. It then happened that when I was returning from Suez
from my meeting with General Gazit on October 27, in the dusk
of the late afternoon, I met General Gamassy and his party on the
road. He asked me whether he was expected in Suez and if I knew
anything about the negotiations he was to hold with the Israelis. I
answered that I had not heard anything and that General Gazit had not
mentioned a meeting, either. Thus General Gamassy returned to Cairo
empty-handed.

The matter remained obscure for a long time and the Egyptians were
apparently accused of never having arrived at the first meeting, contrary
to the agreement. Much later, during his trip to Finland in 1981,
Kissinger asked me what I knew of the matter. It became clear that
there had been a breakdown in communication and therefore I had not
been able to give the right counsel to General Gamassy.

Meanwhile, on the following day, Saturday October 28, there
was a new attempt. This time I had given clear instructions to the
Commander of the Finnish battalion, Lieutenant-Colonel Aulis
Kemppainen. He was to be present at the meeting as a representative
of the UN without participating in the talks. From my own staff I
sent the Irish Captain Joseph Fallon to act as a guide to General
Gamassy. He was to attend the meeting and report to me what had been
said. This was the start of Captain Fallon's career as my trusted and
skilful military aide.

At the first meeting between General Gamassy and the Israeli General
Aharon Yariv, agreement was reached about the details of the supply
convoy to the 3rd Army. It was agreed that the Egyptians would not
drive the trucks in Israeli-occupied territory; instead they would be
replaced by UNEF soldiers who would drive the supplies to the western
bank of the Canal. There the Israelis would inspect the loads of food,
medical supplies and water. Then Egyptian soldiers would load the
supplies on ferries and transport them to the 3rd Army on the eastern
bank of the Canal. Both the Red Cross and the UN would be present
at the loading point. Yariv agreed to 125 truckloads of supplies. In later
negotiations held in Washington the number of trucks was increased

by 50 and, provided that the transport went well, by yet another 50.

UNEF Headquarters named these supply transports Operation Kilo. The loading point was situated at the former UNTSO Observation Post Kilo, north of Suez and near El Kubrit. My headquarters also gave an order to the Austrian, Finnish and Swedish battalions to provide a total of 75 drivers for the operation. The Egyptian trucks arrived at Kilometre 101, the Israeli outpost, by 9 a.m. The first ten vehicles, which all were water-tankers, driven by UNEF soldiers, moved to the loading point under the command of Captain Fallon. It all started slowly because the Israelis were very suspicious and inspected the loads extremely thoroughly. But little by little the pace quickened and during the first two weeks 168 truckloads were moved.

The talks between General Gamassy and General Yariv continued, with UN representatives as witnesses. There were four meetings altogether and the UN was represented by the Commander of the Austrian battalion and Captain Fallon. On the agenda were many military and political questions which later were discussed in more detail in the tent at Kilometre 101. According to Captain Fallon's notes, General Yariv emphasised the importance of an effective cease-fire based on the functioning of UNEF; an undelayed exchange of prisoners of war; free navigation in the Suez Canal and the Strait of Bab el Mandeb; the establishment of communications between local commanders; the rapid definition of cease-fire lines; the setting up of a 10 km.-wide buffer-zone between the fighting parties, and a ban on the fortification of first-line positions.

General Gamassy, for his part, highlighted the fact that the cease-fire obtained from 27 October; that UNEF should interpose itself between the parties; that the 3rd Army should freely receive supplies, and that this should be extended to the city of Suez. He thought that the supply arrangements should become permanent and also demanded that Israel withdraw to the cease-fire lines of 22 October. General Gamassy was not sure about the idea of a buffer-zone but wanted instead to discuss Resolution 338, i.e. the withdrawal of Israel to the 1967 borders.

None of these proposals made any progress in the first negotiations, but the seeds of many new ideas were sown. As a gesture of good-will the Egyptians agreed to repeated Israeli requests and released Lieutenant Avidan, who had been imprisoned for years and was badly wounded.

The author and James Jonah leave UNEF HQ for a meeting at Km. 101 on the Suez-Cairo road.

Beginning of the talks at Kilometre 101

The Egyptian Minister of War had asked me to come to see him on 10 November. The matter was urgent. Thanks to the shuttle diplomacy of Dr Kissinger, Egypt and Israel had reached their first agreement, the Six-Point Agreement. The Minister of War showed me the text according to which:

A. The cease-fire must be scrupulously observed.
B. Discussions would begin on the return to the 22 October positions

within the framework of the disengagement of forces under the auspices of the United Nations.

C. The town of Suez would receive supplies.

D. The 3rd Army would have a free flow of non-military supplies.

E. The UN was to establish two checkpoints along the Cairo-Suez road in order to replace the existing Israeli checkpoints.

F. After that the prisoners of war would be exchanged.

The Minister of War also told me that according to the agreement the military delegations of the parties would sign the document the following day, on 11 November 1973. The signing would take place in the Sinai desert, at Kilometre 101 on the Cairo-Suez road. The outposts of the Israeli forces west of the Canal extended to that point. After the signing, negotiations on the implementation of the agreement would begin.

The parties had asked me to act as a witness at the signing ceremony and to chair the meeting thereafter. It was surprising that I should be given the role of chairman and at first my position was somewhat unclear. The negotiations were to take place "under the auspices of Commander UNEF".

Israel had always emphasised the necessity of face-to-face negotiations. They thought that negotiations should not be carried out under the auspices of any third party. No outsider was needed to take part in – to say nothing of chairing – the negotiations. The Egyptians, however, had a totally opposite view of the matter. What was it that caused the Israelis to accept my presence and my *de facto* chairmanship of the meetings at Kilometre 101? Perhaps this pragmatic solution was adopted because no results had been achieved at the recent meetings between Gamassy and Yariv.

As the representative of the UN, I was also responsible for the practical arrangements of the meetings. The Finnish battalion, commanded by Colonel Reino Raitasaari, had done an excellent job. Three British-issue military tents had been erected at Kilometre 101. In the middle was the meeting tent with an U-shaped table covered with grey military blankets. On each side were the tents of the delegations, to which they could withdraw for consultations. The Finns were also prepared to cater for the negotiators if need arose. An international military police unit, to which all UNEF battalions had sent representatives, had been established to keep order. This was more than necessary because the event attracted more than 400 representatives of the media.

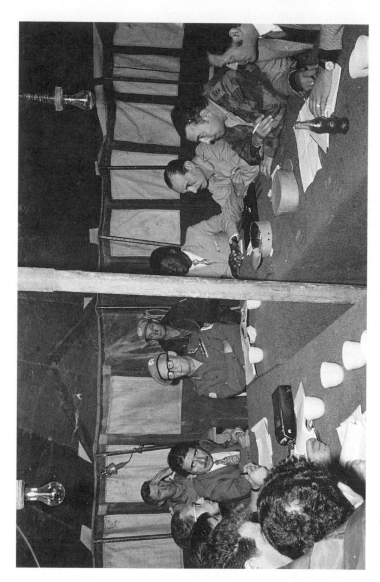

Signing of the six-point accord, 11 Nov. 1973. *From left*: Gen. Yariv, Rémy Gorgé, the author, James Jonah, Gen. Gamassy, Col. Howeidi, Fawzy El-Ibrasi.

The head of the Egyptian delegation was General Abdel Ghani El Gamassy, Chief of Operations of the October War. He soon became Chief of Staff and later Minister of War. The Israeli delegation was led by General Aharon Yariv, former Head of Intelligence and a sharp-witted theoretician. Despite their differences in character and background, they both were first-class officers.

In the UN team I was assisted by James Jonah, Rémy Gorgé and Captain Joseph Fallon. Occasionally Ramon Prieto was with us too.

The new job as Chairman of the negotiations worried me a bit. For the first time in the history of UN peace-keeping, the Force Commander had been given this extremely responsible and time-consuming assignment in addition to his many other duties. Personally I had no previous experience of international negotiations and nobody could clearly define my new job. Should I be simply a silent witness and let the parties sort out their problems among themselves? I soon realized, however, that the Chairman must assume a more active role. During the discussion it was my duty to ensure that the parties understood each other, because language difficulties and different styles of presentation hampered mutual understanding.

There was nothing wrong with Gamassy's English. In fact it was very good. But Yariv's knowledge was superior. He spoke like a professor *ex cathedra*. I often noticed that his presentation exceeded the comprehension of the others. I was then obliged to interrupt and to say, "General Yariv, now I did not quite understand. Please, can you present your case in a simpler way or illustrate it with examples."

I tried not to interfere with the discussion as long as it went well. Only when it had reached an impasse did I adjourn the meeting and hold separate talks with the parties to clarify the questions and to find out what concessions they were prepared to make. Then I presented a compromise proposal, which was usually accepted because it came from the UN. The same proposal would have been rejected had it been made by either of the parties. Thus I had become a *de facto* mediator between the parties, although I had not been officially appointed to the job.

At the beginning the atmosphere in the meetings was icy. The parties did not address each other directly but only through the Chairman. For the Egyptians it was out of the question to sit down at the same luncheon table with the "enemy". But they accepted my compromise proposal that coffee and sandwiches would be served during the meeting at the actual conference table. The excellent coffee and the delicious sandwiches prepared by the Finnish battalion seemed to taste good to all the participants. I think that food was an important factor in the success of the negotiations. Hungry participants are angry participants.

Fortunately the atmosphere improved quite soon. Human factors began to have an effect. In the cramped conditions of the tent it was difficult to remain formal for very long. Furthermore it happened that for some strange reason the heads of the delegations began to like each other and their mutual respect grew stronger every day. It was obvious that the parties had succeeded in selecting the most suitable principal negotiators, a fact that was very important for the success of the meetings.

The Egyptians were horrified by the thought that photographs would appear in the newspapers of the Arab world, depicting senior Egyptians greeting "enemy" officers. This was surely what lay behind the following story.

General Gamassy and an aide were on their way from Cairo to the first meeting at Kilometre 101. The General was apparently very nervous. Finally the ADC had the courage to enquire what was the matter. "Who is going to enter first and to greet first?" was the reason for the General's worry. When they arrived at the meeting-place, I was outside the tent to receive the guests. Gamassy then presented his important questions to me. According to the story I replied, "The representatives of the UN are already inside the tent. The delegates of the parties will be led to the tent in alphabetic order, first the Egyptians and then the Israelis. When everybody is seated I shall get up and say: 'Good morning, gentlemen!' and all will reply: 'Good morning, General!'" I was pleased to note that Gamassy looked quite relieved.

As the meetings continued, photographs could not be avoided. There were hundreds of journalists and representatives of radio and television networks thronging the area. The pictures which Gamassy had been so afraid of were published in due course and caused bad feelings in the Arab world. I had sent a number of the photographs to the heads of the delegations as a memento of the historic encounter. When I met Gamassy the next time in his office at the War Ministry I asked whether the pictures had arrived. "They are in the safe behind seven locks," was Gamassy's somewhat sombre reply.

The signing ceremony was over in ten minutes. After a short intermission the meeting started to discuss the points of the agreement and their implementation. It became clear that Israel in any case did not intend to return to the positions of 22 October as was stipulated in Paragraph B. This was sad news to the Egyptians, but they could hope that this whole issue would become irrelevant as soon as the Israelis would agree to begin their withdrawal. No wonder that there was no success on the other points either.

The second meeting started on the following day, 12 November, at noon. Before the meeting I decided to go to greet the delegations, which had already arrived. In the Israeli tent I asked General Yariv what news there was from Jerusalem. He answered rather rudely, "Listen, General Siilasvuo, I did not come here to negotiate with you. When we now for the first time in the history of Israel meet the Egyptians face to face, it is my intention to negotiate only with them."

When I pointed out that paragraph E of the agreement dealt with the task of UNEF, Yariv replied that he was naturally prepared to discuss that matter with me. I could not understand Yariv's behaviour except as some kind of protest against my presence. Perhaps he did not accept my way of chairing the meeting either. Had I been too active and would it be better to stand aside while the parties negotiated?

In the Egyptian tent my reception was cordial. Gamassy handed me a list of the Israeli prisoners of war held by Egypt and told me that I could hand it over to Yariv at a moment I considered propitious. I knew that the list was hot stuff. Public opinion in Israel had for some time vociferously demanded information about the fate of the imprisoned soldiers.

The meeting started and as the first item we dealt with paragraph F, or the exchange of the prisoners, which in Israel's view was the most important matter and held the highest priority. It was a difficult and for the Egyptians also a delicate matter. In no circumstances did they want their more than 8,000 prisoners of war to be returned by road through the military lines. This would psychologically have a bad effect on the front-line troops and the whole Egyptian people. The Egyptians wanted their prisoners of war flown to a different airfield in the rear.

Israel had no other demands apart from an immediate return of their 240 prisoners of war. The matter was discussed in great length but with no results. The main reason probably was that I had not been able to explain clearly enough to the Israelis what the Egyptians really wanted. What the Egyptians had in mind was a package deal. They were particularly interested in paragraphs C, D and E of the agreement, covering the supply transports to the town of Suez and the 3rd Army and the transfer of the Cairo-Suez road to the control of the UN. In return for these three points they were prepared to arrange the exchange of prisoners mentioned in paragraph F.

Manning of the UN checkpoint at Km. 101, 11 Nov. 1973.

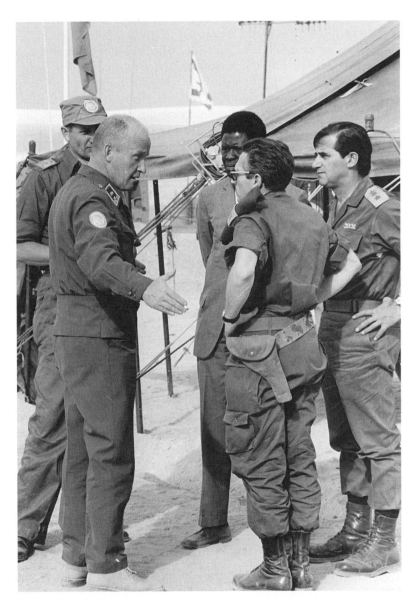

Separate meetings with the parties were held outside the tent. Here the author discusses a point with Gen. Yariv on 14 Nov. 1973. *Also present*: Col. Raitasaari, James Jonah and Col. Dov Sion.

As the second meeting was coming to such an unsatisfactory end I decided to speed up matters. According to paragraph F the exchange of prisoners of war could take place only when the UN had established checkpoints on the Cairo-Suez road in the area occupied by Israel. Henry Kissinger had agreed upon this with Golda Meir and Anwar Sadat and the matter was clearly expressed in the agreement. I decided that there would be two checkpoints: one at Kilometre 101 near the meeting-site and the other at Kilometre 119 closer to the city of Suez. I supposed that they would only have a symbolic significance, because the militarily superior Israel would in fact continue to control the road. But symbols are important in peace-keeping. Experience had often taught me this. I also thought that UNEF had the right to set up these checkpoints and that I did not need to ask permission from anybody.

I had given the Commander of the Finnish battalion an order and necessary instructions in good time, so that he was able to make the preparations before the end of the meeting. I announced to the meeting that the checkpoints would be set up the very same day. General Yariv pointed out that this could lead to difficulties and that Israel would in no case withdraw from its checkpoints.

As we stepped out of the tent we faced a tableau presented by Colonel Raitasaari. Oil barrels, with UN markings and painted blue and white, were lined across the road. On the roadside opposite the Israelis a UN checkpoint had been set up. After a short military ceremony the first guards took up their places manning the checkpoint. At least the meeting which had started so badly had an impressive end. The list of the Israeli prisoners of war was still in my pocket. The negotiations had been fruitless and I did not see any reason to give it to the Israelis. At the end of the day I sent a detailed report of the meeting to the Secretary-General. Apparently the Permanent Representative of Israel was also informed about the list of the prisoners of war.

Incident at Checkpoint Gamma

The setting up of the second checkpoint started later in the afternoon when Colonel Raitasaari had returned to his headquarters in Suez. According to my instructions this checkpoint was named Gamma and was set up at the crossroads at Kilometre 119 about 6 km. from Suez in the direction of Cairo. On the other side of the road there was already an Israeli checkpoint.

The checkpoint had to be set up in a hurry because night falls early in the Sinai desert in November. However, at about 5 p.m. everything was ready, a lieutenant with his half-platoon in position, the tent ready and the UN flag erected. A war of words between the Israelis and the Finns had started as soon as a hole for the flagpole had been dug in the roadside. For the Finns the hostility of the Israelis was something new because until then relations had been good. It came as a surprise, as everything was supposed to have been in order.

Not more than half an hour had passed when Raitasaari received a message that about 100 Israeli soldiers had invaded Gamma, removed the flag, lifted the tent on the Finnish truck and presented an ultimatum: either the Finns withdrew immediately or they would be detained. The situation was difficult because the Israelis had several armed personnel carriers and bulldozers. However, my order was clear. There was no alternative but to try to keep Gamma in one way or another.

Raitasaari immediately went to the site of the incident. He observed the situation, placed the guard again at the checkpoint and restored the UN flag. Thereafter he returned to his headquarters, which was some 5 km. away. It was clear that more men were needed, so he quickly assembled all available men from his headquarters: cooks, clerks, signalmen and others. The enthusiasm was so great that even patients in the hospital lined up to join. Ninety men were gathered in this way. It was already dark and in order to avoid mishaps Raitasaari wisely enough decided to leave weapons in the barracks. Closer to his objective, he drew up his men in the form of an ancient Greek phalanx, all in close array, the Commander and officers in the first rows and other ranks after them. The phalanx rapidly approached Gamma.

The Israelis were flabbergasted. What could be done to an unarmed group of Finnish soldiers approaching in a determinedly threatening manner? With the sheer strength of its numbers, Raitasaari's phalanx broke through the thin line of the Israelis. Both sides had to resort to fists. Here and there one could hear Israeli rifle butts being wielded. The bulldozers appeared next. Raitasaari ordered his men to sit down on the road in front of the bulldozers. Gradually the machines were withdrawn and the situation calmed down a little.

In the meantime I had sent a protest to the Israeli military authorities, while the Secretary-General had demanded through the Israeli Permanent Representative that the Israelis withdraw and the UN checkpoints be allowed to function. Early in the morning, at about 4 o'clock, I went myself to the site of the incident to find out what was going on. There was clearly a good deal of tension; the Israelis and the Finns eyed each other angrily. The Israeli Brigade Commander, however, came to have a few words with me. Somebody brought coffee and gradually the atmosphere became more relaxed. Suddenly I received an urgent message from Tel Aviv. The Israeli Defence Minister, Moshe Dayan, wanted to see me immediately.

I had to return quickly to Cairo and from there, together with James Jonah, take a UN flight to Tel Aviv. Dayan was furious and the beginning of our meeting was extremely unpleasant. I had never before seen him lose his temper so badly. "It is unheard of for you to begin to operate in areas which are under my control!" he shouted.

I tried to answer that the establishment of the checkpoints was an independent task given to me by the agreement and that the exchange of the prisoners of war could not be carried out before the setting up of the checkpoints.

"Firstly you have misinterpreted the agreement," Dayan said. "You shall not force your way into my areas, it will not work." Then he added, "If you want to operate in my areas, you must co-ordinate the matter beforehand."

When I replied that I had co-ordinated this matter with General Yariv, he exploded once again and shouted, "Yariv is nothing, Yariv is nothing. If you wish to co-ordinate, you co-ordinate with me!"

Gradually Dayan's wrath quieted down and the tone of the conversation became more normal. At first, I had been completely bewildered and remained silent, letting the Defence Minister shout. Now I politely and gently put forward my opinion that the checkpoints which had been set up should remain intact. I was prepared to co-ordinate the movements of UNEF troops with the Israeli liaison officers when routine action was in question. But I added that the establishment of the checkpoints was an extraordinary duty which I had to carry out. However, we could not reach an understanding, as neither of us would move from our positions.

When I left Dayan's office I was accompanied by our Chief Liaison Officer, General Avnon, and Ambassador Mordechai Kidron, a senior and respected official of the Foreign Ministry whom I knew very well. I said to General Avnon, "I am very much for co-ordination but not if it means asking for permission." Ambassador Kidron for his part said to me that he thought he knew me and that I was the last person who could have played such a trick. I answered that in that case he couldn't know me very well.

Many stories about the stormy encounter with Dayan circulated afterwards. James Jonah said that in New York an Israeli diplomat had asserted that he had interrupted Defence Minister Moshe Dayan in mid-sentence. "This is not true," Jonah had answered, "but he did interrupt me. And he is not my Defence Minister or the Defence Minister of the whole world."

Later in the afternoon I called Secretary-General Waldheim from Jerusalem. He agreed that it was unnecessary to subject the relationship between Israel and UNEF to further strain and continue waging a private war against Israel. There was also the risk of casualties. UNEF had shown determination and made its intentions perfectly clear. Now it was time to progress in the negotiations and reach an agreement in this matter too. I proposed that the Finnish battalion should temporarily close down the checkpoint and be ready to reopen it as soon as Israel had had second thoughts.

At New York Headquarters the matter apparently had been re-evaluated because later that same night I received an order that Checkpoint Gamma could now be closed but should be reopened again in the morning. Colonel Raitasaari acted accordingly. Fortunately, the whole question was solved by itself in the negotiations the next day.

I was criticized by some people for being too soft in this question of Gamma. My own experience showed many times, however, that a certain flexibility is necessary in the relations between the UN and the parties. One must show determination, but there must be a realistic limit to it, for hitting your head against a wall only makes matters worse. Instead of resorting to force one should use diplomatic means in peace-keeping. An agreement with the parties must be achieved through negotiation.

I have described the fisticuffs at Checkpoint Gamma rather extensively. It may seem in retrospect a trivial incident. But in fact it had a great effect on the attitudes of the parties and the status of UNEF. The Egyptians were delighted: finally somebody had had the guts to oppose the militarily mighty Israel. Perhaps the Israelis, too, in their innermost thoughts had to admit that there was something in this UNEF. Altogether, the parties' respect for UNEF and their confidence in UNEF's ability to carry out its duties increased considerably. This was important because no UN force can succeed without the respect and confidence of the parties. Although I have always emphasised the priority of diplomatic means, the incident at Checkpoint Gamma also taught us another lesson: if a UN force never strikes back it cannot gain the respect of the parties.

I saw clear signs of the changing attitudes of the Egyptian authorities at the decisive meeting of 14 November. Whatever knotty detail which the Egyptians had been unable to accept at previous meetings, could now be solved in one sentence from the head of the delegation, General Gamassy: "UNEF may take care of this," or "General Siilasvuo may decide this."

The third meeting

After a stormy intermission the third meeting in the now-familiar tent at Kilometre 101 was able to start on 14 November at 10 o'clock.

Before the meeting began, I came upon a thoroughly indignant Colonel Raitasaari. He said that he had come straight from Checkpoint Gamma, where Israeli soldiers were again harassing his men and violently opposing the re-establishment of the checkpoint. They had even pulled the UN flag from his hands. All this had happened despite the presence of the Israeli Liaison Officers, General Avnon and Lieutenant-Colonel Avivi. They had explained that the Finns were supposed to leave the area.

I completely lost my temper (perhaps following Dayan's example the day before) and an Israeli captain who happened to be close by got a scare when I shouted, "I shall get this man Avnon!" I did not know that Avnon had already arrived and was just coming out of the Israeli tent. I shouted to him, "Why the hell do you harass my people?"

"Please calm down, General, don't you remember that Dayan told you yesterday afternoon that Checkpoint 119 must be emptied?" he said.

I answered, "Don't you remember that I told Dayan that Checkpoint 119 will remain on its site?"

Other matters were also discussed and Avnon promised to check with Tel Aviv. Finally, I said to Colonel Raitasaari in Avnon's presence, "You take care that the Finns·stay where they are!"

"Yes, Sir!" was Raitasaari's answer.

The brush with Avnon relieved the stress a little and then I went to greet the delegations.

In the Israeli tent General Yariv enquired in a very friendly manner whether the list of the prisoners of war had already been in my possession the day before and why I had not handed it over to him. When I explained the matter he said that the meagre results of the previous meeting were probably his fault. He had not realized that the Egyptians had some kind of a package deal in mind.

"Please help us now in today's negotiations," was his appeal. He had quite obviously received new instructions.

"By all means. That is why I am here," I answered.

Yariv added that Prime Minister Golda Meir had given him an unprecedented earful on the previous day.

The meeting started and General Yariv asked permission to take the floor as the first speaker. I could see from the faces of the Egyptians that they could hardly believe their ears when Yariv started to speak: "I am probably the person who yesterday torpedoed our previous meeting. I apologize for that. Let's try now to join our efforts to solve the problem of the exchange of the prisoners of war."

And so it happened. The atmosphere was bright and nobody even mentioned the incident at Checkpoint Gamma. In this spirit of agreement the details for exchanging the prisoners were agreed upon. Representatives of the International Red Cross undertook to take care of the airlift. Now the only thing missing was the long-awaited list of prisoners of war. Finally both Yariv and Gamassy came to thank the UN team. They thought that an agreement would have taken much longer to reach without our assistance.

The successful arrangement of the issue of the prisoners of war paved the way for a smoother dealing with the other points in the agreement. The supply transports to the 3rd Army continued as agreed. Now a new supply system for the town of Suez had to be arranged. About 100 drivers were needed for that purpose. An unloading point for foodstuffs, guarded by UNEF, had to be arranged near the railway station in Suez, where the Israelis could inspect the incoming goods. After the departure of the UN convoy, Egyptian civilian workers and trucks would arrive at the unloading site and carry out the reloading and the distribution of the goods.

Discussions about a suitable site for the unloading point lasted some time. It was difficult to find a place that would satisfy the Egyptians, who resented the pedantic attitude, suspicion and desire to humiliate which the Israelis showed during the discussions. Finally the participants went outside the tent to examine in daylight the aerial picture which the Israelis had brought with them. A suitable place was selected but one could see how difficult it was for General Gamassy to force himself to look at a picture of an Egyptian town taken by the Israelis.

On November 15 at 8 a.m. the matters agreed at the previous day's meeting were implemented. Checkpoint Gamma was functioning again and the first convoys left for the city of Suez and the 3rd Army. The first exchanges of prisoners of war were carried out. In seven days the International Red Cross transported 8,301 Egyptian and 241 Israeli prisoners of war.

The message of thanks from the Secretary-General warmed our hearts:

To: UNEF Cairo for Siilasvuo
Date: 14 November 1973
Number: 327

I extend to you and your staff my warmest congratulations on the agreement which was reached today. I am sure you will continue to display your skill and ingenuity and to use your good offices in making today's agreement into an effective reality.

Please also express to the Finnish contingent my warmest appreciation of their courageous and admirable conduct in very difficult circumstances at Kilometre 119.

Secretary-General

Negotiations at Kilometre 101 continue

As the last four of the six points of the agreement had been settled and the cease-fire mentioned in the first point seemed to be holding, it was time to consider seriously the difficult question of disengagement, or the withdrawal of the Israeli Army to the eastern side of the Suez Canal. This question was first discussed at two meetings between Yariv and Gamassy where I was not present. These were followed by four official meetings on 22, 23, 24 and 26 November.

"Disengagement and separation of forces" was a novel term which Kissinger had utilized as part of his "constructive ambiguity" in order to cover the real nature of the matter, i.e. that the disengagement meant in reality the withdrawal of the Israeli forces. This kind of obscurity sounds Byzantine but perhaps it was justified in an area which in ancient times was a part of the Byzantine Empire.

The Egyptians imagined that they would recover the whole of Sinai in one fell swoop. As this was not possible, they would have been happy

Meetings continue at Km. 101. The author briefing the press after the meeting on 22 Nov. 1973.

Transporting supplies in Dec. 1973 to the encircled Egyptian 3rd Army north of the city of Suez. On the opposite bank, a cleft made by Egyptian engineers using high-pressure water pumps.

with half of Sinai, i.e. with Israel's withdrawal to the El Arish–
Ras Muhammad Line on the Mediterranean at the southern tip of the
peninsula. When even this proved to be impractical, the goal was set
at the strategically important Giddi and Mitla Passes.

Israel for her part proposed at the beginning that both parties should
withdraw from the areas they had occupied during the war and that UN
forces should take over these areas. In other words, the Egyptians
should withdraw to the western bank of the Canal and they themselves
would move as little as possible. They would leave Africa but the
withdrawal to the eastern bank of the Canal would be so limited that
the Canal zone would still remain in their control and could be reached
by their artillery. It would more or less mean a return to the pre-war
situation. It goes without saying that the Egyptians rejected this proposal once and for all.

As the negotiations progressed the Israelis brought forward new
ideas. On November 22 General Yariv explained that Israel would
withdraw from the eastern bank of the Canal if the Egyptian troops
were thinned out on the western bank. He also proposed UN buffer-
zones between the armies. Areas of limited troops and armaments on
both sides of the UN buffer-zone were also discussed. The verification
of the limitations was planned. This task was to go to UN military
observers, who at regular intervals would confirm that there were no
additional troops or armaments.

As meetings continued, a more realistic approach could be adopted.
However, as Chairman I was not happy with the dominant mood of
the meetings. The rigid and icy atmosphere of the first days had changed
to one of a more normal communication. But each party's attitude
towards the other was still characterized by deep suspicion and hostility.
The development of the relations between two former enemies into a
state of friendship and mutual confidence did not progress as quickly as
I had hoped.

I had noticed particularly that the attitudes of the Israelis in the
current negotiations had been unrelenting and that their military conditions were always extremely rigid. I often thought that a more flexible
approach would have been wiser and more far-sighted in regard to
future neighbourly relations. But few victors have distinguished themselves with generosity and magnanimity. "*Vae victis!*" as the Romans
said.

The Egyptians had great difficulties in accepting the Israeli demand
that they should not be allowed to group their forces freely on the

eastern bank of the Canal. This was sovereign Egyptian territory. The Israelis for their part thought that they had every right to take every measure to guard their security. Once General Gamassy asked, "General Yariv, why are you so suspicious? Do you really think that I would send Egyptian infantry deep into Sinai in order to be beaten by your swift and strong armoured divisions?"

The instructions that President Sadat had given his negotiators were apparently very clear: even the worst humiliations must be swallowed because peace was the most important goal and all efforts were to be concentrated in order to achieve it.

Sadat's stature as a statesman was manifest also in his ability to distinguish between trivial and important matters. It was not worthwhile wasting time in quarrelling about small details, but even in the major issues he would sometimes, to everyone's surprise, give in because this could have a positive effect on the adversary. It was probably as a result of Sadat's approach that Gamassy was always amazingly flexible and he had wide power to settle details on his own. Yariv's authority was rather restricted. He had to check the smallest of details with Moshe Dayan or Golda Meir. Sometimes this could be done by phone but often the matter had to be left to the next meeting. In the evening Yariv had to explain the matter to the Israeli government, who made the decisions in important matters.

I could often see on Gamassy's face that he found it a burden to accept conditions which offended the honour of the Egyptians. Gamassy was a man with strong feelings but a still stronger will, which helped him to restrain his feelings. What also helped was his great respect for and loyalty to Sadat. In any case, it became clear during the later negotiations that without Sadat's determination and sense of purpose there would never have been peace in Sinai.

I have already praised Sadat's merits as a peacemaker. I must in the name of justice say that Golda Meir too did much to enhance the peace process. Without her there would have been no results. Her character and background differed greatly from those of Sadat, but in spite of the differences she piloted the people of Israel with courage, determination and dignity through the difficult times after the October War and brought it closer to peace in Sinai.

Although we made some progress in the negotiations and the positions of the former enemies came slowly closer, we began to realize that soldiers were not able to solve the problem of disengagement. It was more of a political than a military matter.

It is true that at the end of November we were close to a solution. Yariv proposed on 26 November that Israel would be ready to withdraw even beyond the passes if Egypt would reduce to a minimum the number of its troops, tanks and artillery on the western bank of the Canal. Egypt showed interest in this proposal and on the basis of it we achieved a solution that was satisfactory to both parties. Without going into details, this proposal was practically the same as the final disengagement agreement completed on the political level in January 1974. We soldiers were satisfied and overly optimistic.

We gave Yariv one additional day to find out what the Israeli government really wanted. Were the Israelis going to withdraw 15, 20 or 30 km. from the Canal, or were they going to slow down the progress of our meetings in the future? Our intention was that Yariv should carry our proposals, which had already been accepted by the Egyptians, to the Israeli government for its approval. We were greatly disappointed never to receive an answer.

I learned only later that in giving its negative decision the Israeli government had followed the advice of Henry Kissinger. (When Kissinger was on a lecture tour in Finland in 1981 I asked him why we had been let down. Kissinger answered that the time had not been ripe for a political solution.) I suppose that another reason for Israel's decision was Moshe Dayan's negative attitude. He had opposed the negotiations at Kilometre 101 from the very beginning because the United States were not taking part in them.

Kissinger's negative attitude

Kissinger's strange attitude towards the negotiations becomes clearer from his memoirs. He writes that we were not intended to discuss the disengagement, that he had come to an understanding with President Sadat that this matter should proceed only after the convening of the Geneva Peace Conference. But in Kissinger's view Sadat's subordinates were more impatient. They wanted success in the negotiations before Geneva. That could be achieved either by concluding a complete disengagement agreement or by forcing the Israelis to withdraw immediately to the October 22 lines – wherever they were. Gamassy had supposedly brought to the Kilometre 101 meetings a new dynamism by pacing the negotiations faster than Kissinger had expected. This sounds strange, because in my view General Yariv and the Israeli delegation were always the more dynamic and active party in the negotiations.

Yet Kissinger was also suspicious of Israel. He thought that there were those in that country who were attracted by the idea of a rapid disengagement even before the beginning of the Geneva conference. For them the negotiations at Kilometre 101 were a means of ridding themselves of the American influence. It may also be, according to Kissinger, that Golda Meir would have had nothing against showing her constituency that Kilometre 101 had brought results.

In my opinion Kissinger's remarks do not sound credible. If the intention was that we should not discuss disengagement, why was it clearly spelled out as our task in the Six-Point Agreement? Sadat had obviously given his instructions to Gamassy on the basis of this agreement. I cannot understand the matter unless the understanding with Sadat which Kissinger mentions was based on a misunderstanding, or unless Kissinger changed his mind later on.

Perhaps Kissinger resented the fact that we became involved in matters which he considered his own speciality. He writes:

> The whole process tested our patience. For one thing, we never knew exactly what was happening at Kilometer 101. We got different reports from the Israelis, the Egyptians and the UN as to what was going on in the tent where these extraordinary meetings were taking place. Their only common feature was being at least forty-eight hours behind events. Frequently we had three versions of a deadlock to choose from – often four. And deadlock over disengagement was the last thing we wanted, since the separation of forces in the Sinai was the centerpiece of our strategy. On the other hand, we were not, to be frank, too eager for a break-through at Kilometer 101 before the Geneva Conference. As I cautioned Ambassador Dinitz [of Israel] on December 3: "Suppose Yariv comes out a great hero on disengagement, what do you discuss on December 18 [at Geneva]?

I am surprised that the UN version of events was not good enough for Kissinger. It was, at least, an impartial and truthful description of the negotiations. I think that Kissinger's appraisal of the meetings at Kilometre 101 is characterized by his lack of respect for the UN, so typical of a representative of a big power, which we experienced from time to time. Perhaps Kissinger's well-known self-assertive charcter also plays its part in his sour statements.

Rumours about Kissinger's negative attitude were already current in the tent during the negotiations. We heard from State Department sources that at the beginning he was not aware of what we were talking about. The reports from Kilometre 101 did not have the first priority on his reading schedule. Then one day he saw by mistake a report on the day's meeting. "My goodness, they are talking sense. This was not my intention at all. This must be stopped!" was Kissinger's reaction.

I have thought about the answer which Kissinger gave me in 1981 and now I have begun to understand some of his arguments. Perhaps the time at the end of November 1973 really was not ripe for a political solution. Kissinger had already begun to consider the serious problem of Syria. He was afraid that an agreement at such an early stage would tempt Syria's President Hafez al Assad to demand the same. This could postpone the Geneva Conference to a point in the distant future. Moreover, Kissinger wanted to show that the role of the United States was essential for the success of the peace process. Egypt and Israel could perhaps reach an agreement by themselves, but how to get to an agreement with Syria or the Palestinians? In Kissinger's view, in order to lessen the influence of the Soviet Union, it was necessary for the United States to be the indisputable leader of the peace process. For these reasons Kissinger advised the Israeli government to show restraint and it followed this advice for a change. It is possible that Yariv was not aware of all these background factors and therefore gave us too optimistic a picture of the chances of our proposals being accepted.

End of the first phase of negotiations

The first phase of the negotiations at Kilometre 101 had thus come to an end. We had not been able to solve the problem of disengagement conclusively. Despite this, I believe that Anwar Sadat and Golda Meir, the leaders of the parties, not to mention the wider public, were happy with our achievements. Military experts had carefully studied different alternatives for the withdrawal of the Israeli Army and the parties were well-aware of each other's viewpoints. It was now easier to continue negotiations on a political level as the complex problems, including the details, were well-known.

Even Kissinger is prepared to voice his appreciation of the negotiations at Kilometre 101, expressing it in his memoirs thus: "While the talks had ended in an impasse, they had served a very useful purpose in educating both sides about the outer limits of what was possible."

The negotiations at Kilometre 101 strengthened my previous views about the role of a mediator. If the parties have no political will to end the hostilities and to achieve an agreement, even the best mediator will not be able to change their attitudes. The personality, the authority or the skill of the mediator will be of no avail. But if the parties wish to reach an agreement, a mediator with lesser ability and skill will do. The failure of an experienced and skilful diplomat, Gunnar Jarring, in his mission in the Middle East serves as an example. Later I considered the difficulties of Olof Palme of Sweden as mediator in the Iran–Iraq war in this light.

The position of Henry Kissinger was completely different and one cannot compare him with an ordinary mediator. In addition to his great gifts and long experience, he was supported by the political and military might of a superpower. But as we could see many times, even his efforts at persuasion did not always bring results.

As the first phase of the negotiations at Kilometre 101 ended, I wrote a letter home on November 27:

> I do not keep quiet at the meetings but I try to assist in reaching a compromise. Sometimes it brings results but if the Israeli government says "no", a compromise cannot be achieved even if I could speak like Archangel Gabriel. These meetings are always exciting and sometimes dramatic. My presence seems to be of some help, I have noticed to my surprise. And the parties have not been angry with me. All the time I must of course be careful in order not to give an impression of partiality. These meetings are exhausting: two and a half hours of meeting, two and a half hours of driving, a few hours to prepare a cable to New York. In addition, "customers" queuing at my door. Matters tend to accumulate during my absence.

18. The Geneva Peace Conference

Preparations

Just before Christmas 1973 the Middle East Peace Conference began in Geneva. The occasion was historic because for a quarter of a century the Arabs had refused to negotiate with Israel. The armistice negotiations in Rhodes in 1949 had been conducted in separate meetings with each of the neighbours. The representatives of the United Nations, first Count Bernadotte and later Dr Ralph Bunche, had acted as mediators. Now the parties would be face to face in the same meeting chamber. The United States and the Soviet Union would be the sponsors of the meeting. The aim was to discuss a comprehensive peace agreement.

Kissinger has described in his memoirs, in detail and quite colourfully, the preparations for the conference and its course of events. He writes about the objectives of the United States and also presents assumptions about the purposes of the other participants. He asserts that the Soviet Union had been particularly interested in being involved in the conference because, Kissinger thinks, it had persuaded the Arabs to accept the cease-fire by promising to arrange a conference under the auspices of the two great powers where Israel would be forced to make wide-ranging concessions. In my opinion, there is no need to seek such complicated reasons for Soviet participation. As a great power it considered that it had the right and duty to take part in all such efforts to arrange the affairs of the world.

For many Arab states, involvement was difficult to swallow because it entailed the *de facto* recognition of Israel. Many had avoided that until now. In Israel the enthusiasm to participate was great in the beginning but, judging by the press, it seemed to diminish as the date of the conference approached and it began to look as if it would actually happen.

Egypt had certain problems with the conference and its position was delicate. In fact Sadat had already decided at that stage to abandon the policy of co-operation with the Soviet Union and seek an alliance with the United States. In order to keep his options open, however, he needed to approach the matter carefully during the conference. Moreover, he needed to avoid irritating Syria and so reducing the pressure on the Israelis by relieving them of the fear of war. Quite certainly all the participants tried to promote their own national interests in Geneva.

Kissinger, like presumably many others, had no excessive expectations of what the conference would achieve. In any case he had decided to make it the starting point of the peace process which he had planned for so long, to be based on bilateral negotiations, under his leadership, between Israel and its neighbours, seeking not a comprehensive settlement but to advance step by step. The aim of the first phase would be the disengagement of forces in Sinai and thereafter in Syria. The conference was in a way the symbol of this new peace process and at the same time would create a framework for the disengagement of forces. The aim was to try to keep the Russians outside the real negotiations.

Kissinger had prepared a draft for a letter of invitation which the Secretary-General of the United Nations would send to the proposed participants in the conference: Egypt, Israel, Jordan and Syria. The circumstances of the Middle East meant that even the wording of the letter provoked dispute. Everybody wanted to express their long-term objectives in this letter of invitation. Israel proved to be the most difficult negotiating partner, influenced by the fact that it was preparing for parliamentary elections at the end of the month. In the opinion of Golda Meir, the mere mentioning of the Palestinians in the letter was not simply a formality but was evidence of the most sinister intentions. I had earlier remarked that behind Israeli attitudes was a subconscious knowledge that the future of the Palestinians was also a fateful question for Israel. They were afraid that any attempt to solve this issue would threaten the existence of the state of Israel. Therefore the whole Palestinian question had to be fended off. Thus Golda Meir could in some of her speeches exclaim: "Palestinians, who are they! They do not exist."

Dealing with the wording of the letter of invitation reached such an impasse where Israel was concerned that even President Richard Nixon, who was becoming more and more entangled in his Watergate problems, had to free himself momentarily from them. In a letter to Golda Meir he threatened that the United States would be forced to leave Israel to its own devices if the latter's policy were to lead to a new war.

The disputes about the preparations for the conference and the final wording of the letter of invitation could be resolved only during Kissinger's round trip to seven countries of the Middle East in mid-December. From Algeria and Saudi Arabia he sought and got support for the aims of the conference. In Egypt the discussion dealt chiefly with the peace strategy after the conference. In his broad-minded manner Sadat agreed that the Palestinians would not be mentioned in the letter of invitation, but instead there would be a reference to "the invitation of other possible participants in a later phase". In Syria President Hafez al Assad also adopted a positive attitude to the proposed wording, but remarked that it had no great significance because Syria would not attend the conference in any case. More important from the point of view of the peace process, however, was that Syria was willing to negotiate with Israel on the disengagement in the Golan area.

Despite Egypt's *de facto* agreement to all Israeli conditions and the quiet acceptance of Syria, much hard work awaited Kissinger in Jerusalem. The reason for Israel's resistance was above all psychological. It is well-described in Golda Meir's remark on disengagement: "If we are realistic and honest with ourselves, we Israelis, it really means we have come out of this war, which was as it was, by pulling back. That's what you [would] call it by its right name. Just pulling back, that's what it is."

The conference begins

The Geneva Peace Conference, convened after great trouble, was to begin on 21 December 1973. General Gamassy had told me when Foreign Minister Fahmy would be departing for Geneva and I decided to go to see him off. This would be an important meeting for the future of Egypt and the entire Middle East. I wanted therefore to wish him a happy journey and good luck in the negotiations. I greeted the Foreign Minister and his party in the VIP hall of the airport. As he was leaving, the playful Fahmy grabbed me by the arm and began to pull me towards the aeroplane, using gentle pressure. "General, now you come with me! You are needed immediately in Geneva!" I was able, however, to explain that Mr Waldheim would not be pleased if I were to appear before him uninvited and out of the blue.

In Geneva the beginning of the meeting was delayed by a dispute about the seating order. The time reserved for the opening ceremony was already over before a solution that was satisfactory to everyone had been achieved. The participants were then able to make their opening speeches, none of which contained any surprises. They were mainly designed for their domestic audiences and their aim was to make clear why the speakers had attended and what were their objectives. The Peace Conference then ended with the opening ceremony, and no plenary session was convened.

In discussions after the opening it was decided, however, that the conference remained juridically and procedurally in session. The ambassadors of the participating countries and the great powers would remain in Geneva and would form a kind of machinery which would symbolize the continuity of the conference. In the opinion of Foreign Minister Fahmy in particular, it was important to create a framework for the disengagement talks. With this in mind, it was therefore decided to set up a military working group which would continue the negotiations that had broken down at Kilometre 101. This would hold its first meeting on 26 December 1973 and for the time being would be the only one of the conference's planned sub-groups. What Fahmy had said at Cairo Airport, that I was needed immediately in Geneva, proved to be right.

The figure behind the scenes and the main organizer of the peace conference, Henry Kissinger, could be content with the results. The meeting had progressed just as he had planned. Two important Arab states had sent their foreign ministers to negotiate with Israel. Syria, although it was not participating, wanted to preserve its seat and name tag in the conference chamber as a sign that it could join in later. All participants supported the step-by-step peace process advocated by the Americans. The Geneva Conference was clearly an important milestone on the road to peace.

The meetings of the Military Working Group

Christmas 1973 was approaching with full speed. My own holiday preparations had remained non-existent and I had not even had time to buy Christmas presents. Until the last moment I had hoped that I could visit my family in Helsinki at least for a few days, but because of the uncertain situation I had to give up the idea. However, I had written a short Christmas letter home. I had to go to Jerusalem on other business on Saturday 22 December and I rang home from there. My wife asked rather sadly where I intended to spend Christmas. I could not give an answer to that but told her to look at the television news. Perhaps that would give a clearer reply.

An hour after I had spoken with my wife, I received a cable from New York which told me to be in Geneva on 26 December. I returned to Cairo on the day before Christmas Eve and another cable was waiting: I was needed in Geneva on Christmas Eve. Not many hours were left for packing and other preparations. On the morning of Christmas Eve, my assistant Captain Joe Fallon and I boarded an Egyptair plane to Geneva; at 1400 hours we were in the Intercontinental

Hotel in Geneva having a discussion with Under-Secretary Roberto Guyer, whom Waldheim had left as his Special Representative at the peace conference.

Guyer told us the news. The first meeting of the Military Working Group was planned for Boxing Day. Many matters, particularly the question of chairmanship and the presence of the representatives of the United States and the Soviet Union at the meetings, were still open. Both parties wanted me to be the Chairman. Israel had meanwhile announced that it would not come to the meetings if there was a Soviet representative present. On the question of the participation of the great powers, I thought we should try to find a solution that would satisfy everybody. As for the chairmanship, I was not surprised. I had earlier heard rumours that many people were aspiring to that job.

The UN Office in Geneva had assigned a secretary to my service. She brought me the following programme of meetings for Christmas Eve and Christmas Day: that very evening I was to meet the Chargé d'Affaires of the United States, Michael Sterner, and the Egyptian Foreign Minister, Ismail Fahmy. The following day I was to visit the Soviet Ambassador, Sergei Vinogradov; the Israeli Ambassador, Ephraim Evron, and the Egyptian Ambassador, Muhammad Riad.

It was useful to make contact with the representatives of the countries participating in the peace conference and exchange views with them about the forthcoming negotiations. I had met Vinogradov several times during his time as the Soviet Ambassador in Cairo, but everyone else, apart from Foreign Minister Fahmy, was unknown to me until now. With Fahmy we spoke, among other things, about the presence of the representatives of the great powers at the meetings of the Military Working Group. I proposed as a compromise that after each meeting I would give a detailed report on the course of the meeting to the ambassadors of the United States and the Soviet Union. Thus neither of the great powers would need to send its representative to the meeting. Fahmy was pleased with the idea and intended to pursue it further. He also thought that it was self-evident that I should chair the meetings.

A strange but memorable Christmas was approaching. I joked to Fallon that this time we would not spend Christmas with the Christ Child but, rather, at the feet of Ismail Fahmy. However, a Finnish Christmas was in sight. At the airport I had met our UN Ambassador, Klaus Sahlgren, and my old friend, the Embassy Counsellor Leif Blomqvist. We agreed that Fallon and I should join the Christmas Eve meal at Blomqvist's and have a sauna at Sahlgren's on Christmas Day. The right Christmas feeling was preserved.

James Jonah would be arriving from New York on the evening of the Boxing Day. Our working team was about to be assembled and ready for new enterprises.

On Boxing Day morning we familiarized ourselves with the magnificent headquarters of the European Office of the UN. The UN had inherited the Palais des Nations, as it was called, from its predecessor, the League of Nations. It had been built in the 1920s and its interior somehow resembled the Finnish Parliament building, built at the same time. I met the Director-General of the European Office, the Italian diplomat Vittorio Winspeare-Guicciardi. Despite his high rank of Under Secretary-General his job was mainly ceremonial; he received on behalf of the Secretary-General the Letters of Credit of the ambassadors accredited in Geneva and took care of the administration of the house. He had no political tasks. Winspeare-Guicciardi began our conversation by telling me that the diplomatic circles in Geneva were not entirely happy about the idea of my chairmanship. He also had in mind as candidates several trained diplomats from his own staff. I listened puzzled to this talk but decided to keep quiet. I remembered Foreign Minister Fahmy's words on Christmas Eve: the chairmanship was a matter which the parties would decide.

In contrast to their director, the staff at the Palais were extremely friendly and helpful. The Chief of Conference Services, M. Courtois, took us around the building. In these stately marble halls the meetings of the Military Working Group would soon begin. This was a big change from a modest military tent and the harsh conditions of the desert. I wondered anxiously whether the cosy and positive spirit of Kilometre 101 would also disappear. My worries increased when we were shown the different-sized meeting chambers from which we could choose the most suitable. In the smallest one the tables were so broad and the negotiators would have to sit so far apart that loudspeakers would have been needed. I knew, however, that marble halls and mahogany tables do not negotiate, but rather the people around those tables. The negotiations would be continued in the coming days by the same people who had got to know each other in the tent and gradually learned to work together there.

My most pleasant encounters were with the military delegations in their hotels. The Egyptian delegation was now led by General Taha Magdoub, Gamassy's number two man from Kilometre 101. The Israeli delegation also had a new chief; General Yariv was about to leave for other duties and he had been replaced by Major-General Mordechai Gur.

In the first meetings before the end of the year no significant progress was made. Perhaps neither party expected any breakthrough before the Israeli parliamentary elections, which were to be held on the last day of the year. The new chief delegates took each other's measure. General Taha Magdoub proved to be an outstanding negotiator. He was a trusted aide of General Gamassy from the time of the October War and also had negotiating experience, as he had participated in all the meetings at Kilometre 101. Egypt's negotiation position was not one of the easiest, after a war which had ended in a difficult military situation. The difficulties were increased by the harsh conditions laid down by Israel and by the unyielding attitude of its negotiators. But despite everything Magdoub succeeded in achieving quite satisfactory results from the Egyptian point of view. Magdoub's number two in the negotiations was Colonel Ahmad Fuad Howeidi, a sharp-witted and aggressive young officer who had assisted Gamassy and Magdoub at Kilometre 101. An American diplomat on one occasion remarked to the Israelis, "You will have reason to worry when the Egyptians have a few hundred colonels like Howeidi."

Even an outsider could see that General Gur was one of the rising stars of the Israeli Army. During the whole of the October War he had been a military attaché in Washington DC. Despite that, he was a different type from General Yariv, with many faculties that made him a very suitable chief delegate. He quickly succeeded in establishing pleasant relations with his counterpart. General Gur was ably assisted by Colonel Dov Sion, an experienced and capable officer who had been with us at Kilometre 101 and whom I had known from his time as liaison officer to the UN. As the son-in-law of Defence Minister Dayan he had always had good relations with the highest leadership in Israel.

When we started to discuss the disengagement it became apparent that the Egyptians wanted to bring up five principles which would be the basis of the plan. These included the statement that the disengagement should mean the withdrawal of the Israeli Army to a certain line east of the Canal; that this line should be at a distance of about 30 km. from the present Egyptian forward line; that there should be an UN buffer-zone between the Egyptian and Israeli forces, and that the range of the Israeli artillery should not reach the Canal. Israel in other words was to give up the Mitla and Gidi Passes, together with its attempts to restrict troops and armaments which were impossible from the Egyptian point of view.

Israel refused these five principles and for its part brought forward two principles of its own: reciprocity and mutuality. In practice this meant that when one party made a concession in a certain matter, the other should give a similar concession in some other matter. The concessions need not be of a military character only, but a military concession could be matched by a political one. The Egyptians resisted these ideas. They were of the opinion that the Military Working Group was not a suitable organ for dealing with political questions.

After one of the meetings I was presenting my report to Ambassador Vinogradov and complained that it was very difficult to differentiate between military and political matters. We had been given the task of discussing purely military questions, but it had become clear that there was no such thing: every military question had its political aspects and vice versa.

"That is true," Vinogradov replied jokingly, "but the soldiers must remember that the solution is always in the hands of the politicians. If the soldiers are dissatisfied they have no alternative but to mount a coup."

The meeting broke up for a New Year's intermission on 29 December. On the flight from Geneva to Tel Aviv I had the opportunity to acquaint myself better with the Israeli chief delegate, Major-General Mordechai Gur, because we were sitting next to each other on the El Al plane. Naturally I had heard that he was one of the heroes of the 1967 war and an unusual general in the sense that he had written a children's fairy-tale about a cat. He impressed me as strong-willed but at the same time cheerful and positive. Conversation with him flowed easily and we had time to discuss all kinds of matters during the two-hour flight. After the October War he had followed our negotiations from his post in Washington. He described amusingly how he had got his present job: "I was sitting behind my desk and thinking who would be the best person to replace Yariv as chief delegate. Then I suddenly realized that it was I. I grabbed the telephone, called Dayan and he agreed."

I had asked the UN aeroplane to meet me in Tel Aviv. I had also asked Colonel Hogan and Rémy Gorgé to use it to fly from Cairo to Jerusalem as I wanted to tell them the news from Geneva. I learned with pleasure that there was only good news from UNEF.

On the following morning at UNEF Headquarters, I could see with my own eyes that things were in order and there had been good progress during my absence. The energetic General Ibanez O'Brien had acted for me with great efficiency. Now I was home again there were people queuing at my door to have a discussion with me. There were no great problems, however.

On the morning of New Year's Day, my fifty-second birthday, I woke feeling cheerful and energetic. There was need to be energetic because I had a full day's programme: before noon I gave a briefing to the commanders and the senior staff and after that offered a birthday drink to all. At noon I was the luncheon guest of the Canadian contingent. At 1400 hours I had to hurry to meet General Gamassy and an hour later I was already sitting on the UN plane on my way to Tel Aviv. There I had a meeting with Defence Minister Dayan. Only late in the evening did I reach Jerusalem and I still had to draft cables about the day's events to the Secretary-General.

I spent the night as a guest of the Acting Chief of Staff of UNTSO, Colonel Dick Bunworth and at 6 o'clock in the morning departed for Geneva. The Military Working Group was to meet again in the afternoon; after that would be the report-writing and so my work would continue.

At the beginning of January four meetings were held. As an innovation General Gur presented different alternatives for the disengagement plan, calling them "models". One of them looked familiar. It resembled the proposal to which we had received no answer from the Israeli government before the breakdown of the negotiations at Kilometre 101. A few days later, in order to ward off certain misunderstandings, he told me that it really was only a question of "models" and that the Israeli government had no plan ready.

At the meeting of 9 January, which remained the last one at this stage, the atmosphere was somewhat vague. Howeidi remarked that as Israel had now rejected the five principles presented by Egypt, no other alternative remained but for Israel to withdraw to its position of 22 October. We would have to ask experts to tell us where this line was, he added. Finally General Magdoub concluded that a decisive phase now had been reached in the negotiations. The examination of details had been finalized and nothing further could be added to the subject. "We now await the proposal of Israel, because Dayan has said that there is a plan which will be presented soon," Magdoub added.

We, the representatives of the UN, were probably the only ones who did not know anything about this plan of Dayan.

On the following day I returned to Cairo and my intention was to come back to Geneva on 15 January 1974, when the next meeting was scheduled to begin. It was cancelled, however, and I wrote home that "my comings and goings seem to become more and more haphazard. The winds of politics and the travels of Henry Kissinger seem to regulate them." A completely new phase began when we received news that the agreement on disengagement, negotiated by Kissinger, would be signed in the tent at Kilometre 101 on 18 January 1974 at 12 o'clock.

Tension in Sinai

I have already described how the negotiations of the Military Working Group at Kilometre 101 and in Geneva, together with activity on the political front, dominated the period from mid-November to mid-January. At the same time the strength of UNEF increased and its logistics elements began to come into operation. We were able to deploy more troops between the parties. But UNEF's task was not easy, because flagrant violations of the cease-fire had occurred again and our troops were continuously caught in the middle between the parties.

Although the arrival of UNEF troops in Suez and Ismailia had at first pacified the situation, the incidents soon began again. When the firing started by accident, UNEF intervention could often be helpful. But after mid-November the incidents were more often intentional and the parties used them to promote their military and political aims. Then UNEF's attempts at mediation had no effect. Sometimes it looked as if the incident had been initiated on a local level, but sometimes one wondered if it was the result of an intentional change of policy. The parties were worried that the meetings would not produce results and that the war would start again. They wanted, by means of these incidents, to speed up the process and to improve their own negotiating position.

In November there were on an average 15 incidents daily. In December the peak was reached when there was an average of 45 incidents a day. In January the number decreased a little to 36 a day. But these figures give only a hint of the real situation because they include incidents of very different types, from a few minutes' firing by a single rifle or machine gun to exchanges of artillery fire which could last for hours. About two thirds of the incidents took place in the south in the area where the 3rd Egyptian Army was deployed.

The reason for an incident could be, for example, attempts by the

Egyptians to push their positions forwards beyond the original front line, or it could be work on the Israeli fortifications, using bulldozers and excavators. When once again I passed on an Egyptian complaint about these fortifications, which they found particularly annoying, Defence Minister Moshe Dayan asked me to tell the Egyptians that it was the basic right of every soldier to fortify his own defence position. Dayan had apparently changed his mind about fortification, for at the end of October Yariv had proposed to Gamassy that the strengthening of front-line positions should be forbidden.

Although UNEF soldiers were often caught in the crossfire of the parties, we fortunately avoided serious casualties. However, the parties' losses were heavy. Both UNEF and the parties became more and more certain that disengagement should start as quickly as possible. All were tired and frustrated by the deteriorating situation and the continuous firing.

Dayan's disengagement plan

I had naturally read in the newspapers that soon after our last meeting at the beginning of the year Defence Minister Dayan had travelled to Washington. But for once the Israeli press did not reveal what the real purpose of the trip was and what would be the subject of discussions with Kissinger. Only later did it become clear that he presented the so-called Dayan plan, or a new plan of disengagement. The Israeli government had accepted it and at the same time had decided that none of its points would be negotiable. Egypt had either to accept it or to reject it. On closer examination this was not really a new plan; it very much resembled the ideas presented at the last meeting at Kilometre 101 which Yariv had been supposed to present for the consideration of the Israeli government.

According to the plan Egypt could keep the area which it had conquered in the October War, i.e. a zone about 6–10 km. wide on the east bank of the Canal. The Israeli forces would withdraw to a new line about 20 km. east of the Canal. This would mean that Israel would give up its bridgehead on the West Bank. Between the Egyptian and Israeli armies there would be a 6–10 km-wide UN buffer-zone.

Simultaneously, Dayan proposed the "thinning out" of the troops on both sides of the Canal. For this purpose there would be two security zones on each side of the UN buffer-zone. The narrower of them would be about 6-10 km. wide and here the number of troops and armaments would be limited to a few battalions. To the east and west of the narrow zones there would be zones of limited armaments about 30–40 km. wide. Israel's main forward line would be just west of the Mitla and Giddi Passes.

The Dayan plan meant in fact that all Egyptian troops who had crossed the Suez Canal during the war would now withdraw west of the Canal, except for just a few battalions. In Dayan's opinion not a single Egyptian tank should remain east of the Canal and the range of Egyptian artillery and missile batteries should not reach the Israeli positions.

In addition to these limitations on armaments Dayan wanted to impose political conditions on Egypt too: the ending of the state of belligerency between Egypt and Israel, the lifting of the blockade of Bab el Mandeb, a pledge to reopen the Suez Canal and free navigation for Israeli vessels.

In the discussions on the plan, Kissinger told Dayan that although he thought it good and a major step forwards, he could not present it to Sadat on a take-it-or-leave-it basis. He thought that there would be much disagreement over, among other things, the depth of the Israeli withdrawal, the extent of the arms limitations, the ending of the state of belligerency and the promise to open the Suez Canal.

In the middle of these negotiations with Dayan, surprising information was received from Geneva on 5 January. Kissinger was horrified because it appeared that at the meeting of the Military Working Group on the day before, General Gur had presented the Dayan plan for consideration. It was one of the so-called models which he had introduced. There was almost no difference between it and the Dayan plan. How could Kissinger now show the plan to Sadat as a kind of result of American and Israeli co-operation, when the same plan had been introduced in Geneva to the Egyptian delegation as an Israeli initiative? He pointed out to Dayan that it would be very difficult to get the Egyptians to accept anything which quite obviously seemed to come solely from the direction of Israel. The matter was not much improved when General Gur a few days later tried to ease the situation by withdrawing his "model" and by explaining less than convincingly that it had been presented as some kind of illustration of Israeli thinking and was not at all an official Israeli disengagement plan.

Birth of the Sinai disengagement agreement

With all its shortcomings Dayan's plan offered, in Kissinger's opinion, a starting point for a round of talks in the Middle East. He decided to start this round trip in Egypt, because he did not want to give the impression that he was acting as some kind of an Israeli messenger and had come to present an Israeli plan. In addition, he had promised Sadat to present his own plan in January. In this way a phase of shuttle diplomacy began, its aim being the Sinai disengagement agreement.

Sadat received Kissinger on Friday evening, 11 January, in Aswan, where he often spent the winter. In January the climate of Aswan was at its best and I believe that it offered an inspiring environment both for negotiation and for meditation.

During the first meeting Sadat said at once that he did not want to waste time in lengthy discussions on questions of principle. They should go straight to the point. The agreement should be completed within a week because he planned to travel to the Arab countries on 18 January, with the intention, among other things, to promote the lifting of the oil embargo.

When dealing with the contents of the agreement, it became apparent that Sadat had broad-mindedly already given up many of his previous demands. However, he still insisted that Israel should hand back the Mitla and Giddi Passes. He would not accept far-reaching proposals on the limitation of forces and armaments either.

Keeping the Dayan plan as his starting point, Kissinger travelled several times back and forth between Aswan and Jerusalem, until an agreement was reached. This was helped by the open-minded attitude of Sadat which was visible from the very first meeting. Kissinger had the greatest difficulties in Israel, where he was not dealing with a flexible negotiator like Sadat, but with a stubborn and tough negotiating team which defended Israel's real or imaginary interests to the very last. The Israeli negotiators could not, like Sadat, remove obstacles when necessary by a single stroke of the pen. They were under the tight democratic control of the government and even the Knesset. They also needed to gain the sympathy of the strong-willed Prime Minister Golda Meir, who had no confidence in President Sadat's intentions, suspected all things Egyptian and hated any scheme involving Israeli withdrawals. Finally, the negotiators had to take into consideration the free press, which articulated the demands of public opinion.

On the other hand it was well-known that the Israelis very much wanted a speedy withdrawal of their forces. The maintenance of a bridgehead west of the Suez Canal called for mobilized troops and had become a heavy financial burden. Israel knew also that it would become politically completely isolated if the final decision on disengagement were to take place in Geneva.

During the second meeting in Aswan, Sadat made a decision which secured the success of the negotiations. He did not want Israel to dictate to Egypt what its main line was to be on its own territory. In addition the limitations of troops and armaments were too complicated. In order to simplify matters Sadat proposed that only two lines be defined: the forward line of Israel just west of the passes, and the forward line of Egypt 6–10 km. east of the Canal. The area between the lines would be the UN buffer-zone. The limitations on deployment would be expressed in kilometres from the forward line of both parties. Sadat accepted the principle that missiles and artillery would be so stationed that they could not reach the positions of the other side. A suitable number of battalions east of the Canal would, in Sadat's opinion, be ten. He could not accept the complete prohibition on tanks in the Egyptian territory. His infantry units had been training with the tanks and without them they would feel defenceless. Sadat left Kissinger to decide the number of tanks which Israel could accept. The same applied to artillery. Together with Gamassy they would find a type of gun that was compatible with the principle of not reaching beyond the forward line.

However, Sadat did not want to make the commitment on the observance of the limitations directly to Israel. Therefore, it would be better to draft an American proposal that specified the limitations. Golda Meir and he could then sign it.

As for the political conditions, Sadat was prepared to express his intentions in a letter to President Nixon. He could not accept a formal obligation to clear and reopen the Suez Canal, but he could tell Nixon that he would do so as his own decision. He would start the clearing of the Canal after the completion of the disengagement, on condition that Israel did not demand it. The formal ending of the state of belligerency was out of the question. It would lead to an explosion in the Arab world. Instead he could give a solemn promise to observe the cease-fire.

Once again Sadat demonstrated his statesman-like skill by drawing a distinction between the essential and the non-essential. It was essential that Sadat agreed to the Israelis staying west of the passes for the time being, while his idea about the limitations of forces and armaments was ingenious. The rest was less important. Both Golda Meir and he understood that this was the first Israeli withdrawal in 20 years. The details that aroused so many disputes were in fact secondary. If the peace process continued, the number and deployment of troops after the first disengagement would have no significance. If the process did not continue, matters would have to be reappraised anyway.

In Israel one could gradually see signs that Sadat's flexibility and positive approach were changing attitudes. It began to seem obvious that an agreement would be reached. A solution was found to the changes proposed by Sadat. The number of battalions east of the Canal was agreed at eight, which would be 8,000 men altogether.

The government of Israel accepted the plan finally on 17 January at 1500 hours. It looked as if this agreement would be the turning point of the entire peace process. Later that same evening a contented President Nixon could step in front of the press and announce that following the decision of the Geneva Peace Conference Egypt and Israel had concluded an agreement on the disengagement of forces. It would be signed on 18 January 1974 at Kilometre 101 by Generals Gamassy and Elazar. The parties had asked the UNEF Commander Siilasvuo to be a witness to the signing.

Signing the agreement and drafting the plan for disengagement

The information about the conclusion of the disengagement agreement came to UNEF by cable from New York, but a pleased and cheerful General Gamassy also informed me personally about it. I quickly gave instructions to the Finnish battalion, so that the meeting-place would be in order and the coffee and sandwiches ready. The tents at Kilometre 101 had been empty for a long time.

At noon on 18 January the delegations of the parties were present in good time. The head of the Egyptian delegation was General Gamassy and its members were General Taha Magdoub, Colonel Ahmed Fuad Howeidi and the Foreign Ministry official Fawzy El-Ibrashi. The head of the Israeli delegation was the Chief of Staff of the Defence Forces, General David Elazar, and its members were General Avraham Adan, Colonel Dov Sion and the Foreign Ministry official Meir Rosenne. The UN was represented by the familiar team. I was assisted by Rémy Gorgé and Joseph Fallon. On the following day James Jonah arrived from New York as well.

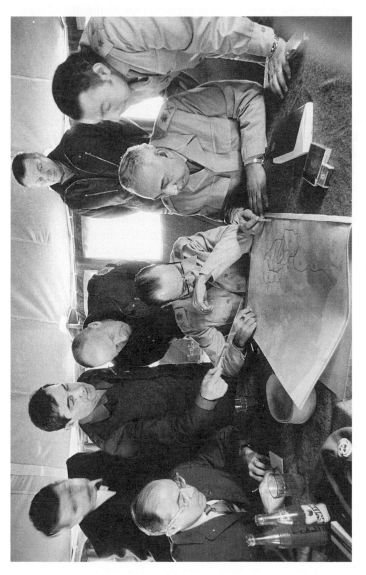

Signing the Egyptian-Israeli agreement on disengagement of forces, 18 Jan. 1974. *From left (seated):* Harold H. Saunders (US National Security Council), Gen. Gamassy, Gen. Magdoub, Col. Howeidi. *Standing:* Rémy Gorgé, Col. Sion, the author, Col. Raitasaari.

Soon the representatives of the US State Department arrived too. They brought with them three sets of the documents of the agreement. The documents were carried by the legal adviser of the State Department, Carlyle E. Maw, already more than 70 years old, a venerable gentleman who had originally been one of the supporting pillars of the legal profession in New York. He had been involved in fighting the forces of nature in Jerusalem, as a snowstorm had blocked all roads and the traffic was jammed. In an Israeli army half-track and wrapped in warm blankets he was able to cross the mountains on the way to Tel Aviv Airport and from there to go on to Sinai. He had with him one of Kissinger's assistants, Harold Saunders, an official of the National Security Council, whom I now met for the first time. Saunders would have a central role in drafting the second Sinai disengagement agreement.

The first encounter, during which the agreement was signed, was ceremonial in character and lasted less than an hour. The fast-acting Israelis had prepared a preliminary outline of the disengagement plan for the consideration of the Egyptians. It was decided to absorb the contents of the documents (see Appendixes 6a and 6b) and meet again on Sunday 20 January.

According to the agreement we were to prepare a detailed plan of disengagement in five days. It was a tough demand, which did not allow for lengthy consideration. The Chairman had to speed up the discussions on these matters to the best of his ability. In these negotiations, however, we kept to our time-table quite well. Not even in the final phase was there any unnecessary haste, but the plan was completed at a leisurely pace before the agreed date.

The proposal on the withdrawal of the Israeli Army, presented by the Israelis at the beginning of the meeting, was used as the basis of the plan. It was indeed a clear starting point for the disengagement. As the planning advanced, the Egyptians for their part presented their own views and demands for change. The basic idea of the plan was the deployment of UNEF troops between the armies of Egypt and Israel after each phase of the Israeli withdrawal. In that way UNEF tried to prevent clashes between the parties and other incidents.

Originally the Israelis proposed that the operation should begin with the withdrawal of the Egyptian 3rd Army from the east side of the Canal through the city of Suez westwards. The Egyptians could not agree to that for psychological reasons, because this would have meant the shameful withdrawal of their soldiers under the eyes of the Israelis.

Neither party wanted to leave its flanks unprotected. It was finally agreed that the Israelis would withdraw to well north of the main road from Suez to Cairo, UNEF would man a temporary buffer-zone between the parties and the road and the 3rd Army would withdraw protected by this buffer-zone.

The purpose of the temporary buffer-zone was to regulate the course of the disengagement and to protect each party's exposed flank. A new term that came into use was "buffer-time": the transition time between two phases of disengagement. Its purpose was to prevent the Egyptian troops arriving too early in an area vacated by the Israelis and thus to avoid disorder. The length of the buffer-time was usually six hours, or sometimes from one evening till the following morning.

The third innovation was the idea of a Forward Headquarters of UNEF which I had developed in Geneva. This was a small liaison team to which each party would send a liaison officer of the rank of colonel. UNEF too was to be represented by an officer of colonel's rank, the Chief Operations Officer, Colonel Tauno Kuosa. I took him with me to follow the preparation of the disengagement plan in the tent at Kilometre 101. He was to be assisted by a group of officers from UNEF Headquarters, including Captain Joe Fallon who had taken part in all the meetings at 101 and in Geneva and therefore was well-acquainted with the details of the agreement and their background. I also asked the Commander of the Finnish battalion, Colonel Reino Raitasaari, to come with me, because I had planned that he would play the principal role in the early phase of the disengagement.

Colonel Kuosa's task was to co-ordinate the functioning of Forward Headquarters. He was to act as an impartial referee of the representatives of the parties, solving disputes over interpretation on the spot if possible and bringing them to me for solution if necessary. He was to investigate violations of the agreement and follow the work of UNEF troops. In addition he was to provide me, and UNEF Headquarters, with a constant flow of information about the progress of the disengagement operation. Israel sent as its representative to Forward Headquarters Colonel Gat, while Egypt sent Colonel Magdoub (the younger brother of the General). Both brought with them junior liaison officers and signals personnel.

In the early days there was much discussion and even dispute about the interpretation of the aerial map annexed to the agreement. It was a small-scale map (1: 363,000) and the borders of the UN buffer-zone, i.e. the Egyptian forward line A and the Israeli forward line B, were drawn on it. The lines had been drawn in rather broad strokes and it appeared that in the terrain such lines could be 1 km. wide. These lines had now to be transferred to the map of the disengagement plan (1: 100,00), for which an Egyptian map of Sinai with texts in Arabic had been chosen. The dispute arose from the question: on whose side of the line should the dominating points of terrain be? Both parties wanted to have as much hilly terrain as possible in their possession, as from there it would be easy to follow the activities of the opposite party. After a quarrel which lasted many days, unanimity was finally reached on the placing of the buffer-zone on the map. The Israelis had brought experts on topography with them, but General Magdoub too proved to be a prominent specialist on maps who skilfully defended Egyptian interests. The task of tranferring the lines from the map to the terrain and marking them with black oil barrels with the letters "UN" painted on in white, was given to the UN.

The results of the negotiations were marked on a map with the inscription "The plan of disengagement of forces." The different-numbered phases of the disengagement were drawn on it, as were the temporary buffer-zones and the final buffer-zone. On the map was glued a separate time-table (see Appendix 7) which contained the timings of the different phases and the movements of the troops. An additional document, the Statement of the Chairman, contained the limitations on forces and armaments which the Egyptians did not want to publicize because of their delicate nature.

After the signing I announced to the press waiting outside that the disengagement would begin on the following day:

Thus we have successfully concluded these meetings at Kilometre 101 . . . I would hope that history may record one day that the initial step towards understanding, reconciliation and peace in the Middle East began here at Kilometre 101.

When the talks began in those gloomy and tense days in October/November last year, the difficulties before us were both grievous and enormous, but we persevered and achieved some results in November. Under the mandate of the Geneva Peace Conference, the parties continued the clarification of views in Geneva in the Military Working Group. It remains my conviction that the talks at Kilometre 101, as well as in Geneva, facilitated the subsequent negotiations at another level which resulted in the agreement signed here on 18 January.

Let me add that I have appreciated with gratification the co-operation of both sides with UNEF. Without their understanding UNEF would have faced greater difficulties in the recent past. As servants of peace we stand ready to play our part in the full implementation of this disengagement plan.

On the same afternoon I held a briefing for the commanders of UNEF contingents at Shams Camp, in the Poles' meeting tent, and gave them a preliminary order on the implementation of the disengagement plan.

19. The first Sinai disengagement

Operation Calendar

At the same time as the plan for disengagement took on its final form in the tent at Kilometre 101, my headquarters was preparing a plan for UNEF's role in its implementation. The operation was code-named Operation Calendar and an operations order was sent to the contingents on 24 January. Because the Israeli withdrawal would begin from the south, it was natural that the Commander of the Finnish battalion would be in charge of the operation in its early phase. However, I wanted the responsibility to remain in his experienced hands as long as possible. Because the resources of the Finnish battalion would not have been large enough for the fulfilment of this task, units from other battalions were detailed to it at different phases. The order also defined the deployment of UNEF battalions in the final buffer-zone east of the Canal. As a preparation for this deployment, the battalions of Peru and Panama were given the job of occupying the first evacuated southern part of the buffer-zone, from where they would later move to their final areas of operation.

The disengagement process started according to plan on 25 January with the redeployment of the Israelis in No. 1 area. Hardly any signs of this movement could be seen from the outside. Only those parts of the Finnish battalion operating in this area could see some extra movement when the Israelis vacated their positions on Mount Gebel Ataqa and reduced their numbers in the southern part of the area and along the Cairo-Suez road.

The Israeli preparations for withdrawal had progressed well. On 28 January at 0800 hours the Finnish battalion, reinforced for this task with detachments from the battalions of Sweden, Senegal and Indonesia, began to take over Israeli positions around the city of Suez, in Adabiya and on Mount Gebel Ataqa. At the same time the Israeli forces withdrew from these areas northwards.

At good old Kilometre 101 the first outwardly visible sign of the disengagement took place at noon on 28 January, when Israel's Chief Liaison Officer, Colonel Gat, handed over the main Cairo-Suez road and the No. 1 area to the UNEF representative, Colonel Kuosa. When I went there myself I saw that the place was full of people. There were official representatives, like the staff of UNEF Forward Headquarters

OPERATION CALENDAR
The First Disengagement Plan in Sinai

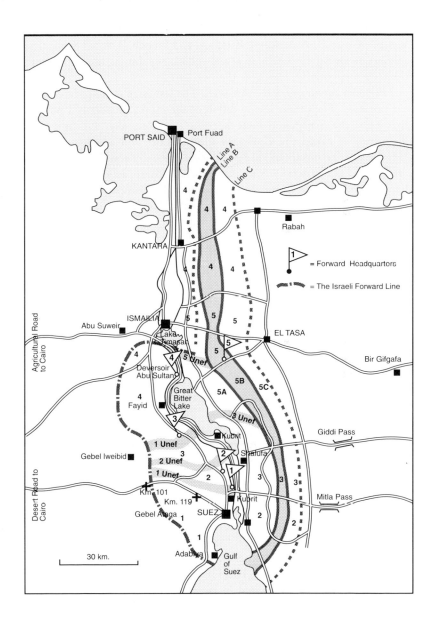

and the Egyptian Chief Liaison Officer, Colonel Magdoub, with his staff. There was a large group of representatives from the world press and the major radio and television companies. There were UNTSO military observers who had come out of pure curiosity. Among them I recognized representatives of the three permanent members of the Security Council: Americans, Russians and French. The tall Senegalese soldiers in their green battle-gear and their new, shining blue berets lent their own decorative touch to the occasion.

The short ceremony was soon over. The last Israelis disappeared over the horizon. The others left in different directions. Suddenly I noticed that only the Senegalese were keeping me company. Nothing was happening. I called the Company Commander and asked in French, "Have you received an order?" "*Oui, mon général!*" "Have you understood the order?" "*Non, mon général!*" Swift action was needed. I told the Company Commander to deploy his company at once. One platoon here near the road, another on that hill and the third on the sand dune a little further on. Only UN vehicles were to be let through: "*Seulement les voitures de l'ONU.*"

At the same time as the last Israeli vehicles were leaving Kilometre 101, the Finnish battalion had begun to man temporary buffer-zone No. 1. But the Egyptians had still to wait the buffer-time of six hours before they could, at 1800 hours, move to the vacated area. Again there was a short ceremony at Kilometre 101 when UNEF handed over the area to the Egyptian Army. A great celebration began. Egyptians were thronging to the area from three directions: from Cairo, from the city of Suez and from the 3rd Army area, behind the Canal. The liberation of the city of Suez and the 3rd Army from the encirclement of Israel was fêted. Magnificent, improvised fireworks started when everybody wanted to shoot in the air for pure joy. Tracer bullets, colourful rockets and light bombs shot through the night sky. In some places the situation was fatally dangerous. A Finnish ranger too was lightly wounded by these "fireworks". The celebration continued on the following days on the main Suez-Cairo road. When the Egyptians were thinning out their troops on the eastern side of the Canal, hundreds of trucks full of shouting and cheering soldiers were on the way to Cairo. It was somehow touching when the soldiers, noticing my car and me on the roadside, shouted rhythmically, "Siilasvuo, Siilasvuo, Siilasvuo!"

Now we had our first experience of how the disengagement plan would function in practice. The Finnish battalion, with the foreign units which had been attached to it, seemed to operate without any problems. The Egyptian soldiers, in their great enthusiasm or perhaps unthinkingly, caused disorders at first. In the early days they several times pushed into the temporary buffer-zone or other forbidden areas. UNEF or the Egyptian liaison officers led them away. But gradually the parties learned the rules of the game of disengagement and the number of incidents decreased. During the entire disengagement period there were very few of these and they never threatened the success of the operation. Thus the Secretary-General could report to the Security Council on 2 February that the disengagement "has progressed smoothly . . . no incidents of major significance have occurred".

The temporary buffer-zones and the buffer-time between the different phases proved in practice to be excellent regulators of the troop movements. Forward Headquarters also functioned well. With the energetic representative of UNEF, Colonel Tauno Kuosa, acting as referee, it carried out its tasks in a flexible but determined manner when needed.

Disengagement continued according to plan. During the second, third, and fourth phases the Commander of the Finnish battalion kept his responsibility for UNEF's role. The battalion's job became much easier when the Egyptians brought more military police to the area to keep order and to control the traffic. In this way the intrusion of the Egyptian soldiers lessened still further. After having carried out their task, the Finns moved on 23 February to their area of responsibility in the southern part of the permanent UN buffer-zone.

The ending of the fourth phase and the beginning of the fifth was a more solemn event than usual, because it meant the transfer of the last Israelis from "Africa" to the eastern side of the Canal. UNEF Forward Headquarters moved in the morning to its new site in Deversoir. I went there myself to meet Colonel Kuosa and the Commanders of the Swedish and Austrian battalions, to whom the responsibility for the UNEF role in the regulation of the operation was transferred now. Here Colonel Gat handed over to UNEF the No. 4 temporary buffer-zone.

The Israelis celebrated the significance of the day by a parade held near the causeway built at Deversoir. I later received a description of this parade from military observers who were present. The tank company which had secured the withdrawal was assembled for inspection. The Israeli Commander made a short speech. The Israeli flag was lowered and finally the tanks of the company rolled along the causeway across the Canal and towards the east. There was an absolute carnival atmosphere on the site. The tanks were decorated with small flags and the soldiers shot rockets of different colours into the air. One could understand the joy, because many soldiers had been waiting for a long time to return home to their families and to peacetime work.

The final phase of the operation continued on the eastern side of the Canal with Swedish, Austrian and Indonesian resources, and the last move into No. 5 area was carried out on 4 March. The permanent buffer-zone was now completely in the possession of the UN and the UNEF battalions had been deployed in their own areas in the zone to perform their new duties.

Now there remained the inspections of the areas of limited troops and armaments. Partial inspections had been conducted as disengagement progressed, but the first inspection of all the areas was to be held on 5 March, according to the agreement. This time the inspection was carried out by UNTSO military observers assisted by liaison officers from the parties. The inspection showed that on neither side were there any additional troops or armaments.

On 5 March, commenting on the completion of the disengagement operation, I said that the parties had fulfilled their agreement to the letter. I added that I had seen a definite change in attitudes during the past months and the parties now had more confidence in each other.

Four days later I gave a special order of the day to the UNEF soldiers. In it I termed the disengagement "a first important step towards a final solution to the Middle East problem" and went on to say:

> I am extremely pleased to report that this complex and delicate operation was carried out on schedule and without a single significant incident. This accomplishment resulted from the devoted and professional spirit of each and every member of UNEF involved in this historic operation.
>
> I am fully aware of the frustrating difficulties which faced you on some occasions . . . It is to your credit that these were overcome so effectively.

Thus a politically and militarily important operation had ended in great success, chiefly because of the following factors: a reasonable and careful plan prepared in the tent at Kilometre 101; the regulation of the disengagement operation punctually carried out by UNEF troops; the excellent functioning of UNEF Forward Headquarters; the will and determination of all the three parties, Egypt, Israel and UNEF, to conquer the obstacles and bring the operation to a happy ending.

With regard to UNEF's reputation, the success of the disengagement

Members of the Peruvian battalion placing barrels to mark the buffer zone, Feb. 1974.

A Panamanian having just received a letter from home, UNEF buffer zone, Feb. 1974.

operation was an excellent achievement. We had stabilized our position as an effective and trusted partner in the eyes of the parties. We had succeeded in promoting equally the interests of Egypt and Israel. This augured well for the future.

A successful operation has its price, too. The Egyptians in particular suffered heavy losses of killed and wounded in the vast minefields of Sinai. UNEF also sustained casualties. On 14 February a Finnish captain drove over a mine and lay wounded in the middle of a minefield. The truck of the rescue patrol sent out to help him drove over an anti-tank mine. Sergeant Risto Jaakko Latva Hakuni and Sergeant Risto Tapani Majasaari, who had been in the cabin, died instantly. All six soldiers who had been on the frame of the truck were injured, four of them seriously. A memorial service was held at Shams Camp in Cairo. The coffins of the deceased, covered with Finnish flags, were placed on the open frame of the Sisu truck. On top of the coffins were the blue UN berets and a mass of flowers. In my memorial speech I said:

> United Nations soldiers, you have come here from different parts of the world, to bring peace to the troubled area of the Middle East and to save human lives. You have been successful in your work, as we are now entering the last phase of the disengagement process between the Israeli and Egyptian armed forces. The first important step towards peace will soon be completed.
>
> We all knew, however, that the task of UNEF would be dangerous. Until very recently there was continuous firing in the Suez city area and around Ismailia town. It was almost a miracle that there were only minor casualties among UNEF troops during that period. With the disengagement a new element of danger came into the picture: the hundreds of thousands of mines which the parties had laid in the former battlefields.
>
> Today we pay tribute to the memory of two young Finnish soldiers who lost their lives in one of these minefields. They were ready to sacrifice everything to rescue an officer, a comrade-in-arms, who had been injured in the same minefield. By their behaviour and their courage they set an example to be followed by all of us.
>
> Blessed be the peacemakers because they are the children of God.

Operation Omega

Parallel to the disengagement process, UNEF was also carrying out a somewhat gruesome operation code-named "Omega". Its purpose was the recovery of the bodies of Israeli and Egyptian soldiers killed in the October War from the battlefield now under Egyptian control, and their return to their home country. The initiative came from Israel and at first the Egyptians could not understand why so much attention was directed to what was, in their view, an insignificant matter. Dead bodies should be buried on the battlefield as the Egyptians had always done.

In the same way as in Finland, where we tried to bring back our dead to bury them in their homeland, in Israel too there were deep emotional values connected with the matter. It was important for practical reasons as well, because according to Jewish law it was difficult to handle questions of inheritance and the widow could not remarry if the body was not found or there was no other valid evidence of the death. In addition, the unprecedently great number of the fallen had stirred up emotions at home and the government had speedily to do its best to calm these feelings.

The matter had been discussed several times without results. The Egyptians were extremely suspicious and claimed that the Israelis were only trying to spy in their areas, using this issue as a pretext. During the discussions I tried to dispel these suspicions. When the disengagement operation started, the Egyptians finally decided to permit the searches. Negotiations on the matter were held at Kilometre 101 towards the end of January. Israel was represented by General Herzl Shafir and the Army Chief Rabbi Piron. As the representative of Egypt, assisting General Magdoub, appeared our old acquaintance Brigadier Adlai Sherif, the former Liaison Officer to UNTSO who had now been transferred to handle humanitarian questions and was in contact with the International Red Cross. The latter was represented in the negotiations by Marcel A. Boisard, Head of the Red Cross Cairo Office. I had appointed Major Alan Windsor of Australia from UNTSO to represent me. He carried out this delicate task with dedication and skill.

The Israelis prepared carefully for the searches. The total number of their killed in action was about 2,700, of whom almost 700 were missing. By interviewing the superiors and the comrades in arms of the fallen, they had got a fairly clear picture of where to look for the bodies. There were bodies on both the east and west side of the Canal.

Each Israeli search patrol consisted of unarmed soldiers and a rabbi, assisted by an UNTSO military observer. When the searches began at the end of January there were 12 patrols in action. Many difficulties occurred at first because the local commanders resisted the incursion of the patrols into their areas. But with UNEF's efforts these difficulties were gradually overcome. The searches lasted for months and the Egyptians were obliged to extend the time allowed for them.

New methods had to be devised for intensifying the searches because public opinion in Israel was not satisfied with the results. Then help came from an unexpected quarter. The eye of an Israeli police officer was caught by an article in a British magazine describing the use of dogs by the Lancashire police in the search for dead bodies. An Israeli police officer was sent to London to request assistance and the British authorities took a favourable attitude to the matter. Police Sergeant R. Dean with Rick, a five-year-old German shepherd dog, and Police Constable Overton, with the eight-year-old Rufus, flew to Tel Aviv and joined Operation Omega on 18 February. According to the contract the dogs were to search for bodies for three weeks, but the results were so good that the contract was extended by five weeks. Then it was time to return to England. In the meantime other policemen and dogs took part in the searches, but at the end of May Sergeant Dean and his Rick returned once more and worked together until early July, when Operation Omega ended.

On a trip through Sinai from Israel to Egypt I once happened to come across the site where the dogs and their handlers were working. I was given an interesting briefing on the use of dogs for the recovery of bodies. These dogs had been trained in Britain especially to search for the victims of crime. Training was done with pig carcasses, which resemble the human body. Dogs can detect a body buried at a depth of up to two feet. Police Sergeant Dean told me that in Sinai he and Rick had found more than 100 bodies. A dog, however, does not have enough patience to search for more than 15–20 minutes at a time. Fortunately, in Sinai there are all sorts of things that engage the dog's interest: a lizard might appear, or some other little animal which can be chased. After that distraction the dog will recover the power to concentrate on its real work.

The Israelis did not publicize the final results of Operation Omega. I assume, however, that the majority of the killed were found, or sufficient evidence of their death was gathered. The highest authorities of

Israel many times expressed their satisfaction at the success of the operation and thanked UNEF for its significant role in the final result.

Deployment in the buffer-zone

When the disengagement process was completed in early March 1974, there were three sectors 10 km. wide from north to south (see map p. 279). The middle one was the buffer-zone, manned by UNEF. On each side of this were the areas occupied by the armed forces of Egypt and Israel, where the number of troops and armaments was limited by the agreement.

Having come through its task of supervising the disengagement with honour, UNEF now had the continuing responsibility of maintaining the cease-fire and preserving the balance, as required by the negotiations. The buffer-zone had to be manned and entry to its area by the forces of the parties prevented. In addition UNEF was to verify with regular inspections that the parties were adhering to the agreed limitations on troops and armaments.

The buffer-zone was under UNEF's complete control. There was no civilian population in the zone and the entry of outsiders was not allowed without special permission. The buffer-zone was wide enough adequately to separate the parties from each other and the fire of light weapons would not reach from one side to the other. This was also true of artillery, because in the areas of limited arms there were no long-range guns. Consequently, accidental breaches of the cease-fire were not possible; the opening of fire would have meant that the party concerned had intentionally decided to violate the agreement.

The buffer-zone was 165 km. long. It was a sand desert covered by dunes, except for the northernmost tip which was an inaccessible salt lake. Often the dunes were very high and hampered movement. The lack of a road running from north to south inside the buffer-zone made the operation more difficult, with the roads in the areas occupied by the parties having to be used for logistics transportation. Inside the buffer-zone, movement was possible only with four-wheel-drive cars.

The defective road network was not the only factor hindering movement. Sandstorms in the early months of the year covered the roads completely. The Polish engineers tried their best to clear them, but there were far too few people and equipment to do this properly.

The move to the buffer-zone also meant that UNEF needed to cross the Canal more frequently, particularly at the cities of Suez and Ismailia.

The Egyptian Army had several pontoon bridges built over the Suez Canal. We could use them and the causeway at Deversoir quite freely. The situation became more difficult only when the Egyptians began to clear the Canal and it was opened to traffic at the beginning of June 1975.

Describing the conditions faced by UNEF troops deployed in the desert, Brian Urquhart said the area

> contains very few buildings, if any, and certainly no trees. It's all sand. The climatic conditions at the moment in the area are fairly dismal for troops living under canvas; it is extremely cold and very wet. In fact, there was a case of frostbite in Rabah the day I was there – a sentry – which is something one doesn't associate necessarily with the desert.

UNEF's Chief of Staff, Colonel Patrick D. Hogan, said that despite the dangers, the lack of comfort and the distance from their homes, the UNEF soldiers accepted all this because they had "a sense of purpose" as members of the United Nations peace-keeping operation.

I had myself noticed on my inspection tours of the different battalions that despite the dismal conditions, bad food and inadequate housing nobody complained; the troops were enthusiastic and their spirits were high.

Immediately after disengagement was completed, UNEF had six battalions in the buffer-zone. Counting from the north they were the battalions of Ireland, Peru, Sweden, Indonesia, Senegal and Finland. This was, however, meant to be a temporary arrangement and more troops were transferred to the area during the next two weeks. After the transfers there were nine battalions: from north to south, the battalions of Ireland, Panama, Peru, Sweden, Indonesia, Ghana, Austria, Senegal and Finland. Most of them manned between five and seven positions each along the eastern and western borders of the buffer-zone. The Swedish and the Finnish battalions each had eleven positions.

All of the battalions had a forward headquarters in the buffer-zone. The main headquarters, logistics elements and reserves were in bases outside the zone. The bases of the Northern Brigade and the battalions of Ireland, Panama and Peru were in Rabah, in Israeli-occupied Sinai. They obtained their supplies directly from Israeli firms.

The bases of the Swedish and Indonesian battalions were in Ismailia and those of the Southern Brigade and the battalions of Austria, Senegal

UNEF BUFFER ZONE AND DEPLOYMENT OF TROOPS 27 MARCH 1974

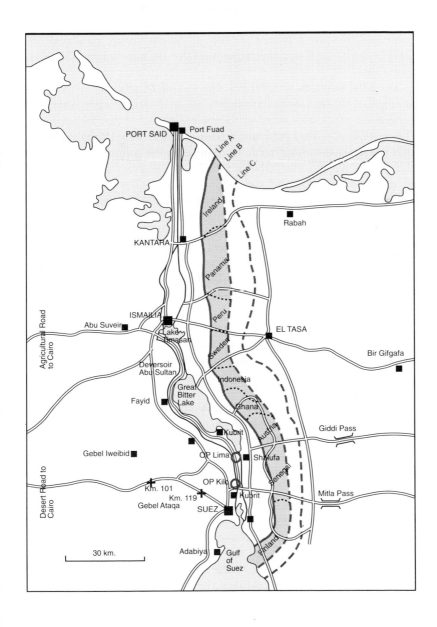

and Finland in Suez. The battalion of Ghana had its base in the former British barracks in Fayid. All these troops were supplied from Egypt.

The Nepalese battalion was in Shams Camp in Cairo as a reserve. It was training its personnel and waiting for the arrival of its new vehicles and radio equipment. The Canadian and Polish logistics contingents continued to operate from their base in Shams Camp. Headquarters UNEF was still in Cairo and preparations for the move to Ismailia were going on.

The total strength of UNEF at the end of March was 7,000. The strength of the battalions stationed in the buffer-zone was 4,000. The permanent positions manned by them were located so that they covered the entire area, paying particular attention to guarding the lateral roads that ran across the buffer-zone. In addition to the permanent positions, the battalions and the UNTSO military observers assisting them patrolled the area day and night.

Particularly in the view of the Israeli authorities, a very important part of UNEF's task was inspecting the areas of limited forces and arms. This was carried out by UNTSO military observers under the authority of Headquarters UNEF. For the execution of the task the Egyptian and Israeli authorities had divided the areas into sub-sections where the liaison officers assisted the UN patrols. The inspections were carried out once a fortnight; those on the prohibition of missiles once a month.

It was a serious shortcoming that the Americans did not give UNEF aerial photographs or other information gleaned from the reconnaissance flights they carried out above the buffer-zone and its vicinity, passing this information only to the parties. These data would have greatly facilitated the work of our inspectors. They could have compared the results of the aerial reconnaissance with the situation in the terrain and in this way our reports would have been more accurate and trustworthy. The lack of information led UNEF on one occasion into an awkward situation in relation to the parties. In early March the Israeli Defence Minister showed me an aerial photo taken of the Egyptian area of limited deployment and asserted that there were three times more guns than the agreement permitted. He wondered why UNEF had done nothing about this. Our own inspectors were sent to investigate the matter and they confirmed that there were too many guns in the area. By studying the same photograph with the Egyptian Defence Minister, it appeared that there had been an error based on misunderstanding. According to the Egyptians a battery consisted of twelve guns, while in the opinion of the Israelis it comprised only four.

The UN Security Council extends the mandate of UNEF, 8 April 1974. The current Council President, Talib El-Shahib of Iraq, opens the session. *Beside him* sits Secretary-General Kurt Waldheim. *Behind them*: Under Secretary-General Brian Urquhart and the author.

The Egyptians quickly removed the additional weapons. The whole incident, and the suspicion it caused, could have been avoided if UNEF had had at its disposal the aerial photos and information given to the parties.

After this violation of the agreement, complaints continued to be presented to UNEF but they were minor. Most of the breaches were on the Egyptian side, probably because the local commanders had a great temptation to exceed the permitted numbers of troops and armaments. The Suez Canal was a great natural obstacle and very difficult to cross. In an emergency the transfer of additional troops across the Canal would have been very slow. The Egyptian highest command understood that it was politically necessary to adhere to the agreed limitations, but the local commanders did. not understand this and imagined that it was their patriotic duty to mislead the inspectors of

UNEF. There was thus a kind of continuous competition going on between the inspectors and the local commanders, which sometimes led to funny exchanges. Once the inspectors were counting random samples of troop-strengths near Kantara and came to an Egyptian field bakery where some 50 bakers were busily working. The Egyptian Liaison Officer explained that these were all civilians. Then the Arabic-speaking inspector heard the bakers, very offended, shouting: "We are all good soldiers!"

On the Israeli side the situation was completely different. There was no natural obstacle between the front line and the rear and troops could be quickly moved from the rear to the front when needed. Therefore in the Israeli areas of limited forces and armaments there was often not even the agreed number of troops and weapons.

As a legacy of former battles, there was a large number of minefields in the area, which hampered movement and continually caused casualties. The Polish engineers at once began the work of clearing the mines but this progressed slowly. There were hundreds of thousands of mines and the maps supplied by the parties were deficient. During the first five months five UNEF soldiers were killed and 15 were wounded in mine accidents. Little by little the Poles got better mine-clearing equipment, including mine-clearing tanks, from their home country. But the task of clearing was so immense that the battalions themselves had to get involved too. For this purpose, for example, the Finns obtained two mine-clearing tanks from the Egyptians on loan. It took several months before mine-free routes had been cleared and the uncleared minefields marked.

By maintaining the cease-fire UNEF visibly improved the atmosphere between the parties. But I believe that the verification activities of UNEF regarding the troop and arms limitations were still more important. The inspections showed that the parties tried scrupulously to adhere to the agreement and no significant violations took place. UNEF's careful and trustworthy verification operation obviously enhanced the confidence between the parties.

On 8 April 1974, the Security Council extended UNEF's remit for another six-month period, as recommended by the Secretary-General. In his report calling for the extension of UNEF's mandate the Secretary-General declared:

The establishment of the United Nations Emergency Force by the Security Council at the height of the crisis in the Middle

East in October 1973 is a milestone in the history of the United Nations.

Less than 30 hours after the decision of the Security Council, the first elements of UNEF arrived in the mission area. Their arrival, and the immediate actions taken by them, served to defuse a highly explosive situation which could otherwise well have had major consequences for world peace.

The contrast between the extremely tense and violent situation that existed in October 1973 and the quiet now prevailing in the Egypt-Israel sector is clear testimony to the effectiveness of the Force in implementing the agreements reached on the diplomatic level.

Although quiet now prevails in the Egypt-Israel sector, the situation in the area remains unstable and potentially dangerous. The disengagement of Egyptian and Israeli forces is only a first step, although a very important one, towards the settlement of the Middle East problem. The continued operation of UNEF is essential not only for the maintenance of the present quiet in the Egypt-Israel sector but also to assist, if required, in further efforts for the establishment of a just and durable peace in the Middle East.

Finally the Secretary-General expressed his gratitude to the governments contributing troops to UNEF and the many others who had given assistance to the United Nations in one way or the other. Last but not least he thanked the commanders, officers and civilian staff of UNEF for the exemplary manner in which they had performed their important and difficult duties.

I had been invited to come to New York and be present at the meeting of the Security Council. It was a pleasant duty to represent a successful mission on that occasion, and for me the visit was really a continuing celebration. The only sad aspect of the day was the death of the President of France, Charles Pompidou. At the session each Council member at first eulogized the deceased and thereafter moved on to speak of the important role played by UNEF, paying tribute to its officers and men and those who had been killed or wounded in discharging their duties.

After the session Messrs Guyer and Urquhart organized a reception in the meeting- and map-room on the 38th floor to mark the occasion of UNEF's first six months. All the ambassadors of the members of the Security Council and the contributing countries and highest UN authorities had been invited to the reception. I thought that the atmosphere of the occasion was very pleasant, because the guests expressed their warm appreciation for the activities of UNEF. But some criticism was expressed too. The Soviet Ambassador, Jakob Malik, came to talk with me and his first words were, "General, your peace-keeping force is very costly!" I replied that I had read in the papers that the expenses of Israel alone in the recent war had amounted to $6 billion. I thought that the expenses of Egypt and Syria together must have been still higher. Therefore, if somebody comes to say that UNEF is too expensive, I become very, very angry. Ambassador Malik did not remain to continue the conversation with me.

The question of UNEF's funding came up in another context during my visit to New York. It arose from the fact that in his first report the Secretary-General had proposed that $30 million would pay for our expenses in the first six months. In January 1974 we were told that all this money had been used and that we could not have new vehicles, tents, tankers and other materiel till May, at the start of a new budgetary period. The total expenses of the first year amounted to $80 million. I asked the Secretary-General why he had quoted such a small sum in the first place, although it had been widely known that it would not be enough for the needs of UNEF. The Secretary-General explained that the sum seemed, politically, more likely to be accepted. I wanted to ask whether it would not have been better to propose that the great powers give up the idea of establishing UNEF, if getting money was so difficult.

20. Disengagement on the Golan

Preparations for the agreement

The political negotiations on the Sinai disengagement agreement had been completed on 18 January 1974 and the preparations for the implementation of the agreement were continuing in the tent at Kilometre 101, when the Secretary of State of the United States, Henry Kissinger, two days later made preliminary contact with the government of Syria in order to clarify the possibilities for negotiations.

In his memoirs Kissinger says he had guessed that it would be difficult to reconcile two arch enemies. It was also hard to imagine two nations less suited to being the subjects of diplomatic persuasion and mediation. Kissinger had already been to Damascus for the first time in December, when he had tried to persuade the Syrians to join the Geneva Peace Conference. He had then realized the deep distrust that prevailed between Syria and Israel. In fact it was no wonder that this was so. These two peoples had for long competed for a position of authority in the area of the Greater Syria of Ottoman times, and therefore had lived in deep hatred for each other.

Kissinger had also become acquainted with the President of Syria, Hafez al Assad, whom he considered very intelligent and having a wicked sense of humour. He quite obviously took to Assad, or at least appreciated him very much. In Syrian terms Assad was not radical at all, but rather a man of moderation. He used the Soviet Union as a supplier of arms, but was no Soviet puppet. The Secretary of State's meetings with Assad, who just then was taking English lessons and was obviously eager to learn in other ways as well, often became Professor Kissinger's lessons in Western politics. Kissinger teased Assad that he would be the only Arab leader who spoke English with a German accent.

The negotiations on the Golan disengagement were difficult compared with the Sinai talks. The President of Egypt was sure of his authority and did not need a general consensus to support his decisions. In Syria the question of negotiations with Israel was so controversial that President Assad, in order to preserve his authority, had to build mutual internal understanding daily.

The Israeli leadership had the same problems, but for different reasons. After the parliamentary elections in December it had not been

Agreement signed on disengagement on the Golan, Geneva, 31 May 1974. The author is flanked by Under Secretaries-General Roberto Guyer and Vittorio Winspeare-Guicciardi.

possible to form a majority government. The previous Cabinet led by Golda Meir continued as a minority government. It was difficult to reach an understanding between the governing party and the opposition. It was well known that the slowing-down in finding a solution on the Golan would have harmful effects on the Sinai disengagement. The continuation of the oil embargo would be considered Israel's fault in other parts of the world. But the government knew also that the majority of its people regarded the possibility of peace with Syria as an illusion. The artillery duels continued on the Golan and led to casualties in the Israeli Army.

The peculiarity of political life in Syria, and especially the relations between President Assad and the party leadership, may be discerned in the experiences of General Gamassy in Damascus in January 1974 a few days after Kissinger's first trip. President Sadat sent him to brief President Assad on the newly prepared Sinai disengagement plan.

Gamassy told me that Assad listened to him with interest, made a few additional questions and thanked him kindly. Finally, Assad asked Gamassy to give a similar briefing to the central committee of the Ba'ath Party. Gamassy did as he was asked and the central committee of more than 100 members listened quietly and attentively. However, when Gamassy had finished, a terrible shouting, cursing and abusing started which lasted about an hour. But then things calmed down and at the end Gamassy was thanked for giving a good briefing.

As we have seen, both Syria and Israel had their own reasons why they could not act in a particularly flexible manner in negotiations. In the course of the peace process, each adopted an attitude of "take-it-or-leave-it". So it is even more to the credit of the Israeli government and the President of Syria that the parties were able to overcome their suspicions.

Assad's first proposal on disengagement was at least not modest. Israel was to give up all areas occupied in 1973 and in addition half of the Golan which Syria had lost in 1967. In return Syria would agree to a cease-fire and the separation of forces. But this hard line and the harsh demands were, in Kissinger's opinion, not the significant fact: more important was that Syria was willing to negotiate at all.

After having left Assad's ideas for the Israelis to ponder, Kissinger returned to Washington. There he received Prime Minister Golda Meir's official response. She was ready to present the matter to her government provided that Syria as a first step would send a list of the prisoners of war it had taken.

Based on Golda Meir's letter, Kissinger drafted his first proposal to Assad. According to this package deal, he would deliver Israel's disengagement proposal to Assad as soon as he had received information about the number and the names of the prisoners of war. Details of the disengagement plan would be dealt with in Washington, where both Israel and Syria would send a senior representative, then negotiations on the implementation of the disengagement agreement would take place in Geneva within the framework of the existing Military Working Group. Assad's reaction to Kissinger's proposal was swift. On 7 February he announced that the number of the prisoners of war was 65. The number was greater than Israel had expected and lessened their worries.

At the same time new difficulties arose. The Soviet Union expressed its dissatisfaction with the course of the negotiations. Gromyko stopped off in Washington on his way from Cuba to Moscow in early February.

He blamed Kissinger for the fact that the Americans had consciously kept the Soviet Union outside the peace process, even though there was a clear agreement on co-operation. Now the Soviet Union wanted to take part in the Syrian negotiations, or otherwise great difficulties would follow. The situation seemed alarming, but then it became apparent that Assad did not want the Soviets to become involved in the matter. For Kissinger this was pleasant but surprising news, as Syria was an ally of the Soviet Union.

However, the situation was slightly troublesome when Kissinger arrived in Damascus on 24 January, because Gromyko appeared there at the same time. But the shrewd Syrians did not bring their guests to the same house or the same table. Once again it was obvious that Syria was not a Soviet satellite; instead it was courageously promoting a completely independent policy in an affair that was of great importance to it. This was realized by Kissinger, who had to change his previous thinking. In the United States, where people are inclined to see things in black and white, it was thought that Syria was held on a tight leash by the Soviet Union. The Israelis encouraged such views, although many of its experts were surely aware of how things really were. It was in Israel's interest to stress the Soviet threat and present its own role as the outpost of the West.

Personally, I had always thought that Syria had been driven into the Soviet camp by necessity. From discussions with the Syrians I understood that this alliance was as little popular as it had been in Egypt. The Syrians were clearly jealous of the Egyptians, who had succeeded in expelling their Soviet military experts and changing sides. General Tayara remarked to me after the October War that Syria, unlike Egypt, had kept its distance from the Russians. It had received technical assistance but had never let them inside the operations rooms. I also believe that the Syrians suffered from the technical backwardness of Soviet weaponry. Moreover, they could not understand the extraordinary caution and slow reactions characteristic of Soviet policy.

Syrian officers, like their Egyptian colleagues, had had great difficulties in adapting themselves to Soviet military training. Many of them had spent four or five years in the military schools of Leningrad and Moscow and spoke Russian well. However, these had been difficult years because their cultural background was so very different to that of their hosts. It was hard to get used to the Western order in the Soviet Union, where the most important thing was hard work. The officers from the Middle East enjoyed their comfort and thought that an officer was a gentleman who should not have to work too hard.

The phase of preliminary shuttle diplomacy, which had started in early February, ended at the beginning of March. The attitudes of the parties were extremely suspicious and difficult and their proposals very far from each other. Israel wanted to keep about one third of the ground it had occupied in the October War. Assad's unconditional demand was that Israel should withdraw from the town of Quneitra and some other areas that it had conquered during the 1967 war. Although the results remained meagre, the peace process itself had begun. There was special reason to be glad, because the Arab oil ministers, as a consequence of these negotiations, announced that they would end the oil embargo on 18 March 1974.

In mid-March the representatives of the parties, Defence Minister Moshe Dayan and General Hikmat Al Shihabi, arrived in Washington as agreed. No significant progress occurred; although both parties, in their own opinions, made immense concessions.

The protracted Cabinet crisis in Israel began to make negotiations with Syria more difficult. The problems became acute in early April when the Agranat Commission published its findings about the errors of the first phase of the October War and the acts of negligence preceding it. Golda Meir's Cabinet resigned but continued as a caretaker government. It was planned that Itzshak Rabin, the victorious Chief of Staff of the 1967 war, would form a new government. Moshe Dayan would be forced to step aside.

At the end of April Kissinger arrived in the Middle East and began negotiations in earnest on the disengagement of the Syrian and Israeli armies. On his departure he could not have guessed that this would lead to 34 tiring days and nights of shuttling between the capitals of the area. Damascus alone he visited 13 times. It was unprecedented for the Foreign Minister of a world power to sacrifice so much of his time and effort to act as a mediator in the quarrels of two small countries.

The basic problem in the negotiations was a dispute on territories. Israel could not understand why it should give up land which Syria had lost in the war. For the Syrians, however, it was impossible to conclude an agreement with Israel as long as it held areas which legally belonged to Syria.

The fate of the town of Quneitra was one of the central questions of the negotiations. For Assad, Quneitra was the symbol of success. Its return would show that he had not achieved less than Sadat. Apart from military considerations, Israel thought that this could set a dangerous precedent. If they gave up Quneitra now, what would the Syrians demand next?

In the final phase of this shuttle diplomacy, a document that had been used already in the Sinai agreement, the so-called American proposal, brought a solution to the territorial question of Quneitra. At this stage the suggestion was that the town should be totally under Syrian administration, with a demilitarized zone set up about 200 metres west of its inhabited area. The Israeli forward line would run along the eastern slopes of two dominating hills in front of Quneitra, but weapons whose range could reach the town would not be allowed in this zone. North and south of Quneitra the line would be straightened out so that the Israeli positions would not encircle the town. Israel and Syria accepted this proposal on 18 March 1974.

At this point it was thought that agreement was close. But problems remained. It had already become clear that disengagement on the Golan would be more difficult than in Sinai. In Sinai the operation took place far from the capitals, in the middle of a desert. While Sinai was uninhabited, tens of thousands of civilians would return to the Golan. Police and administrative arrangements would be needed. The civilian inhabitants were probably the chief reason that Assad did not want a UN peace-keeping force on the Golan, but would have been content with a few hundred unarmed military observers. Israel's minimum demand was for an armed peace-keeping force 3,000 strong. The narrowness of the area was not conducive to the establishment of a UN buffer-zone that would be wide enough.

The question of the prohibition of Palestinian activities proved to be the most difficult issue of all. In Sadat's case this question was irrelevant because there were no Palestinian guerrillas on Egyptian soil. In Syria the matter had no great practical significance either, because Assad had not previously allowed Palestinian action to be launched from his territory. But giving public guarantees on the Palestinian question sounded politically impossible. Syria's position in the eyes of the Arab world would become untenable.

Yet, by working in a patient but tough manner, sometimes persuading, sometimes threatening, the last problems were overcome and the agreement began to take form. In Kissinger's opinion, Israel was the more difficult partner throughout the negotiations. In emphasising the importance of the agreement, he remarked that failure in the negotiations would mean the end of the United States' dominant role in the peace process. It would also mean the end of the policy of the United States as a supporter of Israel and would lead to a new crisis and possibly to a war.

On 29 May President Nixon was able to announce to the world that the negotiations had led to an agreement between Israel and Syria, which would be signed that day at the meeting of the Military Working Group in Geneva.

Kissinger's shuttle diplomacy had required extraordinary patience and exceptional skills in mediation. The results were worth the trouble. The participation of the most radical Arab country in the negotiating process gave hope for a more positive approach from the other Arab states in the future. Israel had less reason to worry about that, because its security had clearly improved. President Sadat too was relieved, as his pioneering position as the father of disengagement had been strengthened. He had been criticized for his policy by other Arabs. Now, however, he could start to plan the next stage of disengagement in Sinai.

The Military Working Group meets in Geneva

For the first time after the January meetings, members of the Military Working Group began to assemble in Geneva on 31 May 1974. Joe Fallon and I left by an Egyptair direct flight from Cairo at 8 o'clock in the morning. We did not see the Egyptian delegation; perhaps it would arrive by a special plane. I wondered on the plane what the composition of the Syrian delegation would be.

In Geneva we met the Special Representative of the Secretary-General, Roberto Guyer, who was obviously pleased to see us. Our arrival at least brought a kind of refreshing change to the frustration caused by idleness. There were no other sub-groups of the Peace Conference operating apart from the Military Working Group. Although the Soviet Ambassador, Sergei Vinogradov, and the Special Representative of the Secretary-General were present, the United States, for example, was represented only by a Chargé d'Affaires.

At a luncheon given by the Egyptian Ambassador many details were clarified. Syria would not have a delegation of its own at the meeting. The Syrians felt that direct negotiations with Israel were something so terrible that they had to be somehow concealed from publicity. As a solution the Syrians had invented the fiction that they were joining the Egyptian delegation and would operate under the wing of General Magdoub. Syria's representatives were General Adnan Tayara, whom

I knew well as the Liaison Officer to the UN; the legal adviser of the Foreign Ministry, Tarazi, one of the best known Syrian jurists, and Lieutenant-Colonel Omar. Magdoub and Tayara were good friends from earlier times.

The seating order of the UN representatives at the signing ceremony caused disagreement. Roberto Guyer wanted to be present and thought that he, as the representative of the Secretary-General and as the most senior in rank, should have precedence at the negotiating table. Such disputes were not entirely unknown in UN circles. Because I did not want to be involved in the quarrel, I asked James Jonah to settle the details. He began to arrange things in his usual energetic manner. The matter was further complicated when the Director-General of the European Office, Vittorio Winspeare-Guicciardi, also wanted to be present. Jonah then found a clever solution: my seat as the Chairman would be at the centre of the table but I would be flanked on each side by a high-ranking United Nations Under Secretary-General. But after the signing the senior UN representatives would leave the chamber. The parties did not want them to be present at the ordinary meetings.

In good time before the meeting the delegations assembled in the beautiful chamber where once the Council of the League of Nations held its sessions. The Israeli delegation was led by General Herzl Shafir, whom the Egyptians knew from the time when he had searched for the bodies of Israeli soldiers in UNEF's Operation Omega. Continuity in the delegation was represented by Colonel Dov Sion and the Foreign Ministry official Meir Rosenne. At the back of the chamber plenty of members of the media were present.

When all were seated I called the meeting to order and gave a short opening statement. I said that it was with a feeling of profound joy that I convened the meeting of the Military Working Group of the Geneva Peace Conference on the Middle East for the purpose of signing the agreement on the disengagement of Israeli and Syrian forces and to work out procedures for its prompt implementation. I continued:

Owing to an exceptional feat of diplomacy unparalleled in the annals of international relations, the foundation has been laid on which a reliable structure of peace could be built and strengthened. We all owe a debt of gratitude to all those who have devoted enormous energy, thought and time in negotiating this agreement.

Although the present agreement is not a peace treaty, no one can deny that it represents a milestone in the unceasing efforts to achieve a just and lasting peace in the Middle East. We are all, I am sure, aware of the fact that a good deal remains to be done in the furtherance of this goal, but this agreement gives us encouragement, that with perseverance, tenacity, flexibility, understanding and the will for peace, we can dare to express the hope of further progress in the search for a just and lasting settlement.

Even though the harsh realities of the problem may yet present us with occasional setbacks in the tortuous and difficult road towards normalization and reconciliation among the peoples of the Middle East, I have the strong conviction that this historic agreement may well turn out to be that giant and courageous step that brought us to the threshold of a new era of trust, justice and peace in the Middle East.

In the spirit of these solemn considerations I invited the representatives of Israel and Syria to sign the agreement.

I heard on the following day that the thanks I had expressed in the opening speech had come to the attention of Henry Kissinger. I sent him with pleasure a copy of my speech, which he had requested. He certainly deserved the thanks.

After a short intermission following the signing ceremony, we began preliminary discussions on the actual issues. General Shafir proposed three points as a basis for the negotiations: the time-table for disengagement, the return of the bodies of the fallen and the evacuation of broken-down vehicles from no-man's-land. One could see here again the Israelis' great concern for their dead, which the Syrians had difficulty in understanding. The Syrian representative, Tarasi, stressed in his statement that the withdrawal of the Israeli forces should be the main subject of the negotiations. On the basis of the views of the parties I proposed that the working group should concentrate on the formation of the methods of disengagement and should deal with the issues proposed by Israel in the course of the discussions. My proposal was accepted. At the same time it was decided that the day's meeting would be considered as the first official meeting, because according to the agreement that was to be held 24 hours after the agreement was signed. The second meeting, it was decided, would be held on the following day at 1600 hours. Now we would have time to familiarize ourselves with the agreement and its Annex, which concerned the UN force. (See Appendixes 8a and 8b.)

The agreement provided for the separation of the opposing armies on the Golan Heights and the complete withdrawal of Israeli forces from the area occupied in the 1973 war. In addition to this Israel had agreed to give up a small area at the Rafid road crossing which it had occupied in the Six Day War of 1967. To enforce the permanent separation of the Israeli and Syrian troops a kind of buffer-zone was formed, which in this agreement was called the area of separation. The UN force was stationed in this area. In addition the agreement defined the areas of limitation on armaments and troops on both sides of the area of separation (see map p. 272).

To supervise the disengagement operation, it was decided to set up a United Nations Disengagement Observer Force (UNDOF). The name of this force betrays the fact that it was the result of a compromise. During the negotiations Israel wanted the UN presence to consist of a strong armed force, while Syria wanted only unarmed military observers. Thus the result was a combination of a few armed soldiers (about 1,200 men) and 90 military observers. After disengagement was completed, UNDOF's task was to supervise the observance of the cease-fire and to verify by regular inspections that the limitations on armaments and forces were not exceeded.

The area of separation was under Syrian administration and Syrian civilians were allowed to return to this area. In carrying out its mission, UNDOF would comply with generally applicable Syrian laws and regulations and would not hamper the functioning of local civil administration.

The task of the Military Working Group was due to be completed within five days, so there was no time to be wasted. We had a good start in the basic questions when General Shafir presented maps relating to the disengagement plan at the second meeting. The different phases of disengagement and the location of the temporary buffer-zones of UNDOF were marked on these maps. At the third meeting General Tayara accepted this plan, proposing a few minor changes which Israel later accepted. When we had arrived this far, General Magdoub proposed the setting up of a committee to prepare final maps for the signing ceremony.

The talks also dealt with issues connected with disengagement which could not be expressed only by maps and time-tables. Many of these questions, for example the limitations on armaments and troops, were in the opinion of the Syrians so sensitive that they did not want to include them in a public protocol. Therefore the Chairman registered these questions, as in the Sinai agreement, in a document called the Statement of the Chairman (see Appendix 9). This paper was read on the last day of the meeting in the presence of Generals Shafir and Tayara and they announced that the parties had accepted it.

The Statement of the Chairman gives some kind of an impression of the issues that were considered at the meetings. The only thing that cannot be seen from it is the unusual thoroughness in the handling of such questions as prisoners of war and the bodies of the dead. Much time was also spent in pondering the armament and troop limitations. Agreement on the practical details of disengagement was much speeded up by the 17-point programme which the Israelis presented at the penultimate session. Because it very much resembled the Sinai plan, this was accepted quite quickly and painlessly. Again a Forward Headquarters was to be set up, to which the parties would send their liaison officers. In the same way as in Sinai, this would regulate the course of the disengagement process. In connection with the deployment of UNDOF, close co-operation with the parties was particularly stressed.

When I look today at the issues covered in the Statement of the Chairman, I note the seemingly pedantic and over-particular manner in which many details were studied. The diminishing numbers of troops during the disengagement period are noted down to the last tank and gun. The tasks, armaments and vehicles of the Syrian police are covered in detail. I remember that the police formed the subject of endless discussions. In everything one could see the deep distrust between the parties and the illusion that security would increase if only the limitations were defined in great detail and UNDOF had the task of verifying them. It was hard for me to understand such endless distrust and I could hardly bear the continual hair-splitting. A detailed scheme of limitations would not resolve the situation on the Golan or ensure the success of UNDOF. Only increasing trust between Israel and Syria would calm the tension, while UNDOF would succeed only if the parties had the political will, based on mutual interests, to maintain peace.

The atmosphere of the meetings was not as positive and easy as in the negotiations that I had previously chaired, yet it would have been unrealistic to hope for any special warmth to be created between Syria and Israel. It was in fact a miracle that the Syrians were present at all. Perhaps the reason for their presence was that the Syrians wanted to bring about an agreement and Hafez al Assad, as a wise and realistic

The author discussing the disengagement on the Golan with Gen. Adnan Tayara, senior Syrian delegate.

leader, realized that this would not happen without negotiations in Geneva. In any case they tried to give the impression that they were not really present at all, but were only following from the side-lines how the Egyptians were handling their affairs. General Tayara, who is by nature quiet and unassuming and does not irritate anybody by his behaviour, usually did not open his mouth. At that time his English was not very good and therefore he was satisfied with giving some statements in Arabic. But together with General Shafir he observed carefully at the map table the different phases of disengagement. Judge Tarazi, who was soon to become a member of the International Court of Justice in The Hague, brought his own positive contribution to the meetings. He was particularly happy that, following the good old traditions of Kilometre 101, we had arranged for coffee and sandwiches to be served during the breaks in the meetings. For 30 years, he said, he had participated in different meetings of the UN and now for the first time coffee was served.

General Shafir was taking part in the negotiations of the Military Working Group for the first time, and he did not quite succeed in his job. Firstly, his English was rather deficient and therefore he had difficulties in expressing himself. I often realized that the opposite side did not understand what he was trying to say. Perhaps it was because of his insufficient grasp of the language that he sometimes sounded harsher and more aggressive than he had meant. But perhaps it was because of his personality that he easily lost his temper and raised his voice. This did not further mutual understanding.

General Magdoub had a completely opposite effect on the smooth running and the atmosphere of the meetings, which were positively influenced by his confidence-inspiring, jovial appearance and fine sense of humour. At the same time, Magdoub was a skilful and shrewd negotiator who got everything possible out of the opposite side, despite the weak negotiating position of the Arabs. Behind his broad back the representatives of Syria had quite an easy life and they got off quite well thanks to Magdoub. Magdoub was helped by his great experience of earlier negotiations, particularly of the Sinai disengagement talks. He certainly gave the Syrians a reliable picture of the possibilities and problems of the plan under negotiation. Without Magdoub the agreement might not have been accepted.

All in all, the negotiations went off without very great difficulties. The favourable result was affected firstly by the fact that on the political level the negotiated agreement was very detailed and that the major causes of the quarrel had already been resolved. Secondly, we all, excepting the Syrians, had behind us the Sinai agreement and its much more complicated disengagement agreement. On the Golan the military situation was simpler than that in Sinai.

According to the very tight time-table in the agreement, disengagement was to begin within 24 hours of the completion of the working group's task, i.e. on 6 June 1974. Therefore we had to get UNDOF operational as soon as possible. We in UNEF had prepared ourselves for that all spring. I had established a working group to plan the disengagement force for the Golan. As a general instruction I said that this should be set up solely from UNEF resources. Both military and civilian personnel should be used as economically as possible. This meant that UNDOF was in a way a child of UNEF and the principle was that

UNEF should take care of the new force like a father takes care of his child.

The work of the planning group was necessarily somewhat vague, because we had no knowledge of the strength of the new force or the width of the buffer-zone, nor were we allowed to reconnoitre on the Golan. The lack of accurate information did not present us with too much trouble when we took as the basis for our planning a brigade of three battalions which was larger than the probable force. I selected the battalions of Austria, Peru and Nepal, because they all had experience of mountain conditions. The Headquarters of the Northern Brigade, under the command of the Peruvian General G. Briceno, would be used to lead the new force. To the logistics component of the force small units would be added from the Canadian and Polish logistics contingents of UNEF.

Following the task it had been given, the Military Working Group completed its work, according to schedule, on 5 June 1974. The representatives of Israel and Syria signed the disengagement plan, marked on a map, and the actual process of disengagement could start the following day.

In my final speech I congratulated the Israeli and Syrian representatives in particular for their co-operation and understanding throughout the Geneva talks, and I added:

I am sure I discern a sign, however feeble, of a desirable change of attitude. Prevailing in all our discussions was a readiness to find areas of accommodation to meet the legitimate interests of both sides. I feel that it was this development and the wealth of experience gained in the talks at Kilometre 101, that enabled us to make rapid progress in our work.

We must constantly remind ourselves that we have only taken the vitally important initial steps in a long and difficult journey towards a just and lasting peace in the Middle East. The two Disengagement and Separation of Forces Agreements, both in the Egypt-Israel and Israel-Syria sectors, should now create the proper atmosphere for tackling the outstanding political problems. Certainly, we are all eager with hope that the constructive and positive attitude that dominated our meetings will offer encouragement to all those engaged in the continuing search for a just peace in the area.

As far as the United Nations is concerned, UNDOF stands ready to render all necessary assistance to the parties in the implementation and strict observation of the Separation of Forces Agreement.

I ended by saying that I had already taken steps to make UNDOF operational within the time specified in the disengagement plan.

Disengagement is achieved

After the meeting had ended, the UN negotiating team had to hurry to Jerusalem. The time-table for disengagement was so tight that there was no time to be wasted. The new Commander of UNDOF, General Briceno, was on his way to Damascus where he intended to establish his headquarters in the UNTSO building. Besides him, Colonel P.D. Hogan, appointed as the temporary Chief of Staff of UNDOF, and Dennis Holland, UNDOF's temporary Chief Administrative Officer, had come to meet us as well. Colonel Kuosa and Captain Fallon travelled with UNDOF High Command to Damascus on the following morning to begin the preparations for disengagement. James Jonah and I flew to Cairo later that same day. The Secretary-General, Kurt Waldheim, was coming to visit UNEF. I had also to take care of other matters pertaining to the setting up of UNDOF, which had still not been settled. For instance, it was necessary to attach a professionally competent officer with English as his mother tongue to the Operations Branch of UNDOF. I spoke of this to the Commander of the Canadian contingent, General LaRose, who promised to look for a suitable officer for the job.

At the same time as we prepared ourselves to complete the present round of talks in Geneva, UNEF Headquarters in Cairo put the finishing touches to the operational plan for UNDOF. According to the signed agreement it would include the battalions of Austria and Peru, and a Canadian-Polish logistics element. The total strength would not be very great, about 1,250 men altogether. This figure included the 90 military observers who would be transferred from UNTSO to UNDOF. I had decided to station the Austrians in the mountain area of the northern sector of the Golan, in the foothills of Mount Hermon. The town of Quneitra would also be part of their area. The Peruvians, whose battalion was smaller, would be placed on the high plateau of the southern sector. As a possible location for UNDOF Headquarters I had thought of the town of Quneitra, where the HQ would be in the UN's own area and close to the troops. At the request of the Syrians,

however, I ended up with Damascus as the location. The merit of this
alternative was that there it would be easier to arrange proper accommodation for the headquarters.

For the Canadian logistics unit accommodation was found on the
Israeli-occupied Golan in an abandoned military camp from the time of
the Second World War. The headquarters and reserves of the Peruvian
battalion would also be stationed here. This Camp Ziouani was in
miserable condition. It was also known as Camp Roofless, because the
tin roofs of its long brick barracks had either been stolen or had gone
with the wind. After repairs the camp became quite good, however,
and in places even cosy. For the Polish logistics unit and the headquarters of the Austrian battalion we found, after a long search, a
suitable camp on the Syrian side near Wadi Faouar. This camp too
needed thorough repairs.

The intention was to bring UNDOF by road transport to the
Golan – a considerable operation because the distance was more than
600 km. The advance parties were flown by UNEF's Canadian Buffalos
to Damascus. Difficulties in carrying out the transport plan appeared
when the Israeli authorities told UNEF that the Polish logistics unit
would not be allowed to drive through Israel and Polish trucks could
not be used for the transportation of other troops. The argument for
the prohibition was that Poland and Israel had no diplomatic relations.
In addition, according to the Israelis, the Poles were so unpopular in
Israel that their security could not be guaranteed. I instructed UNEF
Headquarters to protest strongly against the prohibition. The responsibility would be totally Israel's if UNEF was now forced to abandon
its plan and UNDOF could not be brought to its area of operation in
time. I spoke about the matter to the Israeli negotiating delegation as
well and finally the matter was settled.

Israeli fears of the threat to the security of the Poles proved to be completely unfounded. The appearance of the Poles on the roads of Israel
aroused much attention. Many former Polish Jews came out to see the
Polish soldiers, bringing them flowers and presents. They also seemed
to enjoy speaking with them in their mother tongue. This unexpected
and excessive friendliness considerably slowed down UNDOF's progress and its first detachments arrived at their destinations later than
calculated.

On the last day of May, at the same time as the Israel-Syria disengagement agreement was signed in Geneva, all firing stopped on the Golan.
UNTSO military observers confirmed this good news. Since the end of

the October War they had continued to man their former observation posts in the areas which the war had not reached and had set up a number of new posts on the edges of the vast Israeli salient. Soon the Austrian and Peruvian battalions began to deploy in the area. They pushed between the Israeli and Syrian forces, with the Austrians settling down in the Sasa area and the Peruvians along the cease-fire lines leading from Quneitra to the south.

Disengagement began on 14 June 1974 and continued for four weeks. According to the plan, the operation was carried out in four phases. In each phase Israel handed over to UNDOF a part of the territory occupied by it and on the following morning UNDOF then handed this over to the Syrians. In the last phase on 24 and 25 June Israel vacated the area of separation and UNDOF was permanently stationed in it. On the following day the Syrian civilian administration began to work in this area again. Finally the UNDOF military observers inspected the areas of limited troops and armaments and on the following day went on to inspect the 20 and 25 km. zones. This marked the end of the whole disengagement process.

The entire operation proceeded without greater mishaps. Right in the final phase, on 25 June, a serious accident did take place, however. Early that morning an Austrian truck drove over a mine in the area of separation, near Mount Hermon. Four soldiers were killed and one wounded. After the accident we reached an agreement with the governments of the parties that a 500-strong Syrian mine-clearing unit was allowed to work in the area of separation. Although much work was done to clear patrol paths for UNDOF soldiers, the mines remained a continuing threat.

Having completed the disengagement process with honour, UNDOF defined and marked the borders of the area of separation. This was not entirely successful everywhere, because among the military observers there was no real expert on maps. Small but annoying disputes arose over the delineation. They were never resolved. I thought to myself that in future we would get professional surveyors to do the job.

UNDOF at work

Now UNDOF could embark on its real duties. Its aim was to keep all military units outside the area of separation, as stipulated in paragraph 7 of the Statement of the Chairman. For that purpose permanent positions were set up along the lines and regular patrolling was begun.

AREA OF SEPARATION
OF THE TROOPS
ON THE GOLAN IN 1974

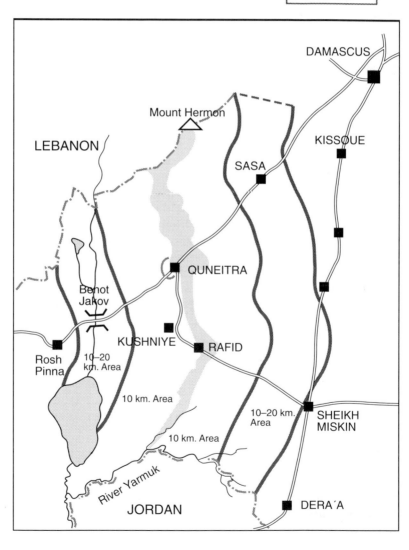

Equally important was the verification of the limitations on armaments and troops, carried out by UNDOF inspectors every second week.

In the beginning many kinds of errors and incidents, caused mainly by inexperience, occurred. Some of them nearly led to fatal consequences for UNDOF's future. The worst error was caused by the fact that the eastern border of the area of separation cut through several roads running east to west, so that the connecting roads were either in the area of separation or far in the rear. As a consequence, one morning a column of black Syrian limousines drove, obviously in error, through a checkpoint inside the area of separation. An Austrian lieutenant, who was present, tried to stop the cars. When all else failed, he jumped on the bonnet of the first car and at gunpoint forced the passengers out. The Defence Minister of Syria and several generals in full uniform were in the car. The situation was most embarrassing, to say the least.

The Syrians were deeply offended by the incident and threatened that UNDOF would have to go. I spent more than a week in Damascus in order to clarify the matter. I tried to explain the situation and to apologize. Fortunately, feelings gradually calmed down and the matter was settled. Almost as difficult for me was to explain the matter to the Austrian battalion. In the view of the Austrians the Lieutenant had acted fully in accordance with the instructions which had been given. My argument was that an officer had been put in charge of the checkpoint because it had been hoped that he would not simply carry out instructions, but would also use his common sense.

On another occasion in UNDOF's early days, there occurred an incident that caused the Israelis justifiable irritation. In the area of separation there were a number of fortified stone-block bunkers, built by the Israelis. It had been agreed in Geneva that UNDOF would take them into its possession and man them. This had, in the main, happened but then it appeared that UNDOF did not need them all. The Syrians often said to me that these empty bunkers should be destroyed. They were afraid that in the possible case of a renewal of hostilities the Israelis could make use of them. I talked to the Israelis about the matter, but it got no further. UNDOF also studied the possibilities of destroying the bunkers by using explosives. In the middle of these rather slow discussions, Syrian bulldozers suddenly appeared on the spot. The Peruvian officers and soldiers stood passively by as the Syrians made short work of razing the bunkers to the ground. The Syrian activity was so surprising and fast that there was no time to do anything. The situation was, from UNDOF's and my point of view, embarrassing.

In August 1974, a Canadian Buffalo flying from Ismailia via Jerusalem to Damascus, crashed near the Syrian village of Ad Dimas, hit by an anti-aircraft missile. All nine of the Canadians on the plane were killed. This very sad accident touched my family too, because my wife had been a passenger on the plane on its leg between Ismailia and Jerusalem.

During the first months I had to go to Damascus frequently and spend lengthy times there. I tried to advise and guide the inexperienced UNDOF Commander and his staff. General Briceno tried his best, but he was perhaps not the most suitable person for this kind of job. He was an officer of commando troops and apparently a very courageous man. His hobby was car-racing. He would talk with pleasure about the highlight of his career, when he was sent to the presidential palace to apprehend the previous President of Peru and to bring him to the ship which was awaiting him in the harbour. The General's real problem was his deficient English, which meant he had difficulties in keeping contact with the authorities and in commanding an international force. He was, however, always in a good and optimistic mood, and when we met would assure me: "I am learning!"

The Peruvian battalion returned home in July 1974 and was replaced by a battalion from Iran. General Briceno left in December and the Austrian Major-General Hannes Philipp was appointed to replace him. He took command of UNDOF in an energetic and skilful manner. Now my task was made much easier. Of course it was necessary to continue the visits to Damascus and to hold meetings with the Syrian authorities and the staff of UNDOF. But my worries were over, because I knew that UNDOF was now in reliable hands.

At the same time, the situation on the Golan was clearly calmer. The problems were minimal. Most were caused by Syrian shepherds grazing their flocks near the line with Israel. Often they crossed the line either unknowingly or because the grass was greener on the other side.

Quite insignificant also were some limitations on the freedom of movement. The Poles were still not allowed to visit Israel. The Syrians for their part also tried to limit the movement of other nationalities from Syria to Israel and back. Both parties from time to time restricted the movement of the inspectors in the areas of limited armaments and troops. One could say that the problems were always small. It was everywhere apparent that Israel and Syria were trying to avoid creating tension and therefore they scrupulously adhered to the agreement that had been concluded. This made UNDOF's task much easier.

21. Life in Sinai, 1974-5

The Secretary-General visits UNEF

In connection with the Golan disengagement, the Secretary-General made a short visit to UNEF on 7 and 8 June 1974. First we took him to see the arrangements in the buffer-zone. Waldheim was clearly disappointed by what he saw. He had probably imagined that UNEF soldiers would stand along the borders of the buffer-zone shoulder to shoulder with their rifles pointing threateningly. Instead he saw only an almost empty sandy desert, where the positions were often many kilometres apart. I noticed again that Waldheim was not interested in how things were but in how they looked.

While sitting in the car on our way to Ismailia, I told the Secretary-General about the dismal conditions in which UNEF soldiers had had to work at first.. But the battalions had now greatly improved their conditions with their own handiwork and resources. I thought that for the sake of morale and the comfort of the troops it would be a good idea to arrange for the soldiers to have a week's leave, for example in Alexandria. I mentioned that in UNEF I in the 1950s and 1960s such leave, paid for by the UN, had been arranged. Waldheim was not at all pleased with my proposal. First, it was too expensive; secondly, the soldiers had not come here to have a comfortable life, and thirdly, such leaves did not occur elsewhere, in the Austrian Foreign Ministry for instance.

In Ismailia we visited the base camp of the Swedish battalion which was beautifully situated on the shore of Lake Timsah. We were received at the gate of the camp by the Battalion Commander, Colonel P.O. Hallqvist, a guard of honour and scores of Swedish soldiers with cameras. Close to the shore, on a green lawn, was the dining tent and a cosy open-air restaurant. The soldiers of the battalion had collected money among themselves and bought comfortable rattan easy-chairs, tables and colourful parasols for the restaurant. The scene was like a sunny beach in a popular tourist resort. It did not impress Waldheim; probably it was too unlike the harsh military life and dismal accommodation he had experienced with the German Army during the Second World War. He muttered to me angrily that this was not a military camp but a leave centre.

The Secretary-General's mood did not improve when Colonel

Hallqvist in his briefing criticized the UN logistics arrangements quite strongly, giving as an example the fact that, despite the hot weather there had been for some time, UNEF had even now been unable to . provide soft drinks and beer for the troops. Pointing at the beer cans on the tables of the mess tent and at the Colonel's rather respectable belly, Waldheim remarked, "You at least have got your share!" He did not want to listen to the Colonel's explanation that the Swedish government had sent the beer and the soft drinks.

I do not think that Waldheim's visit left the Swedish battalion with any pleasant memories. In his own memoirs Colonel Hallqvist writes:

> The Secretary-General did not make any strong impression during the quarter of an hour which he offered to the Swedish Battalion. It looked as if he had come to show himself and to let himself be photographed, and not to be disturbed by complaints and other irritating points of view.

The atmosphere improved temporarily when we came to our next stop, the new logistics camp at Ismailia. The preparations for the move of the Canadians and the Poles had just started. No unit had yet moved because most of the buildings of the camp had fallen into ruin and needed thorough repairs. The Poles, who wanted to offer their important guest a luncheon in conditions compatible with his rank, had worked day and night to get at least one building into a tolerable shape for a visit. They had succeeded very well in their work. The luncheon was elegant and the atmosphere pleasant.

Led by General Holmes, we moved from the luncheon to the Canadian area. It was if possible in a still worse condition than the area assigned to the Poles. Many of the buildings were charred black after a fire. Near one of such ruined houses General Holmes gave his own briefing. He said that after the Polish eyewash we would now get acquainted with harsh reality. As everybody could see, the conditions were such that Canadian soldiers at least were not used to working in them. He continued his briefing by saying that the Canadians had not arrived here to clean and to build, but to take care of the logistics needs of UNEF troops. At this stage the Secretary-General interrupted General Holmes's briefing by saying, "Work more and complain less!" An unpleasant altercation started which continued in asides. The Secretary-General was angry and he considered General Holmes's behaviour disrespectful. I heard that the matter was later discussed in New York on the diplomatic level. General Holmes's behaviour was perhaps not quite appropriate but factually he was right. It was at least partly the fault of the Secretary-General that the UNEF budget had been so under-estimated and that therefore it had not been possible to begin the necessary construction work in the logistics camp.

On the following day the visit continued in the southern part of the buffer-zone and the city of Suez. In the area of responsibility of the Finnish battalion, the Secretary-General inspected a company of honour and a position. At the command post in Ayun Musa he listened to the Battalion Commander's briefing and left the Finnish area through the command post of the 1st Ranger Company. Here the important visitor looked satisfied. Perhaps the conditions there were, in the opinion of an old *Wehrmacht* officer, harsh enough.

The visit ended with a lunch at the base camp of the Austrian battalion in the city of Suez. Half of the battalion was already on its way to the Golan but the other half was still only preparing for departure. The atmosphere at the luncheon table was cheerful and lively. Among his own people the Secretary-General looked content and happy.

Changes in deployment in the UNEF buffer-zone

The establishment of UNDOF at the end of May meant the departure of the Austrian and Peruvian battalions from the buffer-zone. The gaps they left behind were filled by the neighbours of the departed battalions widening their areas. Thus the battalions of Panama and Sweden divided the Peruvian area between themselves and similarly the battalions of Ghana and Senegal shared the area of the Austrians.

The UNEF Office in Rabah was established to replace the departed headquarters of the Northern Brigade. The Nepalese Colonel A. Rana was appointed the Chief of the Rabah Office, whose task was to co-ordinate the functioning of the northern battalions, to assist them in logistics problems and to lead the inspections arranged for the verification of the arms limitations on the Israeli side according to the disengagement agreement. UNEF Headquarters had direct control over the inspections on the Egyptian side.

But the lessening of UNEF troop numbers did not end here. In early June the Irish government decided to recall its battalion. A disastrous act of terrorism had taken place in Dublin and therefore the country's military preparedness had to be strengthened. (The return of the battalion probably increased the preparedness only symbolically because its men were dispersed to their original units all over the country.) For us the departure of the Irish was a great loss. The Nepalese battalion relieved the Irish in the buffer-zone. It was a pleasant task for the Nepalese because they were thoroughly bored with their reserve duties in Shams Camp.

The Nepalese battalion could not stay more than about two months in the buffer-zone, for it had to return home in mid-August. Nepal was making preparations for the coronation of its King and the battalion was needed in the festivities. The deployment of UNEF was now changed so that the Swedish battalion moved to the most northern sector of the zone. I wanted to have in this area, which had turned out to be a very demanding sector, as experienced and reliable a battalion as possible. The Finnish battalion remained in the southernmost sector. In conclusion the deployment of UNEF on 1 October 1974 was, from north to south: the battalions of Sweden, Panama, Indonesia, Ghana, Senegal and Finland.

Lastly UNEF had to give up the Panamanian battalion as well, towards the end of November, "on the basis of an agreement with the Panamanian government". The reason was never announced, but I believe that the small Panamanian Army had difficulties in maintaining a whole battalion abroad. After the departure of the Panamanians the remaining five battalions had to widen their sectors further.

The fall in the number of battalions from ten to five was a serious cut for UNEF. The remaining troops really had to strain themselves to perform wider tasks than before. For example, we were forced to give the battalions guard duties outside the buffer-zone. At first New York Headquarters tried to provide new battalions to replace the departed ones, but politically suitable and willing participants were not found. Later it was realized that the decrease in UNEF's strength lessened expenses and made the passage of the new budget easier.

The contingent commanders, who had to struggle continuously with the difficulties caused by their increasing tasks, were not pleased with the reductions. I had a different view, however. In my opinion the battalions could take care of their additional duties by rationalization and reorganization. The experience of the coming years was to prove me right.

We move to Ismailia

My apartment in Cairo was reasonably comfortable and even cosy during the winter months. Compared with the hotel, it was almost like a home. The burden of work had gradually lessened and now there was occasionally time for leisure. However, life was monotonous – my wife was still in Finland because of the schooling of our youngest son – although the guest book reminds me that even in a home without a hostess guests were received, mainly our own people from UNEF.

Welcome and refreshing guests did arrive from home too. In March my mother and sister came for two weeks. Then in April, when the tulip trees blossomed in Cairo, good old family friends arrived. The visits of the spring season were rounded off by the Defence Affairs Committee of our Parliament. It had been the guest of the Finnish battalion in Suez and now it was the turn of the Ambassador to receive the visitors.

At the end of May my wife finally returned from Finland and it was not before time. In my letters I had assured her that our apartment was so well-furnished that nothing new was needed. At once she noticed a serious shortage, however. There was not a single flower vase in the house. Together with the driver she went to the bazaar and bought more than ten vases as a start. The other more serious shortcoming of the apartment appeared quite soon afterwards. The summer of 1974 was suffocatingly hot in Cairo, as always. Now our apartment, which in the winter months had been so comfortable and cosy, was as hot as an oven. We kept the window shutters closed all day so that at least in the evening the rooms would be a little cooler. Life was easier for me because during the day I was away in my air-conditioned office in Merryland Villa. My wife and my youngest son, however, perspired and suffered.

During the worst heatwave the air did not get cooler even at night. I stayed bravely in the bedroom, pretending to myself and others that a human being should not pay attention to such trifles as heat or coldness. Mother and son, who suffered from heat more than I, tried to sleep on folding cots on the balcony under the star-studded sky, but after a night of broken sleep they would awake in the morning in a pool of sweat. The much-increased air traffic after the winter also disturbed our sleep. The flightpaths of aeroplanes taking off and landing were just above our house and the terrible noise tore the soul.

We all wished impatiently that the move to Ismailia would finally materialize. The decision to move headquarters had been made in

January and the repair work had started in the early spring. But progress was extremely slow. Everything should have been ready when the summer began but one agreed deadline after another was passed. The lack of enterprise and passivity of the Chief Administrative Officer and his assistants seemed totally incomprehensible. I could not reach any other conclusion but that the slowness was intentional. They did not want to give up the comforts of the Sheraton Hotel. The CAO excused the delay by saying that he and his colleagues were used to certain standards and they could not content themselves with field conditions like the soldiers. When a few weeks later he presented as his last pretext the lack of teaspoons in the new dining-room, I could no longer control my temper but gave him a thorough lecture. In the case of this Chief Administrative Officer this was, however, of no avail, because he could be influenced neither by fair means nor by foul. I could only hope that he would return as soon as possible to his hobbies as a pensioner. He was of no help here. Even Lansky was now ready to admit that he had erred in the choice of personnel.

At the beginning of August the staff was at last able to move to Ismailia. Finally we all had good working and housing conditions in the same area. At least the soldiers were very happy. My family too was happy. A beautiful home behind a high brick wall was waiting for us in the headquarters compound. It was not a magnificent palace owned by top executives of the Suez Canal Company, of the type where for example President Sadat often resided, but was the residence of a middle-level official of the Company. There was room enough for our needs, about 200 square metres altogether. On the ground floor there were a large living room, a dining-room, a study, a kitchen and an adjoining breakfast room. Upstairs there were three bedrooms and the bath- and shower rooms. A large terrace, screened with tight mosquito nets, opened onto the garden, where we had our own mango trees and bougainvillea.

In the second week of August my wife and I travelled to Finland to celebrate my mother's eightieth birthday at the family villa in northern Finland, near the city of Oulu. It was a refreshing break in my busy and heavy working schedule, although I could not stay longer than two weeks. My wife remained in Finland to take care of practical matters and only returned to Ismailia at the end of September. A house without a hostess is always sad and at this time she was particularly needed, to complete the arrangements for our new house and to entertain guests. UNEF's own people and outsiders too were queueing to visit. I thought it was cosier and more polite to receive these guests at home than to arrange parties at UNEF's Kilometre 101 mess.

Life in Ismailia was not easy to begin with. The town had been deserted for seven years. The elegant houses built by the French, and their beautiful gardens, had fallen into decay. The difference was great when compared with the pre-war urban scenery that I remembered well from my first trips through Ismailia to Cairo in 1957. Then the city really was a pearl of the Canal zone. The inhabitants, however, began gradually to return, the first shops opened their doors, the houses were painted and the gardens refurbished. Slowly Ismailia was returning to normality.

The UNEF Headquarters compound had its own problems in the early days. The electricity supply broke down every now and then because of overloading. We would have to sit in the dark with no air-conditioning. Life was suffocating because of the heat, There was a continuous shortage of gas bottles, when the refrigerators and gas ranges did not work. The mosquitos attacked and spread malaria. We all took malaria tablets and wished that President Sadat would visit his villa as often as possible, because before his arrival the Egyptians sprayed insecticides above the irrigation canals and other humid areas.

Some other animals were a nuisance at first too. Packs of wild dogs ventured into our compound during the night and would howl threateningly. No wonder that when I left for a couple of days in Damascus or Jerusalem, my wife slept in the upstairs bedroom with a large knife under her pillow. The feeling of security improved considerably when we were able to arrange a Ghanaian guard in front of the house.

One evening we were sitting after dinner in the living room in romantic candlelight because of the usual black-out. Some ladies, good family friends from Finland, were visiting. My colleague of many years, Tatsuro Kunugi, the legal adviser of UNTSO, had also dropped in. Suddenly he asked my wife whether we had a pet animal or what was it that was sitting under the little table? On closer examination it appeared to be a big, furry rat, observing us with bright, cheerful eyes. The ladies made the appropriate noises and Mr Kunugi asked why it was that American and European ladies always screamed when they saw a rat. In Japan people reacted to rats, as to any other animal, without showing terror or disgust.

The rat war continued on the following day. We noticed that a rat was making a nest under the bidet in the bathroom, and had even taken a towel as material for the nest. To deal with it a trap was found: a real, old fashioned, box-form article, made of wire. Soon the rat was sitting in the trap eating a piece of cheese. My wife took the trap out and said to the Ghanaian soldier, "Do something!" Now the ladies began to worry about the fate of the rat. I comforted them by saying that the soldier had opened the door of the trap and let the rat out. That is what I would have done anyway.

In the mornings my wife drove to the city for shopping. The meat was purchased separately from the excellent meat bazaar in Heliopolis, but in Ismailia there was a good vegetable and fish shop. My wife's Arabic improved fast when she had to buy from the very friendly but non-English-speaking fishmonger "*etneen kilo samaka sola*" (two kilos of sole) or "*wahed kilo gambari*" (one kilo of shrimps). There was much more fish and many more varieties than in Israel. It was brought to Ismailia from three directions: the Mediterranean, the Red Sea and the Suez Canal. The amount of fish in the Canal had increased immensely during the seven war years, for navigation had not disturbed them and fishing was strongly forbidden to Egyptian and Israeli troops. Only some military observers, quietly and unknown to the parties, had gone fishing there.

One of our first dinner guests was Colonel Raitasaari, the Finnish Battalion Commander. He noticed with astonishment how my wife from time to time disappeared into the kitchen for a while. "Is it you who is serving and even cooking here? Shouldn't you concentrate on entertaining the guests?" he said and continued, "We have professional people in the battalion who would come with pleasure to help you." This was a good idea. At many dinner parties thereafter a working team from the battalion cooked and served a tasty and elegant meal. The guests definitely formed a favourable impression of the skills of the Finnish UN soldiers. I believe that the latter for their part enjoyed the task, which brought them from the Sinai desert to have a glimpse of the great world. They brought folding cots with them and were accommodated in the basement of our house. In the courtyard of the UNEF compound new films were shown every evening and at least there they met people whom they would not have encountered in the buffer-zone every day.

On one occasion it was the turn of General Taha Magdoub and other senior liaison officers to come for a visit. We had been invited to their homes and enjoyed their generous Oriental hospitality. We thought hard about how to arrange the luncheon so that we would not be put to shame. I told my wife that she had a free hand concerning the different courses, but there should be so much food that when the guests had had three helpings the table would still look untouched. Apparently the lunch was a success because the guests stayed for seven hours.

As a consequence of the move to Ismailia we had to rearrange our contacts with the Egyptian authorities. UNTSO had originally had a liaison officer of the rank of lieutenant-colonel in Cairo, who acted as the representative of the Chief of Staff but on a lower level also took care of the affairs of Ismailia Control Centre. Now the main task of the Liaison Officer in Cairo was to handle the contacts with the UNEF Commander and his military and civilian staff. Since the autumn of 1973 the liaison officer's job was held by the Swedish lieutenant-colonel P.G. Björlin, an experienced military observer whose personality was particularly well suited to this task. Over the years he established warm relations with the Egyptian liaison officers, Defence and Foreign Ministries, airport, police and customs authorities. Under his control, matters seemed to run themselves. I was glad that the Swedish authorities allowed him to continue in his job in the early 1980s.

The volume of work to be handled increased so much that one day Björlin asked for an assistant. He had already found a suitable person for the job, an American military observer. Björlin really needed an assistant, but I thought that instead of one he should have two, a Russian in addition to the American. This was a better solution for political reasons. So it was done and the arrangement proved to be excellent. The representatives of the competing great powers worked well together, now competing only in the sense of striving to be the best in the job. This was surely one of the most successful decisions in personnel affairs I made in UNEF.

The office of the Cairo Liaison Officer was located in Merryland Villa, which was preserved as the Cairo base of UNEF. I kept my former office, where I could receive guests when necessary. The upper floor of the villa became a guest-house where the senior officials of UNEF could stay overnight. This was a very practical arrangement because now the Cairo hotels were again full of businessmen and tourists. My wife and I had a comfortable suite there for spending the night when we had to attend diplomatic receptions and dinner parties and wanted to avoid overnight trips back and forth from Ismailia to Cairo many times a week. There were plenty of these parties, because almost every country in the world had an embassy in Cairo. It was especially polite and useful to visit the embassies of the great powers and the contributing countries.

Naturally, our relationship with the Finnish representatives was on a more personal basis. It was pleasant to visit first the Malinens, whom we knew already from our time in Poland, and later, after 1975, Mr and Mrs Joel Pekuri, with whom our friendship was so close that we were godparents to their baby girl. Through the energetic Ambassador Pekuri we also became involved in the Society of the Egyptian Friends of Finland and became friends with its chairperson, Laila Takla, who also chaired the Foreign Affairs Committee in Parliament and furthered Finland's cause in Egypt with great enthusiasm.

Our social life was busy. According to our guest book there was no end to visitors; people from UNEF and foreigners were in the majority, but to our great pleasure guests also arrived from home. Our middle son, Lauri, his friend Riitta and our youngest son, Pekka, came for a Christmas leave. Close family friends came to stay too, but most of the visitors were officials representing the army and the Defence Ministry. The Parliamentary Ombudsman also came for his yearly inspection trip to the Finnish battalion. But most of the visitors came from the troop-contributing countries, from the Canadian Defence Minister, James Richardson, to Stanislaw Kania, who soon after his visit became the new party boss in Poland.

Despite all the seeming vivacity the nights and even the days in Ismailia could be, especially for my wife, monotonous and even lonely. No wonder that she sometimes sighed that she was too old to be a pioneer woman of the Wild West. Fortunately there was another general's family in Ismailia from the very beginning, the Commander of the Canadian contingent and his wife. The Canadian government had acquired a beautiful house for them at the Canal in downtown Ismailia. After General Holmes, Canada was represented during our time by the Generals Bob LaRose and Blake Baile. It was quite natural that two lonely families in Sinai would find each other. Our friendship remained strong even after our move back to Jerusalem.

My wish to return to Finland had been discussed with the Finnish authorities since January 1975. Then I received information from the Defence Ministry that my appointment to the job of Chief of Training had been discussed with the Commander-in-Chief and that it could take place in April. In April I was informed that Waldheim had asked, at the request of the parties, for a new extension for me, at least till July. In any case it began to look as if my time in Ismailia and perhaps my whole service with the UN would come to an end in the near future. My wife and I ardently hoped that the final decision would be made soon.

Three incidents

At the beginning of 1975 three unusual incidents happened in the buffer-zone. The first of them took place in the north, in the Swedish battalion's sector, and the two others in the south, in the area of the Finns. In all three UNEF had to resort to the use of force.

In January the Swedes noticed that the Israeli Army had set up an observation post on a hill that was more than 1 km. inside the buffer-zone. A skylift had been built on the frame of a tank. The height of its hydraulic ladder was 35 metres. The skylift offered an excellent view of the Suez Canal, about 20 km. away, and with high-powered binoculars one could accurately follow the traffic in the Canal zone. The Swedes established their own position next to the skylift and reported the incident to UNEF Headquarters. I made a strong protest to the Israeli authorities but they did not react in any way.

One night the Swedes saw that the Israelis had started to construct an asphalt road from their area to the skylift. The energetic and decisive Battalion Commander, Colonel Lars-Eric Wahlgren, gave an order that the road should be cut off in the morning. A barbed-wire obstacle was built across the road and this stopped the traffic. I visited the site and found the measures taken by the Swedes appropriate.

The matter was developing into a question of authority. Defence Minister Shimon Peres did not want to admit that Israel had caused the incident, but blamed me for the severe measures taken by the Swedes. He was particularly inflamed by the report that Colonel Wahlgren had pointed his pistol at the Israeli soldiers. In his opinion, the matter should have been handled through negotiation. Peres also accused us of partiality, because we let the Egyptians keep watch-towers inside the buffer-zone. Now Gamassy in his turn intervened. He had heard about the skylift from reports in the Swedish newspapers. If the Egyptians had had watch-towers in the UN zone he was ready to remove them as soon as the Israelis had withdrawn their skylift.

Weeks passed and the matter did not progress, although I negotiated alternately with Gamassy and Peres. Finally the Israeli Chief Liaison Officer, Colonel Shimon Levinson, asked me to come with him to the Swedish battalion's area to study what could be done in the matter. We went with the Battalion Commander to the site of the skylift. After that Levinson wanted to talk to me confidentially. He proposed that I should allow the skylift to remain inside the buffer-zone. If this was done, he had the authority to assure me that the Israelis would soon move it away. I decided to agree to Levinson's proposal.

I told my decision to the Battalion Commander and his closest officers. I said that the Swedes, with their decisive and tough action, had made clear what the opinion of the UN was on the Israeli operation, which ran counter to the agreement. Now it was no longer worthwhile prolonging the incident. The UN's view would not be presented any more clearly by doing that. We should let my negotiations with Levinson have their effect and give Israel the chance to act without losing face. I realized at once that most of the Swedes did not understand my decision at all, nor could they accept it.

A few days passed and still nothing happened. Then came the enthusiastically expected visit of Defence Minister Eric Holmqvist to Israel; he was, among other things, due to visit the Swedish battalion in the buffer-zone. A few minutes before the arrival of the Defence Minister's convoy of limousines through the gate of the battalion's camp, the Israeli skylift began to withdraw.

In February 1975 there was an incident in the Finnish battalion's sector to which the Egyptian authorities reacted in a surprisingly passionate manner. The battalion's patrol found fresh footprints on one of its daily tours near the eastern border of the buffer-zone and, following them, came across an Egyptian patrol – an officer, and two men – hidden in the bushes. The Finns tried to prevent the patrol from fleeing and had to open fire. In the skirmish that ensued, the leader of the patrol, a captain, was wounded in the foot. The Finns brought the wounded Captain straight away to the battalion hospital, where the Medical Officer gave first aid. From there the Captain was transported to the Egyptian hospital in Suez. The wound proved to be serious and the foot had to be amputated.

When the action of the Egyptian patrol was investigated, it was found that it was returning from reconnaissance of the Israeli side. Because of the long distance it had been obliged to stay overnight in the UN buffer-zone. The patrol's equipment included a compass, a radio and binoculars for night-time observation.

The command of the Egyptian 3rd Army and the local liaison officers reacted very angrily to the incident. The Finns were to be punished hard for this unheard-of crime. Their movement across the Canal and on the roads of the area was limited. The Finns also had to give up their quarters in the city of Suez and move to live in tents. The liaison officers even explained that the final aim was to expel the Finns from Egypt.

I presented General Magdoub with my protest against these restrictions. In his opinion, Egypt could not allow the arbitrary actions of the Finns in its own sovereign territory. By wounding a captain who was a hero of the October War, the Finns had insulted the honour of the officer corps of Egypt. The soldiers concerned had to be punished. I said to Magdoub that I could not accept his assertions. Egypt had itself caused the incident by sending a patrol through the UN area to Israel, in contravention of the agreement. The Finns could be blamed, at the most, for not having been able to take care of the matter without resorting to arms. For this I presented on behalf of the Finns my regrets and apologies.

I also told Magdoub that by examining the shooting incident more closely, some extenuating circumstances had become evident. The young soldier who had fired the warning shot was a newcomer who had been in the battalion only ten days. In the fist-fight with the Egyptian Captain he had broken a finger and was assured that the Captain had tried to catch his weapon only in order to shoot at him. But the matter was difficult to prove and I saw that Magdoub looked suspicious.

Even before the meeting with Magdoub I had already taken other steps in consequence of the incident. The members of the Finnish patrol were sent from Egypt to Cyprus, where they were assigned to the Finnish battalion there. Colonel Raitasaari and I were agreed that this was necessary. It was feared that the Finns would become targets of actions of revenge by the Egyptians. As far as the Finns were concerned, this was not a punishment; they could continue their UN service in the Finnish battalion in Cyprus. I also suggested that the Finns in Sinai should show consideration and sympathy towards the wounded Captain.

For a week the Finns had to suffer restrictions on their movement. Then on 26 February some other Finns and I were invited for dinner at the headquarters of the Egyptian 2nd Army in Ismailia. The host was, to the surprise of everybody, the Chief of Staff of the Egyptian Army, General Gamassy. Before the dinner he asked me for a confidential discussion. In his quiet and friendly manner he presented the Egyptian view of the incident. I for my part expressed my apologies for the exaggerated actions of self-defence by the Finns. At the end I said that

I wanted to ask one question: "What was the Egyptian patrol doing in the UN buffer-zone?"

"Nothing," Gamassy replied, "and therefore I have decided that the restrictions will be lifted as of tomorrow morning."

Our discussion was then followed by a meal of reconciliation, or "*sulha*", characteristic of the Arabs. The atmosphere was relieved, several speeches were given and finally the Commander of the 2nd Army gave each of us an elegant set of pens as a present.

Incidentally, this was my first visit to the headquarters of the 2nd Army. It was located in the former barracks of the British Royal Air Force, a continuation of the UNEF logistical compound manned by the Canadians and the Poles. I was surprised by what I saw. The office of the Army Commander was like a set from a Hollywood movie, with its fine carpets, plush furniture and magnificent curtains. Similarly, the officers' mess, where the dinner was served, was grand compared with UNEF's modest messes. The entire area had been recently thoroughly renovated and was in an excellent condition. I asked Magdoub from where the unusual luxury and expensive presents originated. We were after all living in a poor country and in field conditions. He answered cryptically that the 2nd Army had a special fund for these purposes.

I was glad that the incident which had for some time soured relations between the Finns and the Egyptians was now settled. It showed how careful an UN force must be in its actions. It must avoid giving the impression of behaving like an arbitrary colonial master. Even when it is only carrying out the undisputable tasks given by its mandate, it must ensure that the parties do not feel insulted. On the other hand, the shooting incident had favourable consequences as well. The patrolling attempts by the Egyptians stopped, or at least diminished. I also believe that despite the anger it caused, the authority of UNEF increased in the eyes of the Egyptians. The Israelis too must have taken note of the fact that UNEF was performing its duties in an even-handed way. Both in Egypt and in Israel it was demonstrated once again that UNEF would not tolerate illegal activity in its area.

The third incident that deviated from the daily routine happened in the Finnish battalion's sector in April 1975. Bedouin families began to arrive there from the Egyptian side, one after the other. They came with their camels, goats and sheep, erected their tents and settled down as Bedouin traditionally have done in Sinai. On closer examination the Finns noticed that among the Bedouin were familiar-looking faces, men who had earlier been seen as junior officers in the liaison office. Somebody even suspected that they had seen an officer of colonel's rank. The Battalion Commander, Colonel Raitasaari, began to be worried. Had the Egyptians the intention of establishing in his area some kind of a base from where they could carry out reconnaissance of the Israeli side? Raitasaari spoke to me about his worries. We came to the conclusion that the Bedouin must be transported away from the buffer-zone in a friendly but decisive manner. Raitasaari said that he would prepare the matter, but thought it would be better if he was on leave when the actual operation took place. If the Egyptians posed questions about the transfer, there would be nobody present who could give an answer. So it happened that one evening the Finns, with the support of the Indonesians and with Polish trucks, transferred the Bedouin back to the Egyptian side. Nobody asked any questions afterwards.

The real highlight of the spring of 1975 was the opening of the Suez Canal for navigation. The clearing of the Canal and the reconstruction of the technical apparatus were finalized and on 5 June 1975 President Sadat, in the presence of prominent invited guests, declared the Canal opened.

In view of the circumstances the opening was grand. In the conditions of poverty after the October War the luxury of the original opening could not be fully matched. Then the Viceroy Muhammed Ali had invited as the principal guest the Empress of France, Eugenie herself, and for the festive banquet cooks and waiters had been imported from the best restaurants of Paris and Nice. On this occasion a series of triumphal arches, decorated with giant pictures of Sadat, had been built in the cities along the Canal. The largest arch, which was like something the Pharaohs might have built, had been erected at the mouth of the Canal.

Sadat's main guest was the 14-year-old Crown Prince Reza Pahlevi, whose father, the Shah of Iran, had donated a large sum of money for the reconstruction of the Canal zone. Guests had been invited from all the seafaring countries. The government of Finland was represented by Ambassador Pekuri and its business community by Mr Uolevi Raade, the President of Neste, the state-owned oil company.

President Sadat, clad in a white admiral's uniform, declared the Canal open to international shipping and received from the representatives of the army a document by which the Canal zone was transferred from the military authorities to the possession of the Suez Canal Company. It was really an impressive symbolic gesture. After eight years of war the Canal zone moved into the era of peace, in which a new war would not easily recommence.

During the ceremony one could see that Sadat was ecstatic. He wrote afterwards that: "Every time I visit a Canal town, the memories of June 5, 1975, rise before my eyes." And he continued, "Nowadays I am never happier than when I am on the banks of the Suez Canal. I sit there for hours on end in a small log cabin watching the progress of work on new projects and the ceaseless reconstruction effort."

Appointment as Chief Co-ordinator

On his trip to the Middle East in June 1975 Secretary-General Waldheim also stopped in Israel. I went with him to meet Prime Minister Itzhak Rabin. Our discussion related mainly to world politics and to the tasks of the UN in Sinai and the Golan. Finally the Prime Minister said that the last item on his agenda was General Siilasvuo. A rumour had come to his ears that the General was returning to Finland. "What is the Secretary-General going to do in this matter?" the Prime Minister asked and continued, "We cannot allow General Siilasvuo to depart yet."

Secretary-General Waldheim explained that following the customs of the UN he could not put obstacles in the way if somebody wanted to leave UN service for personal reasons. "But in this case you should create obstacles," the Prime Minister replied.

When we left the Prime Minister's office, Waldheim whispered to me, "Couldn't you stay here for a couple more months?" I answered that I had been obliged so many times to cancel my planned return home with the Finnish authorities that I could not do it any more. If he thought that my remaining here was necessary, he should explain it to the Finns. Waldheim promised to do that.

I was really in a difficult position. I had been trying to return home since the spring of 1974 and had always had to give up my plan because of the demands of the Middle East situation. Now once again the Secretary-General contacted the Finnish government and soon after that I received a cable from Helsinki, asking me to come home for consultations. In the discussions at the Defence Ministry, the Director-General of the Ministry, Lieutenant-General Kai Sarmanne, the Chief of the General Staff, Lieutenant-General Paavo Junttila, and other senior officials were present. It was agreed that I should now make a decision:

either I should return to Finland in the near future or definitely remain in UN service.

The idea of returning home was tempting. A demanding job was waiting there; all the alternatives which had been presented to me sounded good. I had already been away for eight years without interruption. UNEF was little by little more able to function efficiently. Therefore the task of Commander of UNEF did not offer new challenges any more. The living conditions in Ismailia were very trying. They were too much for both the physical and mental strength of my wife and myself. But there were important factors that weighed heavy on the other side of the balance. The parties seemed to wish that I should continue. Their requests did not seem to be mere empty politeness; in their opinion I still had important tasks before me.

But I did not want to stay in the Middle East on the same footing as before. I wanted to be officially appointed to direct the functioning of all three peace-keeping operations, UNEF, UNDOF and UNTSO. Unofficially I had from the very beginning carried out this duty. Secondly, I wanted to have my headquarters in Jerusalem at Government House. It would be easier to take care of the job from there than from distant Ismailia. My third wish was the rank of Under Secretary-General of the United Nations which, in my opinion, the new and more demanding job required.

In early July Waldheim wanted me to discuss the matter in Geneva. He had with him Under Secretaries-General Urquhart and Davidson. The latter was the highest administrative official of the UN. To start with, the Secretary-General presented me with a strong appeal, hoping that I would sacrifice my personal interests for the sake of international peace. He stressed that all the parties wanted me to stay in the Middle East. Waldheim was ready to accept my conditions but pointed out that the reorganization would require the acceptance of the parties, the Security Council and the budgetary committee of the General Assembly. In order to speed up matters I should clarify the views of the parties on the new arrangements.

When we then discussed the title of my new appointment, Waldheim proposed the name of Supreme Commander but Messrs Urquhart and Davidson, and also myself, preferred Chief Co-ordinator. They suspected that the title Supreme Commander would not be accepted by the Security Council; I thought that it sounded pompous and over-emphasised the military side of the job. In my opinion the new appointment had a more political and diplomatic character, which the title of Chief Co-ordinator would describe better.

Then we discussed the practical arrangements of command. We recognized that all three of the operations that were now functioning had different starting points and tasks. Therefore they could not be unified but should maintain their operational identity. I said that I understood this and did not want changes in the present practice, according to which UNEF, UNDOF and UNTSO sent their situation reports, summaries of incidents, inspection records and other routine documents directly to New York, with a copy to me. But major questions, like methods of operation, changes in deployment and organization, and the personnel affairs of the senior officers should in the first instance be sent to me for consideration.

The matter was delayed, however, and became more complicated. Difficulties appeared within the organization and moreover the Egyptians were not happy with the idea of my moving away from Ismailia. In their opinion, the Co-ordinator's duties could be carried out from there with the aid of modern communications and transportation equipment. The Secretary-General, who was on his way to a meeting of the African states in Kampala and from there to the European Security Conference in Helsinki, stopped for a day in Cairo. At a dinner party given by Foreign Minister Fahmy he succeeded in obtaining Fahmy's and Gamassy's final agreement to the restructuring of my job.

During the dinner an amusing exchange of words took place. At one point Waldheim asked me over the table, "General, are you ever nervous? I have never seen you nervous." I answered, "No, usually I am not nervous, but sometimes I am very, very angry." The Foreign Minister overheard our conversation and said, "Yes, we know that."

On Friday evening after Fahmy's dinner I received a cable from Jerusalem: Defence Minister Shimon Peres wanted to meet me on Sunday, 27 September. On Saturday morning I saw off my superior, Secretary-General Waldheim. Fahmy once more expressed his regret that I intended to move away from Egypt. He also accused me of cunning when I answered, "If I were an Arab, I would promote all measures which would strengthen the international character of Jerusalem."

On Sunday morning, 27 September, I flew to Israel. I had with me Under Secretary-General Roberto Guyer, to whom Waldheim had entrusted the task of explaining his talks in Cairo to the Israeli authorities. It appeared, however, that Foreign Minister Yigal Allon had no time to receive the representative of the Secretary-General; instead Guyer had to content himself with presenting the matter to Ambassador Mordechai Kidron. I continued immediately by car from the airport at Tel Aviv to the Ministry of Defence. Peres interrogated me thoroughly, asking about the meeting between Sadat and Waldheim, the intentions of the Egyptians, the attitude of the Syrians and finally he wanted to know my evaluation of the situation. I said that Sadat was pessimistic and thought that the Israelis were lacking the political will to conclude an agreement on a new process of disengagement. In Peres's view the Israeli offer was generous and the Egyptians should be ready to meet concession with concession, or *quid pro quo*. He asked what could be the reason for their unwillingness to make political concessions. I answered that in the opinion of the Egyptians the October War, although it ended in a partial military defeat, was a political victory for them, or the *quid pro quo* on the basis of which they were demanding Israeli withdrawal. As my own evaluation of the situation I said that I was still hopeful, because the agreement that was presently under negotiation was in the interests of both parties and the breaking off of the negotiations would lead to a new war.

It was always pleasant to visit Shimon Peres. He was not as reserved and reticent as Dayan, but the conversation was vivid and covered many areas. He was clearly a very civilized person and had read much. This was evidenced, for instance, by the many newly published books on his desk. I did not believe the assertions of his opponents that these were just there for show. Another field where Peres was a real expert was in weaponry and war matériel. This became apparent when a foreign Defence Minister was visiting him. I was often invited to be present when the minister came from a country contributing troops to UNEF. Often a rather embarrassing situation was created when Peres knew more about the visitor's own war matériel than either the Minister himself or his military adviser.

In early August we had come so far that the UN Secretary-General sent a letter to the President of the Security Council regarding the co-ordination of the three peace-keeping operations in the Middle East. He said in his letter that the co-ordination of their functioning and administration would be of advantage to all concerned. Using the same arguments which had been agreed in July in Geneva, he said that UNEF, UNDOF and UNTSO could not be unified but that they should maintain their operational identity. He believed, however, that it would be useful if a greater degree of co-ordination could be established between the three operations. Such an arrangement should also make it possible, to some extent, to streamline the administrative and logistical set-up. In the light of the above the Secretary-General proposed to appoint me as the Chief Co-ordinator of United Nations Peace-keeping Operations in the Middle East, and the Chief of Staff of UNTSO, Major-General Bengt Liljestrand, as the Commander of UNEF. In view of the restricted nature of UNTSO's activities, it could be run adequately by its existing staff. The Chief Co-ordinator and his small staff would utilize the existing accommodation, communications and facilities of UNTSO Headquarters. General Siilasvuo would continue as necessary to discharge his functions in relation to the Military Working Group of the Geneva Peace Conference and would be responsible for liaison and contact with the parties on important substantive matters relating to peace-keeping in the Middle East. In mid-August the Security Council accepted Waldheim's proposal on the reorganization of the command.

At the end of August Major-General Bengt Liljestrand arrived in Ismailia full of enthusiasm and ready to take over his new task as the Commander of UNEF. I moved back to Government House in Jerusalem, from where I had two years earlier departed for Egypt: two intense and busy years which I had very much enjoyed. But now the time had come to do something new. The change of location was also a refreshing experience. After the hot and humid Ismailia it was a relief to breathe again the fresh mountain air of Jerusalem. My wife had been in Finland since July but she planned to return in September. Our home would again be in good order because she intended to send from Finland, by the Finnish battalion's air transport, the necessary carpets, paintings and other decorative items.

The small office of the Chief Co-ordinator also began to take shape. My political adviser, John Miles, was already in Jerusalem. Colonel Pierce Barry was arriving from Ireland as my Senior Staff Officer. The Operations Branch of UNTSO would serve the Chief Co-ordinator as well, while UNTSO's Chief Administrative Officer and his Communications and Transport Chiefs would take care of my administration on top of their UNTSO duties. The permanent staff of my office also included my secretary Maria Zingaretti and the drivers Pekka Lyytinen and Göran Carlsson.

It would be interesting to see how my office would function. My position was at least in theory rather weak because none of the three operations were under my direct command. In fact I could only give their commanders advice and influence them by my personal contribution. But in practice the co-ordination functioned well, in my opinion, and my advice was generally followed, perhaps because I had more experience of the conditions of the area and in peace-keeping than anybody else. I also had close and confidential relations with the governments of the parties and I kept in touch with them on important questions related to peace-keeping. I knew from experience how they wanted matters to be handled. The operational business of co-ordination had fortunately started well, when I was instructed on 4 September to go again to Geneva, where the Military Working Group would begin to consider the second disengagement plan for Sinai. This too was part of the duties of the Chief Co-ordinator, according to the recent decision of the Security Council.

However, I had hoped that we could also start the streamlining of the administration, which the Security Council's decision had allocated to the Chief Co-ordinator as a new task. The co-ordination of the administration, and its rationalization to some extent, were in my opinion important objectives and I hoped that by doing this we could achieve flexibility, efficiency and financial savings. I thought that the situation was especially favourable for innovations. My Chief Administrative Officer of many years, Dennis Holland, was returning from sick leave to resume service in UNTSO. I thought that he and I together could plan and implement changes in administrative arrangements. In many administrative fields it was better to treat the Middle East as one entity, as we had always done in UNTSO. Examples of functions which transcended the borders of states were communications, procurement and the repair workshops for radios and vehicles. Holland had more experience, more seniority in office and more personal authority than the other administrators of the area. I imagined that matters would run smoothly if he were only given the necessary authority.

Unfortunately, the co-ordination of the administration did not progress in the way I had hoped. Under Secretary-General Davidson, so I suspect, had not briefed his subordinates about the results of the talks in Geneva. The decision on the reorganization of command came as a total surprise to them. George Lansky in particular was offended because a decision had been made behind his back in matters which belonged to his field. He decided to resist the new arrangements by every means.

The administrative arrangements were discussed on many occasions.

Brian Urquhart and George Lansky came out at the end of September for the particular purpose of discussing and definitively confirming the details of the reorganization. The Commanders and senior staff of UNEF and UNDOF were also invited to the negotiations. Those in the field seemed to understand what I was trying to achieve, but I realized again that Lansky considered the changes unnecessary. I tried to persuade him to come round to my way of thinking. Holland and I prepared comprehensive and detailed plans and memoranda to clarify our views. But the attempts were in vain because Lansky did not want to give Holland the necessary authority, nor did he put the Chief Administrative Officers of UNEF and UNDOF under an obligation to follow his advice. Holland told me later that on one occasion he had received greetings from Lansky in New York, saying that Holland and I should be living the happy lives of country gentlemen. There would be no unnecessary worries and no new heart attacks for Holland.

I was very disappointed by the development of the whole affair. I knew from experience that directing and supervising the administration from New York did not work. Because no authority had been delegated to us, nothing would change. I guessed that, particularly regarding UNEF, there would be many unfortunate errors, because its administration was complicated and the conditions still difficult. In UNDOF the situation would be easier, helped by the fact that its energetic Commander also directed the functioning of the Chief Administrative Officer.

My presentiments proved to be right. One of UNEF's first problems was to return the buildings of the Suez Canal Company, which had been in its possession, to the lawful owners. The administration of UNEF dealt with this problem so clumsily from the point of view of both UNEF and the Egyptians that it developed into a real diplomatic scandal. In the end representatives had to come from New York to clarify the matter before an acceptable solution could be found. Sadder still was the situation in UNEF when a person whose incompetence was widely known was appointed as its last Chief Administrative Officer. It seemed almost incredible that Lansky could nominate such a person as the administrator of the largest and most difficult mission of the UN. I thought it was unpardonable.

When in 1979 UNEF was recalled and its immense property had to be either stored, transferred to UNTSO or UNDOF, or sold, this same person was still in the job. The task proved to be completely overwhelming for him and got out of hand. Large parts of the property were stolen or disappeared into the wrong hands. Those who were present thought that irreparable harm, including great economic losses, was caused to the UN. I was sorry that UNEF, which had discharged its duties in such a splendid manner, should come to such a miserable administrative end.

22. The second Sinai disengagement

Diplomatic preparations

The disengagement of troops in Sinai and the Golan initiated the move from the state of war to a state of peace. In fact real peace was still very far off but the immediate threat of war had receded and the situation was more stable and balanced. In Sinai the Israeli troops were 15–20 km. away from the Canal. The civilian population was able to return to the big cities of the Canal zone: Port Said, Ismailia and Suez. The clearing of the Canal was begun with the resources of the United States and French navies and soon the Canal could be opened for navigation. The ocean-going ships isolated for years in the Great Bitter Lake could finally continue their journey.

In the Golan progress was not as favourable. The evacuated civilian population did not return to the area supervised by UNDOF. But here too the situation had clearly stabilized after the uncertainty and fumbling of the early stages. Israel and Syria tried earnestly to adhere to the rules of the agreement. Even the Syrians would hardly start a war on their own. That Egypt would participate in a new war was very unlikely, because of the changed situation in the Canal zone. The local situation was thus very favourable to the continuation of the peace progress.

However, the experience of the recent negotiations had already shown that peace does not make progress with local resources alone. The powerful contribution of the United States had been needed to persuade the parties to take the road of peace. Behind the influence of the United States was not only its position as a great power, but its special relationship with Israel as well. The Arabs had also realized that the United States could influence Israel's policy.

Despite the favourable conditions the future of the peace process did not look promising, however. The United States' administration was still struggling in the aftermath of the Watergate scandal and seemed to have lost its initiative. I knew that the new Israeli Prime Minister, Itzhak Rabin, had already, when he was Ambassador in Washington, expressed the view that Israel was not in a hurry to make peace and that every year gained in the delay was in the interest of Israel. The only one who was in favour of a speedy continuation of the peace effort was

President Sadat, but he too had to be satisfied with slow progress, despite his energy and initiative.

Nixon's personal role as the promoter of peace in the Middle East was great. Therefore his trip to the area in June 1974 was a magnificent triumphal procession arranged by the grateful parties. He visited Egypt, Saudi Arabia, Syria and Israel. I had the opportunity to follow his progress while he was in Egypt. Exultant crowds received the visitor as a great friend and benefactor of Egypt. Even a few months earlier he would have been treated as the worst enemy. Now nobody wanted to remember that the Americans under his leadership had strongly supported Israel in the recent war. The trip was perhaps the only bright memory from the last phase of his presidency. Yet it was only outwardly bright. The ostentatious arrangements for the trip, the homage and direct adoration rendered to Nixon, were not in harmony with his own mood. He was troubled by ominous forebodings, because his own future looked gloomy.

My wife and I had been invited to a banquet hosted by President and Mrs Sadat in Heliopolis in the Royal Palace of Kubbeh. We had never before been inside this castle, which was closed to the general public. Built in the last century, the palace, with its hundreds of rooms, had become a little dilapidated, but the garden, illuminated for the occasion, looked fabulous. It was so large that we had to drive several kilometres from the gate to the main building. Then we waited a few hours in the hot Cairene night and finally the host and hostess and the guests of honour arrived. President and Mrs Sadat seemed to be in splendid mood but the guests were clearly tired. Mrs Nixon in particular seemed to be in another world. She was expressionless and absent-looking as she gave her hand and said, "Greetings!" Slightly to one side stood Foreign Minister Ismail Fahmy entertaining Henry Kissinger. Fahmy waved me to come closer and then introduced me to Kissinger, whom I now met for the first time.

Such a glorious party had probably not been seen in Cairo since the days of King Farouk. The dinner was set at small tables in the palace garden. Everything was new, refined and perfect. Even the table-cloths and napkins and the splendid gowns and headdresses of the waiters were new. For the comfort and wonder of the guests, the sandy paths of the park had been covered with Oriental carpets. All this splendour, however, felt somehow vain and empty, when one remembered that the guest of honour was about to lose his office and was in fact already only a figurehead without any real power. He spoke with his host about the future, in which he himself would no longer have a part to play.

After the dinner there was all kinds of entertainment. On a stage in the garden the show alternated between folk dances, Egyptian songs and Oriental dances starring Nagva Fuad, the most famous of Egyptian belly-dancers. The programme seemed endless and the extremely exhausted guests went to bed only at 3 o'clock in the morning.

One could see from all the festive arrangements of the Egyptians that this was not only a demonstration of gratitude and honour to the President of the United States; they also wanted to stress the decisive role of the host, Anwar Sadat, as the man of peace. The visit of the President of the United States gave this effort an unusually splendid framework. The millions of people bordering the streets were in an ecstasy. Egypt had changed its political line. This was the end of destructive wars and the beginning of a new and happier era of peace.

In Israel and Syria I was not able to follow personally the reactions caused by President Nixon's visit. I had to stay in Egypt because the Commander of the Senegalese Army was visiting the buffer-zone and Secretary-General Waldheim arrived in Cairo on 16 June, when Nixon was in Jerusalem. But the press described the events in Israel in detail, and later both Nixon and Kissinger told us more in their memoirs.

In all the other places visited during the trip, the leaders had wanted America to continue and even speed up the peace process. Israel was the only country where its continuation was called into question. The new Prime Minister, Rabin, stressed that peace must be relative to security. It could not be based only on Israel's continuing withdrawal from territory without reciprocal measures from the Arabs. To change the attitudes of the Arabs completely required much time. Therefore, in Rabin's opinion there was no hurry to make peace.

Nixon for his part wanted to advise Rabin that he had before him two alternatives: the career of a politician, where safety is best and no risks are taken, or the courageous attitude of a statesman who does not evade new initiatives on the road to peace. Speaking to Rabin and his most important ministerial colleagues, Nixon emphasised this point very strongly. He said that the times were past when Israel was the only protegé and best friend of the United States and its hostile neighbours were considered as American enemies. The President added that surely many people, both in Israel and among the American Jewish population, thought that it would be best to return to these good old times with an attitude of "Let's give enough arms to Israel and it will take care of the rest". I don't believe that this is the right policy, Nixon said. I don't believe that it is good for the future, because time is running out.

Nixon wanted to show in the final stages of his presidency that, despite the Watergate scandal, he was strong in foreign policy, which was still the most important field of action of the President. His success in foreign affairs did not bring with it the forgiveness of Congress; Nixon was forced to resign. But in the Middle East the results of his work were clearly seen. There the peace process had had a good start.

At the beginning of August, former Vice-President Gerald Ford became President of the United States of America. He had hardly any experience in foreign policy. Therefore it was certainly in the interest of continuity that he asked Henry Kissinger to continue as Secretary of State. Many asked, however, whether Kissinger could be as useful as he was during the time of the determined and strong President Nixon. We would soon see how things would develop.

Despite Israel's obstruction, the United States had just had no other alternative but to continue the step-by-step policy as a mediator between the parties. Delaying would have weakened the position of the United States in the eyes of the Arab states. Striving for a comprehensive settlement in the Geneva Peace Conference would have been a second possibility, but it would have brought the Soviet Union back to the talks and this nobody wanted. It would have been reasonable to suppose that the next round of negotiations would be between Israel and Jordan, but it became apparent that not even the smallest border changes on the West Bank were possible. Political resistance in Israel was very strong in this respect. Egypt and Syria had both benefited from the previous agreements but tiny Jordan, who behaved well and did not participate in the October War, was left out in the cold. President Sadat stressed the priority of the new phase of disengagement in Sinai. In his opinion, perhaps, Jordan did not deserve anything.

Something really needed to be done, but the Jordanian question proved to be more difficult than expected. Questions related to the West Bank could not be resolved by a Cabinet decision, but the matter should be given to the people to decide in new elections. Nonetheless, strong pressure was directed at King Hussein. He would be severely criticized in the other Arab countries if he agreed to anything less than complete withdrawal from all the occupied territories. There was the additional threat that the PLO would be declared the sole representative of the Palestinians. This in fact happened at the Rabat summit meeting in October 1974. Hussein could no longer speak for the Palestinians and the United States had to give up promoting the "Jordanian alternative" (making Jordan the Palestinian homeland).

Thus there was nothing that could be done but to concentrate on a new Sinai disengagement process. The Rabat meeting had also shown that Egypt was no longer the unquestioned leader of the Arab world that it had been in Nasser's time. It had to be careful in planning its new political steps. This was probably the reason why Sadat's demands were so tough: as the price of concluding a second agreement with Israel, Egypt should get the areas of the Mitla and Giddi Passes and the oil fields of Abu Rudeis. Nothing less would equal the risks Egypt had taken in its relations with the Arab world. But Israel did not intend to make concessions either and its new government seemed to have no new line in its foreign affairs. The Americans complained even to me that the Israel government was weak and quarrelsome. Prime Minister Itzhak Rabin, Foreign Minister Yigal Allon and Defence Minister Shimon Peres argued about whose opinion was decisive. Golda Meir could be difficult as a negotiating partner, but when she had once made a decision, it held. It was not as clear that Rabin would be able to lead a quarrelling government and a divided people through the difficult times ahead, particularly when Shimon Peres was only waiting for the moment when he could begin to direct the affairs of the country.

During the six months after the Rabat summit the Americans tried to clarify the intentions of the parties and to moderate their demands. Egypt was adamant in its demands relating to the Sinai passes and the oil fields. The income from the latter was of great importance to the poverty-struck Egypt. It was almost as great as the fees from the Suez Canal which had been collected since June. But for Israel the Sinai oil was important too, because it had satisfied about half of the total oil needs of the country.

Moreover, Sadat hoped that the new disengagement agreement would be military in its character, not just political. He did not want to give the Arab world the impression that he was about to detach himself from the fighting front. Israel's wishes were completely different. It wanted to separate Egypt and Syria definitively from each other and so render impossible another combined attack like the October War. Therefore it wanted Egypt to make political concessions as a counter-weight to Israel's continued withdrawal: Egypt should declare that it was ending the state of belligerency between the two countries and the new agreement should be of long duration. Furthermore, Israel would not give up the passes or the oil.

In an interview with the newspaper *Haaretz* in December, Rabin said that Israel should postpone the negotiations till after the presidential elections in the United States in 1976. He also spoke about the next seven years seeing new alternatives to oil being developed. Thus the Arabs' influence in world affairs would decrease and the pressure on Israel would be eased. One could once again see clearly from Rabin's statement that in his opinion delaying the solution would be in Israel's interest.

In December there was a clear deterioration in relations between Egypt and the Soviet Union. When the Foreign Minister and the Chief of Staff of Egypt returned from a short trip to Moscow, it was announced that Brezhnev's planned visit to Cairo was cancelled. Now more than ever Egypt needed proof that giving up its policy of co-operation with the Soviet Union had been a wise act. In the view of the Israelis, too, a new situation had been created. The preconditions for the disengagement negotiations had improved.

At the beginning of 1975 Kissinger decided to continue talks in the Middle East and visited the area in February and March. Before the trip in February, Sadat publicly supported his efforts and said that the United States now held all the trump cards. Israel also eased its demands a little. Rabin said in an interview that the Egyptians could perhaps get back the oil fields and even the passes if they would give a guarantee not to start a new war.

The February trip remained only a fact-finding tour and did not bring additional concessions. The trip in March was to be decisive but to the annoyance of Kissinger it also ended without results. There were disputes over many details which seemed small. Israel was adamant in its demand that Sadat, using binding legal terms, should declare an end to the state of belligerency between Egypt and Israel. Sadat was ready to express the same thing, using the term "abandonment of the use of force". It was difficult to understand what could be achieved by such hair-splitting over terminology. One could not believe that Israel was willing to reach an agreement. On 23 March Kissinger announced that his mediation effort had failed. The following day President Ford for his part declared that the United States would now begin to reappraise its policy on Israel. It sounded like a punitive measure.

Every indication was that both the President and his Secretary of State were incensed at Israel's obstruction of the second Sinai disengagement. In Kissinger's opinion, the Israeli government was short-sighted, incompetent and weak. Instead of a determined foreign policy Israel had an internal political system which only produced fruitless impasses. Somebody like David Ben Gurion or Golda Meir could lead Israel, but the triumvirate of Rabin, Allon and Peres was not able to do so. Each of the three was pulling in a different direction. The government and the people of Israel apparently had a better opinion of the policy which had been carried out.

The reappraisal of the United States' policy on Israel following the breakdown of the negotiations in March lasted almost three months. A group of the best known and experienced American experts on foreign policy, convened to help Kissinger, ended by recommending the return to Geneva and drafting a special American peace plan. When the matter was studied further and the attitudes of the parties clarified, it was found that the new ideas had no support. Finally it became apparent that there was no other realistic alternative than the tried and tested policy of the gradual approach.

In June Gerald Ford and Anwar Sadat met in Salzburg. The Presidents got along well with each other; the atmosphere of the meeting was pleasant and open. They spoke about the future Sinai agreement. Sadat was for an agreement but his conditions were the same as before: Israel had to give up the oil and the passes but it was not allowed to demand the end of the state of belligerency. Then Prime Minister Rabin met with Ford and Kissinger in Washington. The latter expressed the wish that Israel should be a little more positive in the future negotiations. Rabin was already willing to end the heavy and expensive controversy with the United States. His tough attitude in the spring to Kissinger's demands had increased his popularity; now he could afford to be more flexible.

Towards the end of June the Israeli leadership apparently came to the conclusion that no additional concessions could be extracted from Sadat and that it would be unwise to resist the United States endlessly. If the Americans wanted an agreement, they could pay a good price for it. Israel would agree to withdraw to the eastern slopes of the passes but would maintain the highest points above the passes. In order to secure itself from surprise attacks Israel also demanded an American surveillance unit in the area of the buffer-zone.

After mid-August Kissinger arrived in Israel for the last time. During the weeks before the visit the agreement had been prepared energetically. Above all the planners concentrated on commitments in which the United States bought Israel's acceptance of a new withdrawal in Sinai. Now they were close to a solution. Only a few details needed additional attention. The most important of these were the accurate location of the new Israeli forward line, the amount of military and financial aid to be given by the United States and the technical details of the surveillance station to be manned by American civilians. Much dispute continued over the details, although by now it was clear that Israel wanted to reach an agreement.

In the end, on the last day of August, after a long final session, the final differences of opinion between the United States and Israel were settled and the agreement was ready to be initialled by the parties. It was decided to sign it in Geneva on 4 September 1975.

In Israel the Chief of Staff of the Defence Forces, General Mordechai Gur, and Ambassador Avraham Kidron put their initials on the edge of the document of agreement. Four hours later the Chief of Staff of the Egyptian Army, General Mohammed Ali Fahmy, did the same in Alexandria, where Kissinger had already arrived from Israel. President Sadat made a speech on this occasion, in which he greeted the agreement as a turning point in the conflict between the Arabs and Israel. He said that he had told President Ford on the phone that he had not been completely satisfied with the achievements until now. He had told President Ford to initiate a parallel withdrawal on the Syrian front and to start a dialogue with the Palestinians because without them peace could not be achieved in the area.

The Military Working Group meets again

After the completion of the agreement the Military Working Group was convened for the third time. We would meet again in Geneva, where the agreement would first be solemnly signed and then the preparations for the disengagement plan would start. The plan was to be ready on 22 September 1975.

When we convened on 4 September, the Egyptian delegation led by Magdoub was the same as before. No changes had been made to the UN trio either; I was assisted as before by James Jonah and Joseph Fallon. The latter had already finished his service in the Middle East but the Irish military authorities had, at my request, returned him to the ranks of UNTSO for this special duty.

The Israeli delegation was led by General Herzl Shafir, well-known from the Golan disengagement talks. Apparently in order to stress the political character of the new agreement, Israel sent along with Shafir a senior official from the Foreign Ministry, Mordechai Gazit, who had recently been appointed Ambassador to France. The legal adviser of the Foreign Ministry, Meir Rosenne, continued as a member of the delegation and the new members were General Avraham Tamir and Colonel Shimon Levinson.

Before the talks I was a little worried about the composition of the Israeli delegation. I knew already that Shafir was not one of the best negotiators, because of his personality. Would his abruptness make the atmosphere of the meetings too tense? I was also slightly worried about Ambassador Gazit. I had earlier become acquainted with him as the Director-General of the Foreign Ministry. His sharp intelligence and energy had made an overwhelming impression on me. How would the combination of Shafir and Gazit work? The Egyptians, moreover, were not at all pleased with Meir Rosenne's presence. They remembered from earlier meetings his Zionist zeal and endless legal hair-splitting. General Tamir I did not know but he seemed a matter-of-fact and unassuming person. I was particularly glad that Shimon Levinson, our Liaison Officer for many years, was to join us. With his sense of humour and jovial character he would surely have a soothing effect on his more brusque colleagues.

As I opened the signing ceremony on 4 September 1975 I wished the delegations welcome to the Palais des Nations. I said that the documents to be signed were the agreement between Egypt and Israel, the annex to the agreement and a map which was part of the annex. The ceremony was over in a few minutes. It ended rather awkwardly because it appeared that Israel could not sign the agreement. The United States Congress had not yet accepted the idea of locating an American surveillance unit in Sinai. Israel did not dare to take the risk of taking that on trust, and so announced that it would only sign the agreement later, when acceptance by Congress was certain. Fortunately Israel assured us, however, that the time-table for the agreement would be adhered to, as agreed with Kissinger.

After the signing we had three days to acquaint ourselves with the documents (see Appendix 10) and to prepare ourselves for the ordinary meetings, which were to begin after the weekend on 9 September. In principle the agreement followed the line of the previous disengagement agreements. It contained nine articles in which firstly the parties committed themselves scrupulously to observe the cease-fire and to resolve their disputes without resorting to the threat or use of force. In addition the parties again expressed their determination to reach a final and just peace settlement by means of negotiations.

Second disengagement in Sinai: negotiations begin, 4 Sept. 1975. Israel is represented by Generals Tamir and Shafir and Messrs Shlomo Gazit and Meir Rosenne; Egypt by Gen. Magdoub and Col. Howeidi. The UN team consists of the author, James Jonah and Joe Fallon.

The essential aims of the agreement were expressed in the fourth, fifth and seventh articles. According to these, UNEF should continue to be deployed between the parties as before. The buffer-zone manned by it would be much broader. The lines describing the deployment of the parties were again marked on a map. Egypt would allow non-military cargoes destined or coming from Israel through the Suez Canal. The agreement would remain in force until superseded by a new agreement.

As an annex to the agreement there was a detailed description of the permitted amounts of troops and armaments; the arrangements for aerial reconnaissance; the early warning and surveillance installations, and the tasks of UNEF. At Sadat's demand the number of permitted troops was slightly more than in the previous agreement. The total number of infantry was now 8,000 men divided into eight battalions, there were 75 tanks, and the number of artillery remained at 72 pieces. Neither party was allowed to station or locate in their areas weapons whose range could reach the other line. The parties were not to site anti-aircraft missiles within an area 10 km. east of line K and west of line F, respectively (see map p. 315). The parties were allowed to conduct aerial reconnaissance over an area reaching up to the middle line of the buffer-zone (previously these activities had had to end at the forward edge of the buffer-zone). The aerial surveillance previously carried out informally by the United States would now become public. It would be carried out about twice a month by Lockheed SR 71A reconnaissance aircraft, which would take aerial photographs of the entire area from the height of 70,000 feet. An excellent improvement on the previous practice was that now UNEF was to have at its disposal the results of this American reconnaissance. It had been embarrassing that until now the photographs they took had been given only to the parties.

A new feature was that Israel was allowed to leave its working surveillance station in the UN buffer-zone after its withdrawal. This powerful and technically complex installation with its many optical and electronic surveillance devices was situated near the Giddi Pass on the Umm Khuseiba hill. In compensation Egypt was allowed to build a similar surveillance station near the Mitla Pass. The Americans promised to provide the necessary technical devices.

An unprecedented move was the agreement that the United States would participate in the surveillance arrangements in Sinai by setting up their own early warning and surveillance system in the area of the passes. This installation was established by the State Department and was named the Sinai Field Mission.

Taking into consideration that the traumatic experiences of the Vietnam War were still fresh in the minds of the Americans, it was surprising that the United States Congress agreed to this project. Careful studies were needed, however, before Congress was assured that the project could be carried out. But it particularly stressed that the matter in question was a civilian activity and not a new involvement of the armed forces in a military conflict.

The Sinai Field Mission altogether involved 163 United States citizens, who were all civilians. Twenty-three of them were permanent civil servants of the State Department. To this group belonged the leadership of the Mission and the observers or the operational personnel. A contract was drawn up with a Texan company to take care of the administration, communications, transportation, workshops and other logistics requirements of the Mission. In the service of this company were communicators, mechanics for the technical equipment, drivers and kitchen personnel – a total of 140 people.

The intention was that the Americans would set up three manned watch-stations and four unmanned electronic sensor fields in the Giddi and Mitla Passes. The watch-stations would be manned day and night by two operators, who would monitor anything that the sensor fields detected and would observe the whole area, using binoculars, telescopes and night observation devices. Acoustic, strain, seismic and optical devices would be used in the sensor fields: all these had been developed for the war in Vietnam.

Many people wondered why Israel considered the American presence in Sinai so important. Could it not trust the security offered by UNEF? Had not their previous experiences of this Force been positive? Having accepted UNEF as an essential part of their disengagement arrangements the parties had reason to co-operate. In Sinai the violations of the buffer-zone had been minimal, or inadvertent, and the zone had helped to increase confidence in the ability of UNEF to keep the peace.

The main value of the Sinai buffer-zone was that it reduced the risk of unforeseen clashes. Nadav Safran, writing in *Foreign Affairs* in October 1974, judges that at best the UN troops complicate the decision of a potential attacker by forcing him to choose between ordering them to step aside, and thus giving warning to the opponent, or driving through them and incurring opprobrium in the eyes of the world. UNEF was never put to a test in this manner, but we know what happened in south Lebanon in 1982, where the UN force was passive and weak and the attacker did not care about world opinion. The presence of the American Sinai Field Mission in the middle of Sinai had of course a strong restrictive effect on attacks from either side.

Some people thought that the main reason for Israel's persistent demands for a concrete presence from the Americans was the fear that the security offered by UNEF was too weak and unreliable; therefore a presumably more effective system, like the Sinai Field Mission, was required. Later it became apparent that the additional security offered by the Sinai Field Mission was, except psychologically, rather modest. The size of the unit was very small and the area it covered a tiny part of the vast Sinai desert. It was not located on the best hills from the point of view of observation. Had it been better stationed it might perhaps have seen too much on the Israeli side. Its technical apparatus was surprisingly modest and old-fashioned: Israel's own devices on the nearby Umm Khuseiba were technically much more advanced. Thus the Sinai Field Mission could only supplement Israel's own and UNEF's early warning system.

One could also assert that no matter how competent the UN force was militarily, its political limitations were so great that more reliable assistance was needed. Whatever the reason was, Israel wanted "warm American bodies" as the best guarantors of its security. The real surprise in this connection was that the Americans agreed to Israel's request.

After the signing ceremony Jonah, Fallon and I met the Israeli delegation at a dinner given by General Shafir at their hotel. We talked about the time-table and agenda of the meeting. On the following evening the Egyptian Ambassador invited us to his home to speak with General Magdoub and his assistants about the same matters. After this my team, on the basis of the discussions, started to draft a detailed plan for the negotiations of the coming two weeks. I could guess beforehand that two weeks would be a very short time for the preparation of such an extensive and complex plan. Kissinger had left many more open questions than in the previous disengagement agreements. Our competence and negotiating skills would be put to a hard test. We finished the draft proposal of the programme on Saturday evening and gave it to the parties to study. The Sunday was free and I was able to go with Leif and Marianne Blomqvist to admire the surroundings of Geneva and to eat in a small restaurant in the French area.

Our proposal for the programme was brief, only about two pages long. The first dealt with the general principles of the negotiations (see Appendix 11). The second, which was more important, contained a list of detailed questions to be negotiated. There were scores of them. We proposed that the talks should begin from the so-called southern area (the area south of line E and west of line M), because the Israeli withdrawal would commence there (see map p. 315). The Sinai oil fields were situated in the southern area. In the next phase of the negotiations the matters of the northern area would be dealt with (the area between lines F and K).

We also proposed that the Chairman, when opening the first meeting, would give a short statement. After that the Egyptian and Israeli representatives would each present a general statement on the functioning of the Military Working Group. After each meeting a detailed agenda for the next meeting would be prepared and the parties were requested to submit their proposals for additional questions in good time. These would be presented to the meeting on 19 September. Following tradition, the representatives of the press were allowed to be present at the opening phase of the first meeting, as well as at the final ceremony of the negotiations. After each meeting a press release accepted by the parties would be given to the press.

On Tuesday morning, 9 September, I called the meeting to order and gave my short statement. I said that the solution of the Middle East problem was made difficult by an immense diversity of interests and conflicting perceptions of what constituted a just and lasting peace. I expressed the wish that the agreement, which was the result of strenuous efforts, would change the atmosphere, keep Sinai quiet and further the finding of a comprehensive settlement. At the end I added my satisfaction that the agreement strengthened the role of United Nations peace-keeping in the implementation and supervision of the agreement.

I then asked the members of the press to leave the negotiating chamber. Ambassador Gazit and General Magdoub presented their short initial statements on behalf of the parties. After that I delivered to the Egyptians the Israeli proposal relating to the southern area, which General Shafir had given to me. The general discussion started gradually and I noted that matters started to progress in the previous manner which had been tested and proved good. Soon I realized that I had been completely mistaken about Ambassador Gazit. He seemed to have a respected position among his countrymen and he had a balancing and positive effect on the functioning of the delegation. I learned to appreciate his role highly. I was pleased to learn that the appreciation was mutual; one day Gazit came to me and said he thought I knew that Israel in the past had particularly hoped for face-to-face negotiations with its Arab neighbours without the assistance or presence of an intermediary. It was not known how negotiations would progress without a middleman, but it was difficult enough even in the present manner, he said.

The presence of another middleman was the real innovation of this round of talks. This was an official of the United States National Security Council, Harold Saunders, who for years had been a member of Henry Kissinger's negotiating team and who had thus also taken part in the political negotiations of this agreement. He was fully familiar with the documents in hand and knew the agreement better than any of us. Harold Saunders was not present in the negotiating chamber but he had an office next to it. From there he gave us wise advice and we all waited our turn to see him. As he was very pleasant by nature he was eminently suitable for his role as an intermediary. It was quite natural that the parties should follow his advice because he represented the main sponsor of the peace process. The further the negotiations progressed, and the more difficult the matters dealt with, the more important Harold Saunders' role became. I believe that the parties agreed with me that his assistance was invaluable. Without it our work would have been still more difficult.

There were altogether 21 meetings. There were two meetings almost every day for two weeks. We even met on a Saturday, after the termination of the Sabbath. The working days were long because after the meetings the parties prepared their proposals for the next day's meetings and communicated with their governments. The UN too had its preparatory work and a cable had to be sent to Waldheim after each meeting. The only day off was the Jewish Day of Atonement, Yom Kippur, which happened to fall on Monday 15 September. Surely most of us used it as a day for reflection and remembered the exceptional Yom Kippur two years ago. Religious rules also had an effect on the Egyptian delegation, because the Moslems were just then observing Ramadan, the month of prayer and fast. That lover of good food, General Magdoub, was not allowed to eat during the whole day until sunset. But everybody drank coffee, although this was not, strictly speaking, permitted. The coffee habit formed at Kilometre 101 was continued, thanks to the staff at the Palais des Nations, and was popular with both parties. During the coffee-breaks numerous private discussions were held between the parties and many difficult questions were even solved.

Not much time was left for social life. I dined with the Blomqvists in another French village and had a sauna with Ambassador Sahlgren. I was particularly pleased to meet my old friend, Veikko Pajunen, the star reporter of the *Helsingin Sanomat*, who had moved from Bonn to Geneva and offered me, besides a witty and refreshing conversation, delicious *Quenelles de brochet* and flambéed kidneys in one of the most elegant eating places in Geneva. I was also quite delighted to meet my first political adviser, Miguel Marin. He was in Geneva as the legal adviser of a UN commission on human rights in Chile. As usual Marin was full of life and glad that even as a pensioner he had an interesting and challenging job.

The delegations met socially too. One evening we were invited to a working dinner at the home of the Egyptian Ambassador. Besides Magdoub's delegation, Harold Saunders was present as well, "our pleasant and skilful backer", as I described him in a letter to my wife. In a later letter I described the Israeli party:

> During this last negotiating tour the gratitude shown by the parties has been particularly gladdening. On Saturday 20 September the Israeli delegation gave in our honour a dinner to which Under Secretary-General Roberto Guyer, on a transit trip here, was also invited. Mordechai Gazit gave such a beautiful speech that I could not believe my ears.

The pace of the meetings was at first slow and the sessions were relatively short. I began to be a little worried: would we succeed in dealing with everything on time? In the final stage we were obliged to speed up the tempo and the last four meetings were long. It was strange that all the time we managed really important questions with little talk; the decisions almost made themselves. Yet what were, in my opinion, insignificant details were chewed over for hours and from one meeting to the other.

One such question was the numbers and equipment of the Egyptian civilian police in the southern sector. The force of 3,000 policemen proposed by the Egyptians at the second meeting was considered much too large by the Israelis, who suggested 100 policemen. The number was bargained over as in the best bazaar and towards the end of the same meeting the Egyptian proposal had fallen to half, or 1,500 policemen, while Israel had tripled its offer to 300 policemen. The matter was still

unresolved at the eleventh meeting and the seventeenth ended with
Israel proposing 700 policemen. Egypt wanted to add to this another
200 unarmed policemen. The matter was finalized at the penultimate
meeting; the 700 proposed by Israel remained the final decision. The
attention that the matter aroused and the tough disputes it caused
continued to trouble me and I decided to follow the development of the
numbers of the police in the southern sector. There was never more
than a fraction of the permitted maximum. My suspicions had been
right and the matter was not as important, even to the Egyptians, as
had been presented at the meetings.

Another thorny, and in the view of the Egyptians sensitive, matter
was the question of the civilian population living in the northern area
along the coastal road near the Mediterranean. Some of these people had
been evacuated by the Israelis to El Arish and some had fled to Egypt.
Now the population was to be allowed to return to its home area. In
the opinion of the Israelis this involved a major security risk and they
demanded all kinds of rules to control the population. The Egyptians
did not want even to discuss the matter. It was an internal Egyptian
affair which they would decide independently, for Sinai was sovereign
Egyptian territory. Obviously no progress was made on this issue and
there was a danger that the entire plan would founder because of this
detail. Finally I devised a means to solve the problem. I drafted a letter
describing the position of the civilian population. General Magdoub
would sign this letter in his capacity of Chief Liaison Officer to the
UNEF and not as the head of the negotiating delegation. He would
address the letter to me as the UN Chief Co-ordinator. In the draft it
was said that in order to facilitate the task of UNEF in the northern
area, Magdoub would give some information about the numbers and
the domiciles of the population which was moving there. The Egyptian
authorities would give the inhabitants identity cards which UNEF
would certify with its stamp. Using these cards, the inhabitants could
move in and out of the buffer-zone. An administrative centre would be
set up in the town of Kantara in order to take care of their needs.
Magdoub signed the letter, which I had shown beforehand to the Israeli
delegation for its acceptance. In this way the matter was finally settled.

The third matter which caused differences of opinion concerned the
setting up of the Joint Commission. According to the agreement this
Commission, under the chairmanship of the Chief Co-ordinator, was
to resolve the problems which arose in the implementation of the agreement and assist UNEF in the fulfilment of its mandate. The whole idea

THE SECOND UNEF BUFFER ZONE
1976 – 1979

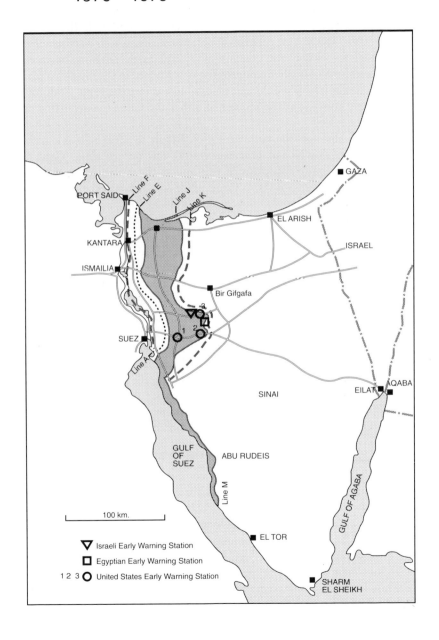

GAZA

Line F
Line E
PORT SAID
Line J
Line K
EL ARISH

KANTARA

ISRAEL

ISMAILIA

Bir Gifgafa

SUEZ

1 2

AQABA

EILAT

SINAI

Line A

GULF
OF
SUEZ

ABU RUDEIS

Line M

100 km.

GULF OF AGABA

EL TOR

▽ Israeli Early Warning Station

☐ Egyptian Early Warning Station

1 2 3 ○ United States Early Warning Station

SHARM
EL SHEIKH

was invented by the Israelis. They wanted the Commission to have a permanent headquarters in the buffer-zone. The parties' liaison officers would be continuously present there and good communications links would be built. I thought the idea good, but the Egyptians resisted the idea of permanent arrangements, which in their view resembled too closely the conclusion of diplomatic relations between Egypt and Israel. Finally a compromise was reached in the matter: a permanent headquarters would not be established but the Joint Commission would convene at the request of either the Chief Co-ordinator or the parties.

Halfway through the negotiations it began to look as if we were working too slowly and that we would run out of time. General Magdoub was quite conscious of this and at the eleventh meeting he encouraged the participants to forget their small disputes and to speed up the discussions. He also urged us to hold longer meetings in order to reach agreement on the issues in two or three days. Magdoub listed the unresolved matters as follows: the number of the civilian police; the civilian population in the northern area; aerial reconnaissance; general deployment; the hand-over of the oil fields; the early warning system, and the Joint Commission. I too remarked that the participants grew tired of the continuous debate on the same matters. General Avraham Tamir at one point looked completely disgusted as he whispered to me that as a military man he could not stand this kind of idle talk. He was also so tired that during the coffee-breaks he preferred to withdraw to the furthermost corner of the room and laid down for a short rest. General Tamir seldom opened his mouth during the meetings and it was not easy to guess on the basis of his unassuming appearance how great an influence he had on his delegation. In his appearance he reminded me of the famous TV detective Columbo, who solves every problem. No wonder that he later played an important role in the Camp David negotiations.

Despite our speeding up, the two last meetings became long-drawn-out marathon sessions. The twentieth meeting lasted 16 hours, with only a few coffee and sandwich breaks in between. In the last meeting, which lasted three hours longer, I had to stop the clock before midnight. Thus we could seemingly end the meeting before the deadline given in the agreement, so that there was no need to change the dates mentioned in the agreement. We continued struggling with the last questions until 5 o'clock in the morning, before everything was resolved. I then gave the parties one and a half hours for shaving and changing and announced that the solemn signing ceremony would take place on 23 September 1975 at 0630 hours.

Tired but happy, the delegations convened once more in the negotiating chamber. We others prepared ourselves to sign the documents and the maps; the Israeli delegation would only initial them, as had been agreed. I began with a short speech expressing my gratification at the fulfilment of our task with honour. It had required long working days and sleepless nights. It would not have succeeded without the determination and co-operation of the participants, as well as their taking into consideration the vital interests of the other party. I thanked the delegations for the understanding and consideration shown to me. I considered it a privilege to have been able to chair the meetings of the Military Working Group for the fourth time. Despite the deep suspicions and misunderstandings which had made the road to Middle East peace so stony, I had noted throughout that the basic need to communicate with each other, so characteristic of human beings, was the only basis for mutual confidence. Having at the end thanked the staff of the Palais des Nations, I asked the participants to sign or initial the documents.

We remained a while longer in the Palais to say goodbye to each other. The map specialists of the Israeli delegation had prepared a copy of the map annexed to the agreement as a gift to everybody. All signed them as a souvenir. The UN delegation also had something to give. We had prepared an informal combination of the protocol and the Chairman's Statement. Thus there was no need to read these two documents side by side, trying all the while to fit the two together. The atmosphere at this short farewell party was relieved and joyful. People joked at the table, sometimes with a slight edge. The witty Colonel Howeidi, when extending the map to Dr Meir Rosenne said: "Meir, you are not only difficult, you are most difficult."

When the ceremony was over and I had rested a little at the hotel, I decided once more to visit Leif Blomqvist at the Finnish delegation to the European Security Conference at Rue Lausanne. The visit almost ended fatally. When I came down the steps to the entrance hall of the building I was dazzled by the sudden sunshine to the extent that without noticing I walked into a huge glass window which broke into thousands of splinters. I ran up the stairs back to the first floor, where the friendly secretaries of the Finnish delegation gave me first aid. Fortunately my wounds were almost non-existent: a few scratches to my forehead and one hand. I had already begun to worry about who

would pay for the damage, but I was assured that firstly I was a guest
of the Finnish government and secondly that the place was probably
insured. Leif Blomqvist said that he would not let me walk alone
anywhere any more. He promised to accompany me back to the hotel
and later to the airport. Only when I came downstairs again did I see
what had really happened and was frightened at the terrible destruction.
A glass pane about three metres square had been complete smashed. I
had had a lucky escape. Later in the day I asked my companion at the
airport whether someone had been found to pay for the broken glass.
He told me no, because it had not been discovered who had broken
the window.

Our arrival at Jerusalem was a joyous occasion. A representative of
the Israeli Foreign Ministry was at the airport to meet me and brought
me a congratulatory telegram from Foreign Minister Yigal Allon in
New York. At the same time he gave me a luncheon invitation from
Prime Minister Rabin. This was a rare honour. I knew Rabin from
before, because I had met him often in the 1960s when he was the Chief
of Staff, and later too at many diplomatic parties. In the early 1970s I
had followed his activities as the Israeli Ambassador in Washington
and admired his exceptional honesty and military bluntness, unusual
qualities in a politician or diplomat.

Now I had to go first to Cairo, however, to meet Foreign Minister
Fahmy and General Gamassy. On the same evening I returned to
Jerusalem because the Israelis wanted to arrange a tour of familiarization
to Abu Rudeis, the centre of the oil fields at the Red Sea. The Finnish
battalion was supposed to deploy there in November as the first step
in the new disengagement process. I was also pleased to hear that Brian
Urquhart and George Lansky would arrive in the area at the end of
September. I hoped that my position as the Chief Co-ordinator and
the reorganization of the command would now be able to take their
final form.

An exceptionally free and cheerful atmosphere prevailed at Prime
Minister Rabin's luncheon. One could see from everything that the
Israelis were satisfied. An important intermediate objective on the road
to peace had been achieved. The Prime Minister's speech was overwhelmingly friendly. When he spoke of the stopping of the clock at
Geneva he related the story of Joshua, who at the time when the
children of Israel were settling down in the promised land stopped the
sun and the moon during the battle against the Amorites when he
wanted more time to win the battle. As if this had not been enough

as a parable, Rabin went on to tell a story about a rabbi who performed miracles. The rabbi was travelling by train on the eve of the Sabbath and for some reason the train was late. It was possible that the train would not reach its destination before the first stars appeared and the Sabbath began. There was a danger that the pious rabbi would unintentionally become a desecrator of the Sabbath. Then the rabbi performed a miracle: Friday continued on the track while the Sabbath began only in the places speeding by on both sides of the train. The Prime Minister's luncheon, and his speech, were a beautiful and memorable end to a difficult negotiating period.

UNEF's third phase, autumn 1975 to summer 1979

The tasks given to UNEF by the new disengagement agreement were more complicated than before and its buffer-zone much wider. First the new lines had to be marked in the terrain. I had asked the Swedish government, through the Secretary-General, to send experts to define these lines in the terrain, as I had become thoroughly fed up with the earlier quarrels over the exact location of the lines. At that time the work had been carried out by military observers. In order to determine where the new lines lay, Colonel Olof Johansson from the Geodetic Survey Board of Sweden and five of his engineers started their work in October 1975. When the course of the lines had been defined, UNEF battalions marked them in the terrain with oil barrels. The work was immense because there were 600 km. of lines altogether. With great devotion and care, using the most modern geodetic devices, the Swedes completed their work in January 1976 to the great satisfaction of the parties and the UN.

In November 1975 the second disengagement process could start. In order to co-ordinate its operation, UNEF had again set up a Forward Headquarters, where it was represented once more by Colonel Kuosa and Captain Fallon. The Commander of UNEF, Lieutenant-General Bengt Liljestrand, embarked on his duties with enthusiasm and made the preparations with great care. As a new idea he prepared a clear description, well-illustrated, of the different phases of the disengagement plan and as an annex to it an instruction which was distributed to each UNEF soldier. It was drawn up in the languages used by UNEF troops: English, Finnish, French, Polish and Swedish. Now at least everybody knew into which phases this complex operation would be divided, the task of UNEF and how it should be carried out.

The first phase of disengagement, involving the southern area, was completed before the beginning of December. The agreement put me personally under the obligation of supervising the hand-over of the oil fields and equipment to the Egyptians. In the northern area the disengagement started in January 1976 and ended on 22 February. As before, UNEF supervised the redeployment of troops using temporary buffer-zones and the buffer-time as its means of supervision. The Forward Headquarters functioned in all phases as a trusted channel of communications and liaison between the parties.

After the completion of the disengagement operation, UNEF started to carry out the permanent duties the new agreement had given to it. In the southern area UNEF had to ensure that no soldiers were allowed to enter the area and that no military installations or fortifications were built. For this purpose UNEF set up checkpoints and observation posts and carried out patrolling on land and in the air. The UN also controlled the two buffer-zones of the area and the common use of certain road sections by permanent control stations and escorts. The Finnish battalion was in charge of the main part of the southern area and the Indonesians of the smaller part. In the large buffer-zone of the northern area, which was manned from north to south by the battalions of Sweden, Ghana and Indonesia, the activities continued very much in the previous manner. Again, battalions of UNEF manned observation posts and checkpoints and sent patrols.

To cope with its increased duties, UNEF was strengthened so that all four battalions got an additional company of 150 men. Furthermore, Australia sent UNEF four Huey Iroquois helicopters for patrolling the area. For the additional air transportations Canada sent an extra Buffalo and the UN rented a small Malaysian Skyvan transport plane.

In order to guard the coast of the southern area, UNEF was supposed to receive four patrol boats with crews from Iran. It soon appeared, however, that the Egyptian Navy strongly opposed this idea. No foreign vessels were needed in the territorial waters of Egypt, because it would only cause confusion. Apparently the Navy's opinion had not been asked during Kissinger's negotiations. Gamassy asked me to come to discuss how Egypt could quietly get rid of this paragraph of the agreement. Gamassy thought that I could best help him in this matter by doing nothing and he said that the UN was a master in this field. I said for my part that it would help me greatly if the Egyptians could persuade the Iranians not to send the vessels. Gamassy thought that this would be easy. Thus it happened that the patrol boats never arrived and nobody said anything about them.

UNEF paid particular attention to the verification of the limitations on troops and armaments. The areas of limitation were supervised by inspections every second week. For this purpose the Egyptian and Israeli authorities had divided these areas into sectors where their respective liaison officers assisted the inspectors. UNEF was also given full information on the results of American aerial reconnaissance, interpreted by experts. This was a great improvement on the practice of the first agreement, when UNEF had not been allowed to see the aerial photos except when one party complained about violations by the opposing side. The results of the ground reconnaissance improved considerably because of the close co-operation between UNEF and the American experts. Not only did UNEF receive the same written reports, maps and aerial photos as the parties, but at joint meetings it could point out the areas from where information was lacking and request additional information. After that, the ground patrols could confirm the results of the aerial reconnaissance.

Thanks to improved verification methods UNEF could prevent violations better than before and persuade the parties to adhere scrupulously to the agreement. Complaints did not cease completely but those that were made were of a minor character, often due to a misunderstanding or differing interpretations of the agreement.

In conclusion I would say that the limited arms and missile-free zones were useful complementary features in the overall security arrangements, despite the fact that these arms limitations were not always observed, that the inspection procedures were not foolproof and that verification of the missile-free zones had little meaning when missiles could readily be wheeled in and out and launching pads could easily be prepared. On balance, the system of limited arms zones added to a sense of security by extending the buffer-zone and making it harder for the parties to launch attacks on each other. It was at least a partial deterrent to resumption of hostilities. More importantly, any significant build-up would sound the alarm and provide some warning against surprise attack. In the UN circle, we were very happy about the excellent co-operation between our inspectors and the American officials who were in charge of the air reconnaissance. It made the inspection results more reliable and strengthened the confidence between the parties. The Americans, for their part, often expressed their satisfaction with the arrangement. They pointed out that for the first time in the history of military intelligence "spy flights" were an honourable part of international co-operation.

The Joint Commission was always convened when needed, under my chairmanship in the buffer-zone. The first meetings were held before the beginning of the disengagement operation and in them we handled details of matters already decided at Geneva as well as new problems that had arisen. The following list of matters handled at the second meeting on 11 November gives an idea of the Commission's function: aerial reconnaissance in the Gulf of Suez; water supply at Abu Rudeis; the establishment of the Forward Headquarters; the return of the Bedouin to the southern area; disposition of certain oil field equipment; minefield maps; use of the roads in various sectors, and six similar matters. After the meeting the Chief Co-ordinator drafted a list of the decisions and gave this to the participants so that they could be followed. Especially in the early days, the Joint Commission convened at least once a month and its role was very useful from the point of view both of the parties and of UNEF.

There was a hiatus in the Middle East peace process after the second Sinai disengagement operation was concluded in February 1976. The situation in Sinai stabilized to the extent that even the mandate of UNEF could be extended by one year at a time, instead of six months as before. The government of Israel thought that it had done enough for the cause of peace. Now it was time for a pause.

Members of the UN forces could also breathe easily for a while. Now medal parades became the most important happenings. Battalions competed enthusiastically to arrange them. We could admire Indonesian music, fakirs' tricks and Balinese plays and dances. My wife and I were judges in a competition between Senegalese companies to produce the best seasoned lamb cooked over a fire. At a party given by the Ghanaian battalion we danced to the tune of "Silent night, holy night" because it was the only waltz which the battalion's famous band, The Hot Barrels, had mastered. But all guests were surely unanimous that the Finnish medal parades were in a special category because of the imaginativeness of their arrangements. It is true that no other battalion was deployed in an area offering such a majestic and beautiful backdrop for its parades. The parade was arranged in a special "medal wadi", or dried-up river-channel, bordered on both sides by high, steep mountain walls. The scenery was like something from a cowboy film. To the surprise of the invited guests, the parade field was completely empty at first. But soon the trumpeters appeared on the top of the mountain wall. Then, observing closely, one could see that the parade troops were climbing down ropes from the mountains to the wadi, where they lined up in parade formation in the normal manner.

I also had the opportunity at this time to meet Israel's new leading personalities. Foreign Minister Moshe Dayan I knew of old but Defence Minister Ezer Weizman was a new acquaintance. There was a captivating charm in the appearance and character of this scion of a famous family, a former Air Force Commander. He also had the relaxed manner of a fighter pilot. No wonder that he was later able to establish close and warm relations with another former officer, Anwar Sadat. Weizman did not have a strong political background behind him and perhaps he did not have the seriousness and strong will required for the post of Prime Minister. But he had other traits which in the course of future peace negotiations would further the achievement of a solution.

I was surprised that Prime Minister Begin wanted to see me several times. I remarked his great politeness, careful dressing and pedantic mode of speech. Begin, who had been educated in Poland, at once wanted to know about the Polish UN soldiers. I said that they were very disciplined and in that respect the real Prussians of UNEF. I added that the Poles still held traditions in great esteem and the two most important matters were honour and fatherland. When I said these two words in Polish, Begin asserted that he had completely forgotten his Polish. Apparently the knowledge quickly returned, because during the Camp David negotiations I saw a press photo where Begin and Zbigniew Brzezinski were playing chess and speaking Polish. Most often it appeared that the actual purpose of my visit was to discuss some violation of the agreement on the part of the Egyptians. Begin wanted me to take as his message to the Egyptians that "*Pacta sunt servanda*": agreements should be adhered to. Years later the Egyptians could have sent the same greetings to Prime Minister Begin when the autonomy for the Palestinians, agreed at Camp David, did not progress at all.

Now I had time for my family and friends too. My wife and I abandoned tourism and historical excursions and went instead for weekend breaks to Gaza, which had become dear to us. There the UN had a much improved beach club, whose life-guard and barman were both great characters. There was another reason for trips to Gaza. Our good friend Magnus Ehrenstrom from Sweden had been appointed the regional director of UNRWA. During his colourful military career in

Canadian Defence Minister Barney Dawson visiting Government House, April 1977, talking with Mrs Siilasvuo and the author.

The new commander of UNEF, Gen. Rais Abin (Indonesia) being introduced to Israeli Defence Minister Shimon Peres, March 1977.

The UN enters the satellite age, 1977, with a parabolic antenna in the garden of Government House. It is in contact with a European communications satellite orbiting over Africa.

the Swedish Army he had trained soldiers in Ethiopia and commanded the UN battalion in Gaza in the 1960s. Magnus had strong links, with Finland. His famous ancestor was the first city planner of Helsinki in the early nineteenth century. As a young volunteer he himself had joined the Finnish Army during the Second World War. He was one of the best international civil servants I ever met and took care of the affairs of the Palestinians with energy and skill. For us the friendship with Magnus and Kerstin Ehrenstrom meant a great deal. I learned many things from Magnus which helped me in my own work.

We were also able to renew relations with other old friends. We often met Colonel Shimon Levinson and Ambassador Rehavam Amir and their families. We travelled to Haifa to meet our Consul Avraham Nemes and his wife. On the way back we stopped at Herzlya and exchanged views with Ambassador Matti Kahiluoto and his wife Ingrid. On our trips to the West Bank we often visited the town of Beit Jala, the Christian neighbour of Bethlehem. There were two reasons for the visits. All the lady guests of the family were taken to the local handicraft centre where beautiful dresses embroidered in the Byzantine style were for sale. More often than not our road would lead to the old house of the Shehadeh family at the highest point of Beit Jala. There with his family, his mother and sister, his wife and children, lived our friend Edmond, a physiotherapist. Of his ten brothers we also knew the surgeon, the baker and the butcher who all lived in Beit Jala as well. Each of them worked in their own field for the Palestinian people. Edmond devoted himself particularly to the care of handicapped children. All members of the family were devoted Christians and belonged to the Greek Orthodox Church.

During the visits to our Israeli and Palestinian friends we felt sorry for both of them. Even for an outsider it was depressing and frustrating to feel the hatred and distrust between them. The road to peace seemed hopelessly slow. In our opinion those who thought that time was on their side were definitely wrong. We were convinced that without negotiations between all concerned, there could be no solution. Our only hope was that the peoples of the area would finally realize this.

23. The peace offensive of Sadat, Begin and Carter

Carter's plans for peace

The true apostle of peace and its energetic promoter, the President of Egypt, Anwar Sadat, gradually became tired of the lull which had continued since February 1976. He feared that the entire peace process would founder if matters were not speeded up. He also believed that the Sinai agreement, which he called the third stage of the peace process, would be the last effort in the present policy of small steps. Now it was time to find a comprehensive solution to the whole Middle East conflict. Therefore Sadat embarked on the preparations for his great peace initiative. In his view it was time to break down the immense psychological wall that had grown up between Israel and the Arabs. This wall had been built up over the years by suspicion, hatred, fear and misunderstandings.

The year 1977 was a time of changes in the United States and Israel. Jimmy Carter was inaugurated as President of the former in January, while the rightist Likud Party won parliamentary elections in Israel and interrupted the era of the Labour Party's dominance which had continued since the establishment of the state of Israel. Itzhak Rabin was replaced as Prime Minister by Menachem Begin in May. Now Sadat would be the only one to represent continuity in the peace negotiations. One could hope, however, that the newcomers would bring with them new ideas and new energy. Vision and imagination were now really needed.

People in Egypt were worried about the new development in Israel and General Gamassy said to me that in his opinion the new government resembled a war cabinet. I answered that I could not yet say anything about the other members of the Cabinet, but advised him to follow closely the activities of the new Foreign Minister, Moshe Dayan. I said that I was sure of his future important role in the peace process. I also told him about the conviction of many Israelis that Begin would be the only one who could give back Sinai to Egypt.

In the United States the new group directing foreign policy, besides the President, comprised Vice-President Fritz Mondale, Secretary of State Cyrus Vance and the National Security Adviser, Zbigniew

Brzezinski. They believed that the deadlocked situation in the Middle East in 1977 could gradually deteroriate and cause unfortunate results from the point of view of world peace. A new war could break out and lead to a conflict between the superpowers which would be worse than the one that was narrowly avoided in 1973. Therefore it was thought that the United States could best improve the security of its ally Israel by continuing the peace process. In the United States it was thought, as Sadat did, that the time of the small steps policy was over.

President Carter also had in mind new ideas besides the security of Israel. In a press conference in May 1977 he said that without a homeland for the Palestinians there could be no reasonable hope of solving the Middle East question. In the following months Carter personally speeded up the matter by meeting the Israeli Prime Minister, the President of Egypt, the King of Jordan, the Crown Prince of Saudi Arabia and the President of Syria. At this stage the aim of the United States was to continue the Geneva Peace Conference. Carter tried to persuade the Arabs to make concessions so that the conference would have a better start. In particular he tried to influence the leadership of the PLO, through intermediaries, so that it would recognize Resolution 242. In the view of the Americans, the objective of the conference should be the comprehensive settlement of the Middle East conflict, normal peaceful relations between Israel and its Arab neighbours, withdrawal to secure and recognized boundaries and the establishment of a Palestinian entity, based on self-determination. To me the idea of continuing the peace conference seemed completely unrealistic. It had no chance of succeeding. If it could be convened at all, it would probably end on its first day in a great shouting match.

Soon it became clear to the Americans too that reconvening the Geneva conference was an impossible idea. Secretary of State Cyrus Vance was the first to realize this on his trip to the Middle East in mid-summer. The disagreements between the parties made such a conference impossible to arrange. No agreement could be reached on the participation of the Palestinians; the demands of the PLO were, as usual, extremist; Israel strongly opposed all American proposals. But the failure to restart the conference was mainly due to the unscrupulous establishment by Israel of new settlements in the West Bank, completely disregarding Carter's appeals. The aim of the new Prime Minister, Menachem Begin, seemed to be to create rapidly a situation in the West Bank which would prevent even partial territorial arrangements. During the autumn it became clearer than ever that the peace conference was not a realizable alternative. The hopes for the progress of peace vanished once again.

Sadat in Jerusalem

Sadat's courageous new initiative changed the whole miserable political situation at one stroke. In a speech in the Egyptian Parliament on 17 November he revealed the surprise solution which he had prepared in secret. It was an Initiative with a capital I, as he says himself in his memoirs. During his historic trip to Jerusalem he would pray in the Al Aksa Mosque during the great Moslem Bairam feast and the high point of the visit would be his speech in the Knesset.

The news aroused all kinds of feelings. The Foreign Minister of Egypt, Ismail Fahmy, angry at Sadat's proposal, resigned in protest, but I have the impression that the majority of the people were satisfied. In other parts of the Arab world reactions ranged from incredulity to blind rage. In Israel there was no limit to the joy of the people. I was able to experience how the hearts of an entire people could be filled with sincere delight.

When Sadat's plane landed on 19 November 1977 at Ben Gurion Airport, a large group had gathered there to receive him: the Israeli Cabinet, members of the Knesset, the Diplomatic Corps and the highest civil servants. Protocol placed me between the diplomats and the civil servants and I became aware that standing next to me was General Gur, my negotiating partner for years. There were also hundreds of journalists present. When the door of the aeroplane was opened, another large group of correspondents and cameramen disembarked. Then I saw at the top of the stairs my old friend, the Chief of Protocol Rehavam Amir, and noticed his happy expression. I had known him in Warsaw, where he had been the Minister of Israel. When he was later appointed as Israel's Ambassador to Helsinki, he told me that the reception of Sadat had been the high point of his diplomatic career.

When Sadat greeted his hosts the atmosphere was spontaneous and warm on both sides. He embraced Golda Meir and spoke with his former adversary Moshe Dayan. To many others, like General Ariel Sharon, he seemed to have something to say. When he saw me, he stopped for a moment and said, "I came here to make your job a bit easier, General."

The rest of the visit my wife and I followed on the TV. In honour of the historic day Israeli Television was, exceptionally, broadcasting a

'I came to make your task a little easier, General.' President Anwar Sadat of Egypt greets the author at Tel Aviv airfield, 19 Nov. 1977. *On Sadat's right*: Israel's chief of protocol, Rehavam Amir.

The Mena House conference, Cairo: negotiations of the Military Working Group. *Behind table, from left*: the author, Eliahu Ben-Elissar (Israel), Alfred Atherton (United States). *Facing the Israeli delegation*: Esmat Abdel Meguid (Egypt).

colour programme instead of its usual black and white pictures. We saw and heard Sadat's great speech in the Knesset and his exclamation which appealed to feelings: "No more wars!" Anwar Sadat's and Golda Meir's television conversation made a very strong impression on me personally. Two grandparents first exchanged small presents, for Sadat's daughter had given birth to a daughter at the same time as he had prayed in the mosque. After that Mrs Meir said how happy she was at Sadat's visit. She had not awaited anything so long and so devotedly as the day when an Arab leader would arrive in Jerusalem and would be ready to negotiate with Israel. She said that she was certain that through negotiations a solution could be reached that would satisfy both parties. Finally Golda Meir said, "I admit that we have this Palestinian problem but with joint efforts we shall be able to solve it." In my opinion this was surprising talk from the previous Prime Minister, who not long ago would not admit that the Palestinians existed.

Sadat's visit had important consequences for the everyday life of our family. First our Palestinian cook gave notice. He could not continue working for a family that so obviously was on the side of Israel and President Sadat. A few moments later the devoted friend of Israel, the Finnish Hertta, announced for her part that she could not stay in such an Arab-minded house. Fortunately, after more careful consideration, Ata cancelled his resignation a few days later. Hertta, whose character was stronger, kept to her decision and to our regret left the house. When at the point of departure I bade farewell to Hertta and thanked her for excellent service, she said to my wife, "The General is lying here. He has learned to lie so well in his job." For a long time we did not hear anything of Hertta. But a few years later, when we were about to return to Finland, she came to work with us again and gave us invaluable help in the preparations for our departure.

What were the political results of Sadat's visit? Sadat himself was very content, although the first contacts with Begin did not fulfil his wishes, for the vicious circle that had tortured the Middle East had been broken and he had agreed with the Israelis that the October War would be the last war between the two countries and that mutual security questions should be discussed around a negotiating table. Sadat's main objective was to resolve the Middle East conflict in such a way that Israel, by withdrawing from the areas occupied in 1967, would create the circumstances in which a better future for the Palestinian people could become possible.

In Sadat's opinion the conditions for peace were good. He had achieved his political aims in the October War. The shame of 1967 had been avenged and the invincibility of Israel made questionable. Egypt and Israel were, finally, equal negotiating partners.

Over the years we had followed Sadat's consistent and determined activities in the pursuit of peace. He tried to overcome the obstacles in the way of peace in the most realistic and pragmatic manner. In negotiations he kept in mind the great objectives for the future and was therefore able to give up seeming short-term interests. Broad-mindedly he swept aside the meanness and short-sighted obstruction of the opposite party and of his own aides.

By 1977 Sadat realized, however, that the building of peace is not advanced by normal means. The departure for Jerusalem was then a revolutionary idea. It demonstrated his exceptional creative inventiveness and great courage, lifting him from being a brilliant leader in the Middle East to the ranks of the great statesmen of world history.

Sadat guessed that the other Arab leaders would not understand his decision to visit Israel and therefore he did not ask their opinions in advance. He could hardly have foreseen, however, that in their very narrow outlook the Arab world would react with such negative fury as in fact it did. Despite everything, Sadat was ready to expose himself to danger and later had to pay for it with his life.

The Military Working Group at Mena House

The bilateral meetings at the end of 1977 and the beginning of 1978 proved to be more difficult than the optimists had assumed. The first to begin was the meeting of the Military Working Group in Cairo around Christmas. We met in the historic Mena House Hotel, at the foot of the Giza Pyramids, where during the world wars Winston Churchill and many other celebrated people had lived. Perhaps it was hoped that the natural beauty of the hotel's surroundings would have a healing influence on the atmosphere of the meetings and inspire the participants to positive contributions. The Egyptians tried their best in this respect because their conference arrangements exceeded everything I had experienced before. The meeting chamber was splendidly luxurious and the delegations had at their disposal stylish suites, cosy guestrooms and gourmet meals. The greatest surprise, however, was the vast press room, where, just by pushing a button, one could make telephone contact with the ends of the world in the blinking of an eye.

Unfortunately all this remained useless outer ostentation because, despite these efforts, the meeting had no concrete agenda. Firstly, the meeting was not even on a ministerial level. Despite its military name the delegations were headed by diplomats: the Egyptian Ambassador Esmat Abdel Meguid and the Israeli Eliahu Ben-Elissar, the Chief of the Prime Minister's office. The United States was represented by Assistant Secretary of State Alfred Atherton and I for my part represented the UN. It became apparent that the heads of the delegations had no independent authority or clear instructions. In addition Israel's representative was, because of his pomposity, less than suitable as a negotiator and aroused instinctive resistance in the opposite party.

The working group continued to meet after the New Year. In the two last meetings the parties presented, among other things, their proposals on the end of belligerency between Israel and Egypt and spoke at length about the nature of the peace. Unanimity was not reached on any issue. There was an immense gap between the opinions of the parties on essential matters like the withdrawal of Israel, relations with the Palestinians and the settlements on the West Bank.

During the Christmas holidays there was an intermission and my wife and I had time to visit the Finnish battalion on the Red Sea. We flew by the UNEF plane from Ismailia to Abu Rudeis. We had with us the Assistant Secretary of State and Mrs Atherton, to whom we had offered a lift to the American Sinai Field Mission's base near the Giddi Pass. They wanted to spend Christmas with their countrymen in the Sinai desert. For us it was great fun to visit the Finns at any time, but nowhere else in the Middle East at Christmas time could one find such a homelike atmosphere despite the exotic surroundings. We took part in the many festivities at the battalion, attended Christmas service and ate Finnish Christmas food. We relaxed in the excellent guest-house and enjoyed the magnificent scenery of the area. All in all our visit to the battalion was such a refreshing and cheerful experience that I did not wonder at all at Hammarskjöld's way of spending Christmas. As far as I know he flew especially from New York to Gaza at many Christmases to spend the holiday in the company of Swedish soldiers, saying that it was a means of keeping in touch with his Swedish roots.

Tired with the slow progress of the negotiations, Sadat tried to give clear tasks to the Military Working Group. He and Begin held a summit meeting to decide on the outline of the peace process on Boxing Day in Ismailia. Sadat was exultant at arranging the meeting and said that this was the happiest day of his life. The happiness was short-lived, however. Despite the agreeable atmosphere of the talks between Sadat and Begin, the real contribution of this meeting too was minimal. It was decided to continue discussions in two working groups. The Defence Ministers would be the representatives in the Military Working Group, while the delegations to the Political Working Group, which would convene in Jerusalem in January, would be headed by the Foreign Ministers.

The Political Working Group in Jerusalem

In the third week of the New Year the Political Working Group met at the Hilton Hotel in Jerusalem. Israeli Foreign Minister Moshe Dayan and the new Foreign Minister of Egypt, Mohammed Kamel, represented the parties of the conflict. Kamel was a career diplomat whose last posting had been Bonn. Secretary of State Cyrus Vance had arrived in Jerusalem to head the American delegation. The issue of UN representation raised problems, for the strong criticism by the Soviet Union and the Arab world caused Waldheim to wonder whether the UN should be present at all. I favoured participation because in my view the question was now whether the UN would be allowed to participate in the Middle East peace process in the future. The Egyptians in particular considered it important that the UN should at least send an observer to the meeting. So after much weighing of pros and cons it was decided that I should act as the observer.

Now the situation began to take on an air of comedy. Waldheim was extremely worried that my chair would be too close to the edge of the round negotiating table. This could give a false impression of the position of the United Nations at the meeting. As the meeting opened, Waldheim was travelling in the region. He phoned me in the middle of the night once from Tehran and once from Athens in order to ensure that my chair would be at least one and a half metres from the edge of the table. Otherwise people could get the impression from TV and press pictures that the UN was a participant and not just an observer at the meeting.

So the meeting got underway but unfortunately the results this time were meagre too. President Sadat had demanded that a list of principles be drawn up. Both parties presented their own version of this list on the first day of the negotiations. Secretary of State Vance for his part presented the meeting with a joint statement, given by Presidents Carter and Sadat in January, which was in line with the opinions expressed earlier by the United States. Its main point was that the "Palestinians had the right to participate in deciding their future".

In the evening Prime Minister Begin gave a banquet to the participants in the meeting. In his speech he said, among other things, "Peace cannot be established should Israel agree to restore the fragile, breakable, aggression-provoking and bloodshed-causing lines preceding the fifth of June 1967." This was too much for the Egyptian Foreign Minister, who ostentatiously marched out of the room.

This incident presaged a bad end for the meeting and, indeed, President Sadat put an end to the negotiations and called his delegation home on the second day of meetings. He was utterly tired of Israel's obstructiveness. This road had now been travelled to the end, he said.

Now the ball was again in the Americans' court. They had to resign themselves to the fact that a comprehensive settlement would be possible only after many years. Therefore they had to be satisfied that Sadat's peace initiative would be realized as an Egypto-Israeli agreement which at the same time would try to promote Palestinian aspirations. At least they could get the conservative Arab countries to join the negotiations and to assure the Palestinians that the United States was advocating their right to self-determination. Sadat had made his trip to Jerusalem in order to help Carter, whom Begin's fanaticism had driven into a corner. Now Sadat had to be helped so that Egypt would achieve its basic aims. However, this had to be done in such a way that the Palestinian question was not forgotten, otherwise Egypt would become a traitor in the eyes of the Arab world.

Israel's objectives were, in the opinion of the Americans, clear from the very beginning: they wanted a separate peace agreement with Egypt which would drive a wedge between Egypt and the other Arabs and allow Israel to continue the occupation of the West Bank and Gaza.

However, people in Israel worried about the consequences and durability of the agreement. This is illustrated by my conversation with President Ephraim Katzir at the Independence Day reception in May 1978:

"Israel is now facing difficult decisions which involve great risks. Tell me, General Siilasvuo, can we trust the Egyptians?"

I answered the President that in this world I would not trust anybody.

"What do you mean?" the President asked, surprised.

"Has Israel been able to trust the British, the Russians or the French? Can you in the end trust your good friends the Americans?" I asked the

President and continued: "I think that Israel should try to create such economic and other relations with Egypt that it would be in the interest of Egypt to adhere to the agreement."

The Camp David negotiations and agreement

The idea of a summit meeting with Sadat and Begin had occurred to President Carter in February 1978. Planning, contacts and trips to the Middle East took time, however, and it was only in September that these three and their assistants convened in Camp David, the President's holiday resort. After very difficult and tough negotiations which lasted 13 days, unanimity was finally reached. The documents agreed at Camp David did not constitute a final agreement, but formed the framework of negotiations on the arrangements for the transition period in the West Bank and the conclusion of the peace agreement between Egypt and Israel. The greatest merit of the documents was the creation of a basis for the peace agreement. The greatest weakness of Camp David was that no clear agreement was made on a moratorium on West Bank settlements. The credit for the success goes above all to Carter's toughness, determination and negotiating skill. Without him no agreement could have been achieved.

The title of the first document was "The Framework of Peace in the Middle East". According to this, the search for peace must be based on Resolution 242 in its entirety, the Charter of the United Nations, the respect for the independence of every state in the area and their right to live in peace within secure and recognized boundaries. The first document's objective was political and economic co-operation and good neighbourly relations between the states of the region.

Negotiations on the future of the West Bank and Gaza were to start between Egypt, Israel and the representatives of the Palestinian people. These negotiations should proceed in three stages. Firstly, a transitional period of five years was needed for the arrangements. In order to provide full autonomy to the inhabitants of the occupied territories, the Israeli military government would be withdrawn as soon as a self-governing authority had been freely elected. In the second stage Egypt, Israel and Jordan would agree on the election of the self-governing authority and its powers and responsibilities. Palestinians would participate in the negotiations as members of the Egyptian and Jordanian delegations. Israeli troops would be withdrawn, except for a few to be deployed in specified security locations. To maintain law and order a strong internal police force would be established, which might include Jordanian citizens.

When the self-governing authority or administrative council had been established and inaugurated, the transitional period of five years would begin. No later than its third year, the third stage of negotiations would take place to determine the final status of the West Bank and Gaza.

Thus Israel succeeded completely in watering down even the reasonable demands of the Palestinians and making the achievement of even small improvements as difficult as possible. It was not solely Israel's fault, however, that the agreed negotiations never commenced. The other reason was the hostile attitudes of Jordan and the PLO to the results of Camp David. It was said that they could not be accepted because they gave too little to the Palestinians. As a result of the everything-or-nothing policy, once more nothing was achieved and the inhabitants of the West Bank and Gaza were left suffering.

After Camp David, autonomy became a subject of lively conversations. We talked about it during the visit of the Ombudsman of the Finnish Parliament, Dr Jorma S. Aalto, in March 1979. During his yearly visit to the Finnish battalion he also dropped in at Government House in Jerusalem to see us. On the following day the Ombudsman of the state of Israel, Dr Nebenzahl, gave a luncheon in honour of his opposite number in the beautiful Mishkenot Sha'ananim restaurant. Also present were other Israelis, among them Meron Benvenisti, the well-known promoter of Arab-Israeli co-operation. The conversation moved on to autonomy and I remarked that I wished the Israelis would be as generous and enlightened as the Russian Emperor Alexander I, who gave autonomy to us Finns in 1809. I then explained the development of our autonomy and concluded: "There was a special trait characteristic of Finnish autonomy; Russian settlements were not imposed on us." At this the Israelis said that they did not care to hear any more about it.

The second document to emerge from Camp David was entitled "The Framework for the Conclusion of a Peace Treaty between Egypt and Israel". In this it was stated that the parties agreed to negotiate a peace agreement between themselves which would be signed within three months of the Camp David meeting. It was also agreed that the negotiations would be under a United Nations flag (this was later forgotten) at a location to be mutually agreed. Israel would withdraw completely from Sinai and Egypt would limit the number of its forces there. A UN force would be deployed in Sinai to carry out supervision and verification duties. Israel would have the right of free passage in the Suez Canal, the Gulf of Aqaba and the Straits of Tiran. After a peace treaty was signed, and after the interim withdrawal to the El Arish-Ras Muhammad line was complete, normal relations would be established between Egypt and Israel, including full recognition and diplomatic, economic and cultural relations. The halving of Sinai, which was first mentioned at the early meetings at Kilometre 101, was now about to materialize.

The peace treaty between Egypt and Israel

Despite the success of Camp David, the peace treaty was not achieved very quickly. New differences of opinion appeared. They were caused especially by the arrogant behaviour of Prime Minister Begin soon after the signature of the documents. In an interview given to an American TV network he said that Israel had the right to remain in the West Bank for an indefinite period of time, even beyond the agreed transition period, and to continue to establish settlements. The cause of peace was not advanced and the situation remained deadlocked over the New Year.

Now President Carter was obliged to become personally involved in affairs. On his trip to Egypt and Israel in March 1979 he succeeded in mediating the last disagreements on the road to a peace treaty. The solemn signing of the treaty took place in the Rose Garden of the White House on 27 March 1979.

The agreement came into force on 25 April 1979 and provided that upon completion of a phased Israeli withdrawal over three years, UN forces and observers would assist in security arrangements on both sides. The agreement stipulated that "the parties will request the United Nations to provide forces and observers to supervise the implementation of the security arrangements." The intention was to use UN forces and observers to perform a variety of tasks, including the operation of checkpoints, reconnaissance patrols and observation posts along the borders of and within the demilitarized zone and ensuring free navigation through the Straits of Tiran. UN forces would also be stationed in certain areas adjoining the demilitarized zone on the Egyptian side and the UN observers would patrol a certain area on the Israeli side of the international boundary. In an annex to the agreement the United States undertook to organize a multinational force of equivalent size if the

United Nations was unable to carry out its duties as envisaged by the agreement.

The intention of the parties was to have UNEF perform the above mentioned tasks. This was not possible, however, because the PLO and many Arab countries strongly opposed the peace treaty. In the Security Council the Soviet Union opposed it too and the Council decided on 24 July not to extend the mandate of UNEF. The role of the United Nations in Sinai was about to come to an end, as I had already feared in January 1978 when my participation in the meeting of the Political Working Group proved to be so very difficult.

In accordance with the peace treaty Israeli forces withdrew from northern Sinai east of El Arish on 29 May and the Egyptians took this area under their control. UNEF no longer participated in this operation except by letting the Egyptian troops enter the buffer-zone and the limited forces areas. It also arranged escorts for the parties in these areas when the withdrawal of the Israeli forces was taking place. During the process UNEF withdrew from the northern part of the buffer-zone and handed it over to the Egyptians. UNEF continued to operate as before, except in areas which were controlled by Egyptian forces. It also arranged escorts for non-UN visitors and for personnel from the parties who travelled to the early warning stations and back.

After the termination of UNEF's mandate in July 1979 the battalions of the various countries were repatriated quite quickly. Only a Swedish guard unit and parts of the Polish and Canadian logistics unit remained in the area to take care of the termination of UNEF's role.

UNEF II had been an exceptionally successful peace-keeping force. It was a great loss from the point of view of both the world organization and the future political development of the Middle East that it had to be terminated as a consequence of the, in my opinion, short-sighted policy of certain Arab countries and the Soviet Union.

24. First days of UNIFIL

The situation in Lebanon and the Israeli offensive in 1978

Ever since civil war had broken out in Lebanon in 1974, I had heard and read about several proposals to set up a UN force. The Lebanese government in particular hoped that such a force could put an end to the cruel war and restore law and order in the country. The situation was indeed chaotic. The government had practically no say whatsoever in the running of the country. As a result of the civil war the army was completely disbanded. Lebanon could hardly be considered an independent sovereign state.

However, the idea of setting up a UN force had several opponents. I myself was one of them, as I was very sceptical of the chances that such a force would have. I knew from experience that peace-keeping was sufficiently difficult when the force was operating in the stable conditions of Sinai or the Golan, deployed between two disciplined armies which were under the leadership of two responsible governments who shared a favourable view of the UN force. The task would most certainly be more difficult in civil war conditions, such as in Lebanon, where the government was weak and the UN force would be at the mercy of factions that were led from abroad. I could also imagine that the countless Palestinian fighters active in Lebanon would further complicate matters, for as early as 1969 the Arab summit had passed a resolution that Lebanon was to allow Palestinian activity against Israel to be conducted from its territory. As a result of this resolution the Palestinians had in a sense set up a state of their own in southern Lebanon. We later learned from experience that every different faction there, Christian or Moslem, Palestinian or Lebanese, left-wing or right-wing, was irresponsible and showed no respect for the UN flag. One thing all the factions had in common was an unwillingness to stop fighting.

These were my arguments for opposing a UN force and I presented them to the authorities in Israel and Lebanon, to foreign ambassadors and to other visitors in Jerusalem. I did not think that the UN ought to be given an impossible mission. I related my views to senior US State Department officials when I visited Washington DC in October 1977. I said that a severe setback in Lebanon would mar the reputation of UN peace-keeping operations and hamper their future usefulness.

Although an official proclamation of the cessation of the civil war was issued in October 1976, when Elias Sarkis was elected President, the situation in Lebanon did not improve. A new government was set up and asked the Arab League to send troops to stabilize the situation. However, this Arab Deterrent Force did not accomplish its mission. Furthermore, it gradually lost its international character and became a solely Syrian force. The reason for its lack of success was to some extent its mode of operation; instead of diplomatic persuasion, the Syrian troops resorted to the use of force. They were under the misapprehension that the battling factions could be forced to peace. The same reasons led to the complete failure of the American-French-Italian multinational force in Beirut in 1982. Only the Italian contingent escaped reprisals, because it was the only one to refrain from colonial-style measures. The American and the French troops, despite their extremely violent tactics, did not gain any military or political benefit; they did, however, inflict great losses and suffering on the local civilian population.

The situation in southern Lebanon continued to be unstable and fighting did not cease completely. Matters deteriorated further when the Syrian force started to move south. The Israeli government threatened severe retaliation if the Syrians crossed the so-called Red Line south of the River Zahrani. The Syrians did refrain from crossing the line, whether because of the Israeli threat or for other reasons. The Lebanese government did not have much influence in the south, nor had it shown very much interest in southern Lebanon before the civil war. Now the government suddenly proclaimed that it wanted to bolster its influence in this area, although I did not notice that it actually took any concrete action in this matter. There were occasional skirmishes between the Christian Militia, supported by Israel, and armed units of the Lebanese National Movement, a loose configuration of Moslem and left-wing parties supported by the PLO. At that point the PLO was clearly the prominent group in the south and it had set up a number of armed strongholds there. Israel always retaliated severely when the PLO undertook guerrilla activity against it.

The Tel Aviv area was the target of an unusually violent terrorist attack on 11 March 1978. It left 37 dead and 76 wounded civilians. The retaliation was also more severe than usual, for Israel invaded Lebanon. On the night of 14/15 March a large Israeli force crossed the border and within a few days had occupied the whole area south of the Litani River, with the exception of the town of Tyre and its environs. The

only solution Israel had been able to develop for the Palestinian question
was an extremely violent one. President Sadat's plea in the Knesset:
"No more wars!" had already been forgotten.

The establishment of UNIFIL

In the Security Council on March 15 the Lebanese government strongly
condemned the Israeli attack. It did not consider itself responsible for
the Palestinian strongholds in southern Lebanon and it had no connection with the recent terrorist raid. It claimed that it had used all possible
means to influence the Palestinians and the Arab countries in order to
bring the situation under control. Israel's negative attitude in regard to
the deployment of the Syrian force deeper in southern Lebanon had
prevented attempts to intensify control of the border area. The Security
Council put the matter on its agenda.

Suddenly things started to happen and the United States proposed
that a UN force be set up in southern Lebanon. Prime Minister Begin
was on his way to Washington to negotiate about peace in the Middle
East. Greater issues than the Lebanese problem were at stake. The
whole peace process might come to a standstill if Israel was not offered
an honourable route for retreat from Lebanon. Nothing was too high
a price for President Carter to pay for saving Israel's face and his own
peace plan. Once again it was to be seen that the words of warning of
State Department officials were of no avail in such a situation.

On March 19 the Security Council passed Resolution No. 425
(1978), which had been submitted by the United States. It called upon
Israel to cease its military action against Lebanon and immediately
withdraw its forces from all Lebanese territory. It also decided to
establish UNIFIL, or a United Nations Interim Force for southern
Lebanon, whose task was to confirm the withdrawal of Israeli forces,
restore international peace and security and assist the Lebanese government in ensuring the return of its effective authority in southern
Lebanon.

The same afternoon the Secretary-General submitted a report to the
Security Council in which he presented the terms of reference,
guidelines and plan of action for its establishment. The force was to set
up and maintain itself in an area of operations to be defined in the light
of those tasks, and it was to use its best efforts to prevent the occurrence
of fighting and to ensure that its area of operations was not utilized for

hostile activities of any kind. UNTSO's military observers in the area were to co-operate with UNIFIL.

In the first stage of the operation UNIFIL would confirm that the Israeli forces withdrew from Lebanese territory to the international border. After this it would commence operations within an area that would be defined in negotiations with the parties. UNIFIL would supervise the cessation of hostilities, ensure the peaceful character of the area and take all necessary measures in order to restore Lebanese sovereignty. In his report the Secretary-General also pointed out that as a first step towards implementing the Resolution of the Security Council, it would be necessary to agree upon certain arrangements with Israel and Lebanon. He also presumed that both states would co-operate completely with UNIFIL in this regard.

While the Security Council together with the Secretary-General continued to discuss the make-up of UNIFIL and other practical matters, the Ghanaian Major-General Emmanuel Alex Erskine, who had been appointed Force Commander, began preparations for setting up the force on the field. Once again the Secretary-General adopted the proven practice of appointing the Chief of Staff of UNTSO to command a new force. Erskine had four years' experience with the UN; he had started out as my Chief of Staff in UNEF in the spring of 1974 and been appointed Chief of Staff for UNTSO two years later. UNIFIL's interim Chief of Staff was the Irish Colonel William Callaghan, second in command in UNTSO, who some years later became the Force Commander of UNIFIL. The rest of the headquarters staff was recruited from UNTSO military observers in the area. This was also an old and proven custom.

The first thing General Erskine did was to set up a command post for UNIFIL in the border village of Naqoura, where UNTSO already maintained an outpost and which had originally been built by the French as a border and customs station. Next the observers started to reconnoitre the area. The situation was naturally, in the aftermath of the Israeli offensive, very tense. The greater part of the area was in Israeli hands and the majority of PLO troops had retreated to the city of Tyre, which was encircled, and north of the Litani River to strongholds in Beaufort Castle and the town of Nabatiye. Extensive shooting continued between the PLO and the Israelis. Another action, which had been tested already in the setting up of UNEF II, was the deployment of a Swedish and an Iranian company as UNIFIL's advance troops. The Swedish company came from UNEF and the Iranian from

UNDOF. The other contingents were to come from France, Nepal, Norway, Fiji, Nigeria, Senegal and Ireland. By the beginning of June UNIFIL's strength had reached 6,100.

In his first report the Secretary-General had already instructed me to get in touch with the Israeli and Lebanese governments and negotiate with their representatives about the arrangements concerning the Israeli withdrawal and the boundaries of UNIFIL's area of operations. This fell in naturally with my duties as Chief Co-ordinator. On the Israeli side I met with the Minister of Defence and the Chief of Staff. In Lebanon I negotiated with the Foreign Minister and the Commander of the Army. Israel took the view that the area of UNIFIL's operations should contain the area they had conquered, with the addition of Tyre, Beaufort Castle and Nabatiye. I pointed out to General Mordechai Gur, who was serving his last days as Chief of Staff, that UNIFIL's area would be more united and easier to control if its boundary ran along the Litani River and thus included the Tyre encirclement. However, UNIFIL would not necessarily need to occupy the latter sites. I added that it might be difficult for UNIFIL to expand its area when the mighty Israeli Army had not been able to do it. General Gur admitted that continuing the advance would have cost Israel a great number of additional casualties. Later I discussed the same subject in Beirut. It was interesting and surprising to hear that the Lebanese government shared the Israeli view. UNIFIL's area should definitely embrace Tyre, Beaufort Castle and Nabatiye.

The PLO was a third important factor to be considered in defining the boundaries of UNIFIL's area of operations, although the Security Council Resolution had not named it as a party. To make up for this defect, and in order to ensure the co-operation of PLO Chairman Yasser Arafat, at the end of March the Secretary-General issued an appeal for a general cease-fire. It was addressed to all parties in the area, including the PLO. He further instructed General Erskine to contact the PLO. This confirmed the division of labour that was adhered to later on: Erskine dealt with contacts with the PLO and I concentrated on contacts with the Lebanese and Israeli governments. After the meeting between Erskine and Arafat the PLO issued a commitment to co-operate with UNIFIL. Arafat did not clearly express his views on UNIFIL's area of operations, but it could be understood that he was not in favour of a UNIFIL presence in areas of central importance to the PLO, such as Tyre. We would soon see whether Arafat would keep his promise about co-operation with UNIFIL.

Besides the PLO there were other armed factions in southern Lebanon which did not recognize the authority of the central government. Officially UNIFIL could not have contacts with them. Many of them supported the PLO, some were pro-Israel. All of them, however, were parties to the local conflict and could not be disregarded. One of the largest groups was the previously mentioned Lebanese National Movement, a grouping of Moslem and left-wing units in league with the PLO. Its armed units were under joint command with the PLO. When difficulties occurred UNIFIL usually attempted to influence the Lebanese National Movement through the PLO.

On the opposite side there was the so-called Christian Militia, led by the renegade Lebanese Army Major Saad Haddad, a pint-size Quisling from southern Lebanon. The Militia was also known as the *de facto* force, because it did exist even though the UN could not recognize it. At this early phase we could not foresee what great problems this force would eventually cause. When difficulties did occur we contacted the Israeli authorities, because Major Haddad was their minion.

The establishment of UNIFIL was a fairly smooth operation, much easier than setting up UNEF five years earlier. We had learned our lesson from the mistakes we made then. The resources of UNTSO, UNEF and UNDOF were available, and if need arose materiel could also be drawn from UNFICYP warehouses in Cyprus. Local procurement, maintenance, communications and transport were easier to organize in the economically and technically developed Israel and Lebanon than in Egypt. The first new troops to arrive were the French battalion and logistics units, which arrived in Beirut on March 23. The battalion was part of the French 3rd Paratrooper Regiment; its home garrison was Carcassonne. It was an élite troop of young enlisted soldiers. The battalion was the first French unit on Lebanese soil for 35 years. A few days earlier, when President Valéry Giscard d'Estaing had briefed the battalion, he had stressed the point that France had a special mission in Lebanon. At the UNIFIL compound I met the Battalion Commander, Colonel Jean Salvan, a veteran from Indochina and Algeria. We viewed the terrain in front of us and he asked me, "Where is the enemy?" I replied that, as far as I knew, the UN did not have any enemies here.

UNIFIL's new Chief of Staff, General J. Cuq, had arrived together with the battalion, and he came with General Erskine to meet me in Jerusalem. We sat in our living room in Government House and Erskine and I briefed the newcomer on the situation in Lebanon and we talked about the future of UNIFIL. I formed a favourable impression of General Cuq, although I was slightly put off by his habit of lacing his speech with "the government in Paris thinks so and so about this matter, and the government in Paris thinks so and so about that matter". I put an end to these remarks by asking General Erskine whether he had any idea what the government in Accra thought about these matters.

Supervision of the different phases of the Israeli withdrawal took place without mishap. In fact UNIFIL coped with its tasks better than many had expected and in the early stages it managed to fulfil its mandate at least to some degree. Normal conditions and peace were restored to the area it controlled. Tens of thousands of refugees started to return to their villages fairly early on, shops and schools reopened their doors and farmers started to till their fields again. I thought that for these accomplishments alone UNIFIL's soldiers had earned their pay.

Early problems for UNIFIL

UNIFIL's problems became apparent at an early stage and as time went by they only became worse. First of all the PLO failed to keep its promises of co-operation; I doubt if they were ever meant to be taken seriously. Maybe Arafat just wanted to appease the UN and Waldheim. However, a more important reason for the difficulties was the lack of discipline. The guerrillas in the field did not take seriously the decisions and promises made by the supreme command.

The unco-operative attitude of the PLO guerrillas led to serious confrontations in the Tyre area at the beginning of May. On May 1 a group of armed Palestinians tried to infiltrate a post manned by the French near Tyre. When they were challenged they opened fire on the sentries. The sentries shot back in self-defence and killed two of the infiltrators. The PLO took its revenge: during the next days its soldiers ambushed the French at several locations. Three UNIFIL soldiers were killed and 14 wounded. Among the wounded was the Commander of the French battalion, who had been on his way to negotiate a cease-fire after a shooting. He was travelling with a PLO liaison officer, his French Aide-de-Camp and a corporal. Suddenly they were met with machine-gun fire. The Aide-de-Camp was killed outright, while Colonel Salvan and the Corporal were badly wounded. My answer to Salvan's question had been wrong: UNIFIL did have an enemy in Lebanon. Later it transpired that the PLO was not the only one.

There were other problems with the Palestinians. Soon after the Israelis had withdrawn, it appeared that there were some 200–300 armed Palestinian fighters scattered in small groups within the UNIFIL area. The PLO claimed that the guerrillas had been there throughout the Israeli occupation and it insisted that they should be allowed to remain in the area. General Erskine and I found it hard to believe that the guerrillas had been there on a permanent basis; we thought that they had infiltrated UNIFIL's area later on. We foresaw great difficulties. UNIFIL would lose its neutral status and credibility if it treated one armed group differently from the others, so we therefore proposed that the Palestinians should be expelled immediately. However, the Secretary-General disagreed. He dispatched an aide to negotiate with the PLO. Arafat confirmed his previous claim that the PLO would co-operate with UNIFIL and refrain from striking against Israel from southern Lebanon; it would use alternative routes instead. Although a PLO presence in southern Lebanon was strictly a matter between the PLO and the Lebanese government, according to Arafat, the organiza-tion would, as a response to the Secretary-General's plea, make it easier for UNIFIL to carry out its mission. The PLO would especially avoid infiltrating UNIFIL's area of operations. As *quid pro quo* Chairman Arafat demanded that the PLO fighters already in the area should be allowed to remain there and that they should be allowed food and medical supplies, delivered under UNIFIL control. Despite the opposi-tion of UNIFIL's leadership and myself, the Secretary-General agreed to Arafat's demands.

I was very disappointed, because I had learned from experience that in peace-keeping it is not worthwhile playing petty political games in order to achieve secondary goals. In any case, UNIFIL's task had now been deliberately made more difficult and its neutrality had become questionable. In part the concessions to the Palestinians hampered UNIFIL's actions against other armed factions. As could be expected, the presence of armed Palestinians led to continuing complaints from the Israelis. In principle they were completely justified, although UNIFIL in practice was able to keep tabs on the said Palestinian groups. Thus they never posed any real threat to Israel's security.

Another major and constant problem for UNIFIL was the security zone Israel established on the Lebanese side of the international frontier. In June 1978 it became obvious that Israel, contrary to expectations, had no intention of withdrawing completely from Lebanese territory. Before the beginning of the last phase of the withdrawal Israel's new Chief of Staff, General Rafael Eitan, explained to me that their intention was to form a so-called Christian enclave, that is to say a zone of purportedly Christian towns and villages along the border. This zone would not be handed over to UNIFIL, it would instead be controlled by Israel's ally, Major Saad Haddad, the Commander of the Christian Militia. According to Israel he was a representative of the Lebanese government. General Eitan added that UNIFIL was to regard the boundary of the Christian enclave as an international frontier. Thus UNIFIL was unable to extend its control to the frontier between Israel and Lebanon, and in this respect failed to fulfil its mandate. Unfortunately, UNIFIL failed in its final report on the withdrawal to stress the fact that Israel had not completely withdrawn from Lebanon. The reason for this may be that at first nobody understood Israel's intentions and the future implications of the security zone. Had the Security Council been better informed, Israel might have been pressured more strongly to withdraw completely from Lebanon. Now the Security Council acted under the misapprehension that the withdrawal had already taken place and that Israel had fulfilled the requirements of Resolution 425.

Faced with a new situation, I sounded the views of the Lebanese government. I was told that the government recognized Major Haddad as the *de facto* Commander of the Lebanese force until the authority of the government had been re-established in the south. It was obvious that there was within the government some support for Major Haddad's pro-Israeli policy. I was also told that army headquarters would issue instructions to Major Haddad to facilitate UNIFIL's deployment and mission.

During the second half of June UNIFIL attempted to deploy within the enclave. UNTSO's observers succeeded in manning their former observation posts along the border and some new UNIFIL posts were set up. But Haddad's opposition was unfailing. It seemed that the instructions the army had sent were ineffective. Thus UNIFIL failed to improve its position within the enclave.

Gradually Haddad and his band became UNIFIL's most difficult problem and worst enemy. No reliable information about its strength was available, but it was estimated to be in the vicinity of 1,500 men. Its core consisted of 700 deserters from the Lebanese Army. New recruits were local Christians and Shi'ite Moslems from the nearby villages, and Christian Phalangists from the north. Israel trained, equipped and armed the Militia. From UNIFIL's point of view the worst problem was that their arms included tanks and artillery. Israel also paid the salaries of the officers and enlisted men. In the Middle East it has been a time-honoured tradition, evident since the campaigns of Lawrence of Arabia, that no-one did anything they were not paid to do, neither the Christians nor the PLO.

UNIFIL's command had great difficulties in creating a normal day-to-day working relationship with Major Haddad. This was what the Israeli authorities kept suggesting they should do. According to them, improved relations would remove the difficulties. Official relations were, however, out of the question, as the Militia was not an independent party. On the one hand it was purported to be a Lebanese government unit, on the other it was completely subordinate to Israel. Israeli officers sat in Haddad's headquarters as political and military advisers, and they were in charge of operations and policy.

Dealings with Major Haddad were further inhibited by his behaviour and character. In his monomaniac ambition he had proclaimed his enclave the Republic of Free Lebanon, and himself President. He drove around in the enclave with a large Lebanese flag on his jeep. He regarded UNIFIL's troops as suspect alien intruders and accused them of being henchmen of the PLO.

In order to ensure UNIFIL satisfactory freedom of movement and action within the enclave, an agreement had been reached with Israel that UNIFIL could use the main roads five days a week and that UNIFIL's helicopters could fly over the enclave, although permission for this had to be obtained from Major Haddad for each individual overflight. Major Haddad could at will punish UNIFIL or its sub-units by closing the roads and preventing traffic from getting through. This sort of interference was tolerable to a degree, but often Haddad's compulsion to humiliate UNIFIL did not stop at that. UN posts were encircled and overrun by force, both UN and private property was stolen, and UN personnel were threatened and intimidated. Three times the *de facto* forces opened fire with grenade-launchers and artillery against UNIFIL's headquarters and field hospital in Naqoura. This shooting resulted in casualties and great material damages, and often made unbearable the lives of the female secretaries, nurses and unarmed civilian personnel who lived in the headquarters compound.

Knowing how dependent the *de facto* force was on Israel, on several occasions I visited Defence Minister Weizman and applied for Israel's good offices to put an end to the interference and shooting. Sometimes he was willing to ease the situation and put an end to Major Haddad's worst excesses. More often than not he complained that Israel did not completely control the Militia. In such desperate situations I occasionally turned to the American Ambassador, Sam Lewis, and tried to enlist his help. The United States had sponsored UNIFIL and I considered that it had a moral responsibility to support it. Sam Lewis did his best, and often succeeded, but sometimes he too complained that the United States did not completely control Israel.

Towards the end of 1978 the *de facto* force entered a more aggressive phase when it broke through into UNIFIL territory and established permanent posts there. It wanted to expand the enclave and take control of prominent features in the terrain. By acting very fast and boldly UNIFIL sometimes was able to prevent such actions. Often the intruders arrived so unexpectedly and with such force that nothing could be done. Negotiations and persuasion on the spot were of no avail. I then tried to talk with Minister Weizman or General Eitan – with no results. I was told that the positions were necessary for Israel's security. Obviously they were set up as part of an Israeli master-plan, and they were not merely one of Major Haddad's quirks, as we had been led to believe earlier on.

There were few regular Israeli troops to be seen in the enclave immediately after the withdrawal. But gradually they increased their activity, setting up battle positions at selected points, laying mines around the perimeter, undertaking regular patrols and transporting supplies to the positions. Israel's withdrawal from Lebanese territory, which Foreign Minister Moshe Dayan had solemnly proclaimed in his letter to the Secretary-General dated June 13, had increasingly began to resemble a fiction.

The PLO's infiltration attempts began again and increased after Israel's withdrawal in June 1978. Arafat's earnest assurances were forgotten, or the PLO fighters did not want to keep them. Erskine and I had been right in our predictions. One reason for the increase in PLO infiltration may have been UNIFIL's inability to take over the enclave. However, UNIFIL's counter-measures were effective. It set up checkpoints along the incoming roads, stopped and checked vehicles and patrolled the area on foot and in vehicles. According to UNIFIL statistics, 40 major PLO attacks were repelled during the first six months of 1979; during the latter six months 800 attempted cases of infiltration were deterred. These incidents often developed into outbreaks of shooting, ambushes, acts of revenge and a great number of casualties on UNIFIL's side.

UNIFIL's position, between the infiltration from the north and the harassment and humiliation from the south, was difficult from the very start and at times it became untenable. The UN troops were frustrated and the countries that had dispatched contingents followed developments with increasing alarm.

All parties to the conflict criticized UNIFIL severely. The PLO accused it of furthering Israeli aims. Israel, on the other hand, considered UNIFIL militarily inept and most of its soldiers and commanders friends and collaborators of the PLO. Two regrettable incidents, in which a Nigerian and a Senegalese officer were accused of smuggling arms and ammunition to the PLO, were greatly exaggerated in the newspapers. Major Haddad proved to be particularly imaginative in his accusations, as he claimed that UNIFIL's men were guilty of the most bizarre and sinister acts. It is a fact that among an international force of more than 6,000 men there are bound to be some who are guilty of crimes or improper behaviour. They were, however, exceptions, and my opinion is that UNIFIL as a whole managed to remain impartial between the parties. Israel maintained that UNIFIL should have adopted the Israeli attitude towards the PLO, that is, no negotiations and no contacts. UNIFIL could not accept this, for practical and political considerations. The UN had accepted and recognized the PLO as a liberation movement and in practice it was a *de facto* party to the conflict in southern Lebanon. Thus UNIFIL's leadership and the individual battalions required daily contacts with PLO's supreme command and its local representatives. It was the only way to solve mutual problems, investigate incidents and organize cease-fires. The PLO groups within UNIFIL's area of operations were an additional reason for contacts. We had to negotiate mutually acceptable regulations for the conduct and freedom of movement of these groups.

UNIFIL's mandate and the use of force

Both in the Middle East and in the countries that contributed troops there were critics who considered UNIFIL too weak militarily and said that it should be given a stronger mandate. In the very first days of UNIFIL I proposed that it should be provided with some tanks. The first incidents had shown how weak UNIFIL was compared with the PLO and the Christian Militia. My intention was to reinforce UNIFIL's checkpoints and positions against assaults by the armed elements. My proposal was not accepted, however, because tanks were considered offensive weapons. Fortunately, the situation was later remedied by providing the battalions with armoured personnel carriers.

In no other respect did I favour a more rigorous mandate, changes in the composition of the force or increased fire-power. UNIFIL was a peace-keeping force and should remain one. If it had been provided with more troops and fire-power, what would the consequences have been? A stronger and better equipped UNIFIL might have been able to use force against the parties and impose its will upon them, as was required in Chapter VII of the UN Charter. But the political and military consequences of such actions would have been unpredictable and heavy casualties would have had to be taken into account. I do not think that the Security Council and the contributing countries would have been prepared to accept them.

I thought that UNIFIL's mandate was adequate. In previous peace-keeping operations force had only been resorted to in self-defence. This had already changed in 1973, when UNEF II was established in Sinai. A new definition of the use of force, which also applied to UNIFIL, sanctioned resistance to attempts by forcible means to prevent it from discharging its duties. The interpretation of these new regulations was naturally a difficult problem. I was not alone in thinking that UNIFIL's reactions to the provocations of the parties were timid, and that it rarely adopted a strong military stand. Usually UNIFIL gave in to the demands of the parties. This was the case when, late in 1978, the *de facto* forces began to expand the security zone and to set up positions in UNIFIL's area. UNIFIL often passively accepted the situation and reached an agreement with the local *de facto* forces or with the Israelis. Then they called me in Jerusalem and asked me to contact the Israeli authorities in order to remedy the situation. The natural reaction of Minister Weizman and General Eitan was, "What are you complaining about? The matter has been settled on the spot." I tried to explain to UNIFIL's leadership that it would be easier for me to present my case, and my bargaining position would be stronger, if UNIFIL, instead of giving in at once, let the situation develop into a crisis. I could then go to the Ministry of Defence and say, "We have a bad crisis in southern Lebanon. Isn't there any way of working out a solution the UN could accept?"

Some battalions in UNIFIL were known for their swift and firm reactions, and were therefore spared harassment and humiliation. The parties knew that such an attempt could have a bad end. But many thought that UNIFIL as a whole was too soft and susceptible to threats and intimidation. Despite my efforts I was unable to change the prevailing attitudes at UNIFIL's headquarters, especially among the successors of the first Chief of Staff, a tough Frenchman. I am prepared to admit that it is easy to criticize from afar, particularly behind a green-baize desk-top. UNIFIL's Force Commander and his battalion commanders in the field had to evaluate their decisions and the consequences they would have. The risk factors were indeed great. It was obvious that UNIFIL could not start a war with either party, but there were always lesser incidents on a lower level which could have called for the use of force. Some battalions in UNIFIL proved this point. From my personal experience as Force Commander of UNEF II, I knew that a UN force could not gain the trust and respect of the parties if it never struck back.

In trying to help UNIFIL solve its initial problems I was faced with my most difficult task to date. For the first time I was compelled to operate in circumstances where the interests of Israel and the UN were at loggerheads. The underlying reason for this was our contradictory views on the best way of fulfilling Israel's security requirements. The Israeli authorities thought that they had developed a brilliant new system by recruiting a Lebanese renegade and his ragtag band and putting them in charge of the security zone along the border. The great drawbacks of this scheme gradually became evident. It seems that Israel did not allow for the increasing opposition of another group, i.e. the Shi'ite Moslems; the difficulties in controlling the unpredictable Major Haddad; the deteriorating morale of the force, and Israel's tarnished reputation, especially in the countries that contributed troops to UNIFIL.

I said that UNIFIL could prevent the infiltration if it were able to take the whole area under its control. If UNIFIL had not had to spend a great part of its resources and energy in unnecessary squabbles with Major Haddad, it could have concentrated on its principal task, i.e. preventing the infiltration of armed elements. I tried to present these views to Minister Weizman, but on several occasions he made it perfectly clear that Israel did not want any radical changes in the present arrangement. He said that from Israel's point of view the arrangement was ideal. They now had two security zones between Israel and the PLO – first UNIFIL and then Major Haddad's troops. Despite my efforts I was unable to convince the Israelis.

The difficult agenda and the differences in opinion notwithstanding,

the atmosphere at the meetings remained cordial. Both Minister
Weizman and General Eitan were extremely amiable. I sometimes had
the impression that the Minister would have been prepared to compromise, but the army was adamant in its opposition. The Minister
of Foreign Affairs, Moshe Dayan, did not want to become involved in
the issue of southern Lebanon, because the internal division of labour
within the government placed these matters under the jurisdiction of
the Minister of Defence. The Minister of Defence, Mr Ezer Weizman,
did not wield very much influence, because he lacked a political base.
It seems that decisions regarding southern Lebanon were primarily
made within the army. General Yanush Ben-Gal, the energetic Commander of the Northern Group, and General Rafael Eitan, the Chief
of Staff, were behind the planning and policy decisions. Most likely they
also formulated the general guidelines for Major Haddad's activities.

The difficulties of the Lebanese government and armed forces

But the difficulties were not limited to the contacts with Israel; many
more had to be faced in Lebanon. The President of the republic, the
eminent and honest Elias Sarkis, had little power outside his palace
walls. Within the palace he was shown all the respect that protocol
affords a head of state. In the prevailing situation this resembled absurd
theatre. The negotiations in the office of the Prime Minister were often
interrupted by sniper bullets and ricochets from the Green Line. The
whole Cabinet was like a pleasant club for polite and learned gentlemen.
However, the helplessness of the ministers was pitiable and meetings
with them were frustrating and depressing.

I often had to visit army headquarters, the massive and modern
"Pentagon", whose size bore no relationship to the size of the army.
In the past I had met several commanders of the army; they had been
trained by the French and were truly professional soldiers. The new
Commander was, however, completely lacking in resolution and sense
of duty. This was a pity, because exceptional times call for exceptional
qualities in a commander. During one visit I happened to meet a former
subordinate of mine in the General's office: the American Colonel Bob
Day, who had been Chief Operations Officer in UNTSO. He was
now in charge of a delegation of American officers whose job was
to re-establish and equip the Lebanese Army after the ravages of the
civil war. We both agreed that he was indeed faced with a "Mission
Impossible".

When it became apparent that Israel intended to assume control of the security zone for an indefinite period, we concentrated our joint efforts on restoring the authority of the Lebanese government in southern Lebanon. I conducted persistent negotiations with the Minister of the Interior and tried to persuade the government to send administrators and gendarmes to the south. The government's first action was to send a civilian administrator to Tyre and almost 100 gendarmes to central locations within UNIFIL's area. They operated in close co-operation with UNIFIL's battalions, assisted the sentries at checkpoints and acted as interpreters.

During one of Brian Urquhart's visits to the area I met Chassan Tueni, who was the Lebanese Ambassador to the UN and owner of the newspaper *An Nahar* in Beirut. This exceptionally enterprising and talented diplomat was an inexhaustible guardian of Lebanese interests in the UN. His wise and balanced views may have created the false impression that Lebanon had a strong and workable government. It was a pity that he was not in Beirut as a minister. When I asked him why restore the government's authority in the south, when it did not have any in the capital, he answered, "We have to start somewhere, and it may be that the circumstances in the south are more propitious, due to UNIFIL."

Another, even more difficult subject for negotiations was the deployment of Lebanese Army units in the south. The reconstruction of the army was still going on and its leadership was hesitant. There were other obstacles. Major Haddad and the Israeli government opposed the idea strongly. I myself was not particularly enthusiastic about the idea at this stage and I did not press it forward. I did not consider the army ready for redeployment. However, I heard that the American Ambassador in Beirut was strongly in favour of the idea. I had already received reproofs from New York, because I had urged the Lebanese Army to postpone redeployment for the time being. In such a conflict of interests the Lebanese government decided to follow the American advice and to deploy a unit of 700 men in Tibnin. Their march route would be along the Bekaa Valley through the village of Kaukaba and the town of Marjayoun, where Major Haddad's headquarters was located. The unit never got further than Kaukaba. Haddad opened fire with artillery and grenade-launchers, and there was no alternative but to give up.

In 1979 there was a new and better prepared attempt to deploy army units in the south. A joint working group of UNIFIL and the Lebanese Army had examined new alternatives and drafted a thorough plan. The working group's proposal was to fly small teams of Lebanese Army personnel by helicopter into UNIFIL's area. When UNIFIL's mandate was renewed for a further period of five months, the Security Council invited the Lebanese government to draw up, together with UNIFIL, a programme to promote the restoration of its authority in southern Lebanon. The programme contained four main points: an increase in the civilian administrative presence in the south; the introduction of a Lebanese battalion in UNIFIL's area; the consolidation of the cease-fire in the area, and further deployment of UNIFIL in the security zone. Within this programme, a Lebanese Army battalion of 500 men was deployed in the UNIFIL area in April 1979. Major Haddad's forces tried to prevent the deployment with violence. As an act of revenge it subjected UNIFIL's headquarters compound to intense shelling, causing casualties and heavy damage to buildings. This time UNIFIL and the Lebanese battalion stood firm. The battalion was deployed in the Nigerian sector in the village of Arzun.

Despite criticism, which in most cases was exaggerated and one-sided, UNIFIL carried out its duties in a fairly satisfactory manner during those early days. In many respects it did valuable work under extremely severe circumstances. It is obvious that it could not prevent PLO artillery from shooting at targets in northern Israel from positions outside UNIFIL's area of operations. Such shelling took place occasionally, before the cease-fire negotiated by the Americans in 1981. But UNIFIL did prevent armed Palestinians from infiltrating into Israel through its area. UNIFIL statistics show that the one and only guerrilla raid into northern Israel via UNIFIL's area took place in April 1980. I think that this is an admirable record. Despite Israel's claims to the contrary, UNIFIL was an efficient guardian of the security of northern Galilee. Another important achievement was the state of security, peace and normality which UNIFIL was able to create for the population of its area of operations. For this it received the deep gratitude of the local people. The Security Council pondered the necessity for UNIFIL when the renewal of its mandate came up on the agenda at six-month intervals. A continuation of the mandate was usually granted as a matter of course. The representatives of the great powers and the other members of the Council were in agreement that the presence of UNIFIL in southern Lebanon was beneficial and that withdrawing it from the area would create a much more difficult situation.

I myself gradually understood that my reasons for opposing the setting up of UNIFIL were at least partly unfounded. Despite all the difficulties, UNIFIL had proved more useful than I had expected. The UN cannot and must not be too selective when it undertakes new missions. It must not avoid operations that seem difficult or impossible, only accepting those that seem to be certain successes. There is no such thing as certain success, because situations change unpredictably. No-one could have been certain about the fate of UNEF II. Instead of succeeding it too could have failed.

All this also holds true of Finnish participation in peace-keeping operations. The fact that we have taken part in UNIFIL has attracted much criticism. In 1978 Finland was not asked for troops, nor did it volunteer them. I think the reasons for this were simple: we had a battalion in UNEF and we were preparing for operations in Namibia. When in the autumn of 1982 the UN requested a battalion from Finland, the request was granted. My opinion is that it would have been impossible to refuse on the grounds that the mission was difficult and dangerous. If participation in peace-keeping is deemed an essential and important part of our foreign policy, Finland cannot afford to be selective and only accept easy and risk-free missions.

25. Epilogue

When I was about to return to Finland just after the New Year of 1980, I was filled with various thoughts and emotions. I was leaving behind me difficult and responsible duties and an exciting life. It was pleasant to return home after twelve years with the United Nations. It felt good to come back to my own familiar community and start life again as a private person among friends and relatives.

I was happy, even proud, of having had the opportunity to participate in promoting peace in the Middle East. UNEF II had been a tremendous success and it had now been demobilized after a mission well undertaken. Egypt and Israel were taking their first steps on the road towards normal neighbourly relations. The Golan Heights had also been peaceful for a long time, thanks to UNDOF. The venerable UNTSO still had meaningful duties ahead of it.

I was surprised and moved by the warm-hearted farewell I received. By this I do not mean the farewell speeches at official functions, or editorials in the newspapers, but instead the reactions of completely ordinary people. Jewish shopkeepers, whose clients my wife and I had been over the years, did not want to hear about our departure. They were alarmed: "Where do you think you are going? You belong here. Otherwise we will never have peace here." My sympathies had been with these little people, especially families with small children. In Israel or in the Arab countries, they were always the ones who suffered first from war, and all over they were the ones who paid the highest price.

However, I was sad and disappointed about many things. I was disappointed because the Israeli government did not want to change its attitude towards UNIFIL and admit that, in difficult circumstances, it had adequately taken care of the security of northern Israel. Israel's whole policy concerning Lebanon was based on a wrong appraisal of the situation. The Christian Militia caused more harm to Israel than any real increase in security could have justified. Policy-making was for too great an extent in the hands of the military. They could not think of any way other than extreme violence to pacify the area.

I was disappointed with the attitude of the United States towards UNIFIL. It did not give enough support to the UN force when it was faced with reckless acts from Israel and its allies; it seemed to be more important for the United States to maintain its good relations with

Israel. It was an American initiative, and vigorous American pressure, that led to the founding of UNIFIL. I think that the United States therefore had a special obligation to support UNIFIL.

I was disappointed because I had not been able to exert a more determined influence on UNIFIL. I would have preferred it to have been more active, firm and effective on a military level. It would thus have been better suited to fulfil its mission and gain the undivided respect of the parties involved.

I was disappointed with the view the other Arab countries and the PLO took of the Camp David agreement. I am prepared to admit that the way the Palestinian question was resolved in the agreement was very far from their set goals, but it was still the first step in the right direction. The matter could later have been furthered through mutual efforts. As things now stand, the Palestinians gained nothing, nor can they expect a change for the better, at least in the near future. The disagreements and lack of unity within the Arab world meant that its voice was not heard. Thus Israel and the United States could deal with the Middle East without paying very much attention to the Arabs.

I was disappointed with the Soviet Union's unfavourable view of the Camp David accord. I understood that it wanted to support its ally Syria, and also the other Arabs, but by doing this the Soviet Union excluded itself from the Middle East peace process. In addition to this, by abolishing the UN peace-keeping force in Sinai, it had to deal with its replacement, the so-called multinational force, which was drawn from the armies of the United States and its allies. Such a development could not be in the best interests of the Soviet Union.

I was disappointed in many ways with the PLO. It did not match my idea of a liberation organization fighting for the independence of its people. I am not referring to terrorism as such, which has always been an integral part of such a struggle; it was after all utilized by the Jews in the 1940s. But the targets of the PLO's terrorism were ill-chosen and this caused irreparable damage to the reputation of the organization. The rest of the world found it difficult to understand, to say nothing of condoning the PLO's acts of terrorism. But Israel's counter-terror was just as worthy of condemnation, although it was purported to be in the interests of national security. I could not by any means accept attacks on refugee camps in Lebanon, or other more distant targets. They only served to continue the spiralling violence.

In addition to this, the PLO was often helpless, unprofessional and ineffective. One would have thought that more than 20 years would have been long enough to set up a large, well-equipped and trained guerrilla army with able leaders and a fighting spirit. Human resources were abundant in the refugee camps, nor was there any lack of funds. Furthermore, as the policies advocated by the PLO were always examples of fruitless extremism, it became evident that the Palestinian people did not have the leadership they deserved.

I had other reasons to be sorry for the fate of the Palestinian people. On the West Bank and in Gaza their situation deteriorated and nothing favourable could be said of their future prospects. The autonomy promised at Camp David fell through because of Arab opposition, and perhaps even more due to Israel's negative attitude. Furthermore, Israel had adopted the hypocritical position of refusing to negotiate with the PLO, supposedly because it engaged in acts of terrorism. I hoped to the very end that Dayan's idea of an unilateral declaration of autonomy would come through. But the suffering and humiliation of the inhabitants of the occupied territories goes on. In this context I was also worried about the future of the Israeli people, who could themselves eventually meet a sorry fate if and when the repressed situation finally erupts.

These expressions of sadness and disappointment do not merely reflect my own personal impatience and frustration, they also reflect the feelings of the people in the Middle East. The road towards peace was hopelessly slow and strewn with obstacles. Despite the deadlock I do, however, believe that Israel and its neighbours will eventually solve their problems. It would not be the first time some surprising and unexpected changes take place in the Middle East.

The peace treaty between Israel and Egypt has, despite all criticism, proved to be a step in the right direction. Furthermore, it proved that normal relations between Israel and the rest of its Arab neighbours are conceivable. I also think that improved relations between the great powers – which I hope for – would help in finding a mutually acceptable solution.

In my case personal success and disappointments were balanced. I could not wish for more. I consider myself privileged and happy to have had the opportunity tangibly to further the cause of peace.

Appendixes

1. Security Council Resolution 242 (1967) of 22 November 1967

The Security Council,

Expressing its continuing concern with the grave situation in the Middle East,

Emphasizing the inadmissibility of the acquisition of territory by war and the need to work for a just and lasting peace in which every State in the area can live in security,

Emphasizing further that all Member States in their acceptance of the Charter of the United Nations have undertaken a commitment to act in accordance with Article 2 of the Charter,

1. *Affirms* that the fulfilment of Charter principles requires the establishment of a just and lasting peace in the Middle East which should include the application of both the following principles:

(i) Withdrawal of Israel armed forces from territories occupied in the recent conflict;
(ii) Termination of all claims of states of belligerency and respect for and acknowledgement of the sovereignty, territorial integrity and political independence of every State in the area and their right to live in peace within secure and recognized boundaries free from threats or acts of force;

2. *Affirms further* the necessity

(a) For guaranteeing freedom of navigation through international waterways in the area;
(b) For achieving a just settlement of the refugee problem;
(c) For guaranteeing the territorial inviolability and political independence of every State in the area through measures including the establishment of demilitarized zones;

3. *Requests* the Secretary-General to designate a Special Representative to proceed to the Middle East to establish and maintain contacts with the States concerned in order to promote agreement and assist efforts to achieve a peaceful and accepted settlement in accordance with the provisions and principles in this resolution;

4. *Requests* the Secretary-General to report to the Security Council on the progress of the efforts of the Special Representative as soon as possible.

2. Security Council Resolution 338 (1973) of 21/22 October 1973

The Security Council,

1. *Calls upon* all parties to the present fighting to cease all firing and terminate all military activity immediately, no later than 12 hours after the moment of the adoption of this decision, in the positions they now occupy;

2. *Calls upon* the parties concerned to start immediately after the cease-fire the implementation of Security Council resolution 242 (1967) in all of its parts;

3. *Decides* that, immediately and concurrently with the cease-fire, negotiations start between the parties concerned under appropriate auspices aimed at establishing a just and durable peace in the Middle East.

3. Security Council Resolution 339 (1973) of 23 October 1973

The Security Council,

Referring to its resolution 338 (1973) of 22 October 1973,

1. *Confirms* its decision on an immediate cessation of all kinds of firing and of all military action, and urges that the forces of the two sides be returned to the positions they occupied at the moment the cease-fire became effective;

2. *Requests* the Secretary-General to take measures for immediate dispatch of United Nations observers to supervise the observance of the cease-fire between the forces of Israel and the Arab Republic of Egypt, using for this purpose the personnel of the United Nations now in the Middle East and first of all the personnel now in Cairo.

4. Security Council Resolution 340 (1973) of 25 October 1973

The Security Council,

Recalling its resolutions 338 (1973) of 22 October and 339 (1973) of 23 October 1973;

Noting with regret the reported repeated violations of the cease-fire in noncompliance with resolutions 338 (1973) and 339 (1973),

Noting with concern from the Secretary-General's report that the United Nations military observers have not yet been enabled to place themselves on both sides of the cease-fire line,

1. *Demands* that immediate and complete cease-fire be observed and that the

parties return to the positions occupied by them at 1650 hours GMT on 22 October 1973;

2. *Requests* the Secretary-General, as an immediate step, to increase the number of United Nations military observers on both sides;

3. *Decides* to set up immediately under its authority a United Nations Emergency Force to be composed of personnel drawn from States Members of the United Nations except the permanent members of the Security Council, and requests the Secretary-General to report within 24 hours on the steps taken to this effect;

4. *Requests* the Secretary-General to report to the Council on an urgent and continuing basis on the state of implementation of the present resolution, as well as resolutions 338 (1973) and 339 (1973);

5. *Requests* all Member States to extend their full co-operation to the United Nations in the implementation of the present resolution, as well as resolutions 338 (1973) and 339 (1973).

5. Report of the Secretary-General on the implementation of Security Council Resolution 340 (1973)

1. The present report is submitted in pursuance of Security Council resolution 340 (1973) of 25 October 1973 in which the Council, among other things, decided to set up immediately a United Nations Emergency Force under its authority and requested the Secretary-General to report within 24 hours on the steps taken to this effect.

Terms of Reference

2. (*a*) The Force will supervise the implementation of operative paragraph 1 of resolution 340 (1973), which reads as follows:
"1. Demands that immediate and complete cease-fire be observed and that the parties return to the positions occupied by them at 1650 hours GMT on 22 October 1973."
(*b*) The Force will use its best efforts to prevent a recurrence of the fighting.
(*c*) In the fulfilment of its tasks, the Force will have the co-operation of the military observers of UNTSO.

General Conditions

3. Three essential conditions must be met for the Force to be effective. Firstly, it must have at all times the full confidence and backing of the Security

Council. Secondly, it must operate with the full co-operation of the parties concerned. Thirdly, it must be able to function as an integrated and efficient military unit.

4. Having in mind past experiences, I would suggest the following guidelines for the proposed Force:

(*a*) The Force will be under the command of the United Nations, vested in the Secretary-General, under the authority of the Security Council. The command in the field will be exercised by a Force Commander appointed by the Secretary-General with the consent of the Security Council. The Commander will be responsible to the Secretary-General.
It is my intention to keep the Security Council fully informed of developments relating to the functioning of the Force. All matters which may affect the nature or the continued effective functioning of the Force will be referred to the Council for its decision.
(*b*) The Force must enjoy the freedom of movement and communication and other facilities that are necessary for the performance on its tasks. The Force and its personnel should be granted all relevant privileges and immunities provided for by the Convention on the Privileges and Immunities of the United Nations. The Force should operate at all times separately from the armed forces of the parties concerned. Consequently separate quarters and, wherever desirable and feasible, buffer zones will have to be arranged with the co-operation of the parties. Appropriate agreements on the Status of the Force will have to be concluded with the parties to cover the above requirements.
(*c*) The Force will be composed of a number of contingents to be provided by selected countries, upon the request of the Secretary-General. The contingents will be selected in consultation with the Security Council and with the parties concerned, bearing in mind an adequate geographic representation.
(*d*) The Force will be provided with weapons of a defensive character only. It shall not use force except in self-defence. Self-defence would include resistance to attempts by forceful means to prevent it from discharging its duties under the mandate of the Security Council. The Force will proceed on the assumption that the parties to the conflict will take all the necessary steps for compliance with the decisions of the Security Council.
(*e*) In performing its functions, the Force will act with complete impartiality and will avoid actions which could prejudice the rights, claims or positions of the parties concerned.
(*f*) The supporting personnel of the Force will be provided as a rule by the Secretary-General from among existing United Nations staff. Those personnel will, of course, follow the rules and regulations of the United Nations Secretariat.

Proposed Plan of Action

5. If the Security Council is in agreement with the principles outlined above, I intend to take the following urgent steps:

(*a*) I propose, with the consent of the Security Council, to appoint the Commander of the Emergency Force as soon as possible. Pending the Commander's arrival in the mission area, with the consent of the Council given at its meeting of 25 October 1973, I have appointed the Chief of Staff of UNTSO, Major-General E. Siilasvuo, as interim Commander of the Emergency Force, and have asked him to set up a provisional headquarters staff consisting of personnel from UNTSO.

(*b*) In order that the Force may fulfil the responsibility entrusted to it, it is considered necessary that it have a total strength in the order of 7,000.

(*c*) The Force would initially be stationed in the area for a period of six months.

(*d*) In my letter of 25 October to the President of the Security Council, I proposed, as an urgent interim measure and in order that the Emergency Force may reach the area as soon as possible, to arrange for the contingents of Austria, Finland and Sweden now serving with the United Nations Peace-keeping Force in Cyprus (UNFICYP) to proceed immediately to Egypt. I am at present actively engaged in the necessary consultations, bearing in mind the considerations in paragraph 4 (c) above, with a view to making requests to a number of other Governments to provide contingents of suitable size for the Force at the earliest possible time. As the Members of the Council are aware, this is a complex matter in which a number of factors have to be taken into account. I shall report further to the Council as soon as possible.

(*e*) In addition to the countries requested to provide contingents for the Force, I propose to request logistic support as necessary from a number of other countries, which may include the Permanent Members of the Security Council.

Estimated Cost and Method of Financing

6. At the present time there are many unknown factors. The best possible preliminary estimate based upon past experience and practice is approximately $30,000,000 for a Force of 7,000 all ranks for a period of six months.

7. The costs of the Force shall be considered as expenses of the Organization to be borne by the Members in accordance with Article 17, paragraph 2, of the Charter.

6a. The Egyptian-Israeli Agreement on disengagement of forces

(in Pursuance of the Geneva Peace Conference, signed January 18, 1974, at Kilometer 101 by the Chiefs of Staff of Egypt [Gamassy] and Israel [Elazar] and witnessed by UNEF Commander Siilasvuo)

A. Egypt and Israel will scrupulously observe the cease-fire on land, sea and air called for by the UN Security Council and will refrain from the time of the signing of this document from all military and paramilitary actions against each other.

B. The military forces of Egypt and Israel will be separated in accordance with the following principles:

1. All Egyptian forces on the east side of the Canal will be deployed west of the line designated as Line A on the attached map. All Israeli forces, including those west of the Suez Canal and the Bitter Lakes, will be deployed east of the line designated as Line B on the attached map.
2. The area between the Egyptian and Israeli lines will be a zone of disengagement in which the United Nations Emergency Force (UNEF) will be stationed. The UNEF will continue to consist of units that are not permanent members of the Security Council.
3. The area between the Egyptian line and the Suez Canal will be limited in armament and forces.
4. The area between the Israeli line (Line B on the attached map) and the line designated as Line C on the attached map, which runs along the western base of the mountains where the Giddi and Mitla Passes are located, will be limited in armament and forces.
5. The limitations referred to in paragraphs 3 and 4 will be inspected by UNEF. Existing procedures of UNEF, including the attaching of Egyptian and Israeli liaison officers to UNEF will be continued.
6. Air forces of the two sides will be permitted to operate up to their respective lines without interference from the other side.

C. The detailed implementation of the disengagement of forces will be worked out by military representatives of Egypt and Israel, who will agree on the stages of this process. The representatives will meet no later than 48 hours after the signature of this agreement at Kilometer 101 under the aegis of the United Nations for this purpose. They will complete this task within five days. Disengagement will begin within 48 hours after the completion of the work of the military representatives and in no event later than seven days after the signature of this agreement. The process of disengagement will be completed not later than 40 days after it begins.

D. This agreement is not regarded by Egypt and Israel as a final peace agreement. It constitutes a first step toward a final, just and durable peace according to the provisions of Security Council Resolution 338 and within the framework of the Geneva Conference.

For Egypt: Mohammad Abdel Ghani Al-Gamassy, Major-General, Chief of Staff of the Egyptian Armed Forces

For Israel: David Elazar, Lieutenant-General, Chief of Staff of the Israel Defence Forces

Witness: Ensio P.H. Siilasvuo, Lieutenant-General, Commander of UNEF

6b. The "United States proposal" on force limitatations

(signed by President Sadat and Prime Minister Golda Meir)

In order to facilitate agreement between Egypt and Israel and as part of that agreement and to assist in maintaining scrupulous observance of the cease-fire on land, air and sea the United States proposes the following:

1. That within the areas of limited armaments and forces described in the agreement, there will be: (*a*) no more than eight reinforced battalions of armed forces and 30 tanks; (*b*) no artillery except anti-tank guns, anti-tank missiles, mortars and six batteries of howitzers of a caliber up to 122 mm. (M-3) with a range not to exceed 12 kilometers; (*c*) no weapons capable of interfering with the other party's flights over its own forces; (*d*) no permanent, fixed installations for missile sites. The entire force of each party shall not exceed 7,000 men.

2. That to a distance 30 kilometers west of the Egyptian line and east of the Israeli line, there will be no surface-to-air missiles.

4. That the above limitations will apply as from the time the agreement on disengagement between Egypt and Israel is signed by the parties and will be implemented in accordance with the schedule of implementation of the basic agreement.

7. Timetable of first disengagement in Sinai

Phase 1 Friday 25.1. – Monday 28.1

WEST BANK	*Time*
1. Redeployment of Israeli Army in Area 1	25.1–28.1
2. UNEF deploys in Israeli positions in Suez Adabiya and Jebel Ataqua	280800*

* Standard military formulation of date/time (= 8 a.m. on 28 January).

3. Transfer of the Suez-Cairo road and Area 1 to
   UNEF
4. Deployment of Forward HQ in Buffer Zone 1   281300–1800
5. Transfer of Suez-Cairo road to Egyptian Army   291900

Phase 2 Monday 28.1. – Monday 4.2

WEST BANK

1. Redeployment of Israeli Army in Area 2   28.1–4.2
2. Transfer of Area 2 to UNEF   041600
3. Deployment of UNEF and Forward HQ in Buffer   041600
   Zone 2
4. Transfer of Area 2 to Egyptian Army   281800

EAST BANK

5. Deployment of UNEF on Line A in Buffer Zone 2   281300
6. Redeployments:
   (*a*) Egyptian Army in Area 2   28.1–4.2
   (*b*) Israeli Army in UN Buffer Zone in Area 2   28.1–4.2
   (*c*) Israeli Army in Limited Forces Area 2   28.1–4.2
7. Transfer of Limited Forces   041600
   Area 2 for UNEF

Phase 3 Tuesday 5.2. – Tuesday 12.2.

WEST BANK

1. Redeployment of Israeli Army in Area 3   5.2.–12.2.
2. Transfer of Area 3 to UNEF   121600
3. Deployment of UNEF and Forward HQ in Buffer   121600
   Zone 3
4. Transfer of Area 3 to Egyptian Army   130600

EAST BANK

5. Deployment of UNEF on Line A in Buffer Zone 3   050600
6. Redeployments:
   (*a*) Egyptian Army in Area 3
   (*b*) Israeli army in Buffer Zone 3   5.2–12.2
   (*c*) Israeli Army in Limited Forces Area 3
7. Transfer of Buffer Zone 3 to UNEF   121600
                                                       121600
8. UNEF inspects Limited Forces Area 2 of Egypt and   5.2.
   Israel

Phase 4 Wednesday 13.2. – Thursday 21.2.

WEST BANK

1. Redeployment of Israeli Army in Area 4	13.2–21.2.
2. Transfer of Area 4 to UNEF	211200
3. Deployment of UNEF and Forward HQ in Buffer Zone 4	210600
4. Transfer of Area 4 to Egyptian Army	211800

EAST BANK

5. Deployment of UNEF on Line A in Buffer Zone 4	130600
6. Redeployments:	
(a) Egyptian Army in Area 4	
(b) Israeli Army in Buffer Zone 4	13.2.–21.2.
(c) Israeli Army in Limited Forces Area 4	
7. Transfer of Buffer Zone 4 to UNEF	211600
8. UNEF inspects Limited Forces Areas	14.2.

Phase 5 Friday 22.2 – Saturday 5.3

EAST BANK

1. Deployment of UNEF on Line A in Buffer Zone 5	220600
2. Redeployments:	
(a) Egyptian Army in Area 5	
(b) Israeli Army in Buffer Zone 5	22.2–3.3.
(c) Israeli Army in Limited Forces Area 5	
3. Transfers:	In March
(a) Area 5 from Israeli Army to UNEF	031600
(b) Area 5 from UNEF to Egyptian Army	040600
(c) Buffer Zone 5 from Israeli Army to UNEF	040600
4. UNEF inspects Limited Forces Areas	5.3.

8a. Separation of Forces Agreement, 31 May 1974

A. Israel and Syria will scrupulously observe the cease-fire on land, sea and air and will refrain from all military actions against each other, from the time of the signing of this document, in implementation of United Nations Security Council resolution 338 dated 22 October 1973.

B. The military forces of Israel and Syria will be separated in accordance with the following principles:

1. All Israeli military forces will be West of the line designated as Line A on the map attached hereto, except in the Kuneitra area, where they will be West of Line A-1.
2. All territory East of Line A will be under Syrian administration, and Syrian civilians will return to this territory.
3. The area between Line A and the Line designated as Line B on the attached map will be an area of separation. In this area will be stationed the United Nations Disengagement Observer Force established in accordance with the accompanying protocol.
4. All Syrian military forces will be East of the line designated as Line B on the attached map.
5. There will be two equal areas of limitation in armament and forces, one West of Line A and one East of Line B as agreed upon.
6. Air forces of the two sides will be permitted to operate up to their respective lines without interference from the other side.

C. In the area between Line A and Line A-1 on the attached map there shall be no military forces.

D. This agreement and the attached map will be signed by the military representatives of Israel and Syria in Geneva not later than 31 May 1974, in the Egyptian-Israeli military working group of the Geneva Peace Conference under the aegis of the United Nations, after that group has been joined by a Syrian military representative, and with the participation of representatives of the United States and the Soviet Union. The precise delineation of a detailed map and a plan for the implementation of the disengagement of forces will be worked out by military representatives of Israel and Syria in the Egyptian-Israeli military working group who will agree on the stages of this process. The military working group described above will start their work for this purpose in Geneva under the aegis of the United Nations within 24 hours after the signing of this agreement. They will complete this task within five days. Disengagement will begin within 24 hours after the completion of the task of the military working group. The process of disengagement will be completed not later than twenty days after it begins.

E. The provisions of paragraphs A, B and C shall be inspected by personnel of the United Nations comprising the United Nations Disengagement Observer Force under this agreement.

F. Within 24 hours after the signing of this agreement in Geneva all wounded prisoners of war which each side holds of the other as certified by ICRC will be repatriated. The morning after the completion of the task of the military working group, all remaining prisoners of war will be repatriated.

G. The bodies of all dead soldiers held by either side will be returned for burial in their respective countries within 10 days after the signing of this agreement.

H. This agreement is not a peace agreement. It is a step towards a just and durable peace on the basis of Security Council resolution 338 dated 22 October 1973.

8b. Protocol concerning the United Nations Disengagement Observer Force [UNDOF]

Israel and Syria agree that:
The function of the United Nations Disengagement Observer Force (UNDOF) under the agreement will be to use its best efforts to maintain the cease-fire and to see that it is scrupulously observed. It will supervise the agreement and protocol thereto with regard to the areas of separation and limitation. In carrying out its mission, it will comply with generally applicable Syrian laws and regulations and will not hamper the functioning of local civil administration. It will enjoy freedom of movement and communication and other facilities that are necessary for its mission. It will be mobile and provided with personal weapons of a defensive character and shall use such weapons only in self-defence. The number of the UNDOF shall be about 1,200, who will be selected by the Secretary-General of the United Nations in consultation with the parties from members of the United Nations who are not permanent members of the Security Council.

The UNDOF will be under the command of the United Nations, vested in the Secretary-General, under the authority of the Security Council.

The UNDOF shall carry out inspections under the agreement, and report thereon to the parties, on a regular basis, not less often than once every fifteen days, and, in addition, when requested by either party. It shall mark on the ground the respective lines shown on the map attached to the agreement.

Israel and Syria will support a resolution of the United Nations Security Council which will provide for the UNDOF contemplated by the agreement. The initial authorization will be for six months subject to renewal by further resolution of the Security Council.

9. Statement by the Chairman as agreed by the parties [operational plan for UNDOF]

1. A UNDOF forward H.Q. will be established in the area of separation dividing the forces at each phase. Israel and Syria will attach liaison officers of the rank of Colonel to this H.Q. in order to facilitate its task in solving

or settling any problem related to the implementation of the plan of disengagement.

2. Israel and Syria agree not to detain military or civilian personnel of the other side and undertake not to take prisoners of war during the period of implementation of the disengagement agreement. They agree to repatriate at [the] end of [the] same day through the good offices of UNDOF any member of the armed forces or any civilians who may fall in their hands.

3. UNDOF will effect an inspection of redeployment of forces after completion of each phase on dates fixed in the Time-Table attached to the Plan of Separation of Forces and will report their findings forthwith to the parties, in order to determine that both Parties have redeployed their forces in the limited forces areas.

4. Israel and Syria will make available all information and maps of mine fields as far as their respective areas are concerned and the areas handed over by them.

5. Israel and Syria will co-operate with the ICRC in carrying out its mandate, including the exchange of dead bodies, which is to be completed on June 6th 1974.

6. Israel and Syria undertake to repatriate all prisoners of war still detained by them, not later than June 6th 1974.

7. The UNDOF shall deny access to any military forces into the separation of forces area. It will deploy its forces in close co-operation with the Parties to the agreement.

8. UNDOF will determine axes of access and exit for its forces from the Syrian and the Israeli held areas in close co-operation with the parties.

9. UNDOF will assume control, will establish and man observation posts in evacuated Israeli positions. It shall mark on the ground the respective lines shown on the map attached to the disengagement agreement.

10. The UNDOF will assist in the arrangements concerning the return of civilians to agreed locations in the separation of forces area.

11. The UNDOF will be permitted to construct a fenced off patrol road, with the assistance of the Parties, along the separation of forces area, and the use of former positions of both armies which are located in the separation area, between lines A and B.

12. In the Syrian administered inhabited localities of the area of separation, a local police force will operate. It will be responsible for normal police duties only. Police vehicles shall be light, soft and unarmed.

13. UNDOF will effect an inspection of redeployment of forces after completion of each of the phases in order to determine that both parties have

redeployed their forces in the restricted forces areas, so that the remaining forces will be as follows:

(a) That the area of limitation in armament and forces west of Line A and east of Line B will be 10 kilometres in width. In each area, respectively the following are permitted:
(1) two brigades of armed forces, including 75 tanks and 36 pieces of short-range 122-mm or equivalent calibre artillery.
(2) the entire force of each party shall not exceed 6,000 men.
(b) That in the area between 10 and 20 kilometres west of Line A and east of Line B:
(1) there will be no artillery pieces whose range exceeds 20 kilometres.
(2) the total number of artillery pieces permitted is 162 with a range of not exceeding 20 kilometres and 450 tanks of all types.
(3) surface-to-air missiles will be stationed no closer than 25 kilometres west of Line A and east of Line B.

14. UNDOF will carry out the following inspections during the separation period:

(a) Phase 2 – 16th June in No. 1 areas on both sides and in No. 4a area.
(b) Phase 3 – 20th June in No. 2 areas on both sides and in No. 1a and 4c areas.
(c) Phase 4 – 25th June in No. 3 areas and in 2a area and in the area between A and A-1 lines west of Kuneitra and in 4th area.

15. UNDOF will verify during these inspections that the level of forces does not exceed the following:

(a) At the end of phase 1, one-third of the final strength would remain in areas 1 and 4a i.e. in the 10 km areas 2 infantry battalion, 25 tanks, 12 guns of short range on each side of the separation lines.
(b) At the end of the phase 2 on Israeli side two-thirds of the final strength would remain in areas 1 and 4a and 4c and No. 2 areas – i.e. 4 infantry battalions, 50 tanks, 24 guns of short range. On Syrian side the final strength would remain in No. 1 and No. 2 areas within 10 km area and in 1A area;
(c) At the end of the phase 4 – in all the restricted forces areas on both sides of the separation lines (A and B) the final strength – i.e. 2 infantry brigades, 75 tanks, 36 guns of short range and a total of 6,000 men only will remain within the 10 km limit.

16. UNDOF will verify on the 26th June 1974 that the above mentioned limitations of forces are observed by the parties and will effect regular bi-weekly inspections of the 10 km restricted forces areas.

17. UNDOF will verify on the 27th June 1974 that no surface-to-air missile launchers and no missiles are deployed within the 25 kilometres west of Line

A and east of Line B. UNDOF will also verify that in the 20 kilometres area there are no more than 162 artillery guns of a range not exceeding 20 kms and 450 tanks of all types only, and will effect regular bi-weekly inspections.

18. The Israeli Army has stated that strict orders have been given not to cause any damage to civilian property in the area during the disengagement period.

This statement has been read in the presence of General Shafir and General Tayara and both Parties have accepted it.

Geneva, 05 June 1974   (*sgd.*) Lt. General Ensio Siilasvuo
                                                     United Nations

10. Agreement between Egypt and Israel

The Government of the Arab Republic of Egypt and the Government of Israel have agreed that:

ARTICLE I

The conflict between them and in the Middle East shall not be resolved by military force but by peaceful means.

The Agreement concluded by the parties 18 January 1974 [*see S/11198 and Add. 1*], within the framework of the Geneva Peace Conference, constituted a first step towards a just and durable peace according to the provisions of Security Council resolution 338 (1973) of 22 October 1973.

They are determined to reach a final and just peace settlement by means of negotiations called for by Security Council resolution 338 (1973), this Agreement being a significant step towards that end.

ARTICLE II

The parties hereby undertake not to resort to the threat or use of force or military blockade against each other.

ARTICLE III

The parties shall continue scrupulously to observe the cease-fire on land, sea and air and to refrain from all military or para-military actions against each other. The parties also confirm that the obligations contained in the annex and, when concluded, the Protocol shall be an integral part of this Agreement.

ARTICLE IV

A. The military forces of the parties shall be deployed in accordance with the following principles:

1. All Israeli forces shall be deployed east of the lines designated as lines J and M on the attached map.

2. All Egyptian forces shall be deployed west of the line designated as line E on the attached map.

3. The area between the lines designated on the attached map as lines E and F and the area between the lines designated on the attached map as lines J and K shall be limited in armament and forces.

4. The limitations on armament and forces in the areas described by paragraph 3 above shall be agreed as described in the attached annex.

5. The zone between the lines designated on the attached map as lines E and J will be a buffer zone. In this zone the United Nations Emergency Force will continue to perform its functions as under the Egyptian-Israeli Agreement of 18 January 1974.

6. In the area south from line E and west from line M, as defined on the attached map, there will be no military forces, as specified in the attached annex.

B. The details concerning the new lines, the redeployment of the forces and its timing, the limitation on armaments and forces, aerial reconnaissance, the operation of the early warning and surveillance installations and the use of the roads, the United Nations functions and other arrangements will all be in accordance with the provisions of the annex and map which are an integral part of this Agreement and of the Protocol which is to result from negotiations pursuant to the annex and which, when concluded, shall become an integral part of this Agreement.

ARTICLE V

The United Nations Emergency Force is essential and shall continue its functions and its mandate shall be extended annually.

ARTICLE VI

The parties hereby establish a joint commission for the duration of this Agreement. It will function under the aegis of the chief co-ordinator of the United Nations peace-keeping missions in the Middle East in order to consider any problem arising from this Agreement and to assist the United Nations Emergency Force in the execution of its mandate. The joint commission shall function in accordance with procedures established in the Protocol.

ARTICLE VII

Non-military cargoes destined for or coming from Israel shall be permitted through the Suez Canal.

ARTICLE VIII

This Agreement is regarded by the parties as a significant step towards a just and lasting peace. It is not a final peace agreement.

The parties shall continue their efforts to negotiate a final peace agreement within the framework of the Geneva Peace Conference in accordance with Security Council resolution 338 (1973).

ARTICLE IX

This Agreement shall enter into force upon signature of the Protocol and remain in force untl superseded by a new agreement.

Done at Geneva on 1 September 1975, in four original copies.

For the Government of the Arab Republic of Egypt:

Taha EL-MAGDOUB
Major-General
Ahmed OSMAN
Ambassador

For the Government of Israel:

Mordecai GAZIT
Ambassador
Herzl SHAFIR
Major-General

Witness:
Lieutenant-General Ensio SIILASVUO

Annex to the Agreement between Egypt and Israel

Within five days after the signature of the Agreement between Egypt and Israel, representatives of the two parties shall meet in the Military Working Group of the Geneva Peace Conference on the Middle East to begin preparation of a detailed Protocol for the implementation of the Agreement. The Working Group will complete the Protocol within two weeks. In order to facilitate preparation of the Protocol and implementation of the Agreement, and to assist in maintaining the scrupulous observance of the cease-fire and other elements of the Agreement, the two parties have agreed on the following principles, which are an integral part of the Agreement, as guidelines for the working Group.

1. DEFINITIONS OF LINES AND AREAS

The deployment lines, areas of limited forces and armaments, buffer zones, the area south from line E and west from line M, other designated areas, road sections for common use and other features referred to in article IV of the Agreement shall be as indicated on the attached map (1: 100,000 – United States edition).

2. BUFFER ZONES

A. Access to the buffer zones will be controlled by the United Nations Emergency Force, according to procedures to be worked out by the Working Group and the Force.

B. Aircraft of either party will be permitted to fly freely up to the forward line of that party. Reconnaissance aircraft of either party may fly up to the middle line of the buffer zone between E and J on an agreed schedule.

C. In the buffer zone, between lines E and J, there will be established under article IV of the Agreement an early warning system entrusted to United States civilian personnel as detailed in a separate proposal, which is a part of this Agreement.

D. Authorized personnel shall have access to the buffer zone for transit to and from the early warning system; the manner in which this is carried out shall be worked out by the Working Group and the United Nations Emergency Force.

3. AREA SOUTH OF LINE E AND WEST OF LINE M

A. In this area, the United Nations Emergency Force will assure that there are no military or para-military forces of any kind, military fortifications and military installations; it will establish checkpoints and have the freedom of movement necessary to perform this function.

B. Egyptian civilians and third country civilian oil field personnel shall have the right to enter, exit from, work and live in the above indicated area, except for buffer zones 2A, 2B and the United Nations posts. Egyptian civilian police shall be allowed in the area to perform normal civil police functions among the civilian population in such number and with such weapons and equipment as shall be provided for in the Protocol.

C. Entry to and exit from the area, by land, by air or by sea, shall be only through United Nations Emergency Force checkpoints. The Force shall also establish checkpoints along the road, the dividing line and at either points, with the precise locations and number to be included in the Protocol.

D. Access to the airspace and the coastal area shall be limited to unarmed Egyptian civilian vessels and unarmed civilian helicopters and transport planes involved in the civilian activities of the area as agreed by the Working Group.

E. Israel undertakes to leave intact all currently existing civilian installations and infrastructures.

F. Procedures for use of the common sections of the coastal road along the Gulf of Suez shall be determined by the Working Group and detailed in the Protocol.

4. AERIAL SURVEILLANCE

There shall be a continuation of aerial reconnaissance missions by the United States over the areas covered by the Agreement (the area between lines F and K), following the same procedures already in practice. The missions will ordinarily be carried out at a frequency of one mission every 7–10 days, with either party or the United Nations Emergency Force empowered to request an earlier mission. The United States Government will make the mission results available expeditiously to Israel, Egypt and the chief co-ordinator of the United Nations peace-keeping missions in the Middle East.

5. LIMITATION OF FORCES AND ARMAMENTS

A. Within the areas of limited forces and armaments (the areas between lines J and K and lines E and F) the major limitations shall be as follows:
1. Eight (8) standard infantry battalions.
2. Seventy-five (75) tanks.
3. Seventy-two (72) artillery pieces, including heavy mortars (i.e. with calibre larger than 120 mm.), whose range shall not exceed twelve (12) kilometres.
4. The total number of personnel shall not exceed eight thousand (8,000).
5. Both parties agree not to station or locate in the area weapons which can reach the line of the other side.
6. Both parties agree that in the areas between lines J and K, and between line A (of the Disengagement Agreement of 18 January 1974) and line E, they will construct no new fortifications or installations for forces of a size greater than that agreed herein.
B. The major limitations beyond the areas of limited forces and armament will be:
1. Neither side will station nor locate any weapon in areas from which they can reach the other line.
2. The parties will not place anti-aircraft missiles within an area of ten (10) kilometres east of line K and west of line F, respectively.
C. The United Nations Emergency Force will conduct inspections in order to ensure the maintenance of the agreed limitations within these areas.

6. PROCESS OF IMPLEMENTATION

The detailed implementation and timing of the redeployment of forces, turnover of oil fields, and other arrangements called for by the Agreement, annex and Protocol shall be determined by the Working Group, which will agree on the stages of this process, including the phased movement of Egyptian troops to line E and Israeli troops to line J. The first phase will be the transfer of the oil fields and installations to Egypt. This process will begin within two weeks from the signature of the Protocol with the introduction of the necessary technicians and it will be completed no later than eight weeks after it begins. The details of the phasing will be worked out in the Military Working Group. Implementation of the redeployment shall be completed within five months after signature of the Protocol.

For the Government of the Arab Republic of Egypt:	For the Government of Israel:
Taha EL-MAGDOUB	Mordecai GAZIT
Major-General	Ambassador
Ahmed OSMAN	Herzl SHAFIR
Ambassador	Major-General

Witness:
Lieutenant-General Ensio SIILASVUO

PROPOSAL

In connexion with the early warning system referred to in article IV of the Agreement between Egypt and Israel concluded on this date and as an integral part of that Agreement (hereafter referred to as the basic Agreement), the United States proposes the following:

1. The early warning system to be established in accordance with article IV in the area shown on the map attached to the basic Agreement will be entrusted to the United States. It shall have the following elements:

(*a*) There shall be two surveillance stations to provide strategic early warning, one operated by Egyptian and one operated by Israeli personnel. Their locations are shown on the map attached to the basic Agreement. Each station shall be manned by not more than 250 technical and administrative personnel. They shall perform the functions of visual and electronic surveillance only within their stations.

(*b*) In support of these stations, to provide tactical early warning and to verify access to them, three watch stations shall be established by the United States in the Mitla and Giddi Passes as will be shown on the map attached to the basic Agreement. These stations shall be operated by United States civilian personnel. In support of these stations, there shall be established three unmanned electronic sensor fields at both ends of each Pass and in the general vicinity of each station and the roads leading to and from those stations.

2. The United States civilian personnel shall perform the following duties in connexion with the operation and maintenance of these stations.

(*a*) At the two surveillance stations described in paragraph 1(*a*) above, United States civilian personnel will verify the nature of the operations of the stations and all movement into and out of each station and will immediately report any detected divergency from its authorized role of visual and electronic surveillance to the parties to the basic Agreement and to the United Nations Emergency Force.

(*b*) At each watch station described in paragraph 1(*b*) above, the United States civilian personnel will immediately report to the parties to the basic Agreement and to the United Nations Emergency Force any movement of armed forces, other than the Force, into either Pass and any observed preparations for such movement.

(*c*) The total number of United States civilian personnel assigned to functions under this proposal shall not exceed 200. Only civilian personnel shall be assigned to functions under this proposal.

3. No arms shall be maintained at the stations and other facilities covered by this proposal, except for small arms required for their protection.

4. The United States personnel serving the early warning system shall be allowed to move freely within the area of the system.

5. The United States and its personnel shall be entitled to have such support facilities as are reasonably necessary to perform their functions.

6. The United States personnel shall be immune from local criminal, civil, tax and customs jurisdiction and may be accorded any other specific privileges and immunities provided for in the United Nations Emergency Force Agreement of 13 February 1957.

7. The United States affirms that it will continue to perform the functions described above for the duration of the basic Agreement.

8. Notwithstanding any other provision of this proposal, the United States may withdraw its personnel only if it concludes that their safety is jeopardized or that continuation of their role is no longer necessary. In the latter case the parties to the basic Agreement will be informed in advance in order to give them the opportunity to make alternative arrangements. If both parties to the basic Agreement request the United States to conclude its role under this proposal, the United States will consider such requests conclusive.

9. Technical problems including the location of the watch stations will be worked out through consultation with the United States.

(Signed) Henry A. KISSINGER
Secretary of State
of the United States of America

[*Signed separately by the*
representatives of the two parties]

11. Proposed programme for Military Working Group, September 1975

Military Working Group   Geneva, 8 September 1975
of the Middle East Peace Conference
at Geneva

Chairman

Draft proposal

*List of subjects to be discussed and
timetable for meetings*

1. The provisions of the Agreement between Egypt and Israel and the Annex attached to it enumerate subjects to be discussed and agreed upon at meetings of the Military Working Group. A listing of subjects, which is not exhaustive, has been prepared together with a timetable.

Owing to the requirement in the Agreement that the transfer of the oil fields and installations be transferred to Egypt in the first phase in the process of implementation, it has been considered advisable to give priority to the Southern Area (i.e. Area South of Line E and West of Line M).

2. The Chairman will open the first meeting with a short statement. Representatives of Egypt and Israel may wish to make general statements regarding the work of the Military Working Group.

3. At the end of each meeting a detailed agenda for the next meeting will be prepared and submitted to the parties.

4. In addition to the listed subjects the parties are invited to suggest other items they deem necessary. It is hoped that additions to the agenda will be announced before the meeting of 19 September.

5. Press relations. In conformity with past practice, the representatives of the Press will be present at the opening phase of the first meeting. At the conclusion of each meeting, a communiqué for the Press will be prepared in consultation with the Parties. The Press will also be present at the final formal meeting of the Working Group when the Protocol will be signed.

INDEX

The following major topics, which are indicated in the analytical contents list (pp. vii–x), are not included in this index: UNEF II, UNTSO, Egypt, Israel, Jordan, Syria. Likewise the author's career, movements etc. are not indexed.